MW00638450

Cold War Freud

In *Cold War Freud* Dagmar Herzog uncovers the astonishing array of concepts of human selfhood which circulated across the globe in the aftermath of World War II. Against the backdrop of Nazism and the Holocaust, the sexual revolution, feminism, gay rights, and anticolonial and antiwar activism, she charts the heated battles which raged over Freud's legacy. From the postwar US to Europe and Latin America, she reveals how competing theories of desire, anxiety, aggression, guilt, trauma, and pleasure emerged and were then transformed to serve both conservative and subversive ends in a fundamental rethinking of the very nature of the human self and its motivations. Her findings shed new light on psychoanalysis' enduring contribution to the enigma of the relationship between nature and culture and the ways in which social contexts enter into and shape the innermost recesses of individual psyches.

Dagmar Herzog is Distinguished Professor of History and Daniel Rose Faculty Scholar at the Graduate Center, City University of New York, and has published extensively on the histories of religion, gender and sexuality, and the history of the Holocaust and its aftermath. She is the author of four previous books, including *Sex after Fascism: Memory and Morality in Twentieth-Century Germany* (2005) and *Sexuality in Europe: A Twentieth-Century History* (2011), and editor or coeditor of six anthologies spanning issues of war, sexuality, religion, and historical theory.

Cold War Freud

Psychoanalysis in an Age of Catastrophes

Dagmar Herzog
Graduate Center, City University of New York

CAMBRIDGE
UNIVERSITY PRESS

CAMBRIDGE
UNIVERSITY PRESS

University Printing House, Cambridge CB2 8BS, United Kingdom

Cambridge University Press is part of the University of Cambridge.

It furthers the University's mission by disseminating knowledge in the pursuit of education, learning, and research at the highest international levels of excellence.

www.cambridge.org
Information on this title: www.cambridge.org/9781107072398

© Dagmar Herzog 2017

First published 2017

Printed in the United Kingdom by TJ International Ltd. Padstow Cornwall

A catalogue record for this publication is available from the British Library.

ISBN 978-1-107-07239-8 Hardback

CONTENTS

FIGURES

INTRODUCTION

Cold War Freud addresses the uneasy encounters of Freudian theories about desire, anxiety, aggression, guilt, trauma, and pleasure – and the very nature of the human self and its motivations – with the calamitous events of World War II and beyond. While psychoanalysis is often taken to be ahistorical in its view of human nature, the opposite is the case. The impact of epochal historical transformations on psychoanalytic premises and practices is particularly evident in the postwar decades. This was precisely when psychoanalysis gained the greatest traction, across the West, within medicine and mainstream belief alike. For in the course of the second half of the twentieth century, psychoanalytic thinking came consequentially to inflect virtually all other thought-systems – from the major religious traditions to the social science disciplines and from conventional advice literature to radical political protest movements. Psychoanalysis, in all its unruly complexity, became an integral part of twentieth-century social and intellectual history.

The heyday of intellectual and popular preoccupation with psychoanalysis reached from the 1940s to the 1980s – from postwar conservative consolidation to delayed-reaction engagement with the legacies of Nazism and the Holocaust, from the anti-Vietnam War movement and the concomitant inversion of generational and moral alignments to the confrontation with new Cold War dictatorships, and from the sexual revolution and the rise of women's and gay rights to an intensified interest in learning from formerly colonized peoples in an – only unevenly – postcolonial world. The battles within and around psychoanalysis provided a language for thinking about the changes in what counted as truth about how human beings are, and what could and should be done about it. But the possible relationships between psychoanalysis and politics were fraught, and a permanent source of ambivalence.

Sigmund Freud died in 1939 in his London exile. Ever the self-reviser, he had tacked frequently between issues of clinical technique, anthropological speculation, and political opinion. For him, psychoanalysis was, at once, a therapeutic modality, a theory of human nature, and a toolbox for cultural criticism. In the years that followed, however, the irresolvable tensions between the therapeutic and the cultural-diagnostic potentials of psychoanalysis would be argued over not just by Freud's detractors but also by his disciples. And the stakes had changed, drastically. The conflicts between the various possible uses of psychoanalytic thinking were especially intense in the wake of the rupture in civilization constituted by the wild success of Nazism in the 1930s and the unprecedented enormity of mass murder in the 1940s. This was not just because of the ensuing dispersion of the analytic community, but above all because of the stark questions posed by the historical events themselves. Psychoanalysis, it turned out, could have both normative-conservative and socially critical implications. And while its practitioners and promoters careened often between seeking to explain dynamics in the most intimate crevices of fantasies and bodies and venturing to pronounce on culture and politics in the broadest senses of those terms, there was never a self-evident relationship between the possible political implications of psychoanalytic precepts, left, middle, or right, on the one hand, and the niceties of psychotherapeutic method or theoretical formulation, on the other. And neither of these matters matched up easily with the declarations of rupture or of fealty to Freud made on all sides.

In 1949, the first post-World War II meeting of the International Psychoanalytical Association was held in Zurich. World events had kept the IPA from meeting for more than a decade. In Zurich, the Welsh-born, London-based neurologist and psychoanalyst Ernest Jones – President of the IPA, one of the most respected exponents of psychoanalysis in Britain, longtime editor of the *International*

Journal of Psycho-Analysis, and soon to be Freud's official biographer – addressed the audience with a plea to stay away not just from anything that could be construed as politically subversive. In fact, he urged them to stay away from discussion of extrapsychic factors of any kind.

Or perhaps it was more of an order than a plea. Jones directed his listeners to focus strictly on "the primitive forces of the mind" and to steer clear of "the influence of sociological factors."[1] In Jones' view, the lesson to be drawn from the recent past – particularly in view of National Socialism's conquest of much of the European continent along with the resultant acceleration of the psychoanalytic diaspora, as well as from the fact that, at the then-present moment, in countries on the other side of the Iron Curtain, psychoanalytic associations that had been shut down during the war were not being permitted to reconstitute themselves – was that politics of any kind was something best kept at arm's length. Jones' official justification for apoliticism, in short, lay in political events. (This justification was all the more peculiar, as it suppressed the fact that actually quite a bit of writing about such topics as war, aggression, and prejudice had been produced, also by British psychoanalysts, including Jones, in the 1930s and 1940s.)[2] Or, as he framed his argument: "We have to resist the temptation to be carried away, to adopt emotional short cuts in our thinking, to follow the way of politicians, who, after all, have not been notably successful in adding to the happiness of the world." But his was a multifunctional directive. For avoiding discussion of politics and of extrapsychic dynamics had the added benefit of erasing from view Jones' own collusion with Sigmund and Anna Freud, during the war, in the exclusion of the Marxist psychoanalyst Wilhelm Reich from the rescue operations extended to most other refugee analysts (due to Reich's perceived political toxicity). And it had the further advantage of providing a formal repudiation of more sociologically oriented "neo-Freudian" trends that had come to prominence especially in the United States during the war years (and that Jones was interested in seeing shunted). Jones was adamant. While "the temptation is understandably great to add socio-political factors to those that are our special concern, and to re-read our findings in terms of sociology," this was, he admonished – in a description that was actually a prescription – "a temptation which, one is proud to observe, has, with very few exceptions, been stoutly resisted."[3] Many psychoanalysts – in the USA, in Western and Central Europe and in Latin America – would come to heed Jones' counsel, whether out of personal predilection or institutional pressures, or some combination of the two.

More than two decades and ten biennial meetings later, however, at the IPA congress in Vienna in 1971 – a meeting which Anna Freud, two years earlier, had agreed could be dedicated to studying the topic of aggression (the proposal to do so had been put forward by the Pakistani British psychoanalyst Masud Khan, the American Martin Wangh, and the Argentinean Arnaldo Rascovsky) – the eminent West German psychoanalyst Alexander Mitscherlich stood before his peers and demanded that they take sociological and political matters seriously. "All our theories are going to be carried away by history," Mitscherlich told his colleagues, speaking on the topic of "Psychoanalysis and the Aggression of Large Groups" – "unless," as newspapers from the *Kansas City Times* to the *Herald Tribune* in Paris summarized his argument, "psychoanalysis is applied to social problems."[4] One evident context for Mitscherlich's remark was the war ongoing at that very moment in Vietnam. Indeed Mitscherlich went on to provoke his fellow analysts with warnings of how irrelevant their models and concepts of human nature would soon become with a fairly direct reference to that particular conflict: "I fear that nobody is going to take us very seriously if we continue to suggest that war comes about because fathers hate their sons and want to kill them, that war is filicide. We must, instead, aim at finding a theory that explains group behavior, a theory that traces this behavior to the conflicts in society that actuate the individual drives."[5] Mitscherlich also did not hesitate to invoke his own nation's history, noting that "collective phenomena demand a different sort of understanding than can be acquired by treating neuroses. The behaviour of the German people during the Nazi rule and its aftermath showed how preshaped character structure and universal aggressive propaganda could dovetail into each other in a quite specific manner to allow the unthinkable to become reality."[6] Moreover, and pointing to such texts as *Group Psychology and the Analysis of the Ego* (1921) and *Civilization and its Discontents* (1930), Mitscherlich reminded the audience that Sigmund Freud himself had been highly interested in political and cultural phenomena – and thus that concern with extrapsychic conditions and forces would in no way imply a departure from the master's path. Nonetheless, and as the newspapers also reported, "Mitscherlich's suggestion that destructive aggressive behavior is provoked by social factors runs counter to current Freudian orthodoxy – that aggression derives from internal psychic sources that are instinctual."[7] And while Mitscherlich's politically engaged comments "evoked a burst of applause from younger participants [,][...] some of their elders sat in stony silence."[8] An emergent intergenerational, geographical, and ideological divide within the IPA had become unmistakable.

At the turn from the 1960s to the 1970s, the IPA was dominated by a handful of its British, but above all by its American members, many of whom Mitscherlich knew well from numerous travels and research stays in both countries.[9] Why did Mitscherlich's message not find a welcome resonance among his senior confreres? Mitscherlich's barb – "all our theories are going to be carried away by history" – could sting his older American colleagues, and garner notice in the international press, not least because psychoanalysis in the USA was, in fact, at this moment, in a serious predicament. The "golden age" of American psychoanalysis that had run from roughly 1949 to 1969 was about to be brought to an end by the combined impact of: the feminist and gay rights movements with their numerous, highly valid complaints about the misogyny and homophobia endemic in postwar analysis; the rise of shorter-term and more behaviorally oriented therapies, but above all the explosion of pop self-help, much of which would expressly style itself in opposition to the expense and purported futility of years on the couch; and the antiauthoritarian climate in general. The turn inward and the emphasis on intrapsychic, or at most on intrafamilial, dynamics that had been so remarkably successful in the first two postwar decades had, in short, run aground.

Already two years earlier, at the occasion of the IPA congress meeting in Rome in 1969, younger West German, Swiss, Italian, and French analysts and analysts-in-training had organized a "counter-congress" to register their dissent from what they perceived as the authoritarianism and inadequate engagement with social issues of the day among the leaders of the international psychoanalytic community. More than 100 participants showed up for several days of engaged discussion (at a restaurant within a fifth of a mile of the Cavalieri Hilton, where the registered congress participants were housed in upscale splendor). The IPA was accused – as the dollar signs replacing the final letters in the poster criticizing the main "Congre$$" made all too clear – of caring more about lucrative professional self-protection than about excellence in clinical practice, to say nothing of pressing political matters (see Figure 1).[10] Mitscherlich – together with the

Roma, 26, congresso di psi-
canalisi: Elvio Fachinelli (a
sinistra) e Berthold Rot-
schild affiggono un manifesto di protesta. Accanto al
titolo: la principessa Alessandra Tomasi di Lampe-
dusa, ex presidente della so-
cietà psicanalitica italiana.

Figure 1 Marianna Bolko, Elvio Fachinelli, and Berthold Rothschild – coorganizers of the "counter-congress" in Rome, July–August 1969 – hanging a poster critical of the International Psychoanalytical Association congress' program and professional priorities. The accompanying article in the Italian magazine *L'Espresso* covered both the congress and the counter-congress, but was clearly most fascinated by what it described as the counter-congress' claims that American psychoanalysts were "seeking hegemony over the unconscious."

Swiss psychoanalysts Paul Parin and Fritz Morgenthaler – had been among only a tiny handful of prominent senior members of the IPA who had shown support for the counter-congress (although Jacques Lacan had flown in from Paris when he learned how much excitement and media coverage the counter-congress was engendering).[11] And Mitscherlich had also delivered a speech at the main congress in which he expressed sympathy for youth "protest and revolution."[12] In Rome, the young European dissidents, joined by several Latin American, especially Argentinean, analysts (notably also more senior Latin American psychoanalysts had been irritated by their inadequate representation among those regularly chosen to be IPA presenters), launched a network called "Plataforma."[13] This network would link radicals in Latin America and Europe for the duration of the next two decades – a linkage which was deeply to shape the subsequent clinical and conceptual work of the participants.[14]

For, as it happened, psychoanalysis globally was not in decline. On the contrary, what was really going on was that the geographical and generational loci of creativity and influence were shifting. Psychoanalysis was about to enjoy a second "golden age," this one within Western and Central Europe, and (although complicated both by brutal repressions and by self-interested complicities under several dictatorial regimes) also in Latin America.[15] This second golden age, from the late 1960s through the late 1980s, was sustained not least by the New Left generation of 1968 and by those among their elders, Mitscherlich, Parin, and Morgenthaler among them, who were in sympathy with New Left concerns. The New Left was, simply, *the* major motor for the restoration and cultural consolidation of psychoanalysis in Western and Central Europe and for the further development of psychoanalysis in Latin America as well.[16] But it was a distinctly different Freud that these rebels resurrected. Or rather: one could say that there was not one Freud circulating in the course of the Cold War era, and not even only a dozen, but rather hundreds.

We have been living through a contemporary moment of renewed interest in Freud and in the evolution of psychoanalysis. Already in 2006, the American historian John C. Burnham detected the emergence of a "historiographical shift" that he dubbed "The New Freud Studies." Burnham observed that the opening to scholars of a massive archive of primary sources that had long been sealed from public access – especially the collection at the Sigmund Freud Archives at the US Library of Congress – would inevitably stimulate an efflorescence of fresh work. (Much of the material in that collection, which was begun in 1951 and includes a wealth of correspondence from the first half of the twentieth century as well as extensive interviews conducted in the early 1950s with dozens of individuals who knew Freud personally, has indeed, between 2000 and 2015, finally been derestricted.)[17] Burnham surmised that because the history of psychoanalysis had for so long been written by insider-practitioners rather than historians, and that these insiders were unabashedly "using the history of psychoanalysis as a weapon in their struggles to control the medical, psychological, and philosophical understandings of Freud and the Freudians" – and hence tended to produce writing that "had its origin in whiggish justifications of later versions of theory and clinical practice" – the involvement of outsiders would change how the history of the field was told.[18] And so it has been – although it remains critical to add that insider-practitioners have written superb histories as well, and may often have been better positioned to explicate such matters as the evolution of clinical technique (and, of course, there are individuals who are both analysts and historians and bring that double vision creatively to bear).[19]

One of the earliest results of fresh perspectives coming from outside, already in evidence in the midst of the so-called "Freud Wars" of the mid-1990s – wars over scholarly access to the archive but also over the meaning of Freud's legacy – was a far deepened understanding of Freud's own historical contextualization.[20] Sander Gilman's *Freud, Race, and Gender* (1994) signaled a move toward placing Freud more firmly in the antisemitic atmosphere of fin-de-siècle Vienna and the consequences of the "feminization" of male Jews for Freud's theories of women; numerous scholars have since followed Gilman's lead.[21] Mari Jo Buhle's marvelously lucid *Feminism and Its Discontents: A Century of Struggle with Psychoanalysis* (1998) and Eli Zaretsky's pioneering *Secrets of the Soul: A Social and Cultural History of Psychoanalysis* (2004) took the story of the psychoanalytic movement forward, with both paying particular attention to the vicissitudes of its recurrent encounters with feminism and with both offering especially important insights into the development of psychoanalysis in the USA.[22] But Burnham proved correct that additional access to theretofore unseen primary sources would allow a repositioning of Freud's work in a yet richer matrix of alliances, rivalries, and mutual influencings.[23] A stellar example of the insights gained was George Makari's magisterial *Revolution in Mind: The Creation of Psychoanalysis* (2008).[24] And in 2012 Burnham published an anthology, *After Freud Left: A Century of Psychoanalysis in America*, which brought together literary critics and historians to consider the place of psychoanalysis in key phases of US history.[25]

Since then, ever new areas of inquiry have opened up. Among other things, the increasing internationalization of historical research has complicated what we thought we knew about the early diffusion of psychoanalytic ideas. As the British historian John Forrester noted as recently as 2014: "Much of the history of psychoanalysis really is lost from sight – because we have been looking for too long in the wrong places." In particular, Forrester continued – here echoing Burnham – "we have been taking on trust not only the official histories of psychoanalysis, suffering from all the distortions that winners' history always introduces, ... but also the presumption that key figures in later history were also central to the earlier phases of its history."[26] But another broad trend has been to redirect attention beyond Freud, toward post-Freudian actors and the by now nearly infinite permutations of Freudian concepts that have circulated, and been recirculated – and thereby repeatedly modified – and the many uses to which these concepts have been put. As Matt ffytche, Forrester's successor as editor of the journal *Psychoanalysis and History*, noted in 2016:

> Psychoanalytic history may begin with Freud and his colleagues, or thereabouts, but that was simply the opening chapter. What has become increasingly fascinating, for historians and psychoanalysts alike, are the multiple sequels beyond Vienna – in the 1930s, the 1950s, the 1980s and now the 2000s – during which psychoanalysis has reached across various geographical and cultural boundaries, and embedded itself in many other fields, including modern psychology, philosophy, literature, politics and the social sciences and humanities more broadly.[27]

The outpouring of new work within which *Cold War Freud* is situated has developed along two main axes. One encompasses histories locating post-Freudian actors either in national cultures or in transnational political conflicts – including explorations of the role of psychoanalytic ideas in colonial and postcolonial contexts. Among the most significant recent ones are Camille Robcis' *The Law of Kinship: Anthropology, Psychoanalysis, and the Family in France* (2013), Michal Shapira's *The War Inside: Psychoanalysis, Total War and the Making of the Democratic Self in Postwar Britain* (2013), Elizabeth Lunbeck's *The Americanization of Narcissism* (2014), and Erik Linstrum's *Ruling Minds: Psychology in the British Empire* (2016), as well as the anthologies edited by Mariano Ben Plotkin and Joy Damousi, *Psychoanalysis and Politics: Histories of Psychoanalysis Under Conditions of Restricted Political Freedom* (2012), and by Warwick Anderson, Deborah Jenson, and Richard C. Keller, *Unconscious Dominions: Psychoanalysis, Colonial Trauma, and Global Sovereignties* (2011).[28] Also relevant here is the work-in-progress of Omnia El Shakry on "The Arabic Freud: The Unconscious and the Modern Subject."[29] Several books within this cluster are specifically concerned to recover politically committed versions of psychoanalysis. The most noteworthy of these are *A Psychotherapy for the People: Toward a Progressive Psychoanalysis* (2012), co-written by the psychoanalysts Lewis Aron and Karen Starr, and historian Eli Zaretsky's *Political Freud: A History* (2015); among Zaretsky's foci are the historical uses made of psychoanalysis by African American activists.[30] The other cluster of scholarship, at times overlapping with the first, and following on a prior wave of preoccupation with feminist challenges to the psychoanalytic movement, involves the efflorescence of histories pursuing "queerer" readings of psychoanalysis and seeking to make sense of the depth and doggedness of the homophobia that became practically endemic to the psychoanalytic movement, despite Freud's own repudiation of it. This group could be said to have its roots in a special issue of *GLQ* published in 1995: *Pink Freud*, edited by the literary critic Diana Fuss.[31] Since then, it has been growing steadily, although it has tended to draw in psychoanalysts and cultural studies scholars more than historians.[32]

Cold War Freud adds to these studies in multiple ways. Each of the six chapters takes up a different set of at once ethically and politically intense and long-perplexing, even stubbornly refractory, issues. They include: the relation of psychoanalysis to organized religion at the very onset of the Cold War; the tenaciously flexible hold of hostility to homosexuality; the striking time lag in acknowledging the existence of massive psychic trauma in the wake of the Holocaust; the unique trajectory of conflicts over whether aggression might be an innate feature in the human animal as these evolved in intergenerational battles in the aftermath of Nazism; the limits of an Oedipalized model of selfhood for understanding the workings of politics in conditions of globalizing capitalism; and the possibilities of acquiring a critical vantage on the cultures of the former colonizers by engaging the perspectives of the formerly colonized. As this brief list already suggests, the recurrent themes all somehow involve desire, violence, and relations of power. Or, to invoke the words of the venerable conservative sociologist and critic (and Freud expert) Philip Rieff, they each involve humans' struggle to "mediat[e] between culture and the instinct."[33] What is noteworthy as well is that they all demonstrate just how impracticable it was for postwar psychoanalysts to pretend they could be politically abstemious. Ambivalence and caution about politics made sense; thoughtful analysts recurrently declared that it would be absurd to extrapolate from models of human nature developed by studying individuals to groups and nations.[34] And needless to say, there were numerous analysts whose genius lay in their clinical technique and who had nothing much to say about politics, nor should they have been expected to; the extraordinarily gifted Donald Winnicott is perhaps the consummate – most prominent and most enduringly influential – example of this type.[35] On the other hand, however, too strong a renunciation of the world outside the consulting-room caused many analysts to miss – or deny – the inescapable reality of continual mutual imbrication of selves and societies. And what the historical episodes in the chapters that follow reveal as well is that the world kept coming back of its own accord, pressuring all the players in the unfolding controversies to engage in moral-political and not just clinical reasoning, no matter which side of which issue they found themselves on.[36]

Part I of this book discusses the overdetermined trend toward sexual conservatism in the forms taken by psychoanalysis in the postwar USA – manifest in its florid misogyny and homophobia. It accounts for the turn inward, away from critical engagement with politics with the exception of sexual politics. Chapter 1 explores the complex combination of a deliberate desexualization of post-Freudian psychoanalytic theory with the maintenance of Freudianism's titillating reputation, and positions this within an active rapprochement with mainstream Christianity, Catholic as well as Protestant, a Christianity that was itself at that historical moment in the process of being transformed. Psychoanalysis, I argue, so often shorthanded as "the Jewish science," might in fact better be described as undergoing a kind of "Christianization" – even as Christianity, like Judaism, was at that moment also becoming more "psychologized." But this chapter additionally makes an argument for recovering the work of the psychoanalyst Karen Horney – not in the terms in which she is usually understood, especially her feminist challenges to Freud, but for her innovative reflections on how one might better conceptualize the relationship between sex and other realms of life – and then shows how rivalrous irritation at Horney's popularity constrained her successors' maneuvering room in the face of attacks from religious leaders. Chapter 2, in turn, has at its center the problem of psychoanalytic homophobia while also examining the impact of loosening sexual mores and the ascent of competing sexological research – from Alfred Kinsey to William Masters and Virginia Johnson – as heretofore underestimated but key factors in the stages leading up to the eventual abrupt decline of psychoanalysis' prestige in the later 1960s and 1970s, within psychiatry and within US culture as a whole. In addition, the chapter assesses the attempted self-renovation of American psychoanalysis in its tactical shift of focus to theories of narcissism, deficient selves, and character disorders – as it also traces the beginnings of efforts to revitalize psychoanalysis for anti-heteronormative and pro-sex feminist purposes, with particular attention to the ingenious and inspired arguments of Robert Stoller and Kenneth Lewes.

Part II documents the quite unforeseen but profound consequences of the return to political relevance of the Nazi past on both sides of the Atlantic. Chapter 3 charts the clashes that ensued between pro- as well as anti-psychoanalytic psychiatrists in the USA, Europe, and Israel over the often delayed-reaction post-catastrophic emotional damages evinced by survivors of Nazi persecutions and the grotesque violence and sadism pervasive in concentration and death camps. Emphasizing the resurgence of antisemitism and resentment against survivors within West Germany, the chapter examines both the startling appropriation of Freudian concepts by physicians antagonistic to the survivors as well as the eventual creation, by sympathetic psychoanalysts and psychiatrists – through the contingent but crucial conjoining of survivors' concerns with those of Vietnam War veterans and antiwar activists – of the syndrome now known as PTSD (post-traumatic stress disorder). It introduces the distinctive contributions into this debate of Kurt Eissler, more usually known to historians as the founding director of the aforementioned Freud Archives.[37] Yet the chapter traces as well the inherent limits in the diagnostic category of PTSD as it was ultimately formulated, not least as the category was put to the test in Latin American psychotherapists' efforts to provide care for survivors of torture.

Chapter 4 looks at the complicated process involved in returning psychoanalysis to cultural prestige in post-Nazi Germany. The chapter is centered on recovering and reinterpreting the work of Alexander Mitscherlich, the leading protagonist in the project of bringing psychoanalysis back to a land in which it had been denigrated as "Jewish" and "filthy," and it is concerned to bring into view Mitscherlich's particular strategic mix of ego psychological concepts with left-liberal recommendations for tolerance and social engagement. Yet the chapter makes an argument that considerable credit needs to be given to animal behavior expert Konrad Lorenz's bestselling book *On Aggression* for setting in motion an unusually heated nationwide debate not only over whether human aggression was simply natural and inevitable and even a positive (i.e., not a German specialty and nothing Germans needed to be particularly ashamed of) but also, and specifically, over what exactly Freud had initially meant when he suggested that aggression might be a drive comparable in strength and form to libido. In a final section, this chapter explicates the long-delayed but then enthusiastic reception in Central Europe of British analyst Melanie Klein's ideas about innate aggression.

Part III turns to two case studies in what can only be called radical Freudianism. Both chapters are concerned with inventive appropriations of psychoanalytic concepts initially developed by tendentially nonpolitical analysts in earlier decades – but on the basis of thoroughly distinct psychoanalytic models, with one protagonist working from a model of the self as in tumultuous disarray, while the others relied on an assessment of selves as integrated albeit profoundly culturally inflected, and/or as sometimes damaged but potentially reparable. Chapter 5 turns to France to revisit philosopher Gilles Deleuze and psychoanalyst Félix Guattari's countercultural classic *Anti-Oedipus* (1972) – with its giddy but simultaneously earnest splicing of ideas taken not only from the work of such overtly political psychoanalysts as Reich and Frantz Fanon, but also from Klein and Lacan – as well as an array of Guattari's earlier and subsequent writings. The chapter makes a case for Guattari as not just a critic of stultifying existing forms of psychoanalysis – and especially of its much-mythologized icon, Oedipus, and the narrowly familialist framework of interpretation of psychic difficulties for which that icon stood – but also as a resourceful revitalizer of the psychoanalytic enterprise. This enterprise was, under the impact not least of the sexual revolution, feminism, and gay rights as well as anticolonial and antiwar activism, undergoing substantial transformation, and Guattari – reviving but respinning for his present older psychoanalytic theories of the appeals of fascism – also brought his experience working in alternative-experimental psychiatric institutions to his observations of Cold War politics. Chapter 6 reconsiders the pioneering fieldwork of the Swiss ethnographer-psychoanalysts Paul Parin, Fritz Morgenthaler, and Goldy Parin-Matthèy in Mali, Ivory Coast, and Papua New Guinea against the backstory of decades of merger and mutual borrowing as well as disputation between psychoanalysis and anthropology. It discusses the trio's attempts to adapt psychoanalytic ideas about psychosexual stages, ego structure, Oedipal conflicts, defenses, and resistances to study non-Western selves in order to explore the enduring enigma of the relationships between nature and culture and the ways social contexts enter into and shape the innermost recesses of individual psyches. And finally, the chapter recounts the rise of the Parins and Morgenthaler to countercultural fame as it also explores how their cross-cultural experiments in the so-called Third World came to inform the stands they took on the politics of the First (including, notably, the sexual politics).

In its reconstruction of the dialectical and recursive interaction between these older radicals and the many young leftists they would inspire, this last chapter brings forward explicitly a larger argument that is only implicit in the earlier parts of the book. The history of psychoanalysis in general, it seems, has been one of countless delayed-reaction receptions, unplanned repurposings, and an ever-evolving reshaping of the meanings of texts and concepts. In the history of psychoanalysis, what a particular reading, a particular understanding, has facilitated – emotionally, politically, intellectually – has often been more important than what was said in the first place. There has never been an essential, self-evident content to the ideas that traveled into new contexts. Far from offering unchanging truths (or, for that matter, unchanging falsehoods), psychoanalysis has turned out to be only and always iridescent.

Meanwhile, another theme that recurs throughout the book has to do with the history of sexuality. There is no question that psychoanalysis as a twentieth-century phenomenon was utterly enmeshed with cultural conflicts over the status and meaning of sex. After all, the birth of psychoanalysis as a thought-system at the turn from the nineteenth to the twentieth century had been itself a symptom, and by no means just a cause, of an at least partial liberalization of sexual mores in Central Europe – and indeed psychoanalysis was just one of many in a welter of competing and overlapping thought-systems arising at the turn of the century to grapple with issues of gender and desire. Sexologists and other medical professionals, feminists, and homosexual rights activists, as well as moral reformers across the ideological spectrum, fought vehemently over such matters as prostitution and marriage, contraception and satisfaction, perversion and orientation. The emergence of psychoanalysis cannot be understood apart from this wider context; Freud and his first followers, as well as defectors and adapters, were in continual conversation with the trends of the era. Moreover, the subsequent evolution of the psychoanalytic theoretical edifice would be deeply shaped by the oscillation, in later decades – and differently in every country – between sexually conservative backlashes and efforts at renewed liberalization.[38]

What makes probing the history of psychoanalysis such an interesting problem also for historians of sexuality, then, is the fact that psychoanalysis, like the many schools of thought which borrowed from it, did not only theorize sex *per se*, but continually wrestled with the riddle of the relationships between sexual desire and other aspects of human motivation – from anaclitic, nonsexual longings for interpersonal connection to anxiety, aggression, and ambition. For some psychoanalytic commentators, sex – desires or troubles – explained just about everything. For others, the causation was completely reversed: sex was about everything *but* itself; nonsexual issues – including, precisely, ambition, aggression, and anxiety – were continually being worked through in the realm of sex. The puzzle of how to make sense of such matters as the sexualization of nonsexual impulses exercised analysts who were otherwise politically divergent. The question of what exactly people sought in sex – much of which may not, in its origins, have been sexual at all – helped some analysts to develop entirely new frames for analytic thinking. The insistence that the sexual and the economic realms were simply not categorically distinct provided grounds for others for retheorizing the emotional pulls by which all politics functioned. And a fascination with how hetero- and homosexuals alike reworked early traumas in order to turn them into sexual excitement helped yet others to facilitate empathy with sexual minorities and make a mockery of those of their peers who persisted in clinging to prejudicial views.

There is much that we still need to mull about the possible impact of the sexual revolution as a factor in the decline of psychoanalysis' cachet in the USA in the later 1960s and 1970s – exactly the years when psychoanalysis' fortunes were rising again in Western and Central Europe, as well as Latin America. Especially where and when sexual mores relaxed, increasing numbers of commentators claimed that it no longer made sense to assume that sexual repression was a key source of human problems.[39] And yet over and over, in culture after culture, as conflicts over sexuality returned in new forms, perceptive observers and impassioned activists alike found that psychoanalytic concepts, however necessarily adapted, remained indispensable for making sense of human dreams and difficulties at the intersections of sexuality and the rest of life. To be sure, "repression" might long since no longer be the best way to think about the relationship between "the sexual" and other realms of existence. But psychoanalytic concepts would continue to be crucial references for grappling with matters as diverse as: the utter inextricability of social context and psychic interiority; the place of ambivalence and the meaning of conflict in intimate relationships; the apparent complexity – even inscrutability – of the relationships between excitement and satisfaction; and the extraordinary power of the unconscious in fantasies and behaviors alike.

All of this, in turn, raises intriguing questions about the opacity of historical causation in the realm of battles over meaning. Almost all the chapters engage the puzzle of major paradigm shifts in areas consequential for law, policy, and/or cultural commonsense – as well as some of the frequent unintended side-effects of such shifts. How do some ideas triumph and take enduring hold, while others are defeated or lost from view? And how might we explain the fact that very similar, even identical, concepts could be put to use for quite opposite agendas? How was it that a passionate investment in the notion of drives, for instance, could coexist with culturally conservative, tolerantly liberal, or subversive-transgressive political visions?[40] How could a belief in inner chaos animate avowedly apolitical and ardently anarcho-politically engaged projects alike? Simultaneously, and conversely, how was it that individuals working from utterly irreconcilable models of human motivation – for example, analysts convinced of the universality of the Oedipus complex and analysts who found the notion beyond preposterous – could nonetheless find themselves on the same side of a contested political divide? My aim throughout has been to relocate each eventual paradigm shift in the complexity of its originating historical context, to show how terms got set and why – and with what often counterintuitive results. But another aim has been to explore what happens when theories travel and when concepts float loose from their original moorings.

In sum, a reading of several decades of psychoanalytic texts can provide a history of the vicissitudes of human nature, culture, politics, and sexuality not least because psychoanalysis has been not only a (variously proud, defensive, banal, insightful, bizarre, and influential) movement-sect-guild-profession-faith-discipline as well as an interactive treatment technique for emotional troubles. Rather, the practitioners and proponents of psychoanalysis have also, in the movement's long and strange career, generated a set of conceptual tools that remain potentially quite useful for critical political and cultural analysis. Twenty-first-century pharmaceutical and neuroscientific research – often bent on ignoring social context and interpersonal relations and intent on refiguring selfhood as a matter mostly of chemical reactions and/or encoding in the genes – has had very little to say, for example, about such crucial features of human existence as conflicting desires, the instabilities of meanings, or the ever-mysterious relationships between psychic interiority and social context. Psychoanalysis, in all its contradictions, absurdities, and self-revisions, can contribute a great deal on precisely these matters.

Part I

LEAVING THE WORLD OUTSIDE

1 THE LIBIDO WARS

"All is not sexuality that looks like it."
Karen Horney, 1937[1]

In the United States, what counted as psychoanalysis in popular awareness and in expert minds in the first seven or eight years after World
War II went through multiple transformations within a very short time,
in a series of controversies alternately subtle and explosive. One of
the major effects of these controversies was to change the relationship
between psychoanalysis and theories of sexuality, as perplexity about
the nature and place of libido in human lives had an impact on the
form and content of all the major analytic schools developed in the
USA. In fact, one could tell the story of American analysis as one of
multiple (but mutually contradictory) efforts to flee from sex's centrality in the original Freudian mission.

Although heretofore understudied, one of the most significant
dynamics shaping the forms taken by postwar psychoanalysis had to do
with complex changes in American *religious* life. In the postwar years a
distinctive combination emerged of, on the one hand, resurgent religiosity (in the form of heightened attendance at houses of worship and
increased self-identification as a "believer" – a trend also expressly fostered by business leaders and politicians), but also often blended with
assertive patriotism and a diffuse but fervent anticommunism with, on
the other, ongoing secularization (as religion became increasingly "psychologized" and directed toward self-optimization and "the power
of positive thinking") *and* a rising acceptance of religious pluralism

(as Jewish, Catholic, and Protestant forms of piety and self-definition became more similar).[2] Numerous scholars have called attention either to the impact on American psychoanalysis of the nearly 200 (mostly, albeit not entirely) Jewish refugee analysts who landed in the USA fleeing the lethal tentacles of Nazism, or have remarked more generally on the growing role of Jewish intellectuals, also native-born ones, on American cultural life in the postwar era – a process sometimes even referred to as "de-Christianization."[3]

A case will be made here that we also need to understand how psychoanalysis in the USA, although often shorthanded as "the Jewish science," may be better understood as profoundly *Christianized* in the course of the first postwar years. But this point comes with the caveat that such Christianization was of a very particular kind, one born precisely of that peculiar mix of revived religiosity, secularization-*cum*-psychologization, and greater religious pluralism that defined the postwar moment.[4] In short, the phenomenon of profound but conflicted sexual conservatism that came to characterize postwar US psychoanalysis – alongside and in contrapuntal tension with its ongoing titillating reputation – needs to be explored as not merely a product of generalized Cold War trends but also very specifically as one major side-effect of the massive and widely broadcast battles over the relationship between religion and psychoanalysis that marked the years 1947–1953 in particular. Indeed, the religious conflicts would not have been nearly so consequential had they not occurred at precisely the moment when psychoanalysis was poised to become broadly popular with the general US public.

Horney's Theories of Sexuality

As it happens, the psychoanalysis that would suffuse psychiatry and pop culture alike from the early 1950s on (specified as "ego psychology" within the profession, even as what was received by the public was far more of a mishmash of competing tendencies) would take its momentum as well as its authority but *not* its content from the forms of psychoanalysis that had initially been developed in the mid- to late 1930s and early 1940s especially by a group loosely referred to as "neo-Freudian." It was these neo-Freudians who prepared the ground for "the halcyon days," the "golden age" of American psychoanalysis in the first two postwar decades, even as they would be shunted aside and deemed wrongheaded by their successors.[5] Another way to put the point would be to say that the ego psychological form of psychoanalysis that was consolidated and was to become extraordinarily influential over the course of the first half of the Cold War, while still amorphous and subject to ongoing contestation, did not only no longer resemble the psychoanalysis that had first intrigued a handful of medical men and literati in the 1910s to 1920s (and which was strongly associated with sexual reform and bohemian experiments in sexual emancipation), but, more importantly, no longer resembled its more immediate predecessor either: the neo-Freudian psychoanalysis that had first secured truly widespread fascination in the general public, within psychiatry, and, notably, across the social science disciplines in the mid- to late 1930s and early 1940s.[6] These neo-Freudians – while strikingly alert to and actually very comfortable with the progressive loosening of sexual mores they saw as happening in the 1930s to 1940s – nonetheless theorized the relationship between the sexual and other realms of existence differently.

The neo-Freudians stood out above all for their emphases on culture, on social pressures and interpersonal relations, in addition to individual intrapsychic dynamics. The neo-Freudians included German émigrés like Franz Alexander in Chicago and Karen Horney and Erich Fromm in New York, but also the native-born Americans Harry Stack Sullivan in Washington, DC and Maryland and Clara Thompson in New York. While inevitably differing also from each other as well as each evolving over time (Sullivan and Thompson, for instance, were strongly drawn to the work of Sigmund Freud's erstwhile Hungarian associate Sándor Ferenczi and his more active and empathetic approach to patients and his interest in dyadic reciprocity between analyst and analysand), they frequently supplemented the traditional psychoanalytic interest in a patient's childhood with attention to the stresses in the patient's ongoing daily adult life. They often took stands on matters of broad social and political interest (Fromm and Horney in particular), and Horney drew as well on anthropological evidence to buttress her case that cultural conditions powerfully shaped what only looked like biologically driven behaviors. They also, at various moments, were associated with experimentation with shorter-term therapies (notably Alexander and Horney), with popularizing "self-analysis" (Horney), and, especially in the case of Alexander, with a concern with how best to approach psychosomatic problems. Meanwhile, Sullivan, together with his colleague Frieda Fromm-Reichmann, became one of the premier innovators in adapting psychoanalysis to work not only with patients deemed neurotic but also with those diagnosed with schizophrenia and other psychoses.[7]

One of the neo-Freudians' most distinctive shared features is the attention they gave to the problem of *anxiety* and related feelings of existential unsafety – whether understood as arising from cultural conditions in a competitive society or from interpersonal tensions either within the family of origin or in ongoing everyday life – and this, in turn, had major consequences for their ideas about sexuality. As Alexander (Budapest-born, Berlin-trained, and since 1930 in Chicago) would remark in an essay of 1946 as he meditated on the expendability of individuals in the face of constant technological innovation: "The result will be that periodic unemployment will remain with us as a constant source of insecurity and a constant threat to self-esteem, arousing the feeling of having lost one's social usefulness." Tellingly, Alexander simply presumed as self-evident that this state of affairs demanded a fundamental rethinking of the basic tenets of the Freudian inheritance as he went on in the same breath to state summarily: "This insecurity and the frustration of having no opportunity to make use of one's productive capacities are the main source of emotional maladjustment in our times, taking the place of sexual repression which dominated the scene during the Victorian era."[8]

The other neo-Freudians had long since offered numerous variations on this theme. Sullivan, for example, was consistently critical of Freud's core concept of libido and his conviction that infants seek pleasure above all; Sullivan instead emphasized the infant's search for safety and approval as it developed its own sense of self.[9] For his part, Fromm (Frankfurt-born, since 1934 in New York), drawing on his sociological as well as analytic training in a virtuoso 1937 essay, "Zum Gefühl der Ohnmacht" ("On the Feeling of Impotence"), was especially attentive to the helpless rage and fear caused by literal economic insecurity – certainly a compelling theme in a time when memories of the Great Depression were still fresh – but also by an emotionally debilitating ideological climate, whether authoritarian or democratic, that continually implied to ordinary, non-elite people that their fate lay in their own hands (even precisely when, as Fromm noted, the actual causational forces and workings of the economic and political power arrangements in a given society were not only out of their hands but very often inscrutably elusive and quite impossible to decipher).[10]

Horney – who was close to and inspired by both Sullivan and Fromm – combined their insights in her 1937 bestseller, *The Neurotic Personality of Our Time* (see Figure 2). There she explored the contradictions in American culture between "Christian ideals which declare it is selfish to want anything for ourselves" and the continual injunctions to be "'keeping up with the Joneses'" and working on making a "success" of oneself ("which means that we must be not only assertive but aggressive") – and all of this in a context, no less, in which "everyone is the real or potential competitor of everyone else" so that "competitiveness, and the potential hostility that accompanies it, pervades

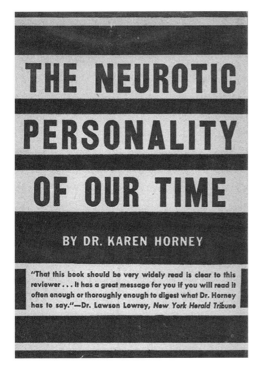

Figure 2 One of the covers of Karen Horney's bestselling *The Neurotic Personality of Our Time* (1937). The endorsement quote is from the eminent American psychiatrist and child guidance expert Lawson Lowrey and declares that "this book should be very widely read." Another edition of the book was adorned with a quote from the British-American anthropologist Ashley Montagu, stating that "Unquestionably this book must be read by anyone who wishes to obtain a really clear insight into the relation between culture and personality."

all human relationships" (including, significantly, close friendships). At the same time, she, too, explicitly rejected Freud's assumption "that the instinctual drives or object relationships that are frequent in our culture are biologically determined 'human nature' or arise out of unalterable situations (biologically given 'pregenital' stages, Oedipus complex)."[11] In her influential follow-up book, *New Ways in Psychoanalysis* (1939), Horney stated even more directly that Freud's "one-sided consideration of the pleasure-principle, implicit in the libido theory" needed to be replaced by a "sociological orientation" in which "the striving for safety" in an inescapably overwhelming environment was the preeminent human aim. And she here argued further – as she spent an entire chapter refuting the idea of the Oedipus complex – that it was not that the Oedipal tale needed to be rewritten; it should simply be dismissed. "The relevant factor in the genesis of neuroses is then neither the Oedipus complex nor any kind of infantile pleasure strivings but all those adverse influences which make a child feel helpless and defenseless and which make him conceive the world as potentially menacing." More generally, Horney found nonsensical what she saw as Freud's tendency to overinterpret everything as sexual – including "the manifold strivings and attitudes which apparently have nothing to do with sexuality – for instance, attitudes of greediness, stinginess, defiance or other character peculiarities, artistic strivings, irrational hostilities, anxieties. The sexual instinct as we are accustomed to regard it could not possibly cover this enormous field." Over and over, Horney was confidently dismissive: "The libido concept is unproved. What is offered as evidence consists of unwarranted analogies and generalizations, and the validity of the data concerning the erogenic zones is highly dubitable."[12]

Horney (non-Jewish, Hamburg-born, Berlin-educated, since 1932 in the USA, first in Chicago and then from 1934 on in New York) had initially made a name for herself in Freudian circles as a highly gifted training analyst (codesigning and directing the Berlin Psychoanalytic Institute's training program as well as working in a hospital and seeing patients in private practice) but also as a perspicacious and irrepressible feminist. To this day she remains best known for her insistence that *if* there was such a thing as female penis envy, then it was caused by differential parental conduct toward children and a girl child's awareness of male privilege (here already one can see the incipient culturalist in her), as well as for her proposition that actually it might well be males who suffered from "womb envy" in the face of women's reproductive capacity – and she had interesting things to say, too, about how apparently deep-rooted in men was the "unconscious impulse to depreciation" of women.[13] But, although this has been much less noted, she also gave extensive thought to the problem of theorizing the relationships between the sexual and other realms of existence.

At first, Horney had attempted to work within the Freudian Oedipal framework – and even though it was constricting in some ways she nonetheless used it to put forward intriguing original aperçus. Thus, for instance, in a 1928 essay on "The Problem of the Monogamous Ideal" (a paper she had delivered at the 10th International Psychoanalytical Congress in Innsbruck), Horney hastened to avow that "there is hardly another situation in life which is so intimately and so obviously related to the Oedipus situation as is marriage" (noting on this basis that inhibitions or rages or possessiveness or guilt or secret hostility toward the partner might have their sources in feelings toward parents, for whom the partner was, she at that point still asserted – and in this respect completely in line with Freud's position – unconsciously a substitute). But then she went on to use this as a springboard to reflect on how the demand for exclusive possession of a partner might have its source not so much in passionate or even anaclitic love as in "analsadistic" and "narcissistic elements" – or, alternatively, in "obsessional compulsion" and denial of one's very own "impulse to seek after fresh objects." Positioning herself as building on the work of Freud (especially his "'Civilized' Sexual Morality and Modern Nervousness" and "Contributions to the Psychology of Love"), but also Ferenczi's "Psycho-Analysis of Sexual Habits," and the sex-radical analyst Wilhelm Reich's 1927 book, *Die Funktion des Orgasmus* (The Function of the Orgasm), she further found it necessary to question "whether (as is so frequently asserted) men have naturally a more polygamous disposition; for one thing, we know so little with certainty on questions of natural disposition." Horney pointed out that not just biological ("seeing that the possibility of conception makes coitus physiologically a more momentous matter for women than for men, is it not to be expected that this fact will have some psychological representation?") but also "historical and social" factors ("the economic dependence of women … the draconic punishments decreed for feminine unfaithfulness," men's demand for a woman's premarital virginity "in order to ensure some measure of 'sexual thraldom' in her") made knowing what was "natural" a matter of the greatest uncertainty.[14]

Occasionally the reflections she squeezed into the Oedipal box sound in hindsight only fanciful, as for instance in one moment Horney suggested that the objects of desire in a child's earliest masturbatory phantasies represented the first unfaithfulness to the beloved and coveted parents and hence became durably associated with guilt and fear, as the dread of parental punishment later became transferred onto dread of the partner's potential rage. But at other moments she was able to use Freud's terminology of stages of sexual development also to make compelling points, as when she called attention to the ambivalent – albeit often disavowed – combination of hate mixed in with love that was inevitable in intimate relations, sometimes precisely in the midst of a monogamous partnership. Thus, in one instance Horney again made reference to the Oedipus complex and unconscious bondedness to parents when she noted acerbically that "the elements of hate can find an outlet" in marriage "not only when the principle of monogamy is violated but when it is observed." Yet in conclusion she also relented and moved on to emphasize that the Oedipal roots of the choice of and attitude toward the spouse had the potential as well to "weaken ... the polygamous tendencies" of *both* partners – so that ultimately "it may become possible for the conflicts to be fought out" and the ideal of "tender attachment between husband and wife" finally to become realized.[15] In sum, as unruly and contradictory as this essay was, and at once stimulated and constrained by inherited logics, it also adumbrated one of Horney's later signal insights: that – as she would put it in her 1937 book – "just as 'all is not gold that glitters,' so also 'all is not sexuality that looks like it.'" For, as she explained further, "A great part of what appears as sexuality has in reality very little to do with it, but is an expression of the desire for reassurance."[16]

Horney was to depart from Freud's theorization of sexuality on at least four grounds (even as she continued to assert, based not least on her commitment to the concepts of unconscious conflict and repression, that "fundamentally my interpretation rests on Freudian ground"). One was her gradually emerging idea that rather than interpreting such character traits as creativity or greediness or anxiety as having a libidinal source and thus in some sense as an expression of originally sexual aims that were then sublimated, misdirected, or repressed, it would be better to understand them as having *non*sexual origins. To some extent, Horney was here creating a strawman of Freud. (Freud himself had over time added to his theoretical edifice the concept of the aggressive drive as a parallel drive to libido – a fact that Horney finessed by picking up on the idea, giving due credit to Freud, that "hostile impulses" were often coupled with "sex impulses."[17] And Freud was in any event hardly a reductive drive-theorist only, as he had already by the mid- to late 1920s at the latest shifted from insistence on the singular significance of the drives to a supplemental interest in "ego functions" and individuals' adaptations to their environments.)[18] Nonetheless, Horney's explicit dismissal of the importance, or even the reality, of libido was certainly to be consequential, as it became a key issue of contention for her adversaries.

Another departure involved the above-mentioned point that just because something looks sexual – and may even involve sexual activity in the narrowest definition of that term – does not mean that its purpose or function is primarily sexual. Sexual activity might rather be seen as serving all kinds of other emotional purposes. A third difference from Freud involved Horney's attunement to historically changing conditions. Just as Alexander's comment of 1946 uncomplicatedly presumed that the "sexual repression" of "the Victorian era" was a thing of the past, so already Horney in her 1937 book took it to be indisputable that mores had loosened. As she phrased the matter:

> The conception of what is normal varies not only with the culture but also within the same culture, in the course of time. Today, for example, if a mature and independent woman were to consider herself "a fallen woman," "unworthy of the love of a decent man," because she had had sexual relationships, she would be suspected of a neurosis, at least in many circles of society. Some forty years ago this attitude of guilt would have been considered normal.[19]

And finally, the fourth count on which Horney diverged from Freud's theories of sexuality – and indeed from Reich's as well, even as she continued to situate herself also in Reich's lineage due to her interest in the Reichian idea of character defenses that individuals evolved in reaction to anxiety – involved the direction of causation between sexual problems and emotional problems. As she phrased this perspective succinctly in the opening pages of her 1939 book: "Sexual difficulties are the effect rather than the cause of the neurotic character structure."[20]

For Horney, a neurotic character structure was produced *not* by conflicts between the ego and libido, but rather by a profound anxiety, an anxiety rooted in the child's powerlessness, warded off from consciousness by elaborate defenses, and subsequently exacerbated by social conditions.

Meanwhile, one of Horney's fundamental arguments remained throughout that men and women alike used sex to get other things they wanted or express other things they felt.[21] And over and over, she tied her elaboration of this idea of sex as instrumental both to reflections on shifts in cultural attitudes ("we have greater freedom in sexual relations and a greater capacity for satisfaction … Frigidity is no longer considered a normal condition in women, but is generally recognized as a deficiency") as well as to the need for a reversed causation in theorizing the connections between sex and all else. In her chapter on "The Role of Sexuality in the Neurotic Need for Affection," Horney thus not only rejected as nonsense the typical Freudian analyst's surmise that sexual desires directed at him- or herself were to be construed "as repetitions of a sexual fixation on the father or mother," arguing that these transference wishes "often … are not genuine sexual wishes at all, but a reaching out for some reassuring contact to alleviate anxiety." In addition, she had the audacity to propose that "a great deal of sexual activity" in the society at large as well might be better understood as "more an outlet for psychic tensions than a genuine sexual drive."[22]

While her feminism was distinctive, the main aspects of Horney's theorization of sexuality were clearly persuasive to other neo-Freudians. Fromm, for instance, in his magnum opus of 1941, *Escape from Freedom*, footnoted Horney as he expounded on how his "own social orientation" differed from Freud's "biological" one. As in his earlier work, Fromm continued to see economic conditions as shaping human behavior, as he also emphasized, similar to Horney's focus on safety, "the need for self-preservation" as "the primary motive of human behavior" and stressed that "because of the imperative need for self-preservation" the economic system under which an individual lived did indeed become "a primary factor in determining his whole character structure." And far more directly than in his prior work, Fromm here expressly distanced himself from "Freud's libido theory," contending, in unambiguously Horneyan fashion, that in general Freud had gotten the sequencing wrong: Freud "mistook the causal relation between erogenous zones and character traits for the reverse of what they really are." Fromm did beg to differ from Horney on whether or not sex was important to people in and of itself: "Although I believe that the discouragement of sexual joy is not the only important suppression of spontaneous reactions but one of many, certainly its importance is not to be underrated."[23] Yet overall, Horney's influence was clearly evident.

By the turn from the 1930s to the 1940s, Horney's impact was culture-wide. To take just one example among many, when in December of 1941 Pearl Harbor was attacked by Japanese forces, an essay Horney wrote about the best means for preparing preemptively for managing anxiety was discussed across the nation.[24] Moreover, Horney's friendships with such luminaries as the feminist anthropologist Margaret Mead, internationally renowned for such books as *Coming of Age in Samoa* (1928), *Growing Up in New Guinea* (1930), and *Sex and Temperament* (1935), and the Yale University psychologist-ethnographer John Dollard, co-coiner, in 1939, of the extensively referenced "frustration-aggression hypothesis," but also author of the widely debated *Caste and Class in a Southern Town* (1937) with its numerous revelations of white men's sexual privileges in the Deep South (including the blatant and apparently socially accepted fact of maintaining sexual relations with Black women alongside their marriages to white women), meant that Horney's ideas frequently showed up in their ongoing work as well.[25] Horney was positively received across the social sciences, as American sociologists too celebrated her as "an outstanding psychoanalyst," embracing her work as "mark[ing] an important step in the highly significant process of freeing psychoanalytic theory and practice from its outmoded formulations" (especially to be appreciated were her insights that "neuroses are disturbances in social relations" and "the libido theory in all its contentions is unsubstantiated") and announcing that, "for years to come, it will probably serve as a standard guide to the newer, more sociological, more realistic Freudianism."[26] And Horney also had fiercely loyal colleagues and students within the New York Psychoanalytic Society and Institute. But precisely this breadth of success and this durable loyalty would prove to be a trigger for her opponents and, already at the time but certainly in hindsight, it was and is impossible to sort out what of the animus directed at her was motivated by professional envy or by misogyny and what by sincere theoretical disagreement.

The brief version of what happened was that a majority of her New York colleagues wanted to restrict the influence Horney had on incoming, and hence still highly impressionable, analytic students and thus – while tensions had been brewing since at least 1939, when *New Ways in Psychoanalysis* was published – in April of 1941 had demoted her upstairs in the sense of restricting her teaching to more advanced students only. Horney reacted by resigning – and taking four colleagues and fourteen students (out of totals of 88 and 110, respectively) with her. Had that been the end of the matter, it is unclear whether relations would have grown as ugly as they did. But Horney did not disappear quietly, and instead – to her ex-colleagues' immense chagrin – launched an "Association for the Advancement of Psychoanalysis" as well as a competing training institute under the name "American Institute for Psychoanalysis." Her ambition was unmistakable and, in the eyes of her former colleagues, unforgivable.

The prominent native-born New York analyst Lawrence Kubie, immediate past president of the New York Psychoanalytic Society, although initially undecided in the disputes as he had once upon a time been something of a Freudian dissenter and open to innovations, changed his tone under pressure from colleagues and took it upon himself to be the point person in setting the record straight.[27] In November 1941, in a statement subsequently published in the *Psychoanalytic Review*, Kubie (albeit anonymously, speaking on behalf of the New York Psychoanalytic Society as a whole) addressed his professional colleagues across the nation as he offered his version of events and expressed indignation that Horney's new institute was succeeding in spreading the idea that it had been "founded as a protest against scientific dogmatism entrenched behind political power within the New York Psychoanalytic Society." Kubie countered with the enumeration of what he saw as the Horney-affiliated group's misdeeds. These included: "an unscientific tendency to form cliques around the persons of individual instructors, and to reject the ideas of others with scant hearing," the generating of "increasing confusion" in the minds of "elementary students," and the "form[ing of] cliques" and a "band of disciples, under the pretext of 'academic freedom.'" Primly, the statement ended: "As the only organization for training in psychoanalysis chartered by the University of the State of New York, and as the only Institute in New York State recognized for such training by the American Psychoanalytic Association, the New York Psychoanalytic

Society and Institute feels called upon to present these facts clearly and unequivocally."[28] Also, in the fall of 1941, when Horney had hoped that the American Psychoanalytic Association would approve of her new organization and deem its training program legitimate, she was disappointed when the New York psychiatrist William V. Silverberg, her ally, lost the election for the presidency of the American Psychoanalytic Association to the influential Kansan psychiatrist and psychoanalyst Karl Menninger. Menninger took the occasion of his acceptance speech to decry the dragging of internecine quarrels among analysts into public view, by which he meant that the neo-Freudians should desist from explicating their differences to a popular audience. Or as he put it, arguments should be "confined to the halls of our meeting places," and no one should attempt "to obtain popular support by appealing to the prejudices and so-called common sense of persons unfamiliar with the details and history of science."[29] The push to exclude Horney from professional prestige nationwide was on, and it would not fully subside until her death in 1952.

Nonetheless, and strikingly, when *Time* magazine in 1946, in its consistent commitment to keeping the American public well informed about developments within and around psychiatry and psychoanalysis, listed what it saw as the six "big-league practitioners" of psychoanalysis in the nation, Karen Horney was still named as one of them. The topics of psychiatry and psychoanalysis were pressing to the fore in the media in that first postwar year not least because of major US government attention. A broad campaign had begun to address the nation's mental health needs and a proposal by "the newly created ... National Advisory Mental Health Council" urged the pouring of "$10,000,000" into expanding the pool of available psychiatrists (at that point numbering only 4,000 across the entire country). In this context the magazine also saw fit to explain to its readers the distinctions and overlaps between psychiatry and psychoanalysis (a sign of how confused it was assumed readers might be): "Psychiatry is a general medical term embracing all types of treatment of mental disease; psychoanalysis, one of the methods, depends on deep probing of a patient's subconscious and past emotional experiences." Horney was the only woman to make the list of six, as *Time* also helpfully elaborated that "Horneyans" were "socially conscious," and that they "dispute Freud's idea that sex is everything and put more emphasis on environment." The other five named by *Time* were: Horney's former

Chicago associate Franz Alexander (who had parted ways with her already in 1934); "Dr. Gregory Zilboorg and Dr. Lawrence Kubie, fashionable Park Avenue analysts"; and "Drs. William and Karl Menninger of Topeka's Menninger Clinic."[30] All five of these men were dismissive of Horney, if not more vehemently contemptuous, in public and in private, whether antagonistic to her all along (for instance, Zilboorg) or in reaction against their own earlier affirmative interest in her work (this applied particularly to Karl Menninger, who had just closed her out of the American Psychoanalytic Association).[31] And the latter four were to become the main strategic players in the soon-to-erupt battle over the harmonizability of psychoanalysis and religion.

The Desexualization of Psychoanalysis

Most scholars who have considered the depoliticization of American psychoanalysis – from Russell Jacoby in 1983 to Eli Zaretsky in 2004 – have referenced the active silencing and expulsion of more radically inclined analysts from the official fold as well as the blunting impact of medicalization on psychoanalysis' critical political potential (in the USA only MDs were allowed to practice as analysts).[32] As Jacoby memorably quipped:

> Next to the quiet, if effective, process of medicalization, the impact of immigration was noisy and catastrophic … The power of psychoanalytic organizations to regulate dissent – and filter out dissenters – paled in comparison with the might of the state to expel or allow entry … The refugees knew the risks … As they filled out their applications for entry permits and visas, their politics evaporated; and what they left off the forms, they dumped in the Atlantic as they crossed it.[33]

Louis Menand in 2011 invoked the Cold War climate of generalized anxiety as both a psychoanalysis-amenable and a conformity-encouraging force, while Elizabeth Ann Danto in 2012 documented the very tangible and extensive redbaiting and intimidating surveillance of analysts – with the foreign-accented émigrés perceived as "queer birds" and especially suspect.[34] And Emily Kuriloff in 2009 and Lewis Aron and Karen Starr in 2013 emphasized that postwar psychoanalysis needs to be understood as itself a "Holocaust survivor" – traumatized and manically intent on fitting into the host society which had, after all, given safe haven to hundreds of analysts and their family members.[35] The enticements to offer either banal pablum or didactic counsel were multiple and quite evidently intense.[36] And it remains indisputable that – despite some significant countervailing efforts to use psychoanalytic ideas for culturally subversive and emancipatory purposes (Herbert Marcuse's *Eros and Civilization* of 1955 and Norman O. Brown's *Life Against Death* in 1959 would be the most notable examples) – the overwhelming trend in the first two postwar decades would be toward an affirmation of normative-conservative values (including especially sexual conservatism).[37]

Two different styles emerged to supersede the neo-Freudians. One was expressly disinterested in sex.[38] For the ego psychologists that began to consolidate their vision in the late 1940s and early 1950s – as systematized by Heinz Hartmann with his coauthors Ernst Kris and Rudolf Loewenstein in New York, and Hartmann's close associate Edward Bibring in Boston, as well as by Karl Menninger's colleague David Rapaport (first in Topeka and then in Stockbridge) – the external world the neo-Freudians had been so concerned with continued to matter, very much, in the sense that the emphasis was placed on an individual's ability to adapt to reality. But the main task of psychoanalysis was to assist a patient in managing intrapsychic conflict. This meant: working on modulating and above all *neutralizing* libidinal and aggressive drives, and above all developing and expanding autonomous ego functions (such as distinguishing between reality and fantasy, controlling impulses and affects rather than acting-out, and integrating synthetically contradictory feelings).[39] Hartmann had no interest in theorizing sex *per se*, but tended to dismiss the topic as having already long since been exhaustively covered by others.[40] The other style that emerged – typified by Karl Menninger's own work, but also evident among such nationally prominent analysts as Robert Knight, Phyllis Greenacre, Leo Rangell, or Ralph Greenson, as well as countless others – insisted on the importance of libidinal themes and restored the Oedipal framework, titillated the reader with sordid or desperate tales, but always directed the story toward a conventionality-reinforcing outcome.[41]

One of the strange misunderstandings held by contemporaries, and one which ended up affecting historiography as well, involved the outraged views of the German émigré philosopher-sociologist Theodor Adorno, whose rupture from his erstwhile colleague Fromm contributed to his intense dislike of Horney as well, and whose hostility to the neo-Freudians would be adopted with like fervor by his close associate Marcuse (who used the conclusion of *Eros and Civilization* and an extended debate in the pages of *Dissent* to settle scores with Fromm).[42] Adorno – in the 1940s still in California exile – found both Fromm and Horney offensively platitudinous. Adorno was surely not wrong to see that, in Fromm and Horney's emphasis on social anxiety and the search for safety in an overwhelming and disempowering world, they also ended up stressing individual accommodation *to* social conditions, rather than encouraging social change. Ironically, this was the same accusation that would later get leveled at the ego psychologists. But in the 1940s and 1950s, the ego psychologists were understood as restoring libido to its rightful place in the Freudian conceptual edifice, and in an important lecture given in 1946 Adorno lambasted Horney specifically as he argued that any "desexualization of psychoanalysis" by definition removed its critical political edge as well.[43] Arguably, the ego psychologists around the far more respected Hartmann – in their own disinterest in the themes of sexual repression or expression and in their emphasis on the autonomous strength and positive adaptation-oriented resources of the individual ego, and despite their later rebuttals of claims that they meant "adaptation" in a conformist way – would be no less contributory to the (generally correct) perception that postwar American psychoanalysis was a normative and normalizing enterprise.[44]

But the main misapprehension absorbed by later historians from Adorno and Marcuse was the idea that Horney was responsible for the "desexualization of psychoanalysis." This view needs to be corrected. On the contrary, although Horney had been unconvinced that there was any such force as "libido," she had extensively theorized both sexuality itself and the relationships between sexual and other realms of existence in ways that were far ahead of her time (and that would only resurface in the midst of the sexual revolution of the 1970s).[45] Instead, although misrecognized in her historical moment, the main impetus for the neutralization in postwar America of whatever sex-radical potential had once existed in psychoanalysis was a battle over whether Freud could be reconciled with Christianity. The ascent of a sex-normative psychoanalysis in postwar America was to a far greater extent than has been previously understood an inadvertent side-effect of this battle.

It was not, however, psychoanalysts who provided the initial spark for the conflict that would end up spreading through the mainstream US media and reaching over the ocean to the Vatican.[46] A Boston-based Reform rabbi named Joshua Loth Liebman had written a book in 1946 entitled *Peace of Mind* which argued for the benefits of being analyzed to all and sundry. It ended up on the *New York Times* bestseller list for three years, even rising to number 1 for 58 (nonconsecutive) weeks. The book's express aim was to reconcile psychiatry and religion. By "psychiatry," however, Liebman specifically meant psychoanalysis (and he blended Freud and Horney as though doing so was completely unproblematic); he himself had been analyzed, and he strongly advocated analysis as the healing method best suited to achieving a lasting cure on the grounds that it got at the root of destructive behavior patterns. By religion Liebman meant a "mature" as opposed to "childish" (these were his terms) faith in a benevolent and glorious God, a God who was powerful but who also – significantly, and in a kind of Social Gospel-inspired, proto-liberation theology way – required human cooperation to bring about a better world. In *Peace of Mind*, he argued explicitly not only that "far from being antagonistic, religion and psychiatry are mutually supplementary," but also that "Sigmund Freud, the founder of psychoanalysis, really had a spiritual purpose, even though he may not have been aware of it."[47]

The book made Liebman a household name across the USA, and his recommendations for achieving greater self-acceptance earned him ads and feature pieces in such venues as *Life* and *Ladies Home Journal* (the latter replete with portraits of his family – which also included an adopted daughter, Leila, a Polish Jewish teenager and survivor of Auschwitz – a striking conjunction of acknowledgment of catastrophe and uplifting messaging) (see Figure 3).[48] The book and the surrounding publicity made him – in the words of historian Andrew Heinze – "decades before Elie Wiesel … the first 'iconic Jew' of postwar America," an individual who pioneered a novel combination of crossover appeal and assimilation with unabashed pride specifically in the Jewish religious heritage, and "the first celebrated Jewish figure identified with the Jewish predicament and the human predicament

Figure 3 Rabbi Joshua Loth Liebman, author of *Peace of Mind* (1946), in a feature piece in *Ladies Home Journal* in 1948. Liebman is shown here with his wife, Fan, and adopted daughter Leila, a survivor of the Auschwitz concentration camp. After more than a million copies had been sold, the cover of the affordable Bantam paperback noted summarily: "This book is treasured in millions of homes for the comfort and inspiration it brings. It blends the great truths of religion with the most helpful insights of psycho-analysis – to guide us in understanding our selves, our loves, fears, griefs and ambitions. Peace of Mind is helping men and women everywhere get more out of life."

after Hitler."[49] In a country in which the notion of a "Judeo-Christian" heritage was just starting to take tentative hold, Liebman did not aim to adapt Jews to the Christian mainstream but on the contrary showed Christians what they could learn from Jews – both from Jewish theological tradition and from Freud.

The book also, and instantly, infuriated a competing celebrity clergyman, Monsignor Fulton J. Sheen, professor at the Catholic University of America in Washington, DC, host (since 1930) of the nationally broadcast nighttime radio program *The Catholic Hour* (in the context of which he received approximately 4,000 letters a week from listeners), and soon to become (as of 1951) Auxiliary Bishop of the Archdiocese of New York.[50] He would later be dubbed "America's Bishop."[51] In March of 1947, Sheen delivered a sermon at St. Patrick's Cathedral in New York in which he took direct aim at – as the *New York Times* reported the next day – "psychoanalysis in general and 'Freudian' psychoanalysis in particular." Sheen made unfavorable comparisons between the couch and the confessional. Confession was healing; it "restores you to relationship with the Heavenly Father." Psychoanalysis, by contrast, could not relieve "the unresolved sense of guilt of sin" from which "most people who consult psychoanalysts are suffering ... Psychoanalysis gives no norms or standards. There are no more disintegrated people in the world than the victims of Freudian psychoanalysis." Moreover, since Freudianism, as Sheen averred, was based on "materialism, hedonism, infantilism and eroticism," any patient who avowed an interest in pursuing a life of "purity" could expect the analyst to be "angry with you." Sheen in addition attacked the psychoanalytic phenomenon of transference. Or, as he put it, the "transfer of the affection to the analyst." This method, Sheen contended, "is only used when the patient is a young and very beautiful woman. It is never found to work among the ugly or the poor." Finally, for good measure, Sheen again worked the class angle, announcing that "most psychoanalysts cater only to the rich."[52]

The situation had been substantially aggravated by the fact that the most famous person Sheen had succeeded in converting to Catholicism – the former *Vanity Fair* editor, successful Broadway playwright, and member of the US Congress Clare Boothe Luce – had in February 1947 begun publishing a three-part essay about her conversion in the popular women's magazine *McCall's*. Luce argued that her bad experience with psychoanalysis was "one of the real reasons I became a

Catholic."[53] In the March installment, read around the country at the same time that Sheen's St. Patrick's Day sermon was being debated, the silliest-sounding and most reductively sex-fixated aspects of Freudianism were skewered. In compressed form, Luce managed to summarize drive theory, the Oedipus complex, and the concept of repression:

> The Freudian child springs from its mother's womb a brat, harboring aggressive and lustful intentions toward Pappa, Mamma, sister, nurse, and, as his little world expands, odd relations and playmates. If these intentions are clumsily or violently suppressed they boil and bubble and fester within him and become "complexes." If in maturity he fails to sublimate them successfully, they break out into anti-social actions which cause him and everybody else endless troubles and heartache.

She also noted, in a perceptive aside, the at-times-uncanny echoes between psychoanalysis and Christianity ("If this is not the doctrine of Original Sin, then I don't know a Catholic doctrine gone wrong, that is, turned into a heresy, when I see one").[54] In short, while Sheen's sermon had not been too explicit about sexual themes even as they were being unmistakably alluded to in the reference to "eroticism," no one concerned with the reputation of psychoanalysis at that moment in the USA would have missed the implicit accusation.

The reaction against Sheen from psychoanalysts of all religious backgrounds was swift. The first to respond publicly would be Lawrence Kubie, once again on behalf of the New York Psychoanalytic Society. Kubie took to the pages of the *New York Herald Tribune* to object to Sheen's "seriously distorted" characterization of "the theories and technique of psychoanalysis" and the way in which Sheen's sermon had caused "the good faith, the honesty and the decency of the profession itself [to be] maligned." Kubie declared Sheen's accusation that psychoanalysis was hedonistic to be "irresponsible nonsense" (as Freud not only was himself an "ascetic," but had consistently emphasized that the "'pleasure principle'" was curbed by the "'reality principle'"). While quite evidently taking his cue from Luce's comparisons of "primitive drives" with "original sin," he also creatively invoked no less an authority than St. Augustine (in whose *City of God*, as it happens, Adam and Eve's disobedience to God caused them to experience "a new motion of their flesh" which their souls could no longer command).[55] Kubie argued that, while perhaps the Church had been the first to identify these "primitive drives," it was psychoanalysis that provided new tools to get beyond conscious grappling with those drives in order to address the *unconscious* level.[56]

Less than a month after Kubie's intervention, in May of 1947, Karl Menninger's brother William – who had been the Army's Chief of Psychiatry during World War II, with the rank of Brigadier General – took to the pages of the *New York Times Sunday Magazine* to provide a complementary but different "analysis of psychoanalysis" and "answer … those who attack it." In contrast to Kubie's delicate discretion, Menninger homed right in on what he perceived to be the main, even if intermittently underacknowledged, subtext of the arguments over the legitimacy of psychoanalysis: sex. Menninger noted that "never before has psychoanalysis been so much a matter of general discussion" and, simultaneously, that many Americans remained, in his view, misinformed. Prime among the misunderstandings, Menninger observed, was the idea that psychoanalysis was "concerned primarily with sex." In response, Menninger developed the influential compromise formation that was to be a hallmark of both his and his brother's approach to the issue of sex's reputed centrality to the Freudian project. Menninger thus oscillated between two in principle incompatible arguments. On the one hand, he made the assertion that sex *was* really very important, going on to endorse the most undiluted version of Freud's original theory of libido: "Actually, sex is the basic and all-pervasive motivation in life, and it must be understood for a healthy mentality." Without needing to mention any of their names, then, he was here positioning himself *in opposition to* the neo-Freudians' rejection of drive theory. Yet, on the other hand, Menninger also contended that the fuss about psychoanalysis and sex was all based on a big misunderstanding; Freud was not really talking about *sex*. "Freud used the word sex as being inclusive of much more than genital activity. This, and the fact that American usage of the word is much more restricted, explains some of the resistance to psychoanalysis." Above all, it was not true, Menninger added, that analysts "interpret all unconscious expressions from a patient in sexual terms." On the contrary, psychoanalysts were all about *reducing* people's sex-focusedness. Far from routing everything back to sex, Menninger – propounding a vision of psychoanalysis as utterly wholesome – declared that an analyst much more frequently "has to point out how the patient's preoccupation with sex is interfering with mature relationship with people and with constructive work."[57]

While Kubie was of Jewish heritage, and Menninger a Protestant, psychoanalytically interested Catholic psychiatrists inevitably took special offense at Sheen's implicit assault on their integrity. A powerful statement was delivered by Catholic psychiatrist Frank J. Curran when, on May 27, 1947, he resigned his post as chief psychiatrist at St. Vincent's Hospital in New York in protest against not only Sheen's aspersions, but also, and even more significantly, in protest against "the failure of the Roman Catholic Archdiocese of New York to clarify or repudiate" them.[58] In the meantime, moreover, and while attending a meeting of the Group for the Advancement of Psychiatry in Minneapolis in June–July 1947 (the group had been founded the year before, under the leadership of William Menninger, for the double purpose of encouraging consciousness about pressing social issues and promoting psychoanalytic approaches among members of the American Psychiatric Association), Curran, together with three other prominent Catholic psychiatrists, issued a press release spelling out their dismay at Sheen's misrepresentations (even as they fudged the issue of the relationship between psychoanalysis and psychiatry by speaking solely in the name of psychiatry): "We take issue with the recent series of public statements attacking psychiatry attributed to Monsignor Fulton J. Sheen ... These statements have been widely interpreted as charging that the science and practice of psychiatry is irreligious." However, they countered, "It is a fundamental tenet of the Catholic Church that there can be no conflict between true science and religion."[59] In addition, the Group for the Advancement of Psychiatry as a whole (at that point representing 126 psychiatrists, approximately 100 of which were present) at the same meeting adopted a resolution which communicated its concern about Sheen's attack on psychoanalysis in particular. Declaring that "medicine and religion [have] assumed distinctive roles in society, but they continue to share the common aim of human betterment," they went on, in a rather unanalytic but determined vein, to stress the upstanding aims of analysis, going so far as to contend that "We believe that a major goal of treatment is the progressive attainment of social responsibility."[60]

The sticking point for many Catholics but also numerous Protestants involved their concern that Freudianism was shorthand for not just an unseemly but a frankly immoral overemphasis on sex. Sex was not the only issue. There were other issues to be sure, including the profound philosophical question of whether humans had free will or were driven by impulses outside their conscious control, as well as the question (which had been set in motion by Liebman's emphasis on self-acceptance and the damages done by neurotic, inappropriate guilt) of whether guilt over misdeeds was actually an ethically highly appropriate emotion. Ancillary debates concerned the grounds on which religion and psychoanalysis could be discussed. Numerous commentators would argue for the compatibility of science and religion. (Erich Fromm, for instance, was to contend that only the humanist elements within each of these were to be respected but that then these would be combinable.)[61] By contrast, Zilboorg, ever the fervent Thomas Aquinas fan, insisted precisely on maintaining the division of labor between science and religion. Freud had only concerned himself with the psyche, never with the soul; why should Catholics take any more offense at Freudians than they did at surgeons?[62] Or again: "It [psychoanalysis] threatens religion no more than the heliocentric theory or Newtonian physics threatened religion. Man's faith and man's need for moral values are not overthrown by scientific discoveries, although they may be destroyed by wars and concentration camps."[63] Others, by contrast, pointed out that of course psychoanalysis and religion were in competition, since both concerned themselves with human behavior.[64]

But the conversation kept circling back to sex, and to the theory of libido. And in this context, Catholic and Protestant critics – either unaware of or ignoring the fact that Freud had moved beyond simplistic drive theory – kept emphasizing that it was Freud himself who was responsible for making psychoanalysis a sex-obsessed, libido-rooted, Oedipally framed enterprise. Already close on the heels of Sheen's sermon, in April 1947, writing in the widely read monthly *Catholic World*, the Catholic historian Thomas Patrick Neill expressly stated that despite Freud's gradual self-revisions (e.g., shifting from topographical metaphors to a structural model of id, ego, and superego), Freud had remained immovable in his conviction that individuals' problems were rooted in childhood and "'were always concerned with sexual excitations and reactions against them.'" ("To the day of his death in 1939 Freud refused to deviate from this conclusion [that neuroses all had a sexual etiology]." For Freud, the "instinctive, irrational, unconscious self called the Id, 'the essence of the soul,' is a pan-sexual entity ... Freud pushes all impulses back to sex-energy, his well known 'libido.' ") This in turn meant that the conclusions drawn by Freudianism were inevitably "strained. They contradict common sense and the traditional intellectual heritage of the Western World. Either Freudianism is wrong, or the Christian tradition is absurd."[65] A year later, the popular novelist Kathleen Norris, again in *Catholic World*, expressed her disgust at the intrusiveness of analysts inquiring into the minutiae of female patients' intimate encounters with their husbands as well as the encouragement to patients (under the auspices of "transference") to fall for their doctors instead, and above all found appalling that in psychoanalysis "all begins and ends with sex. Any reference to God and goodness I have yet to find in books on this subject. And yet the dangers of atom bombs and Communist threats are child's play indeed before the prospect of the unthinkable darkness of a world without goodness and without God."[66] But Protestants too were clearly concerned. In the *Christian Century*, the flagship journal of mainline US Protestantism, a Lutheran worried about Freud's "overemphasis on sexual energy or libido."[67] And *Time*, ever attuned to mainstream concerns, reported summarily in 1948 about the ongoing "catcalls from the public – about Freud's preoccupation with 'sex.' Certainly it helped give psychoanalysis (and with it, psychiatry) a bad name. (Another reason was Freud's personal atheism.)"[68]

One of the oddest, and telling, aspects of the burgeoning dispute involved the unremittingness with which the participants on all sides engaged in a collapsing of, but then again a distinguishing between, psychiatry and psychoanalysis as well as of varieties within psychoanalysis – a clear indication of just how much the relationship between psychiatry and psychoanalysis was at that very moment in strong flux, but was also, and not least through the evolving conflicts over religion, in the process of being settled (but in a very particular way). The general consensus among scholars is that – as Zaretsky put it most succinctly – "After the war the influence of psychoanalysis exploded."[69] Or, as Harold Blum, psychoanalyst and director of the Sigmund Freud Archives, has said: "Indeed, at the time, psychoanalysis had a greater impact upon American psychiatry than it had upon psychiatry in any other time or place in history."[70] And already within the historical moment, psychoanalysts themselves would soon be very proud to announce – as, for instance, M. Ralph Kaufman, psychiatrist at Mount Sinai and president of the American Psychoanalytic Association, would do in 1950: "At this time it is rather difficult to visualize

American psychiatry divorced from psychoanalytic concepts."[71] But the point that requires emphasis is that it was in the midst of the by no means marginal fight over the compatibility between religion and psychoanalysis in the postwar years in the USA that a unique version of psychoanalytic psychiatry was consolidated. And a further point is that the now-you-see-it-now-you-don't quality of the many references to the purported centrality of sexual matters to the psychoanalytic project was a result of this fight as well.

The Menningers

Many things, as it happens, were going on at once – both in front of and behind the scenes. And nobody understood better just how much was at stake than the Menninger brothers. Among the tasks the brothers had set themselves were at least three, all of which they pursued with sustained vigor, alongside their respective Topeka-based jobs managing the Winter Veterans Administration Hospital (Karl) and the Menninger Foundation (William). They were striving to expand the purview and practice of psychiatry across the nation; they were jockeying *within* the American Psychiatric Association to promote psychoanalytic approaches; and – suddenly confronted, at the very moment they were positioned to succeed amazingly at meeting their first two goals, by accusations of impropriety of purpose coming from Sheen, a national celebrity who styled himself as speaking on behalf of the globally powerful Roman Catholic Church – they were hastening to mobilize a counter-campaign that would stress instead the congruence of analysis with faith.[72] As believing Christians themselves, and no doubt specifically also as small-town Midwesterners – and this despite their national profile, their cosmopolitan experiences, and their well-cultivated close connections to individuals at the highest levels of the US government and military (William, for instance, had been utterly instrumental in persuading the Army to focus its psychiatric efforts on rehabilitation rather than diagnosis and discharge, and both men were essential to garnering government support for growing mental health services nationwide) – they understood more acutely, and viscerally, than many other practicing psychoanalysts, whether native-born or émigré, just how fundamental were the concerns of hundreds of thousands of faithful Protestants and Catholics about the (variously threatening or nebulous) phenomenon called psychoanalysis.[73] Not only the immediate and widespread media attention to the controversy as it was happening, also in the religious press, but the multiple dozens of articles and books that would continue to be published in the years that followed, would be a testimony to the extreme volatility of the issues. And the Menningers' views mattered. As the *Time* magazine story in 1948 (with William Menninger on the cover) was to explain, thanks to the Menningers Topeka "is the largest training center for psychiatrists in the world; it trains 15% of all the psychiatrists now being trained in the U.S."[74]

The issue was simultaneously one of belief and of business. Certainly, psychoanalysts were continually worried that their newly won public respect could be tarnished by quacks. As Zilboorg had remarked in passing already in 1939, when first fretting over whether sex could be at the root of a potential conflict between religion and psychoanalysis (a question he – tactically or sincerely? – answered in the negative): "There are purple and red neon signs glowing in some streets of Hollywood which proclaim the virtues of psycho-analysis along with those of hair tonics and sure-fire laxatives. Such conspicuous and cheap popularity is usually a sign of decay."[75] But in the postwar years, with government money flowing in and with psychoanalysis having acquired a surge of prestige within psychiatry not least because of its efficacious use within the military, the financial stakes were even higher. As the analyst-historian Nathan Hale found, "between 1948 and 1961 psychoanalytic institutes received $1,121,030" from the National Institute of Mental Health, while "the Menninger Foundation alone received some $881,584. Two of the largest recipients of NIMH funding were Yale and UCLA, where psychoanalysts headed departments of psychiatry."[76] But none of that was secure or known as of yet when Sheen mounted his campaign of criticism.[77]

In the wake of Sheen's attacks and the ensuing discussion in the press, Karl Menninger – more strongly interested in psychoanalysis than his brother – was caught in a bind. Both he and William had been analysands of Alexander's (Zilboorg, not incidentally, was as well, as was Karl's closest friend, the Detroit-based Catholic psychiatrist Leo Bartemeier, who had been one of the four prominent Catholics to protest Sheen's sermon). He himself had entertained more loosely "psychodynamic" modifications of analytic technique. He himself could well have been mistaken for a neo-Freudian to the extent that he had – again, as had William – really often, and not least precisely in the very successful efforts to expand psychiatric services in the Army and across the country, worked from an "environmentalist" premise.[78] If he argued against Sheen that psychoanalysis was *not* a sex-focused enterprise, then he would sound even more like Horney.[79] The accusations that psychoanalysis revolved around sex were complicated for him to respond to. Menninger wanted to say: We *are* about sex (against Horney). We are *not* about sex (against Sheen).[80] He clearly felt bothered that psychoanalysts continued to be associated with encouragement to non-normative sexuality.[81] At the same time, and while there were also Catholic and Protestant defenses of Freud heard in the press, all too often, as they were being elaborated, they ended up sounding rather more like defenses of the neo-Freudianism with which Karl Menninger felt so competitive.[82]

Meanwhile, undeterred, or even spurred further, Sheen in 1949 slammed back, publishing a counter-book to Liebman's bestselling *Peace of Mind*, pointedly entitled *Peace of Soul*. Pulling out all the stops, Sheen did not hesitate to exaggerate or twist Liebman's views into a (mendacious) caricature – one which combined theologically serious points with unquestionably antisemitic overtones, and mocked Liebman's hopes that human beings could learn to be kinder to each other. Sheen imagined a

> Pharisee (who was a very nice man) ... praying in the front of the temple as follows: "I thank Thee, O Lord, that my Freudian adviser has told me that there is no such thing as guilt, that sin is a myth, and that Thou, O Father, art only a projection of my father complex. There may be something wrong with my repressed instincts, but there is nothing wrong with my soul. I contribute 10 per cent of my income to the Society for the Elimination of Religious Superstitions, and I diet for my figure three times a week. Oh, I thank Thee that I am not like the rest of men, those nasty people, such as the Christian there in the back of the temple who thinks that he is a sinner, that his soul stands in need of grace, that his conscience is burdened with extortion, and that his heart is weighted down with a crime of injustice. I may have an Oedipus complex, but I have no sin."[83]

While in his sermon, Sheen had been undiscriminating in his blanket dismissal of Freudianism, in his book he was repeatedly more differentiated. Thus Sheen at one point tried to clarify that "when I attack sex analysis, I do not mean the theory of Freud, but rather that of the bandwagon climbers who take Freud too seriously and who explain *all* neuroses as repressed sexuality." Yet nonetheless Sheen also stated that the trouble remained that Freud had given such "wide signification … to libido or sex." At another moment, Sheen again conceded that "a distinction must in fairness be made between Freud and Freudianism, a kind of pan-Sexism which reduces everything to sex in a way that Freud himself never intended." Nonetheless, in the interstices, when explicating what kinds of analysis he found acceptable, Sheen also made friendly mention of Horney, hailing her criticism of "an analysis searching only for instinctual causes," expressing appreciation of her recommendations for "self-analysis" (since engaging in it could help avoid actually entering an analysis and thereby running the risk of having a potentially sexualized transference), and listing her, affirmatively, as one of the few analysts who had "abandoned fundamental Freudian ideas," contrasting this with others who continued to show an "exaggerated interest in sex."[84] What Sheen's textual shell game (not all Freudians are sex-obsessed but some are; Freud himself wasn't, but then again he was, overly preoccupied with sourcing all emotional troubles to libidinal repression, etc.) prompted in his opponents was quite apparently an even more urgent desire to offer counterarguments.

Thus, for instance, when psychoanalytic psychiatrists Clarence P. Oberndorf and Sol W. Ginsburg (both friends with both Menningers) in 1950 sponsored a book to promote popular acceptance of psychoanalysis (blurbed on the front cover as "A practical guide by leading authorities, covering personal, family and social problems, with valuable information essential to normal living") – a book which included contributions by Kubie and Karl Menninger as well as Alexander, Anna Freud, and others – they also reprinted a 1948 essay written by Ginsburg on "Religion: Man's Place in God's World" (criticizing Sheen's sermon).[85] And they included an Appendix under the title "Some Common Misunderstandings of Psychoanalysis," the first item of which stated that "Psychoanalysis reduces all emotional disturbances to sex." The refutation of this misunderstanding began with the words, "The most widely held misconception of all and vexing because of its tenaciousness." In rebuttal, the authors maintained: "It is a statement devoid of meaning bordering on the ridiculous and about

as absurd as a pronouncement that 'physics reduces everything to electricity' – except that nowadays nobody would commit such an obvious error." For actually, they affirmed, "if the statement refers to the
sexual functions of the adult, curiously enough, the very opposite is
true: sexual disturbances (unless caused by organic disease) are due
to psychological disturbances, that is, they are symptoms of neurosis,
not its cause."[86] This was, it should be noted, a thoroughly *Horneyan*
idea – yet another indication that actually her theory not only made
quite a lot of sense, but also could be rather useful in the midst of the
fights at hand. Yet in the very next "common misunderstandings" item,
a stance against neo-Freudians (specifically their minimization of the
determinative importance of childhood) was once again pronounced.

Along quite evidently related lines, when in 1951 Karl Menninger was profiled in *Time* magazine, under the headline "Psychiatry
and Religion," the presumed connection in the popular mind between
the psychoanalytic enterprise and an inappropriate preoccupation with
sexual matters was palpable, and it was manifestly apparent that Karl
was on an ongoing crusade to undo those presumptions. "Busy Dr. Menninger practices Presbyterianism as well as Freud," *Time* announced. In
the article, Karl went further than he had ever gone in prior comments
to the press, testifying to his own commitment to the practice of prayer
and, in addition, to his conviction that God heard all prayers, "because
my conception of God is such that everything reaches Him." Always
ecumenism-minded, Karl further explained that group religious worship under the guidance of a "pastor, rabbi or priest" was extremely
beneficial in "furthering interpersonal linkages and enthusiasm in a
common purpose." And once again, in an unmistakable gesture to the
initial terms of the conflict between Sheen and Liebman, Menninger
worked to counter the notion that psychiatrists promoted "a Godless,
immoral philosophy," and he expressly rejected "the common impres-
sion that psychiatry is down on all sense of guilt." As *Time* summarized: "Not so, argues Menninger. It is only false guilt – the patient's
sense of sin about something he did not do – that psychoanalysis tries
to remove." And to round off his remarks, Karl once more expressed
annoyance that "many ministers and laymen apparently assume that
the Freudians are in favor of general sexual promiscuity." In terms very
similar to the ones used by William three years earlier, but with even
more feeling, Karl declared: "This assumption is false, and its reitera-
tion is a lie, a slander ... Psychoanalysts do not favor promiscuity, do

not encourage it, do not attempt to relieve any patient's guilt about it ... Quite the reverse, most of them spend hours and hours attempting to relieve patients from the compulsive feeling of need for these very 'immoralities.' "[87] Few statements could have captured more plainly the strategy being taken by some of the most prominent psychoanalysts to ward off the slightest hint that psychoanalysis had any non-conventional intentions.

Psychoanalysis and the Pope

Finally, in September 1952, Pope Pius XII weighed in, in clear response both to the arguments unfolding in the USA and in Western Europe and Canada (where numerous priests and activist laity who were interested in psychoanalysis had been pleading for the right to be analytically trained and/or had published books arguing for the compatibility of Freud and faith). A Dominican named Albert Plé had started a journal in 1947, a supplement to *Vie spirituelle*, which printed articles on psychoanalysis; the Jesuit Louis Beirnaert (analyzed by Daniel Lagache and under supervision from Jacques Lacan) began to conduct analyses; the philosopher Roland Dalbiez had published a book, to wide acclaim also in Catholic circles, which argued that, while Freud's theories were often eccentric, his method was valuable, and he had been right to point to the existence of the unconscious.[88] Also among the issues being put forward by priests interested in psychoanalysis was the question of priestly vocation and the reasons for choosing a life of celibacy. One articulate proponent of openness to psychoanalysis was the French priest Marc Oraison, who expressed concern that celibacy in some cases might not be truly a choice of faith, but rather a sign of an unstable personality in flight from sexuality; his book of 1952, based on a doctoral thesis completed 1951 on "Christian Life and Problems of Sexuality" that had initially garnered the "nihil obstat" from church authorities and thus had been deemed as containing nothing offensive to faith or morals, received such attention that the Vatican became alarmed and Oraison was asked to retract and self-censor.[89]

Pius was highly cognizant of the tenor of discussion in the USA not least because Bartemeier had come to see him in 1949 expressly in order to ask for permission to take up an offer to become the next president of the International Psychoanalytical Association. Pius, who – as

Bartemeier's memoirs later revealed – was remarkably knowledgeable about the intricacies of psychoanalysis, had given his blessing, urging Bartemeier, in playing this role, to see himself as also bringing honor to Catholicism.[90] In April 1952, however, the debate was once again filling the international media, as a leading prelate of the Catholic Church, Monsignor Pericle Felici, had declared bluntly that any individual seeking or providing "psychoanalysis as a method of cure" was risking "mortal sin." Vatican spokesmen had hurried to declare this simply Felici's personal opinion.[91]

This was the prompt for Pius to spell out his own position. Taking the occasion of a speech to an international gathering of medical professionals in France, Pius got right to the heart of the arguments as he distinguished between one tendency within Freudian psychoanalysis (or as he pointedly called it, "the pansexual method"), which he deemed absolutely unacceptable for any faithful Catholic, and alternate methods of the talking cure – such as some other Freudian ones but also Jungian ones, known to be less fixated on sex – which could be acceptable as long as the doctor and patient steered clear of too much sex-talk.[92] (As the Jesuit Gordon F. George would soon explicate in the pages of the Catholic journal *America*, "the Holy Father" was definitely not including *all* Freudians in his criticism of "the pansexual method" – only the analyst who "manipulates his techniques to bring the patient back again and again to sex, when he suggests sexual interpretations of all dreams and encourages and guides the free association of ideas to sex, then we can surely say that pansexualism has descended from theory into method.")[93] In Pius' own words:

> In order to rid himself of repressions, inhibitions or psychic complexes man is not free to arouse in himself for therapeutic purposes each and every appetite of a sexual order which is being excited or has been excited in his being, appetites whose impure waves flood his unconscious or subconscious mind … For a man and a Christian there is a law of integrity and personal purity, of self-respect, forbidding him to plunge so deeply into the world of sexual suggestions and tendencies.[94]

In his own unique compromise formation, then, Pius expressed himself as being amenable to talk as a therapeutic *method*, even as he remained sharply critical of the overemphasis on sex that he thought was still expressed in too much Freudian *theory*.

Less than a year after his French address, in April 1953, Pius publicly and officially relented even further. *Newsweek* – among many other venues – was pleased to announce that, in a speech to another international gathering, this time to a conference of psychotherapists and psychologists meeting in Rome, "Pius formally approved the use of psychoanalysis as a healing device."[95] The pressure of popular, indeed also pious Catholic, but especially *clerical* interest in psychoanalysis had been quite apparently too strong for an outright prohibition of the practice, as the pope's own reflections on the matter made abundantly clear. Himself speaking in the language of "the ego," "the unconscious," and "the repressed," Pius indicated that "Science affirms that recent observations have brought to light the hidden layers of the psychic structure of man" and that questions about the "dynamisms, determinisms, and mechanisms hidden in the depths of the soul" rightly belonged to the areas of "competence" for therapists and clinical psychologists alike.[96] Or, as the French newspaper *La Dépêche de Toulouse* put the point succinctly, "Freud and Vatican sign armistice. Far from putting it on the Index, the Church now accepts psychoanalysis as a psychotherapeutic method for the soul."[97]

Pius did once again caution his listeners that one could go too far in addressing sexual matters, and he warned that therapists should never usurp the role of priests. But this time he allowed that *some* talk of sex could be beneficial: "There is also an efficacious sexual education which in entire safety, teaches with calmness and objectivity what the young man should know for his own personal conduct and his relationship with those with whom he is brought into contact." Pius actually granted the existence of "psychical sexual troubles"; he just found problematic the idea of dragging into consciousness every possible intimate detail. For: "The indirect treatment also has its efficacy and often it suffices to a large extent."[98]

Conclusion

By the 1970s in the USA, the ego psychologists would themselves have been overturned. And by the 1980s or 1990s at the latest, the neo-Freudians' perspective had risen again. In the 2000s present, a school called "relational psychoanalysis," growing out of the interpersonal approach once pioneered by Harry Stack Sullivan, supplemented by British object relations theorists' emphasis on internalized relations with others, is one of the most influential modes.[99] Indeed, as early as 1998, sociologist of knowledge Neil G. McLaughlin observed: "While neo-Freudians lost the battle for legitimation as a separate school of thought, they won the major intellectual wars in which they were engaged within psychoanalysis." Among other things: "Few contemporary psychoanalysts defend the orthodox libido theory that was the major object of criticism by Horney, Sullivan and Fromm. Contemporary Freudian thought is dominated by the concern with gender and the mother pioneered by Horney, the focus on interpersonal dynamics articulated by Sullivan, and the historical, sociological and cultural factors introduced earlier by Fromm, Horney and Sullivan."[100]

Actually, however, Horney continues into the twenty-first century to be misunderstood above all as a commentator on gender relations more than on sexuality *per se* – and the innovation in her efforts to retheorize the connection, and direction of causation, between sexual and other realms of existence has gotten lost from view. At the same time, it has become near impossible to dislodge the peculiarly pitying presumption – advanced in what is still one of the most oft-cited biographies, Bernard J. Paris's *Karen Horney: A Psychoanalyst's Search for Self-Understanding* (1994) – that Horney's abiding difficulty in life was that her sharp and discerning feminism was combined with ongoing romantic and sexual interest in men. (Or, as Paris puts it, "her compulsive need for men.")[101] Thoroughly missed, for example, is the fact that quite a few of Horney's original questions about the nonsexual sources of sexual behavior would resurface again – albeit without any reference to her – in the 1970s work of such otherwise completely opposed analysts as the (tendentially sexually conservative) self psychologist Heinz Kohut and the (sex-radical and subversive) analyst of sexual excitement Robert Stoller.[102] The endless and intricate entanglements between sexual and other realms of existence, as well as the crucial aperçu articulated by Horney that "all is not sexuality that looks like it," would prove enduring puzzles for psychoanalysts – and indeed for everyone who researches and reflects on sexuality – up until the present.[103]

All of this, however, was still very far on the horizon at the turn from the 1940s to the 1950s. In one sense, Bishop Sheen had been defeated (and not only because, however ironically, he himself had contributed mightily to the trend toward "psychologization" of American Catholicism that he had initially so strenuously attacked).[104] Subsequent Catholic interventions, while continuing – notably – to express concerns specifically about psychoanalytic laxity around sexual mores, were far more mellow on both psychiatry and psychoanalysis and often eager for "rapprochement."[105] Thus, for instance, the Jesuit Francis P. Furlong titled an essay of 1955 elucidating the Pope's 1953 stance and published in the *Bulletin of the Menninger Clinic*, "Peaceful Coexistence of Religion and Psychiatry."[106] And the Catholic psychiatrist Francis J. Braceland – a mentee of Bartemeier's – published an anthology in 1955 entitled *Faith, Reason and Modern Psychiatry: Sources for a Synthesis*. Both Furlong and Braceland's contributors found positive things to say about Freud.

But, from another perspective, Sheen had triumphed. As of the early 1950s, psychoanalysts had become very careful about revealing to a wider public any not utterly normative ideas about sexuality. Perhaps tellingly, the French Jesuit Beirnaert had announced in the pages of the French Jesuit journal *Études* already in 1952 that – as Furlong summarized it – there was only "a very limited school of pansexualism anywhere, perhaps none in the United States."[107] Either appreciating the trend away from too much sex-obsession that he identified in US psychoanalysis or strategically insisting on that trend so as to reduce Catholic opposition (this was, after all, an essay written *before* the 1953 papal statement and intending to help sway Pius), Beirnaert argued that Freudianism had been evolving and was now

> more and more devoted to the totality of the conflicts that upset the personality in its relations with itself, with others and with the world. Freud's theory of instincts leaves plenty of recognition for aggressivity and the need of security. Personality development, instead of being reduced to a mere privileged instinct, is seen as a total growth in the sense of personalization and of socialization. It is less and less concerned with "technique of sexuality." When a treatment is run along these lines, experience shows that it is possible to bring sexual or aggressive conflicts out into the light of consciousness, without violating, in the Pope's words, the law "of personal integrity and purity."[108]

This was a fair summary of what had developed in the USA, due to the work of *both* the "neos" and the "egos."

Nonetheless, sex, after all, and despite psychoanalysts' many protestations, had been one of the main reasons Americans had been at all interested in the first place in that incontestably idiosyncratic system of thought that was psychoanalysis. And alas, one of the great troubles with the ensuing dynamic was that the *post*-neo-Freudian psychoanalysis readers were increasingly treated to would contribute just as much, if not more so, to exacerbating their woes within intimate relations rather than to alleviating them. This would be due not least to analysts' reaction to an unexpected attack from a new quarter.

Nobody but Christian spokespeople had seriously challenged psychoanalysts' hegemony on expert discourse about sex. Nobody, that is, until the sexologist Alfred Kinsey burst onto the national scene. Initially, confronted with the first volume in 1948, some psychoanalysts – Karl Menninger included – were comfortable defending Kinsey's research, even if they made a few critical or qualifying remarks about one or another aspect of the work. Menninger, for instance, assured an acquaintance (the philanthropist Ada McCormick) in March 1948 that "I am sure it [the volume] will be disquieting to many people who are not in intimate contact with the secret lives of individuals as psychiatrists are, but I can only tell you that every psychiatrist that I know of is prepared to accept the Kinsey report as sound … Don't underestimate it – it is very, very important."[109] This tone would change when the second volume of the Kinsey Report, on women, appeared in 1953.

Psychoanalysis in the USA had initially, and adroitly, reconfigured itself in response to widely publicized criticisms from church leaders. Psychoanalysts were wholly unprepared for being outflanked by new competition. In their testy antagonism to Kinsey, US psychoanalysts solidified the misogynist and homophobic views for which they have become so justly notorious.

2 HOMOPHOBIA'S DURABILITY AND THE REINVENTION OF PSYCHOANALYSIS

"We can all be given a diagnosis."
Robert Stoller, 1973[1]

One of the many mysteries surrounding the broad popular success of psychoanalysis in the United States in the first two postwar decades involves the fierce persistence with which analysts insisted on denigrating homosexuality, especially male homosexuality, and the passion they poured into explicating a particular version of femininity – one they insisted must involve sexual responsiveness to men, but on very specifically circumscribed terms. And one of the notable but underexplored facts in the historical vicissitudes of psychoanalysis is that the arrival of the sexual revolution and the subsequent rise of the gay rights and women's rights movements also marked the end of American psychoanalysis' halcyon days and its transmogrification into a still culturally influential but professionally far more marginal niche phenomenon. What remains ill understood is the impact of historical conditions – and psychoanalysts' eagerness for cultural relevance – on the content of psychoanalytic theory.

What has also so far been underappreciated is the astonishingly strong, and recurrent, influence of competitiveness with sexology and with sex rights activism of any kind. Professionals or activists (sometimes overlapping categories) who claimed to speak about human sexuality from a vantage point other than psychoanalysis were vigorously rebuffed. This was so whether the challenger was the German sexologist and homosexual rights activist Magnus Hirschfeld, or the American sex researchers Alfred Kinsey and, later again, William Masters and Virginia Johnson; in each instance, psychoanalysts reacted with a combination of creative flexibility and furious tenacity. This trend was all the more remarkable despite (or because?) of analysts' own ambivalence about centering libido at the heart of their intellectual project.

To put it another way: psychoanalysis' own conflicted relationship to sex explains a great deal both about its fortunes and about the ever-evolving contents of its most cherished concepts. This would become especially evident in the course of the 1970s, as psychoanalysts engaged in an extended debate over whether their patients – or indeed human beings more generally – could best be understood through the framework of Oedipal conflicts or rather were beset by pre-Oedipal problems, including borderline and narcissistic character disorders. The discussion turned on whether it was time to shift "from Oedipus to Narcissus."[2] The label most frequently ascribed to the decade of the 1970s – "the culture of narcissism" – has its tangled origins not least in an intra-psychoanalytic struggle to maintain the post-Freudian animus to homosexuality within a renovated framework that emphasized pre-Oedipal over Oedipal challenges. Reinventing psychoanalysis and reinventing homophobia went hand in hand. But it would be in the context of conflict over this intra-psychoanalytic paradigm shift that innovative counterarguments and a fresh theory of sexual desire and excitement came also to be formulated.

Homophobia after Freud

Beginning already in the midst of the battles over the proper relationship between psychoanalysis and religion, an additional subtle paradigm shift in postwar US psychoanalytic thinking about sex evolved in direct reaction to – indeed *against* – Alfred Kinsey. Kinsey's *Sexual Behavior in the Human Male* and *Sexual Behavior in the Human Female*, published in 1948 and 1953, were widely read and discussed in the US media.[3] Instantly, already the first Report was understood full well, by the general public and journalists alike, as an endorsement, in the guise of scientific empiricism, of a greater "democratic pluralism of sexuality" – as the psychoanalytically inclined literary critic Lionel Trilling put it at the time, evincing considerable distaste and

discomfort at the idea.[4] Through its statistics alone, the Report constituted a frontal attack on the idea of constricting sex to monogamous
heterosexual marriage. But it did more than that. It took ordinary
people's experiences seriously. As the reviewer in *The Nation* noted,
until the first Report, "only two organized groups have been entitled to
talk about sex – the churches and the psychoanalysts." Alfred Kinsey
made it possible for everyone to talk. No wonder, then, that "clergymen and psychoanalysts are among the most militant enemies of the
report."[5] Initially, there were some psychoanalytic responses that were
moderate in tone – intrigued, overall, but including a few criticisms of
Kinsey's method and conclusions.[6] And interestingly, Erich Fromm still
took the occasion of the first Report to restate the neo-Freudian position (with its characteristic assumptions of reversed causation between
sexual and other emotional troubles).[7] But by the time the second
Report appeared, psychoanalysts as a guild had become uniformly and
extraordinarily critical. Among their many objections, psychoanalysts
took special offense at the fact that Kinsey had asserted that there was
no particular difference between men and women in such matters as
their capacity for orgasm, or for marital infidelity, or for sexual interest
in general. And they were incensed that Kinsey actively advanced the
view that homosexuality was a natural variant of human sexuality –
and indeed a remarkably prevalent one.

What had changed with regard to the topic of homosexuality in the half-century since Sigmund Freud had first weighed in on
the themes of sexual desire, aims, and objects? Freud's work was full
of contradictory impulses and recurrent self-amendments, but he was
unquestionably more open and curious about the intricacies of desire
than many of the psychoanalysts who followed in his wake. On the
one hand, there were in Freud's published work the normative assumptions that what he called "a normal sexual life" required: making an
object choice external to the self; connecting the drive for pleasure to
reproductive aims; fusing component instincts and putting any remaining partial (polymorphous, oral, anal) drives into the service of genital
primacy.[8] On the other hand, there were also in his published writings
repeated declarations that: homosexuals were not necessarily any more
mentally unstable than heterosexuals; homosexuals could in fact serve
as analysts themselves; and there was as little prospect of converting
homosexuals to heterosexuality as the reverse.[9] Moreover, and emphatically, Freud declared (in a 1915 footnote added to his *Three Essays on*

the Theory of Sexuality, initially published in 1905): "Psycho-analytic research is most decidedly opposed to any attempt at separating off homosexuals from the rest of mankind as a group of a special character."[10] In general, Freud's conviction about the constitutive bisexuality of all human beings meant that homoeroticism was a possibility within everyone.[11] And in Freud's subsequently published correspondence, it was also evident how often Freud struggled with what he in his own words called an "unruly homosexual feeling" in himself, even as the yearning for the men for whom this feeling in him stirred (from Wilhelm Fliess and Sándor Ferenczi to Carl Jung and Ernest Jones) was not so much a frankly physical one as rather an intensive longing for emotional intimacy and, not least, a yearning that they might express obedience to him as the revered patriarch.[12] One of the few instances in which Freud let himself slip into making a homophobic slur – in a letter to his erstwhile prized associate Jung about the prominent German sexologist Magnus Hirschfeld, leader of the campaign to decriminalize homosexuality – the remark was clearly triggered by competitiveness and irritation that Hirschfeld was not wholeheartedly endorsing the psychoanalytic project and was insisting on the idea of inborn, rather than developmentally acquired, same-sex desire.[13] Such rivalries between psychoanalysis and sexology, and between psychoanalysis and sex rights activism, were to remain a persistent theme.

In the several decades between Freud's *Three Essays on the Theory of Sexuality* and the publication of Kinsey's Reports, moreover, and while the psychoanalytic community, scattered as it was between Vienna, Budapest, Berlin, London, and Paris, had been tending increasingly toward more negative assessments of homosexuality, there was still for a while a lively mix of opinions and theories being explored – in the midst, significantly, of an ongoing effort to profile psychoanalysis in relationship to other then-emerging sexological propositions. Ferenczi, for instance, one of Freud's closest collaborators, veered between: earnest confession of "the homosexual impulses" in himself as well as "the homosexual component that is hidden in everyone"; amused descriptions of how well a particular man he knew was managing his own homosexuality – despite being married to a woman; and a smorgasbord of side-remarks in case studies of patients, ranging from one homosexual patient's "indissoluble fixation on his mother" to another patient's "far-going homosexual bondages."[14] Most consequential for the future, however, was Ferenczi's attempt to distinguish conceptually between different types of male homosexual interest. Reacting, in a talk given in 1911 and published in 1914, specifically to Hirschfeld's theories of a "third" or "intermediate sex," Ferenczi advanced the notion that one should distinguish between subtypes of same-sex behavior. On the one hand, there was what he called "subject-homo-erotism" (evinced by a more feminine man, i.e., by someone inverted in his own gender role and thus an exemplar of Hirschfeld's "intermediate sex"); these types, Ferenczi thought, were not convertible to heterosexuality. On the other hand, he proposed that there was also a form he called "object-homo-erotism" (exemplified by more masculine-appearing men who nonetheless desired other men); these types Ferenczi deemed to be suffering from "obsessional neurosis," and he asserted that they could in fact be converted and could learn to desire women.[15] Yet only two years earlier, in speaking of how the gender of the (male) physician mattered in the transference, he not only had stressed that women patients might bring heterosexual desires to their doctors, but also noted that the "'feminine'" elements within the doctor himself were "enough… for women to bring their homosexual, and men their heterosexual interests, or their aversion that is related to this, into connection with the person of the physician."[16] In other words, Ferenczi was both attuned to fluidity in desire and in gender identification and, however contradictorily, also sorted individuals into categories and then sought to use the fact of fluidity to encourage those he thought capable of changing their orientation to do so.

In Vienna, Berlin, and Paris, also female analysts participated in elaborating antihomosexual sentiment. In the early work of Helene Deutsch (later famous for the concept of the "as-if" personality), there was a stark vacillation between, on the one hand, a genuine, at times intrusive-voyeuristic and at other times almost envious, concern with investigating the sexual practices of lesbians; and, on the other, the eager attempt to develop further Freud's reflections on lesbian object-choice – above all by shifting theoretical interest to the pre-Oedipal stage of the mother-child relationship.[17] In Karen Horney's often impressive feminist critiques of Freud's theories of sexuality, as well as in her eventual skepticism of the validity of libido theory in general, there was at least ambivalence about the status of same-sex desire.[18] Strikingly, Horney's occasional critical comments about homosexual men were accompanied by critical assertions about most heterosexual men as well.[19] By contrast, in Marie Bonaparte's studies of incest and of children's sexual play with each other, there were inserted strongly negative assertions about the pathology of homosexuality.[20]

In Britain, the trend was against tolerance. Ernest Jones had decided in 1921 – in the midst of a dispute within the leadership of the International Psychoanalytical Association over whether homosexuals could become analysts – to throw his influence on the side of rejecting homosexual candidates. While the Viennese, under the leadership of Otto Rank, had called for assessing each case on its own individual merits, the majority of Berliners, led by Karl Abraham, insisted that if psychoanalysis had not cured an individual of his or her "inversion," then he or she was also incapable of being an analyst. Jones sided with Berlin, noting that the reputation of the analytic movement would be at stake. In the eyes of the world, he said, homosexuality was "a repugnant crime: if one of our members committed it, we would be seriously discredited."[21]

While British analysts conflicted constantly with one another over theories and methods, all developed negative views on homosexuality. The one anomaly was Edward Glover, who did hold that homosexuality was a "perversion" and a "regression to an earlier stage of sexual development," but nonetheless found that some homosexuals were no different in their emotional attachments from heterosexuals, and in later years would fight for decriminalization.[22] The other analysts were far more adamant that homosexuality was a pathology. In her drive-centered, pre- (or early) Oedipally focused work with children, Melanie Klein, in her inimitable terminology, described not only six-year-old Erna's "anal love desires," "persecutory phantasies," and "oral sadism," as well as the envy she presumed Erna felt toward "the genital and oral gratifications which she supposed her parents to be enjoying during intercourse," but linked Erna's "hatred" and "paranoia" to her "homosexual tendencies, which had been excessively strong from early childhood onwards."[23] Also little Peter, whom Klein saw at age three and three-quarters, had, according to her reconstructions based on watching him play with toy horses and motor cars, supplemented with inquiries with the parents about when Peter could have witnessed parental coitus (it could only have happened at age eighteen months, while briefly sharing a bedroom whilst on vacation and he had promptly – Klein assumed causation not correlation – begun to regress in his toilet training and smash his toys rather than playing appropriately), developed a "very strong passive homosexual attitude," replete with anxiety-inducing "phantasies in which he was being copulated with by his father."[24] Klein may well have been right about the primal furies, fears, and "phantasies" about body parts, emissions, and activities that young children develop – though her assumptions about the impact of the primal scene surely need to be historicized. But there is no question that, in her interpretations, the word "homosexual" had a censorious valence.

Meanwhile, in Scottish analyst Ronald Fairbairn's writings, and in the midst of his innovative larger project of de-eroticizing the concept of libido and promoting the importance of object relations, there was explicit annoyance at so many male homosexuals' refusal to see themselves as disturbed and disinterest in changing their orientation; in a 1946 essay Fairbairn described homosexuality with clear distaste as "the natural sexual expression of a personality which has become perverse in its essential structure."[25] Conversely, in the more ego- and defense-oriented work of Sigmund Freud's daughter Anna (since 1938 in London), there was the proud pronouncement, as of 1949, that while her father had not believed in the possibility of conversion of orientation, she, Anna, could report excellent success in this area with a number of male homosexuals. Basing herself expressly on Ferenczi's distinctions between "subject-" and "object-homo-erotism," Anna Freud insisted that the most important things to look at in the attempt to arrive at accurate diagnoses and treatment approaches were not men's behaviors but rather their fantasies (especially with regard to their identifications as either passive or active – or, in alternation, both – in the midst of the sexual act). Therapeutic success in "divert[ing] their libido from one sex to the other" would emerge from the analyst's interpretations of these oscillating identifications.[26]

Homophobia in Cold War America

Nowhere was the homophobia as strong as in the postwar USA.[27] In the early postwar years, the dramatically rapid spread of psychoanalytic ideas into the American mainstream via the mass media and popular advice books was marked by an ever more firmly consolidated consensus among analysts that homosexuality was by definition abnormal. It was almost as though it was the one thing that otherwise feuding analysts could agree on. In fact, offering condemnatory views

of homosexuality appeared to be an essential element of psychoanalytic self-marketing in the postwar United States. For example, in 1950,
Elements of Psychoanalysis – a "practical guide" containing contributions from leading analysts in prose accessible to the general reading
public – was advertised as offering help with such typical problems as
"the career woman, alcoholism, impotence, frigidity, homosexuality,
prejudice."[28] From Baltimore, New York, and Boston to Chicago and
Topeka to Los Angeles, and despite ongoing vigorous conflicts in views
with regard to psychoanalytic theory and technique more generally,
there was remarkable accord that homosexuals were disturbed and
needed to be cured – i.e., that they were, in fact, the separate category
of person that Sigmund Freud had insisted they were not. Whether in
the neo-Freudian trend first inspired by the writings of Franz Alexander and then developed further by both Karen Horney (whose followers were more homophobic than she) and Harry Stack Sullivan (the
latter of whom, although homosexual himself, did also publicly make
homophobic pronouncements) or among the ego psychologists around
Heinz Hartmann's respected colleagues Robert Bak and Phyllis Greenacre (especially in their work on perversions and fetishes), whether in
the group around Sándor Radó (whose antihomosexual ideas were
built on his vehement objections to Sigmund Freud's foundational
concept of bisexuality) or in the writings of the eminent non-émigré
psychoanalyst and explicitly Christian "dean" of American psychiatry
Karl Menninger, the psychoanalytic community in the USA generated
a welter of uninterrogated assumptions and declarative assertions that
would shape the conversation about same-sex desire for decades to
come.

The incoherence of the claims about the patheticness and/or
pathology of homosexuality was as palpable as was the imposing confidence with which those assertions were delivered. Male homosexuality
was seen as a way of attempting to avoid castration by the father – or
as a way to unite with the father. It signaled an overidentification with
a seductive or domineering mother – or it was a sign of a profound fear
of the female genitals. It functioned as a hapless way to repair one's
sense of inadequacy as a male – or it was a powerful sexual compulsion
that required better control.[29] The prolific, popular New York-based
analyst Edmund Bergler (possibly the single most sex-obsessed analyst
of his era and also the most punitively normative one, author of such
titles as *Frigidity in Women* [1936], *Unhappy Marriage and Divorce*

[1946], *The Basic Neurosis* [1949], and *Neurotic Counterfeit-Sex* [1951]) declared with authority in 1956: "Homosexuals are essentially disagreeable people ... [displaying] a mixture of superciliousness, fake aggression, and whimpering ... subservient when confronted with a stronger person, merciless when in power ... You seldom find an intact ego ... among them."[30] Not one of his analytic colleagues challenged him.

Analysts were not quite as obsessed with lesbianism, but comparably confused things would be said about it as well. Was the same-sex-desiring woman identifying *with* an emotionally withholding Oedipal father or defending herself *against* her (frustrated) desire for that father? Were lesbians stuck in a still all-too-masculine "clitoridal" phase – or did they have castrating impulses toward their own sons? Or were they above all striving for a return to the undifferentiated mother-child fusion of infancy?[31]

It is difficult in hindsight to assess how much the hostility to homosexuality was driven by the lasting sense, inherited from Freud, that homosexual impulses, however well hidden, existed in every individual, including within the analysts themselves, and how much the animus was driven by the ongoing effort to make psychoanaly sis acceptable to mainstream, Main Street America. For there is no question that the attacks launched especially by Catholic critics of psychoanalysis in the later 1940s and early 1950s – and the ensuing debates about the potential compatibility of psychoanalysis with Christianity – had exacerbated American analysts' ambivalence about how to handle the presumed centrality of sex of *any* kind to the psychoanalytic project. Sex was both the topic analysts thought they were the experts on *and* they were deeply anxious about being too strongly associated with it. And such ambivalence was, of course, both perceptive *and* problematic.

The trouble was that the issue of libido was always palpably present, hovering over the enterprise, at once necessary to the entire conceptual framework and yet continually threatening to make the enterprise seem dirty and tawdry and trivial. *This* was the context into which the Kinsey Reports had burst. No longer skittish about being associated with sex, analysts thrown on the defensive by the Reports' wild popularity rushed both to announce their longstanding expertise on the topic of sex (*we* are the ones who know the most about masturbation, infidelity, etc., they averred) and to denigrate Kinsey's work, directly contesting his views on the normalcy of homosexuality and the reality and strength of female sexual interest. But their largest move, especially after the report on *Sexual Behavior in the Human Female* was released in 1953, was to insist that Kinsey treated humans "zoologically." Kinsey was an ignoramus about *love*.

The Love Doctrine

Thus the Columbia University psychiatrist and psychoanalyst Sol Ginsburg – one of the leading members of the Group for the Advancement of Psychiatry that had been founded by William Menninger – complained about Kinsey's apparent "need to separate sex from love, tenderness, concern with the feelings and needs of one's partner ... such a separation of the genital from other aspects of one's sexual attitudes and satisfactions itself represents an abnormality in individuals."[32] Karl Menninger for his part declared: "As for an orgasm being the chief criterion of sexuality, everyone knows that one orgasm can differ from another as widely as do kisses." The examples he gave were telling: "The orgasm of a terrified soldier in battle, that of a loving husband in the arms of his wife, that of a desperate homosexual trying to prove his masculinity and that of a violent and sadistic brute raping a child are not the same phenomena." And Menninger approvingly cited yet another (anonymous) author who had argued, commenting on the Kinsey Reports, that "Unless the movement toward sexual integration is an expression of love for the other person there can be no normal sexual ecstasy ... Sexual promiscuity or experimentation or athleticizing... without feelings of tenderness and affection is ... destructive.' "[33] In another essay, in the *Saturday Review*, Menninger repeated some of the same arguments and also complained that

> So as far as I can ascertain, Kinsey appears to have heeded scarcely a word of the scholarly analyses and wise counsel of such penetrating critics as [psychoanalysts] Dr. Robert P. Knight, Dr. Lawrence Kubie, [literary critic] Lionel Trilling and numerous others. Kinsey's compulsion to force human sexual behavior into a zoological frame of reference leads him to repudiate or neglect human psychology, and to see normality as that which is natural in the sense that it is what is practised by animals.[34]

Psychoanalysts also confronted Kinsey in public forums. Franz Alexander argued with him onstage in Little Rock, Arkansas in March of 1954 (a fact which prompted Menninger to congratulate Alexander for "your rebuke to Dr. Kinsey" – even as he added, "but I don't think any amount of rebuking is going to cure this guy!").[35] And in May of 1954 Menninger debated Kinsey openly at the meeting of the American Psychiatric Association in St. Louis, Missouri. Once again the arguments centered on whether what mattered most to women was "orgasms" or "love."[36]

Other analysts made variations on this same point. Iago Galdston at New York University attacked Kinsey for praising primitive peoples like the Nepalese Lepcha "among whom 'sexual activity is practically divorced from emotion... like food and drink it does not matter from whom you receive it, as long as you get it' ... In Kinsey's scheme of things there seems to be little room for love."[37] And psychoanalyst Edward S. Tauber of the (Sullivanian interpersonal relations-focused) William Alanson White Institute, meanwhile, found it awful that ordinary Americans rushed to read the Kinsey Reports in order to discover "that their difficulties are statistically 'normal,' despite the fact that their sexual behavior fails to be an expression of real warmth and tenderness." "A healthy psychosexual adjustment," Tauber intoned, "would mean that the individual has the ability to have a durable intimate relationship with a person of the opposite sex ... This would be an adjustment which expressed love and tenderness, and was not an expression of non-sexual aims or sado-masochistic trends."[38] Not a single analyst reacted positively to Kinsey's second volume.

A number of things are worth noting about this phenomenon. One is that it really was new. While homophobic views had been solidifying for quite some time, then, what was novel was the development of what might well be called "the love doctrine." Freud himself, moreover, and significantly, had remarked on the frequent *disconnect* – also specifically among heterosexuals – between love and sexual desire.[39] This claim that loveless sex was pathological was a postwar US innovation. It was consolidated in direct response to Kinsey. (Revealingly, the reaction to the Kinsey Reports was quite different in Continental Europe. There the diagnosis was not that Kinsey lacked a commitment to marital love, but rather that Americans lacked sexual skill, sensuality, and eroticism.[40] And also the homophobia expressed in European psychoanalytic circles was not fixated on love.)[41]

Second is that it was not innocent. There was nothing banal or benign about this disavowal of the extraordinary prevalence of loveless sex also *within* heterosexual marriages and the tone-deafness this displayed especially toward *women's* all-too-frequent sense of alienation within marital sex. Highly ironic, moreover, was the fact that nobody knew better than psychoanalysts themselves just what a wide variety of behaviors and feelings existed among the supposedly so ideal heterosexuals. Reading the psychoanalytic literature of postwar USA, one cannot help but be struck by the prevalence of American men's visits to prostitutes (including across class and racial divides, including at the recommendation of analysts), extramarital dalliances, intramarital miseries, illegal abortions, and sexual fantasies at odds with the normative prototype.

Third, the paradigm would be enormously influential. Psychoanalysis ascended in the decades of the Cold War precisely by offering a mixed, at once secular and religious, "moral sensibility" that reinforced conservative family values under the sign of "health," one that was expressly contemptuous of homosexuality and of any expression of female sexuality outside of marriage.[42] Some people fit the norms effortlessly. But the wastage of lives – the traumas of homosexuals subjected to relentless disrespect and conversion attempts, the sorrows within numberless heterosexual marriages – was immense.[43]

From Oedipus to Narcissus: Homophobia after the Sexual Revolution

All of this would be undone by the sexual revolution: first the Pill, then the deluge of porn, the explosion of public chatter about free love and the ubiquitous incitement to loosen mores even more. What had previously been covert became demonstratively overt. On the one hand, there were intimidating new standards of sexual performance. On the other hand, the women's and gay rights movements would turn what had been the casual power of the misogynist double standard and the privilege of heterosexual masculinity into scandals requiring massive redress.

And not least: the sexual revolution also arrived in the heartland of America with William Masters and Virginia Johnson and their blockbuster book, *Human Sexual Response* (1966).[44] Here, once again, in other words, were sex experts who challenged the sovereignty of psychoanalysis directly. Masters and Johnson explicitly sold their behaviorist sex therapeutic techniques for curing premature ejaculation and anorgasmia as *the* antidote to psychoanalysis. Two weeks in a hotel in St. Louis making daily love with your spouse was certainly marketable as an improvement over seven years on the couch.

Masters and Johnson took empiricism inside the body itself, measuring pulse rates and erections and lubrications and flushed skin, providing data on what bodies really did in the run-up to and in the midst of and in the aftermath of climax. Kinsey had counted orgasms (as though they were pennies or beans or cars on the highway); Masters and Johnson problematized orgasms themselves – men's and women's. And one innovation Masters and Johnson insisted on was the importance of treating the *couple* as the patient, not the individual who manifested the symptom – whether that symptom was premature ejaculation or erectile difficulties for men or lack of orgasm or even vaginismus (painful resistance to penetration) for women. In short, they problematized heterosexuality, without realizing that this was what they were doing. A second innovation was their insistence on the *anatomical*, on physiological functioning rather than psychological dynamics. In their two books – *Human Sexual Response* was followed up with *Human Sexual Inadequacy* (1970) – they deliberately distanced themselves from what they perceived as the uselessness and even harmfulness of the psychoanalytic approaches to marital sexual discordance that had been prevalent in the USA in the 1950s and 1960s, approaches which all too often had exacerbated a couple's misery by blaming it on the wife's inability to "adapt to her feminine role" and/or incapacity to transfer sexual excitation from the supposedly immature clitoris to the purportedly more mature locus of the vagina.[45] Masters and Johnson by contrast promoted the idea, incidentally already advanced by Kinsey, but now backed by the "hard science" of their own inside-the-body empirical studies, that all female orgasms were triggered by clitoral excitation, even if some women experienced them as localized in the vagina or in the entire genital area – or all over the body. And they offered behaviorist therapy that emphasized caressing, communication, and relief from performance pressure – especially for men.

Among other things, the women's movement, building expressly on the findings of Masters and Johnson, engaged in a frontal assault on the core psychoanalytic notion that there was a distinction to be made between clitoral and vaginal orgasms and that only the latter were properly mature – a discussion which caused uproar also within psychoanalytic circles, not least due to its exposition in the pages of the

reu immature or or become actually "—by the present and impending ac- motherhood. But erhood, which we lably think of as a emale capacity and iment, is indissolu- in Freudian thought ian's inferiority to he woman has never n up her longing to enis, and this "un- wish," says Freud, e converted into a ive a child." In fact, s libido slips into means—there is re- her way to put it— tion 'penis = child.'"

Freud is saying is exual energy of fe- lich has existed up gely as an imitative iale libido, can only d by the actuality or ntiality of giving act by which the mbolically obtained. irth to a son is the olete symbolical ap- 1. The new mother's "is great indeed desire for a child finds a real fulfill- especially is this so

child is the supreme aim of woman is a statement having the precise value of an adver- tising slogan," says de Beau- voir) and to a passive accept-

ance of sexuality as male in- trusion. Against this, some feminists, including, under- standably, many Lesbians, ar- gue that the clitoris is in fact the specific organ of female

of justifying male abuse of women as "more food for her nature."

Beyond this constitutional handicap, women are de-

scribed throughout Freud's writings as suffering from many other psychic disabili- ties, moral afflictions and ex- istential disqualifications. They are more envious than men,

"In all his bold explorations of the inner life, women remained dark and unfathomable to him, like planets beyond the range of his instruments."

Figure 4 Cartoon accompanying the essay by theater critic Richard Gilman in the *New York Times Magazine*, 1971. Among other things, Gilman observed: "That fem- inists of almost every degree of militancy respond with such resentment to the word 'psychoanalysis' and, even more violently, to the name Sigmund Freud, comes as a great shock to the average cultivated man." One of the pull-quotes accompanying the essay announced further: "According to women's liberation leaders (and some male critics today), many of the fundamental ideas of psychoanalysis constitute an ingen- ious doctrine of male supremacy, traceable to its founder's own underlying misogyny." Freud himself, in short, was held responsible for the conservative views endemic in postwar US psychoanalytic circles. From *The New York Times*, January 31, 1971 © 1971 *The New York Times*. All rights reserved. Used by permission and protected by the Copyright Laws of the United States. The printing, copying, redistribution, or retransmission of this Content without express written permission is prohibited.

Journal of the American Psychoanalytic Association by the psychiatrist (and former student of Kinsey's) Mary Jane Sherfey.[46] The essay was widely debated (also hostilely, also by female psychoanalysts).[47] Femi- nists additionally criticized the assumptions prevalent in the analytic community that women were intellectually inferior to men and that their purpose was to serve men. And they challenged analysts' more gen- eral disdain for women's professional and sexual agency (see Figure 4).[48]

For their part, gay rights activists were especially incensed by the psychiatric pathologization of homosexuality (within the DSM, the *Diagnostic and Statistical Manual of Mental Disorders*), not least because it was understood to lend the authority of medicine to the legal discrimination against homosexuals prevailing across the USA. From 1970 on, provocative disruptions became common at meetings of the American Psychiatric Association and related organizations. At the APA in 1970, at a panel on homosexuality and transsexualism, the presentation of Irving Bieber, one of the most influential homophobic analysts, was greeted with comments to the effect that "you're a motherfucker," and that if his book "talked about black people the way it talks about homosexuals you'd be drawn and quartered and you'd deserve it." A presentation on aversion therapy to convert homosexuals by the Australian psychiatrist Nathaniel McConaghy was met with loud jeers such as "where did you take your residency, Auschwitz?" At the APA in 1972, on a panel entitled "Psychiatry: Friend or Foe to Homosexuals – a Dialogue," a gay psychiatrist wearing a Nixon mask and a wig, speaking through a voice distortion machine, and calling himself Dr. H. Anonymous (it was in fact the psychiatrist John E. Fryer), gave a presentation explaining the damage done to gay psychiatrists due to their need to remain in the closet (see Figure 5). And in the same year, there was a "zap" at the New York Hilton when the Association for the Advancement of Behavior Therapy met – under the banner slogan "Torture Anyone?" A movement was underway to get the diagnostic category of homosexuality removed.[49]

At the same moment, psychoanalysis in the USA was confronting an abrupt but overdetermined decline in status. One proximate cause was the sexual revolution itself. The normalization of desire that had been one of the major agendas of the postwar American psychoanalytic community was in trouble. Freud's original conviction that human beings were driven by libidinal urges which were then repressed by society – the idea that, however ambivalently, had been reasserted in the shunting-aside of the neo-Freudians, even as it had been supplemented by additional encomiums to ego strength and the individuals' capacity to master those urges – would inevitably be eroded in the face of a society filled with frank sexual stimuli and incitements. The neo-Freudians had challenged the significance of the Oedipus complex most vigorously and directly. But ego psychologists too, while restoring the Oedipal framework, had either left sex to the side (as in the work

Figure 5 The psychiatrist John E. Fryer as Dr. H. Anonymous at the American Psychiatric Association meeting in Dallas in 1972. Wearing a wig and a Nixon mask and speaking through a voice distortion microphone, Fryer – at a panel entitled "Psychiatry: Friend or Foe to Homosexuals – a Dialogue" – reported on his professional positions lost to homophobia and on the devastating damages done by the professionally demanded closeting of same-sex-desiring individuals within the Association. His opening words were: "I am a homosexual. I am a psychiatrist." The event proved to be a key episode in the ultimately successful campaign to get the category of homosexuality removed from the *Diagnostic and Statistical Manual of Mental Disorders* in 1973.

of Heinz Hartmann et al.) or had expounded an explicitly sexually normative framework.[50] By the 1960s–1970s, as sex filled the public sphere, psychoanalysts seemed completely out of step with the public's concerns; neither Freud's earliest ideas nor the subsequently developed theories fit the situation.

Second, there was the rise of self-help and pop psychology, with millions of book titles sold, as well as a more general disrespect for the whole notion of high-minded – and high-handed – "expertise" in a culture that increasingly embraced antiauthoritarianism.[51] The fact that analysts had inadvertently dug their own ditch – since in their efforts to popularize psychoanalytic concepts they had been the progenitors of the self-help boom – did not make the result easier to bear. Third, also within psychiatry, analysis was increasingly felt to be unscientific – at best an art, but certainly not a science – an approach that could not keep pace with biomedical research and discoveries, including pharmacological ones. It was not just the advent of Haldol and Thorazine for those deemed psychotic; also the ascent of Miltown for the hassled businessman, or Valium for the dissatisfied housewife, made talk therapy seem quite old-school.[52] A fourth source of the problem was economic: analysis was simply too expensive, and there was by the later 1960s a proliferating welter of other opportunities (from recreational drug use to "New Age" and other alternative therapies) for dealing with personal and interpersonal ills and the desire for self-improvement and greater life enjoyment.

As it happened, and for a complicated conjunction of reasons, psychiatry in the USA would rescue its own reputation and cultural esteem by dumping psychoanalysis overboard, and binding its professional future to a biomedical research agenda. And it was this particular turn that was to have tremendous consequences for gay rights (so closely intertwined was the homophobic consensus with the psychoanalytic hegemony that was now in trouble). The key figure in this transformation would be the psychiatrist Robert L. Spitzer, who was no particular fan of either feminism or gay liberation. But he was adamantly intent on making psychiatry more scientific and he was open to hearing gay rights advocates make a scientific case for the removal of homosexuality from the DSM.

Spitzer became interested in hearing from experts who could assert that homosexuality should simply be thought of as a "common behavior variant," that homosexuals fell "within the normal range of psychological functioning," that many homosexuals coped just fine in their daily lives and that many were perfectly satisfied with their orientation and not interested in being converted.[53] Studies conducted in the 1950s by psychologist Evelyn Hooker, which had demonstrated psychiatric experts' inability to detect any difference between homosexual and heterosexual men with respect to their "mental adjustment," became newly crucial evidence in this context.[54] At the same time, however, Spitzer was attuned to the concern that the profession should not be seen as capitulating to "outside agitators" and he was committed to continuing to give antihomosexual experts a hearing. He thus organized a panel at the May 1973 American Psychiatric Association convention in Honolulu which pitted psychiatrists who favored removal of the category (their names were Robert Stoller and Judd Marmor – both, as it happens, also analysts – and Richard Green) and the gay rights activist Ronald Gold against two of the most prominent proponents of ongoing pathologization of homosexuality, analysts Irving Bieber and Charles Socarides. While the Honolulu panel was to be an important tipping point, no less important were the several years of quiet strategic planning that had put more liberal and sympathetic psychiatrists into key positions within the leadership of the American Psychiatric Association.[55]

In November of 1973, the Board of Trustees of the APA voted to remove the category of homosexuality from the DSM. This was a major victory for gay and lesbian liberation, even as it also caused many in the psychoanalytic subcommunity of American psychiatry to withdraw from further discussion of the issue in disgruntlement at what was obviously a rebuff to their perspectives, and even as the official shift did not necessarily signal a change of heart in the rank and file of American psychiatry either. (Four years after the vote, 69 percent of the first 2,500 psychiatrists responding to a survey conducted by the journal *Medical Aspects of Human Sexuality* still affirmed that "homosexuality is usually a pathological adaptation, as opposed to a normal variation," and only 18 percent disagreed, with the rest being uncertain. Similarly, 70 percent said that "homosexuals' problems have more to do with their own inner conflicts than with stigmatization by society at large"; and 60 percent said homosexuals were less capable of "mature, loving relationships" than heterosexuals.[56] The love doctrine, as it were – and this despite the sexual revolution – remained a reference point.)

Meanwhile, however, in these same years, analysts in the USA and internationally were reviving with renewed intensity and in new terms a long-running dispute over whether the analytic patient base was moving toward more borderline and narcissistically disturbed patients.[57] British object relations theorists had been shifting analytic attention from Oedipal to pre-Oedipal pathology already since the 1940s. But the 1970s saw an especially heated round of this dispute – coinciding quite specifically with the crisis in US psychoanalytic prestige more generally. Significantly, the dispute coincided as well with the sense that leading American practitioners' longstanding post-neo-Freudian emphasis on the Oedipus complex had been linked to pre-sexual revolution assumptions about sexual repression as a source of difficulty. As the American analyst Edward M. Weinshel noted at the International Congress on Psycho-Analysis held in London in 1975, there was a growing consensus among analysts internationally that primitive and "archaic" aggressions were a far larger element in patients' problems than sex *per se* (even as Weinshel himself – and invoking on this point also Anna Freud – surmised that sexual problems persisted in new forms in the midst of the sexual revolution).[58]

And it was in this context, in turn, that an increasing number of American analysts thought the time had come to shift "from Oedipus to Narcissus."[59] Importantly, the narcissism problem under discussion was not understood in the quotidian sense as meaning self-involvement, vanity, and the advancement of self-interest, but rather, on the contrary, the sign of a profound *deficiency* in self-love. While some of the impetus for rethinking character disorders had come from diverse British object relations approaches and particularly the American Otto Kernberg's innovative adaptation of Melanie Klein's ideas for work with borderline patients, the major lightning-rod figure in the conflicts of the 1970s was the Chicago analyst and developer of self psychology Heinz Kohut.[60] Patients might be filled with inchoate rage and anxiety even when they presented as manipulatively seductive, but whatever sexually provocative or aggressively hostile impulses were being directed at the therapist were, in the Kohutian framework, not strong drives being dealt with in transference with the analyst but rather the breakdown products of a weak and poorly formed self.[61]

This paradigm shift, despite all its various internal contradictions and ongoing areas of controversy, would, however ironically, give both homophobia and sexism new leases on life. The turn to a preoccupation with narcissism was, after all, not just a realistic assessment of a changing client base, nor just a sign of the profession's maturing insight that perhaps all along, for decades, patients had been misunderstood as Oedipally challenged neurotics when really the source of their troubles had lain in severe damage produced in the dyadic dynamics of the pre-Oedipal phase – although those two options were hotly debated in the mid-1970s. The shift to pre-Oedipal issues needs also to be understood in the context of a reaction both to the declining significance of analysis within American psychiatry and to the feminist and gay challenges. Psychoanalysis *had* to reinvent itself.[62]

Just as in the 1950s analysts had not responded directly to the Kinsey challenge, but instead rerouted the discussion to the purported pathology of loveless sex, here too there was a sideways response. Rather than letting go of homophobia, its contents morphed.[63] Analytic discussion turned on new theories that homosexuality had its pathogenic source not in a failure to "navigat[e] the straits of Oedipus," but instead – as Harry Gershman and Charles Socarides among others argued – in the prior failure to establish "a sound and solid gender identity" due to "an incomplete resolution from the mother-child symbiosis that precedes the Oedipal period."[64] In the past, the framework for homophobic arguments often involved the idea that same-sex-desiring individuals had remained fixated in, or had regressed to, an earlier developmental stage (e.g., oral or anal, rather than the purportedly mature and heterosexual genital); Oedipus complex-related castration fears were also often invoked.[65] Now Gershman described homosexuals in a way that resonated powerfully with the kinds of symptoms typically associated with narcissistic character disorders. In Gershman's view, homosexuals were driven by a "compulsive sexuality [that] serves to allay anxiety and inferiority feelings ... It is linked to [the patient's] need for control, to his masochistic self-contempt, and to his need ... to stimulate himself in order to overcome his profound emptiness, resignation, and hopelessness."[66] Socarides too continued to reiterate – and many of his colleagues agreed with him, even if they did not say so as publicly as he – that "the naïve acceptance for social/ political reasons [i.e., due to gay rights activism] of one of the most severe forms of sexual disorder, intimately related to gender identity, abrogates our responsibilities as healing professionals."[67] As he had been arguing since 1968 (basing himself on the work of the ego psychologist Margaret Mahler about an incipiently "schizoid" and "borderline" child), Socarides persisted in insisting that "in all obligatory homosexuals there has been an inability to make the psychological progression from the mother-child unity of earliest infancy to individuation."[68] Pleasure might be experienced by these individuals, but it could not possibly be emotionally healthy: "The perverse acts alleviate feelings of emptiness and diminished sense of self, but the effect is transitory, evanescent, and must be continually repeated with 'fresh partners' in order to provide a sense of temporary intactness of the body ego and an increase in self-cohesion."[69] (Interestingly, and revealing how linked assumptions about heterosexual femininity and hostility to homosexuality could be, Socarides also objected strongly to the rising cultural credibility of Sherfey's Masters and Johnson-based critique of many psychoanalysts' beliefs about differentially valuable female orgasms. If particular vaginas were found to be anesthetic, he opined, this had to be a psychological reaction, not a biological finding – it "reflect[ed] an emotional incapacity to accept phallic penetration and is symptomatic of an unconscious fear. As such, it indicates difficulty in accepting the psychosexual role in the male-female relationship."[70] Here as well, Socarides was by no means the only analyst to stick to this view.)[71] Given all these developments, it is perhaps no surprise that the American *Psychoanalytic* Association did not manage formally to adopt a nondiscrimination policy with regard to homosexuality until 1991 – and the International Psychoanalytical Association did not do so until 2002.[72]

In one last twist, and despite their growing marginalization within psychiatry and their seemingly dwindling impact within American society, analysts' notion that narcissism was the new condition ailing humanity took astonishingly strong root in cultural commentary. Christopher Lasch's hugely successful *The Culture of Narcissism*, published in 1979, is perhaps the best example. Americans in general, he thought, evinced a "dependence on the vicarious warmth provided by others … a sense of inner emptiness, boundless repressed rage, and unsatisfied oral cravings." Lasch was especially contemptuous of both feminism and sexual liberation, scoffing, as so many analysts had, at feminists' complaints about "the myth of the vaginal orgasm" while also noting, not without insight but nonetheless without sympathy, that men were often terrified of women's new "sexual demands," because these called up "early fantasies of a possessive, suffocating, devouring, and castrating mother." And he was resolute in his condemnation of everything associated with the sexual revolution, from oral sex to homosexuality to promiscuity to the celebration of polymorphous perversity.[73] Whether any of this had ever been based on sound evidence about individual analytic patients or about the culture as a whole remains an open question.[74] Yet the diagnosis of what purportedly went wrong in the 1970s, and the damning association of both feminism and loosened sexual mores with "narcissism" – a word thrown around freely even when the term was misunderstood – has stuck.

Stoller's Dissent

One voice stood out with particular eloquence in its dissent from the crescendo chorus insisting on maintaining a sense of privilege and superiority to the perversions and pathology purportedly evinced by unapologetically sexually active women and homosexuals. Robert J. Stoller was the Los Angeles-based psychiatrist and psychoanalyst who, at the APA meeting in Honolulu in May 1973, had offered the most imaginative indictment of the homophobia endemic to his profession. His antihomophobic colleagues Judd Marmor and Richard Green had also made excellent points, among them that "from an objective biological viewpoint there is nothing 'unnatural' about homosexual object choice" (indeed it could be thought of as akin to vegetarianism – a similarly unusual choice in the midst of a world in which "most human beings are 'naturally' meat-eaters") or that labeling homosexuals according to the degree of intensity of their same-sex desires was "unpleasantly reminiscent of the Hitlerian process of trying to determine what fraction of black or Jewish ancestry a person might be permitted to have" (those were both Marmor), or that (as Green pointed out) there were plenty of heterosexuals who used sex neurotically "to control others, as a substitute for feelings of self-worth, or as a defense against anxiety and depression" – and yet there was no DSM category for them.[75]

No one turned the mirror around onto the heterosexual male norm as forcefully – at once mockingly and earnestly – as Stoller did. This mattered tremendously not least because Bieber and Socarides took the opportunity of the Honolulu panel to reiterate the positions they had advanced for years. Bieber repeated his view that "mothers of homosexuals are inappropriately close, binding, often seductive," while fathers "are overtly or covertly hostile" and that thus male homosexuality was an attempt to seek "reassurance and acceptance" from other men; it was, moreover, a form of "sexual inadequacy" like impotence and premature ejaculation: each was a sign of "a network of fears about being effective in heterosexual activity."[76] Socarides, for his part, opined that mothers of homosexuals were "domineering" while fathers were "weak." He additionally – demonstrating once again the apparently felt links between the challenges posed by feminism and gay activism – noted that "orgasm produced by intravaginal penetration" was "basic to elementary human biology" and "not subject to change by social or political movements." Anyone unable to find "orgastic relief" in this framework had a problem – and it was, again, likely due to the inability to make the progression "from the mother-child unity of earliest infancy to individuation."[77]

Importantly, Stoller in this context as elsewhere did not dispense with psychoanalysis (of which he was a passionate practitioner) but rather wed it to a pro-sex feminist and pro-gay agenda. Stoller noted that "there is no such *thing* as homosexuality" and thus there were in any event no grounds for having a diagnosis for it in the DSM. However, if diagnoses there must be, he said – reminding his listeners that there were after all *many* "variants of overt heterosexuality, e.g. compulsive promiscuity, use of pornography, preference for prostitutes, adult masturbation," then indeed "we can all be given a diagnosis." For – even among those who seemed conformist to norms on the surface – "everyone has his own style and distinctive fantasy content that he daydreams or stages with objects." In fact, Stoller was dubious that anyone achieved the purported ideal of "a male preferring a female and vice versa, in which both wholeheartedly enjoy the sexual and loving aspects of their relationship." Although, he conceded, that ideal "may well be buried there in most of us," he observed that it was manifestly evident at best "in only a few." And Stoller went on to propose that if a finer diagnostic schema for sexual preferences were to be developed, then some more realistic examples of such preferences should be chosen. What might some of those preferences be? One has to imagine here the audience, predominantly straight, and at least outwardly propriety-preoccupied. And there was Stoller blithely extemporizing some possibilities: "e.g., heterosexual, monogamous, with accompanying fantasies of being raped by a stallion; homosexual, with foreskin fetishism; heterosexual, with preference for cadavers; homosexual, with disembodied penises (tearoom promiscuity); heterosexual, voyeurism; homosexual [male], expressed only in fantasies during intercourse with wife."[78] The barbed joke was aimed directly at the audience.

In the years that followed, Stoller emphasized the key point that what was erotic for one person was utterly nonerotic for another. While Masters and Johnson had researched arousal anatomically, Stoller was interested in how excitement worked *emotionally*. He was interested in fantasies – both conscious and unconscious – and how in every individual (but *always differently* from how it worked in everyone else) there was an intricate calibration of safety and riskiness, scripted storylines and fetishistic image scraps (with their convoluted combination of dehumanizing abstraction and rehumanizing concreteness) that maximized sexual excitement for that person. In doing so, Stoller was inspired by the social constructionist theories of sexuality developed by the newest Kinsey Institute-affiliated sexologists, the sociologists William Simon and John Gagnon, and especially their theories of "sexual scripts" (which combined sociocultural with intrapsychic approaches); their coauthored book *Sexual Conduct* had been published in 1973.[79] And simultaneously, Stoller found a way creatively to rework for progressive purposes the ego psychologist Phyllis Greenacre's ideas about a fetish as resulting from early trauma as well as the Pakistani British Winnicottian analyst Masud Khan's ideas about perversion and alienation.[80] Drawing in addition on examples from his own practice but also from pro-sex feminist writing on fantasy (for example, Nancy Friday's bestseller *My Secret Garden*), using as his data patients' daydreams as well as masturbatory and during-sex fantasies (whether taken from pornography or self-invented), Stoller began to develop a theory that the point of all fantasies was "to undo frustration, trauma, and intrapsychic conflict" – and that there was often a theme (however well hidden) of desire for revenge for past humiliations.[81]

The intellectual and political implications would be considerable. For one thing, Stoller eroded the boundary between normal and abnormal, instead seeing human beings on a spectrum in which, when it came to sexual excitement, almost no one fit the normative ideal of loving, unhostile relationships – hostility over past hurts was a theme in countless individuals' fantasies (whether they seemed on the surface to be about sadism or about masochism, one's own loss of control or one's power to frustrate and then thrill the other characters in the script), even as each individual's script (continually reworked over the course of a lifetime) was unique. In Stoller's view, painful experiences were at the root of all perversions – but almost everyone was a pervert in some way.

Moreover, Stoller helped rethink the nature of sex itself. The point was to challenge the very notion of sex as a biological drive and instead emphasize sex as an emotionally loaded phenomenon, an activity that human beings sought over and over again not in order to release some kind of built-up tension (in any event an overly masculinist notion) but rather in order continually to re-play, and each time re-solve, a convoluted but pressing inner psychological drama. The theoretical framework also of sexology, in short, would do better to proceed from the mind – its recesses and contradictions – and not from Masters and Johnson-style physiological functions alone. The old Freudian assumption that many problems in life that seemed nonsexual had their (hidden) roots in sexual desire or conflictedness could be turned on its head; the idea now was to take note of how much that was originally *non*sexual was being brought into every sexual encounter. This was a major conceptual shift. The idea, in short, was to shift from drive to drama.

In addition, Stoller was adamantly antimisogynist and anti-homophobic. The women in his essay were as inventive in their perverse imaginations as the men – and he was utterly accepting of their sexual agency, both within and outside of marriage. And Stoller was also articulately scathing about the denigration of homosexuals as somehow different from run-of-the-mill heterosexuals, convinced that if more details on heterosexuals' fantasies were to be collected, "we shall become more lenient or more aware of our hypocrisy when we allege, as in law codes, that all sorts of behaviors that do not damage others must be massively punished. We try to make the outlandish folks function as scapegoats for the rest of us, but anyone – analyst or other – who collects erotic thoughts knows that many citizens, avowedly heterosexual, conspicuously normal ... are also filled with hatred and wishes."[82] Over and over, in subsequent publications, Stoller mocked the idea that homosexuals were narcissists and perverts with "vulnerable" egos and "archaically cathected objects" who were unable to renounce "primitive gratification" and could not master their "libidinal and aggressive impulses" (these were all quotes taken directly from the antihomosexual analyst Socarides) by giving examples of *heterosexual* males who had quite the same problems. A typical Stoller strategy, for example, was to quote Socarides' summaries of homosexual personality structures ("the archaic, narcissistic ego structure makes the ego vulnerable to the impact of libidinal stimulation," etc.) and then go on to describe in affectionate detail a man he called "a cousin, George" as someone

> who has an archaic, narcissistic ego structure that makes the ego ... vulnerable to the impact of libidinal stimulation, and so on. But I also claim that George is not a homosexual. He is a heterosexual. At least he says so, as does his wife, girlfriend, daydreams and choices in pornography, sexual history, and hunger for women's anatomy. I suppose – because I know that he is rather boastful about his erotic prowess, inclined to drink too much when socially

ill at ease, given to telling jokes about queers, smokes big cigars, regularly plays poker with his male friends, and wastes weekends watching football on TV – that we can now claim he is a latent homosexual. Fair enough, since, by the rules of the libido-theory-game, everyone is. Therefore, we need a usable definition of the heterosexual, since the heterosexual has been the baseline of nor-mality against which the homosexual is measured. We cannot use people such as George. He has too many flaws; his homosexuality just oozes out of him. (You might almost say it is what makes him heterosexual.) Worse than that, he is downright pre-Oedipal.

In fact, Stoller concluded with a flourish, "How many happy hetero-sexuals do you know? How many of them are untainted by archaic and primitive narcissistic cathexes?"[83]

Another favorite Stoller tactic was the list that deliberately mixed the unusual with the all-too-common in such a way that no one could avoid feeling called out and put on the spot. A typical example was the enumeration, of "in males, some of the heterosexual realities with which clinicians are familiar." These included:

voyeurism, exhibitionism, satyriasis, preference for prosti-tutes, ... masturbation with pornography as more exciting than using live females, ... klismaphilia [pleasure from receiving ene-mas] (the stimulus delivered by a female), telephone scatologia, ... excitement with other men's wives but not with one's own, and preference for fat women, thin women, tall women, short women, blonde women, red-headed women, steatopygous women, big-busted women, small-busted women, black women, white women, Italian women, Jewish women, Gabonese women, Thai women, women with a cute little penis (a.k.a. clitoris), ladies, actresses, policewomen, poetesses, and women who are jet copilots.

"Where," Stoller asked rhetorically, "is our paragon?"[84]

In sum, Stoller was positioning himself in resistance to three prior movements. For one thing, he diverged from the rise of the bio-medical model of psychiatry promoted by Robert Spitzer's DSM-iii by maintaining a commitment to psychoanalysis as a practice and emo-tions as a focus. Second, he resisted the ongoing misogyny and homo-phobia still prevalent among his fellow psychoanalysts – and, more generally, he pointed out how many similarities could be found across the gay-straight divide. (For instance, Stoller noted how many *hetero-sexual* men apparently had had closely binding mothers and distant fathers.)[85] And third, he repudiated the love doctrine originally developed by analysts in reaction against Kinsey.

Stoller died in 1991. To this day, he remains mostly remembered for his writings on gender identity and his sympathetic work with transsexuals. Apart from an enthusiastic endorsement blurb on his 1985 book, *Observing the Erotic Imagination*, by the feminist psychiatrist Ethel Spector Person (she deemed the book "charming," "serious," and "irresistible"), Stoller's subversive, deeply nonmisogynist and nonhomophobic impulse was ignored almost entirely by his psychiatric and psychoanalytic peers.[86] He was a prominent and respected figure who published in the most important journals, but when his ideas about how hostilities and traumas may be found at the root of perversions were adopted by fellow analysts and other psychiatrists in the USA, it was almost never with the same fiercely compassionate antinormativity that Stoller evinced, but rather with far more conservative agendas. Worse, and however ironically, in the years after his death, prominent analysts assimilated Stoller's ideas about trauma and hostility to *reinforce* a normative – and indeed also overtly homophobic – version of the love doctrine.[87]

Conclusion

It was only in 1991, when the American Psychoanalytic Association passed its nondiscrimination declaration, that openly gay or lesbian individuals in the USA could begin to move toward being certified as analysts and only 1993 when they were permitted to become training analysts as well. In other parts of the world it would take yet longer – and, despite the International Psychoanalytical Association's official move toward nondiscrimination in 2002, in many countries – including Britain, France, and Germany – the matter remained unsettled.[88] The process in the USA had taken years of careful behind-the-scenes negotiations.

Several factors made the formal shift to nondiscrimination possible. One factor was what can only be called "the feminism-ization of psychoanalysis," growing out of the broader feminist revolution in psychotherapy in the course of the 1980s. Feminist critiques of the authoritarianism and misogyny structuring analytic encounters and theoretical publications alike, as well as the rise of pop psych and competing (often shorter-term and more client-centered) therapies had created a climate in which the ideals of empathy and a more democratic alliance between doctor and patient had begun to take hold also in more traditional analytic circles.[89] In fact, even the shift to the narcissistic character disorder paradigm, and despite that paradigm's homophobic uses, had contributed to the growth of a strand within analysis – spearheaded by Kohut but embraced by many others – which emphasized using the analytic space as a (Donald Winnicott-style) "holding environment" more than a place of withholding (the stereotypical analyst's silence interrupted only by the occasional stern interpretation).[90] Another huge factor was the rise, over the course of the 1980s, of ardent enthusiasm for, and sophisticated contributions to, psychoanalytic theorizing among non-MD psychologists, many of them drawn to Sullivanian relational and intersubjective approaches (only some of which were expressly antihomophobic but all of which tended toward the erosion of the analyst's sense of secure superiority vis-à-vis the patient).[91] The 1985 lawsuit, settled in 1989, which at long last permitted the entry of analytically interested psychologists into the American Psychoanalytic Association benefited the Association most of all, as it brought an enormous infusion of energy into what had become a constricted and declining enterprise.[92]

A further significant factor was the broad positive reception among therapeutic professionals and in the mainstream media of the analytically inclined psychologist Kenneth Lewes' landmark study, *The Psychoanalytic Theory of Male Homosexuality*, published in 1988. Lewes documented in detail the preposterousness and absurdism of the antihomosexual theories put forward over the decades since Freud and the cruelty and cowardice that had marked the profession's handling of the topic. And yet another major additional step forward in synthesizing the extant critical thinking would come in 1992, when the sociologist and psychoanalyst Nancy Chodorow published her influential essay "Heterosexuality as a Compromise Formation." Building on her prior feminist work while also drawing extensively on both Stoller and Lewes, Chodorow brilliantly called for treating heterosexuality as just as problematic as homosexuality had been thought to be, and insisted on the importance of pluralizing homosexualities and heterosexualities alike.[93] In subsequent years, Chodorow would also be a key figure in promoting for a wider readership the splendidly perceptive early anti-homophobic essays of relational psychologist Stephen Mitchell, and in making the case for *individualizing* all theorization of gender and sexuality.[94]

The turnaround in professional trends was dramatic. Five hundred psychoanalytic essays and books had been written on the topic of homosexuality before the early 1980s. Of those, as Lewes noted years later when he retrospectively surveyed this landscape, "less than half a dozen claimed homosexuality might be part of a satisfactory psychic organization."[95] As of the early twenty-first century, however, the excitement over the transformation of analysis as it sought to undo its nine-plus decades of post-Freudian contempt for homosexuality would be seen as one of the most vital growth areas within the field. Already the 1990s saw countless workshops, committees, initiatives, conference papers and publications – even journal launchings – that showed how eager the analytic community was to renew itself by *learning from* gays and lesbians.[96] In addition, more and more openly gay and lesbian individuals became analysts.

Nonetheless, this turnaround came with its own set of unintended side-effects: in particular a return, albeit in variant form, of the love doctrine that had initially been invented in reaction against Kinsey, and that was nothing if not an insecure effort to assimilate psychoanalysis into a profoundly repressive and conformist Cold War culture. Or, to put it another way: gay-friendly psychoanalysts in the 1990s and 2000s ended up, and however unexpectedly – not least because of the eventual reception in the 1970s USA, as drive-based versions of Freudianism were in increasing trouble, of (all too often desexualized) object relations theories developed in Britain, *and* because of the resurgence of interest in neo-Freudian concepts – inventing a novel love doctrine of their own.[97] Kenneth Lewes has been most direct in his alarm at the results. Among other things, Lewes has described recent gay-friendly analysts' emphasis on "attachment as a primary motivation," and their concomitant underestimation of the importance of "phallic drives," as evincing a profound disrespect for those who "did not come out as gay because they wanted a relationship or a family, but only the bare, forked activity of sex again and again, in all its variety, anarchy, repetition, and insatiability." Notably, moreover, Lewes has understood "phallic drives" as not only involving sexual desires in the narrowest sense, but also "the derivatives and sublimations of phallic strivings" in healthy ambition and narcissistic self-display.[98]

Lewes' concern – as elaborated in 2005 in the journal *Fort Da* – has been to defend the sexual outlaws and dissidents, the ones who did and do not fit into the new domestic paradigm – not least because he is convinced that talking those patients into believing that what they are most searching for is a singular relationship can only cause profound dependence and above all depression; it shames patients into disowning their own desires. Sex, also specifically anonymous sex, he argued, could after all serve as a life-affirming strategy for warding off despair – and, in Lewes' view, it was by no means incompatible with social responsibility or sound psychological functioning. The preoccupation with relationships, he maintained, deprives individuals of all sexual orientations and preferences of a deeper and more honest understanding of the ways sexual desire and pleasure – or, as Lewes has put it, "the intensity of our sexual lives and imaginations" – need not only be sutured to the couple form, but can also serve as significant strategies of life-affirming resistance to – again in Lewes' words – "social conformity … homogenization, and mediocrity."[99] By no means was Lewes hostile to the dream of love, having concluded a prior essay with a vision of "the promised land all people strive for: the experience of love, which, not checked by fear, shame and humiliation, expresses itself in affection, respect, and gratitude."[100] But in his 2005 essay Lewes was adamant in his concern that the ascent of the relational schools' insistence on "yearnings for attachment and affiliation" as humans' primary motivation could only be damaging to patients who did not fit the normative mold and that, indeed, it should be seen as part of the much longer analytic tradition of flight from and discomfort with sex.[101]

The virtues of Lewes' intervention were many. Among other things, he offered a thought-provoking and original – at once historically contextualized and analytic – explanation for the durability of homophobia within the psychoanalytic profession. In Lewes' phrasing: "The discourse on homosexuality from the Second World War until the 1980s was a neurotic symptom that was maintained with an amount of energy entirely disproportionate to its importance, which served to discharge disowned sexual and sadistic impulses. It helped bolster the fragile self-esteem and cultural identity of psychoanalysts; and it was maintained irrationally in the face of experience and obvious historical fact." Moreover, and pointedly: "Psychoanalysis would have plenty to say about such an aberration if it concerned a patient."[102]

Of even more interest, however, is what Lewes' critical comments also demonstrate, without him necessarily intending it to be so. And this is that there was and is, apparently, absolutely no necessary correlation between a particular psychoanalytic concept (in this case: drives) and the politics that could, and can, be made of it. Stoller had shifted the focus from drive to drama; Lewes retained and ardently defended the value of the idea of drives. Both were creatively antihomophobic. To state the point another way: each and every notion in the Freudian and post-Freudian edifice (from drive to object, from trauma to transference, from ego to unconscious) can be, and has been, used both for malicious and for generous purposes. Nowhere would this become more clear than when also nonsexual political realities pushed their way back into psychoanalytic discussions. If – figuratively – leaving the world outside the consulting-room door had helped to fulfill psychoanalysts' ambitions for cultural success in the first two postwar decades, at the turn from the 1960s to the 1970s that strategy would now cease to make sense.

Part II

NAZISM'S LEGACIES

3 POST-HOLOCAUST ANTISEMITISM AND THE ASCENT OF PTSD

"The murder of how many of one's children must one be able
to survive asymptomatically in order to be deemed to have a
normal constitution?"

Kurt Eissler, 1963[1]

In the monumental reorganization of the *Diagnostic and Statistical
Manual of Mental Disorders* ongoing in the course of the 1970s under
the leadership of psychiatrist Robert L. Spitzer and resulting in the
creation of DSM-III in 1980, an important innovation was the introduction of the category of Post-Traumatic Stress Disorder (PTSD).
Most scholarly accounts of the evolution of the PTSD idea go back to
railroad and industrial accidents at the turn from the nineteenth to the
twentieth centuries and above all to the "shell shock" experienced by
soldiers in World War I. Without a doubt, the renewed high attention
to the phenomenon of PTSD in the second decade of the twenty-first
century due to the USA's recent wars in Afghanistan and Iraq has only
fortified the assumption that the relevant precursor developments that
influenced how the category of PTSD was formulated in 1980 primarily involved the experiences of soldiers, especially the experiences of
veterans of the US war in Vietnam. What most accounts, peculiarly,
skip over or only mention in passing is the crucial role of the aftermath
of the Holocaust of European Jewry in its wholly unexpected, intricate
intersections with subsequent controversies over the USA's military
involvement in Vietnam.[2] PTSD was an "invention-discovery" born of
multiple, overlapping conflicts.[3]

For, as it turns out, *the* catalyst for changing the science of trauma, including the very particular symptoms that we now in the twenty-first century continue to understand as key signs of PTSD (including delayed-reaction onset, numbness of affect, intrusive memories, or hyper-arousal), was a grotesque debacle fought out through the 1950s and 1960s over financial compensation for mental health damages among Jewish survivors of life in flight, hiding, or in the ghettos and concentration and death camps.[4] The battle was ugly, not least because the psychiatrists appointed by the West German government to evaluate survivors regularly rejected their claims, arguing that whatever debilitating insomnia, nightmares, chronic melancholia, fears, fixations, disabling psychosomatic pains, difficulty concentrating, or crippling apathy survivors were displaying must have had their source either in the survivors' *pre*-camp lives – perhaps even in their characters from the time of birth, or in very early life-experiences in their families – or in their difficulties adjusting to *post*-camp life. Anything but the persecutions or the camps themselves.

For it was *against* the doctors who regularly rejected survivors' claims for health damages (many, though not all, gentile Germans, though there were occasionally Jews among the rejecting physicians as well) that survivors sought out second, or third, or fourth opinions from more sympathetic doctors (often, as it happens, German or Austrian Jewish refugee psychoanalytically inclined psychiatrists living in the USA, in various Western European nations or in Israel, although it is noteworthy that there were some important gentile German sympathizer psychiatrists also). And it was up to these more sympathetic doctors to make the case that the origins of the patients' problems lay *in* the persecutions and imprisonments. Very quickly battle lines were established and two opposing sides emerged – arguing their positions in the pages of medical journals as well as directly in the patients' case records, records which were then submitted to the reparations offices and subsequently, in the tens of thousands of cases that were appealed after initial rejections, to courts established in West Germany to adjudicate reparations claims. There would be no simple explanation internal to the history of medicine for how doctors could end up on one side or the other, for most had experienced the same medical training in pre-Nazi Germany. What both the medical journal articles and the case records reveal, instead, is that the doctors' expert medical judgments about the survivors they encountered were deeply shaped by their own (inevitably personal as well as professional) reactions to the patients.

Overlooking the role of the Holocaust's aftermath in the history of PTSD means that we have also missed just how multifaceted – indeed contradictory – would be the invocations and uses of the psychoanalytic tradition within the convoluted transnational interactions among psychiatrists which eventually shaped the specific form which the diagnostic category of PTSD was to take. One main aim of Spitzer's reorganization of the DSM was not only to jettison psychoanalytic approaches in general, a shift which had already assisted in the removal of homosexuality as a category of mental disorder, and which would also lead to the complete disappearance from the DSM of the distinctively psychoanalytic notion of "neurosis" (even as new categories such as "borderline personality disorder" were incorporated). Spitzer was additionally intent on removing any need, or even any opportunity, for speculation about the etiology – that is, theorization of the causes – of psychological conditions. Instead of conjecture about the sources of a particular disorder, DSM-III introduced the phenomenological (and, at the time, it was felt, infinitely more objective) concept of a checklist of measurable symptoms.[5] The redirection of attention away from puzzles about the past – and therefore about causation – and toward the (ideally clearer-to-determine) manifestations of emotional or mental disease in the patient's present was designed to put psychiatry on a more secure scientific footing and make it more comparable to other medical subspecialties. The sole exception to the rule, the only condition for which causation would continue to matter in the DSM-III of 1980 (and up to the present), even as a checklist of symptoms for it was presented as well, would be PTSD.

Psychoanalysis, however, was to figure also in other ways in the impassioned controversies surrounding Holocaust survival. For one thing, the very idea of taking seriously adult, as opposed to childhood, trauma meant a departure not only from mainstream psychiatry but also from the mainstream tradition of psychoanalysis, which with few exceptions tended to the opinion that everything determining a person's later character and behavior had its roots either in an individual's inborn constitution or in early intrafamilial dynamics. For another, many psychoanalysts, particularly those inclined toward ego psychology, were prone toward skepticism that external conditions rather than unconscious motivations drove the production of symptoms, and they often took note of the "secondary gain" patients might be acquiring via their sickness (whether a gain in solicitous attention or a particular balance of power in a relationship or an excuse for not changing their habits). Above all: numerous analysts in the USA and elsewhere had, on principle and in practice, left the real world outside the consulting room. To treat real-world events as consequential for psychic life was anathema.[6] Grappling with the possibility that experiences in flight, hiding, and/or imprisonment in Nazi camps caused psychic damage challenged psychoanalysts' isolation from extrapsychic events. The real world broke in with a vengeance. But it did so only after a delay of many years.

Oddly and ironically, but significantly, it was not initially the sympathetic doctors who alluded to Freud or to psychoanalysis, but rather the rejecting physicians who did so. Their provocative and canny appropriation of psychoanalysis to dismiss the claims of survivors and to put sympathizing doctors on the defensive was strikingly effective. It took time for sympathetic doctors who were also analysts to use their engagement with post-Holocaust and other kinds of trauma as an opportunity also to reinvigorate the psychoanalytic project – which was, after all, entering a phase of deep crisis in the USA during the precise period, from the early 1970s on, when the DSM was being reformulated.

Two further noteworthy themes emerge from revisiting the conflicts over mental health damages to survivors. One is the importance of context for the evolution of theory. In this case, the context was the toxic postfascist climate filled with resentment against the survivors in which the (at once medical, legal, and moral) battle over mental health damages was first fought through and in which in general truth was up for grabs. A second theme has to do with the problem of scientific objectivity and the predicaments of bias. The anti-reparations doctors regularly attacked the more sympathetic doctors for being (purportedly) unobjective and unscientific. In turn, the sympathizing doctors struggled to bring into view and coherence the multi-symptom phenomenon that they first called "survivor syndrome" and "massive psychic trauma" and which eventually, by historical contingency but also by engaged activism – as the doctors working with and on behalf of survivors of Nazi persecutions and camps joined forces with physicians pressing for attention to the emotional difficulties experienced by many veterans of the Vietnam War – came to be called PTSD. On the one hand, this turned out to be a historical instance in which politics (specifically and preeminently, international Jewish organizations' political pressure) literally moved the science forward. But no less significant is a countervailing and complicating point: The sympathizing doctors were acutely aware of the extreme messiness of their evidence.

It has been argued that the rejecting doctors were simply caught in the traditional medical orthodoxy.[7] According to the inherited doctrine, individuals with a previously normal constitution were by definition robust and should recover rapidly from stress; if mental problems continued, there were only two possible explanations. Either there must be a somatic, physiological explanation, or the individual must have been emotionally unstable before. Certainly, these traditionalist arguments were used by psychiatrists to deny effective care not only to concentration camp survivors but also to disturbed German soldiers returning from Soviet POW camps.[8] Reviewing the medical disputes over concentration camp survival, however, reveals that on this subject the rejecters were no innocent traditionalists. The minute the topic of mental health damages to camp survivors entered the medical journals – which it did already by 1957–1958 – the rejecting doctors knew full well what they were doing, and self-consciously used every rhetorical strategy at their disposal to refute their critics and justify their decisions.[9]

Yet the sympathizing physicians were not easy heroes, but rather often maddeningly imperfect. They were caught not only in the binds created by their opponents, but also in their own assumptions about human nature and therapeutic process. Eventually, however, first incrementally and then with ever greater success, their efforts helped to generate a paradigm shift with momentous consequences. In subsequent decades and into the twenty-first century, PTSD has become the diagnostic category of choice for addressing emotional turmoil in our apparently ever-proliferating array of disaster zones of both human and natural making. That these consequences have since in turn had numerous more ambiguous ramifications is the ever-evolving end of the story within which we still live. For finally, as it turned out, the achievement of the sympathizers remained an ambivalent one, fraught with unanticipated complexities.

One purpose of this chapter, then, is to reconsider the medical texts on both sides produced in this moment and in so doing also to reintegrate the history of post-Holocaust trauma into the history of

PTSD – valuable not least because this episode turned out to be one of the most important learning moments for the psychiatric profession in the USA, indeed one which ultimately had global repercussions. But what is no less fascinating to ponder are the predicaments of bias and the intricacy of ideological conflict on display here. Over the first dozen or so years of the dispute, the rejecting doctors set the terms of debate. No one, in those years, could have predicted which side would emerge vindicated.

The Case Against Reparations

The story begins not with the Holocaust itself, but rather in its aftermath. A law triggered the debate over the status of trauma. It was passed in West Germany in 1956 as part of a broader set of negotiations underway since the end of the war between the West German government, the Western Allies, especially the Americans, and international Jewish organizations (like the Conference on Jewish Material Claims against Germany and the United Restitution Organization), as well as the young state of Israel. The law provided for small pensions (and in some cases also therapy) for survivors whose capacity to be economically self-supporting had been damaged by at least 25 percent due to persecution and violence experienced in the Third Reich in flight and hiding, in ghettos, or in camps.

Jews who had lost property under Nazism were able to seek restitution under an earlier law; the law allowing survivors to seek compensation for damages to health was, to put it bluntly, the law for the little people, the ones who had no property to reclaim – often poorer Jews, and often Jews from Eastern European territories, including parts of Poland, that had been part of the German Reich as of 1937. The only property they had, as it were, was their labor power. Hence the need to prove the 25 percent or more diminishment of the ability to be self-supporting – in whatever new land had become their refuge. (The clear model for the law lay in workers' compensation legislation.)

But in case after case, as noted, the initially evaluating doctors said that whatever survivors had experienced in hiding or in the camps was something that someone with a previously healthy disposition *should* have been able to recover from. Anybody having trouble afterward must have been troubled before. Maybe their parents' marriage had not been happy; maybe they were just oversensitive.[10] Or, alternatively – these doctors averred – perhaps the prospect of receiving a pension was causing the survivors to display symptoms of psychological dysfunction; perhaps they were, like lazy workers or malingering soldiers had been imagined before them, best understood as "pension-neurotics" (*Rentenneurotiker*) – that was the literal term used, whether they were producing their (suddenly financially convenient) symptoms consciously or unconsciously. In fact, one West German government-sponsored guidebook for evaluating psychiatrists contended that therapy could only be helpful in cases where no pension had been given, because the granting of the pension itself prevented healing.[11] As survivor, "displaced persons" (DP) leader, and historian Samuel Gringauz would summarize the situation with caustic outrage in 1967:

> The sufferings are [in the rejecting doctors' assessments] caused by constitutional factors, caused by fate, caused by old age, caused by environment, caused by character, caused by simulation, caused by fraudulence, caused by marital conflicts, caused by the milkman, caused-by-anything-you-want, just not caused by the inferno, just not caused by hell. As far as is possible, the human- and soul-murdering inferno of German history should be denied.[12]

Over and over, the doctors who rejected survivors' claims denied that there could have been any causal link between *symptoms* and *experience*.

All of this happened in a cultural context in post-Nazi West Germany of intense public hostility – shared also by leading politicians – toward the very idea of reparations or restitution. As West German Chancellor Konrad Adenauer's close associate, the Christian Social Union's Fritz Schäffer – a conservative Catholic and the second most powerful man in the postwar government – put it with striking lack of inhibition: "If the Jews want money, they should raise it themselves by arranging for a foreign loan."[13] Schäffer was from 1949 to 1957 the head of the Ministry of Finance, and his main assistant, Ernst Féaux de la Croix, was a man given to remarking on his annoyance about the "terrible drama of Israeli-Jewish demands" and the way protests in Israel "swearing revenge" provided the "background music" to the always-delicate diplomatic negotiations over reparations. In his history of the reparations process, Féaux de la Croix noted that while it might sound "distinctly antisemitic" and "strongly exaggerated" to say that reparations were "the price that American Jewry exacted of its president for allowing him to take the Federal Republic as a partner into the community of Western nations," it could "nonetheless not be denied that there was a kernel of truth" in such assertions, and his account was liberally sprinkled with complaints about "world Jewry," "supervision from Jerusalem," and how "Jewry just would not let go." (By contrast, Féaux de la Croix was indignant that "the Jewish press" mentioned the Nazi past of one of the bankers involved in the negotiations, deeming the exposure of this backstory the "most aggressive," "undignified personal defamation.")[14] Minister of Finance Schäffer, for his part, openly stoked public anger against survivors by provocatively prophesying that reparations would so strain the West German financial system that it would "inevitably lead to a devaluation of the Deutschmark."[15] As though – not much more than a dozen years previously – non-Jewish Germans had not been enthusiastically supportive of a criminal regime, and had not benefited directly – with career opportunities and with property – from "Aryanization," Jewish flight, deportations, and murder.[16]

These two – Schäffer and Féaux de la Croix – were the men in charge of managing the entire reparations apparatus. (In the vast majority of instances the claimants were Jews – there were a tiny number of Roma and political resisters that put forward health claims as well.) Schäffer also liked to complain that no one was willing to break the taboo against criticizing the reparations project for fear of being accused of antisemitism.[17] But the taboo was, inevitably, broken all the time, as invoking the idea of taboo was precisely what facilitated the talk. Chancellor Adenauer himself was said to have remarked in a high-level meeting: "The Jews cheat us anyway."[18]

In the wider public and in the media, there was far blunter rhetoric around reparations. Hendrik G. van Dam, the head of the Jewish community in Germany, received hate mail with contents such as: "You get yourself out of Germany as fast as you can! Every second Jew has made false claims and enriched himself ... The reparations must end."[19] A letter written by a pastor in Berlin to the news magazine *Der Spiegel* declared – commenting on a much-discussed case in 1957 in which a schoolteacher had told a survivor "in my opinion far too few Jews were gassed" – that this kind of unfortunate slip was understandable in a situation of unequal rights: "Once Jews had fewer rights than

Aryans. Nowadays a problematic reparations practice has turned the legal situation into the exact opposite."[20] Or, as another letter-writer opined in 1958 – again defending the schoolteacher's remarks: "Once again, the 'Chosen People' are, each and every one, dancing around the 'golden calf.'"[21]

Clever and/or pained counterarguments were also published. "The name of the Law for the Compensation of Victims of Nazism might better be changed into 'Law for the Reawakening and Promotion of Anti-Semitism,'" one letter-writer observed.[22] Another noted sarcastically, "Many of our contemporaries now like to reproach the Jews for the fact that so many of them are entitled to compensation. After all, back then it was obviously due to their self-interested profit-seeking that these mercenary Semites pushed their way so eagerly into the concentration camps!"[23] And yet another reminded readers of "the grotesque deeds of the Nazis, who with ice-cold hearts turned to oppressing entire groups of peoples whose nose did not appeal to them, in order to make fertilizer out of them."[24] But it was apparent from the terms of debate how much dislike of Jews permeated the discourse (by some accounts, everyday expressions of antisemitism had actually risen in the wake of Nazism's defeat), and how greatly put on the defensive the anti-antisemites were.[25]

Every small scandal – and there were scandals – in which a claimant made a false claim or a lawyer appeared to have a conflict of interest or profit too much from representing survivors provided a further chance to link Jews in general with greed and corruption and unseemly self-interest. Jewish organizations were obliged to remind all potential claimants of the danger that antisemitism could be restoked. They urgently warned all involved to avoid even the appearance of malfeasance.[26]

Promptly, three actually separate matters became entangled: what a postfascist government owes the victims of its predecessor (morally, legally); whether reparations in principle were a just concept, but the demands of "world Jewry" were unreasonable and excessive; and whether a few bad apples could be construed as standing in for a group as a whole. In this climate, avid opponents of reparations – like the CDU politician Jakob Diel – could frame their objections in coded but easily understood ways: "What ... simply cannot be accepted," Diel argued, "is the shameless abuse of the good will of the Federal Republic."[27] In a long-running campaign to encourage his party, the governing party, to turn against the entire project, Diel was given to asking rhetorical questions such as: "Can it truly be just that in countless cases individuals covered by the reparations law are better off financially now than if they had never been persecuted?"[28]

While there is always a battle over the truth, this battle is especially acute in the aftermath of great horror. It is especially acute, in short, in a postfascist environment, when people's investments in rewriting reality – massaging, spinning, reinterpreting the facts – are particularly strong. To only feel morally indignant is to miss just how much the idea that *Jews were a problem* was part of the commonsense texture of public discussion in the aftermath of a mass-murderous dictatorship. Moreover, the blatancy of *the hypocrisy around money* is noteworthy. This was also a climate, after all, in which there were not just pensions available for concentration camp guards as well as their widows, but also entire organizations of gentiles dedicated to clamoring that they had been "victims of denazification" ("*Entnazifizierungsgeschädigte*") and/or "victims of reparations" ("*Restitutionsgeschädigte*" – this included people who were distressed that Jews whose property had been lost to "Aryanization" had come back to reclaim it).[29] A journal launched in 1953 was dedicated to expressing vituperative distress over reparations: *Die Anklage* (The Accusation) – the subtitle was "Organ for the Disenfranchised Victims Damaged by the Postwar Situation."[30]

In addition, it is important to keep in mind just how intricate were *the enmeshments of the experts* in the project of denying the recent past. What is notable about post-Nazi West Germany is that the majority of professionals who were authorities during the Third Reich continued to be the authoritative and respected professionals in their fields in the aftermath – with consequences for how younger professionals were mentored, but also with complicated consequences for the daily interactions with peers. Significantly, individuals who found Nazism repugnant nonetheless worked to stay on remarkably courteous professional terms with fully compromised individuals.

As of the end of 1966, a decade into the process, rejections amounted to more than a third of the cases, and indeed on the initial round, before a case went to the courts on the basis of more sympathetic evaluations, the rejection rate had been more than half.[31] The justifications took a multitude of forms. One evaluator in 1960, for example, found a woman who had spent three years in Auschwitz to have "a psychopathic personality with a tendency toward abnormal processing of experience and an inability to deal with life." The expert consensus, the evaluator declared – and here we see the gesture to medical orthodoxy – was that a "normal person" would have recovered six months after liberation at the latest.[32] Other victims were described variously as having "hypochondriacal attitudes" (this in regard to a man who had been in one ghetto and three concentration camps, had been thrown from a truck, and had his mother, sister, wife, and four children killed), or of displaying a "hysterical faulty attitude" and a "hysterical demonstration of helplessness" (this in response to a woman who made strange inarticulate sounds when being questioned about her experiences, which included not only eight to ten hours of heavy camp labor every day – this an evaluator interpreted as providing her with access to somewhat better rations – but also the murder of two children, six siblings, and two grandchildren, who had been torn from her arms).[33] Or, in another case, involving a mother who had lost several of her children in concentration camps and had difficulty sleeping, the evaluating physician declared that "many people are sensitive and have sleep disturbances. This is not a serious disability."[34] There were thousands of cases like this; a significant number of the claimants were written off as suffering from a congenital or endogenous (*anlagebedingte*) "anxiety neurosis." This particular label was freely applied to people who had seen the murder of children, who had lived in near-unendurable conditions in hiding, or who had been subjected to violent beatings in camps.[35]

There was also the case of a Polish Jewish man Z., born in 1913, who had lost wife and child and parents and several siblings, survived the Warsaw Ghetto and the labor camp Falenty, where he was violently abused and from which he then escaped. He hid with a farmer in a pig stall in a coffin-size pit covered with pig dung in which he could neither move nor turn around and where he had to urinate and defecate and was only fed every few days. He became too weak to sit up unassisted; he lay there for 18 months, frequently in terror of the SS contingent coming through with trained police dogs. Only the pig dung piled over his pit kept the dogs from sniffing him out. Years later, he had constant pain in his joints, dizzy spells during the day, difficulty concentrating, and nightmares from which he woke screaming at night. "I should rather have died" was the survivor's own self-assessment; "congenital idiocy" was the diagnosis.[36] In short, the non-sympathetic doctors were endlessly inventive in their determination to refute the claims for restitution.

Meanwhile, and in addition, the doctors intent on rejecting not only specific individuals' claims but the foundational premise on which claims were based started recurrently to impute a lack of objectivity to those physicians who were beginning to insist that it was definitively the persecution and camp experiences that caused psychological damages, accusing these other doctors of "a really very extensive application of subjective interpretations" and suggesting that sympathetic assessments were more the result of the predilection of the assessor than of the facts of any particular case. For example, singling out the work of the Walther von Baeyer clinic in Heidelberg (these were very careful, cautious sympathizers), one of the non-sympathetic physicians, Hermann Witter, sneered that the evaluations of survivors produced in Heidelberg had a "downright artistic design" but that "quite often we find the evidence for the reality-content of the proffered portrait entirely lacking."[37] Or, as another rejecter, Helmuth Lotz, phrased it, sympathetic doctors were indiscriminately handing out a welter of pension-securing diagnoses "without convincing evidence."[38]

Most fundamentally, the very idea of granting a pension for any "neurosis" was declared by the lead researcher on neuroses in West Germany, Ernst Kretschmer, to be "scientifically insupportable [*wissenschaftlich unhaltbar*]." It was precisely the possibility of a pension that caused people to be *unable* to get healthy, Kretschmer averred, citing studies on shell shock from the 1920s. An early official government publication to orient physicians on reparations for the victims of National Socialism expressly promoted the Kretschmer position. It would mean "breeding neuroses in a grand style, rather than healing them," Kretschmer declared, and the government publication reiterated, if any pensions were granted. The whole dynamic driving most neuroses, Kretschmer commented, had nothing to do with past experiences, but rather with future hopes (for money) or with a "hypochondriacal" inability to master one's present. Neuroses *could* emerge from either "familial conflicts or inner problems of character," but *not* from later external events.[39] Another official government publication in 1960 declared: "Only on the ground of a particular psychic and somatic personality structure can damaging experiences lead to manifest illnesses. *The actual experience, as dramatic as it may seem, can thus not be considered to have any causational importance.*" In fact, to the extent that "*experience*" could be considered relevant at all, the authors felt that the "emotional climate" in the first year of life – even if no longer accessible to the claimant's conscious memory – should be included for consideration.[40]

Over and over, the sympathetic doctors were dismissed as having "remarkably little" insight or an "empirical basis" that was "really rather thin."[41] They were derided for having a "naïve-psychological approach."[42] It was "unfortunate" that sympathetic doctors let "affective attitudes" intrude on their judgment; this made a "scientific discussion of the issues almost impossible."[43] Rejecters recurrently accused the sympathetic doctors of using their newly invented diagnostic terms inconsistently. (Among the terms used were "deportees' asthenia," "reactive depression," "exogenous depression," "experience-reactive syndrome," and "experience-based personality change" – in all these cases one can see the effort to emphasize the exogenous experiences; rejecters made fun of the proliferation of terms.)[44] And the rejecters repeatedly demanded evidence of what they called "bridge symptoms."[45] The time lag notable between liberation from the camps and the emergence of psychological distress was seen as suspicious – read as yet another sign that the survivors were motivated by the hope of financial gain. (Nowadays a latency period between experience and symptoms is seen as one of the typical signs of post-traumatic stress; at the time, however, sympathetic experts were repeatedly challenged to explain the phenomenon.)

And finally, there was the peculiar way in which Freudian psychoanalysis appeared and disappeared in rejecters' texts. Sometimes the reference was coded, as when a rejecter text simply flatly announced that "also … classical psychoanalysis" had no answers when it came to the question of the relationships between external experiences and emotional damage.[46] Sometimes Freud seemed advantageous to invoke. The early official government publication, for instance, was pleased to quote Kretschmer invoking Freud for support on the idea that neuroses were a "flight into illness" and that there was such a thing as a "gain from illness [*Krankheitsgewinn*]."[47] Sometimes the slap was explicit – and it is important to note here that the Nazis had continually both denigrated Freud in antisemitic terms *and* simultaneously appropriated many of his ideas as their own.[48] This double move of both denigrating and (mis-)appropriating Freud continued into the postwar era and showed up particularly in debates over whether the simulation of symptoms was "conscious" or "unconscious." Here rejecters liked to propose that perhaps in many cases the survivors were not aware that they were motivated by pensions, that the display of symptoms might "frequently" be the results of "largely unconsciously unfolding processes."[49] In general, as a sympathetic psychiatrist critical of the rejecters' strategies noted already in 1965, "the [F]reudian concept of neurosis ... proved surprisingly useful" for psychiatrists intent on rejecting claims,

> for Freud could easily be quoted as placing the origin of all neu-
> roses in childhood; and further as stressing, in the adult flare-up
> of childhood conflicts which is the essence of neurosis, the impor-
> tance of organ compliance and of secondary gain. He could be
> understood as supporting the idea that neurosis attaches itself in
> a purely external and almost accidental way to the adult trauma,
> but does not derive in a direct and internal way from it. His
> teachings thus appeared to be quite compatible with the classi-
> cal doctrine: the cause of neurosis lay altogether anterior to any
> persecution.[50]

Thus for instance Christoph Jannasch, a rejecting expert, would opine snarkily in 1973 that "Early childhood is decisive for the emergence of psychoneurotic disorders, not only in the primitive Freudian view. The first six years of life lay the crucial groundwork ... The groundwork for an anxiety-neurotic structure, with all its consequences, is laid in the early years of life."[51] Indeed, the double move of both dismissing and deploying Freud would show up most clearly in disputes over whether childhood experiences were more significant for character development than whatever persecutions and imprisonments had occurred later.

Summarizing and protesting this state of affairs, the Israeli psychoanalyst Hillel Klein in 1983 commented in anguish on the contradictory and punitive uses of Freudianism to reject survivors:

> I am ashamed to read the evaluations by my psychiatric col-
> leagues in Germany. They use psychoanalysis to conclude in one
> case: "This child was only two years old; how could he experi-
> ence persecution!," while in another case maintaining, "The boy
> was already thirteen years old and had lived with his parents,
> so he had experienced the so-called warmth of the family nest."
> These paradoxes in the name of Freud and psychoanalysis are still

perpetrated by reputable professors in Germany. I speak in anger, because I believe that many of my colleagues, with their obsessive tendencies, unconsciously identify with the aggressor.[52]

The battle between the two sides got deeply personal, and "objectivity" – especially the relationship between evidence and explanation – became the key point of contention. Rejecters saw to it that doctors considered too sympathetic were denied the right to evaluate survivors. And sympathetic doctors in the USA and West Germany and Israel self-censored and deliberately approved fewer claims for pensions than they thought were medically warranted, so as to retain the right to produce evaluations at all.[53] How did the tables finally turn?

The Case for Reparations

Already in the 1940s, during and after the war, a number of survivor-professionals and soon thereafter a number of other physicians, in numerous countries (including notably France, Poland, the Netherlands, and Norway) had begun to publish on the topic of psychological damage due to experiences of persecution and imprisonment. International conferences of medical specialists working on health damages of persecution and internment were held in Paris and Copenhagen in 1954 and Brussels in 1955. But it was not until the 1956 law went into effect and claims began to be denied that physicians who were convinced of the reality of post-camp psychological damage needed not just to counter the contentions of the rejecters, but also to make fuller sense of their own findings.

Among the issues sympathizers grappled with was the purported comparability between death camp experiences and those of POWs or victims of bombings or expulsions, and thus an argument about the uniqueness of what we now call the Holocaust began to take shape. Hans Strauss, an émigré psychiatrist who was initially a sympathizer and later became predominantly a rejecter (making him a favorite with German authorities and reviled by some US peers), emphasized already in 1957 "the singularity" (*das Eigenartige*) in the chronic depressions displayed by the victims of Nazi persecution and rejected the comparisons with victims of industrial accidents and wars; he subsequently referred to the concentration and death camps as "a psychiatric mass experiment, the like of which should never have been made and will, we hope, never be made again."[51] The widely respected Munich-based psychiatrist Kurt Kolle, one of the most remarkable German sympathizing doctors, opened his 1958 essay on the subject with the words: "The topic is new, there is no precedent." And he went on to observe that "the fate of the Jews of Central Europe can in no way be compared with accidents that happen to people ... [or] to injuries sustained in military service." Even those who were politically or religiously persecuted at least had the opportunity and choice to change their views and adapt to the regime, he noted. Those who were racially persecuted had not the slightest chance. Moreover, he continued, "the Jewish people knew, or suspected, when they were deported and imprisoned, that they were slated for liquidation." After examining more than 200 survivors, 155 of them Jews (the others were political prisoners or Roma), Kolle found a predominance of "chronic depressive conditions" and "nervous disturbances" that "substantively diminish the ability to be self-supporting" and he endorsed the concept of "concentration camp syndrome" that had begun to be developed in other nations, and that, he suggested, was especially notable in individuals who were the sole survivors in once-large families.[55] Another sympathizer, the Mainz-based psychiatrist Ernst Kluge, emphasized key elements of the concentration and death camp experience: the utter guiltlessness of Jews (as opposed to political prisoners who had chosen to resist), the complete powerlessness and continual vulnerability to the most primitive cruelty and sadism, the arbitrariness, the inversion of values in the camps and "diabolization" of the community caused by privileging some prisoners over others and making them co-responsible for the suffering of their fellows.[56] Yet others emphasized the shattering loss of loved ones, the guilt of surviving not just while others died but also at the cost of constant humiliation and degradation.[57] The survivors the sympathizers encountered were, in many cases, simply "broken people."[58] In addition, sympathizers took on directly the prevalent rejecter argument that, if someone could not recover, they must have had preexisting problems. "Can one really expect of every person who becomes a victim of racial insanity that he gets over it with equanimity?" Kolle asked rhetorically.[59]

Sympathizing doctors also grappled with the confounding complexity of the evidence they encountered. As Kolle himself put it, "the causal relationship [between the experience of violence and the

subsequent psychological conditions] ... cannot be reduced to a simple formula"; every single case was different and in each there was
at work "an entangled play of forces."[60] There was a bewildering
variety of syndromes and symptoms, and every attempt to systematize (e.g., by age at onset of persecution, or by the particularities of
the camp, or the kinds of violence encountered) only confused things
more.[61] Certainly, the type of person one had been before *did* shape
how one managed the camp experiences, as arbitrary as the horrors
otherwise were. And indisputably the conditions of post-camp life
mattered as well. Was there a spouse, were there family members
with whom to reunite, was there a new love? Was there meaningful work and social respect? Some survivors had trouble adjusting
in a country (whether Palestine/Israel or the USA or any number
of other nations) where they did not initially speak the language
or were unable to gain a foothold. Meanwhile, how indeed could
the (manifestly common) time lag in the emergence of symptoms be
explained? (Was the interlude in the displaced persons [DP] camps
an ongoingly difficult phase, and that explained why survivors
kept their agonies repressed, only to have them surface later, when
things seemed to have gotten better? Or had survivors actually been
"spoiled" in the DP camps – as one doctor suggested – and this, not
the death camps, was the source of their later difficulties in master-
ing the ordinary challenges of daily life?)[62] And why was it that some
survivors – maybe as many as three-quarters, all told – seemed to
be able to build up some kind of post-camp life, sometimes even a
quite successful one, and showed no particular signs of debilitating psychological damage, while others were completely crumpled?[63]
Throughout, moreover, precisely because sympathizing doctors were
acutely aware that mainstream medical teaching in Germany, already
since before Nazism, had emphasized that lasting, as opposed to
short-term and reparable, psychological damage after a traumatic
experience could only be explained by organic somatic damage like
a blow to the head or long-term malnutrition, some of them deliberately placed strong emphasis on whatever somatic findings they
could locate.[64] Indeed, they too had been trained in this framework
and were thus themselves at times hard put to explain how psychological problems could last even if there were no somatic findings.
This in turn made them even more vulnerable to being accused by
the rejecters of exaggeration, speculation, and inconsistency.[65]

There were courageous sympathizers on both sides of the Atlantic. In addition to Kurt Kolle, one of the most important German defenders of the survivors was the young physician Ulrich Venzlaff, who had been mentored by Gottfried Ewald, the sole psychiatrist in the Third Reich to openly oppose the murder of the handicapped. Venzlaff developed the concept "experience-reactive personality change" (*erlebnisreaktiver Persönlichkeitswandel*) to capture the causal link in the diagnostic category; in an early and much-cited sympathetic evaluation, he strategically praised aspects of the rejecters' doctrine only then to go on to undermine it. His emphasis lay in trying to find language that conveyed the "permanent deformation" (*Dauerverbiegung*) of the psyche caused by intense trauma.[66] A signally relevant figure in the United States was the New York-based William G. Niederland, who worked tirelessly, in hundreds of sympathetic evaluations and in dozens of scholarly essays and media interviews, to achieve reversals of rejections. Among his many contributions were the development and explication of the concept of survivor guilt – a profoundly contested but, as it would turn out, strategically important topic – and the concept of hypermnesia (especially vivid intrusive memories).[67] But one of the biggest contributions he made was to call attention to the point that life in hiding, often under subanimal-like conditions and in constant terror of discovery, could be *as* damaging to mental health as life in the concentration and death camps, and also his insistence that the earlier experiences of persecution in one's hometown – perhaps especially for children being mocked and beaten up and excluded from one's former circle of peers – needed to be taken into account as well.

Notably, moral outrage was not the main tack taken by the most successful sympathizers. Instead, the far more effective strategy was to combine fulsome praise for some small aspect of a prominent rejecter's insight – Niederland and Venzlaff both, for instance, praised Ernst Kretschmer on minor points – only then to go on to declare that, alas, the rejecters were sadly behind the times. They were simply not up to speed on the latest scientific findings.[68]

Eissler's Critique

Perhaps the most searingly articulate critique of the rejecters, however, came from Kurt Eissler, an émigré psychoanalyst in New York who later became director of the Freud Archives, at that time often sought out, like Niederland, as a sympathizer who could provide a second (or third or fourth) opinion in disputed cases. Eissler had worked for the US military during World War II, and this gave him additional authority because he was able to contrast the experiences of combat veterans and survivors. In two essays, the first in German in 1963 (with the provocative title summing up Eissler's scathing critique of the rejecter position: "The murder of how many of one's children must one be able to survive asymptomatically in order to be deemed to have a normal constitution?") and a subsequent essay published in English in 1967 in the *American Journal of Psychiatry* and titled simply "Perverted Psychiatry?" Eissler dismantled the rejecters' strategies piece by piece. Among other things, he emphasized the uniqueness of the racial persecutions, explained the time lag in symptom appearance, and forcefully accused the *rejecters* of a lack of objectivity. In other words, he used their own weapons against them.

In this unprecedented situation, the kind of emotional distance toward the patient that rejecters demanded, Eissler said, was not true objectivity. The incapacity to feel one's way into the novelty and grotesquerie of what the Nazis had done demonstrated, in Eissler's view, a "defect" of objectivity. "I am here arguing that an *adequate* reaction when one is listening [to descriptions of the camp experiences] is to have the reaction: 'this is unbearable.'" Eissler was not asking doctors or judges to feel pity. Rather, he reflected on how any one of those professional men would *himself* react if he was arrested, put into prisoners' garb, forced to do heaviest labor in the worst weather and on the absolute minimum of food, had his children murdered, been hunted by dogs, threatened with being shot, kicked in the head and abused so badly that his face carried permanently disfiguring scars – after three years of this, would he really be so stoic and be able to resume his daily life? As Eissler concluded with deadpan fury in 1963: "It remains a mystery how such a profound malfunction of the ability to identify can emerge among educated intellectuals." It was the rejecters, he said, who had an "emotional conflict" when they were conducting evaluations. The idea that a psyche, a soul, is not autonomous and impervious, that it can in fact be damaged, indeed damaged forever, by external experiences: *this* realization, Eissler proposed, must awaken strong fears.[69] In short, Eissler began to theorize the issue of bias within countertransference – what the evaluators were bringing to their encounters with survivors.[70] Critical self-reflexiveness, in his view, was essential to objectivity. But he was also unapologetically insisting that traumatic events could in fact cause lasting damage to the mind; there need not be measurable damage to the body.

In the 1967 essay, Eissler had his own theories about the kinds of regression to more primitive pre-civilized "archaic" emotions of contempt for the weak and suffering that Nazism had encouraged and that he found persisted after 1945. Ever the psychoanalyst and not just psychiatrist, striving to sort out what it was about the crushed survivors of this particular catastrophe that seemed so to destabilize the evaluators, Eissler noted that contempt for the weak had complex roots, and appeared to be connected, he submitted, "with the whole problem of sadomasochism." A tragic hero, no matter how narcissistic or criminal, was held in awe, and his punishment seemed reasonable. By contrast, the survivor, broken and not vengeful, with no crime to expiate, was denied "the top of that hierarchical pyramid to which Christ has elevated the humiliated and the suffering." Eissler went on to imagine that the hostile evaluators were actually deeply afraid, seeing a survivor, that they themselves, had they been in the camps, might well have reacted to their oppressors with weakness and groveling. By no means granting himself greater virtue, Eissler also reflected that the discomfiture in the face of humiliated people was "something of a universal reaction still very much alive in almost all of us." Nonetheless, his point was that anyone not critically self-aware and able to "control this archaic feeling" should recuse himself, or simply be excluded by the authorities, from the right to conduct evaluations.[71]

Unlike some other sympathizers, whose texts were filled with defensiveness – itself an indication of the imbalance of power at that time within postwar Germany between rejecters and sympathizers, Eissler went on the offense: "Everyone should have only one purpose in this matter: to assist in relieving the sufferings of the victims of persecution. It thus stands to reason that if anyone's personal conviction could in any way make such relieving impossible, he should silently step aside and let those take over the function of 'experts' whose convictions will at least augment the chance that that suffering will be assuaged." And if the biased ones did not step aside voluntarily: "The minimum one may demand, under such circumstances, is that the responsible authorities recognize those who cannot control this archaic feeling and exclude them from the position of experts in matters of compensation for suffering."[72] Eissler's texts became major touchstones in the subsequent battles.

His plea for the rejecters to be excluded was not what happened, however. Unsympathetic evaluators continued their work well through the 1970s and in some cases beyond. What did happen was that the international power balance shifted. One early result of sustained pressure from the Conference on Jewish Material Claims against Germany as well as other international organizations came with a law change in 1965 in which the concept of a "concentration camp presumption" was introduced. Thenceforth, having spent one year in a camp was considered adequate evidence that there must be a link between symptoms and experience. Although rejecters found imaginative ways to get around this as well – for example, by minimizing the assessed percentage of reduction in earning capacity – the law change simplified the claims process considerably. Just as important was the gradual reorientation in the international terms of debate among medical professionals. Only a handful of leading psychiatrists had adapted by the late 1960s. But gradually, though in many cases too late for the survivors, the climate of medical opinion shifted. This was due not least to the ongoing international conferences on survivors' health problems held in various European cities, conferences at which the German rejecters were increasingly shamed and countered. In this altered climate, courts within West Germany also increasingly reversed the initial decisions on appeal. But one of the most important dynamics involved what can only be called the "Americanization" of the debate from the late 1960s on – inextricable from the wider rise of, and indeed a major contributing factor to, Holocaust consciousness in the USA.

Especially significant were the series of conferences in Detroit organized by William Niederland together with his fellow psychiatrist Henry Krystal beginning in 1963 and with results published in 1968 and 1971, at which not only the sympathetic German physician Ulrich Venzlaff was an important presence (and was able to relay American expert trends back to Germany), but which additionally brought together psychiatrists who did not just do diagnosis but also therapy with survivors – a hugely significant topic unto itself.[73] Among other things, the presenters debated the value specifically of psychoanalytic concepts: the masochistic defenses demanded by the camp experience; the confirmation of primal childhood fears and guilts when parents

were murdered; the need to repress anger and aggression for the duration of the imprisonment (not just anger at perpetrators but also anger
at parents for being unable to protect); as well as insights into how
therapists might better manage their own countertransference.[74] The
conference discussions make clear how deeply the sympathizers were
still engaging with the arguments of rejecters (for example, they discussed the case of the woman who had a breakdown *after* she got
her pension, because she felt she was being paid for the child she had
let die while she survived – the example was brought up to prove the
point that it could not have been the desire for a pension that caused
her troubles), as well the sympathizers' initial difficulties in making
sense of the frequent time lag between traumatic event and onset of
symptoms, and the possibility that preexisting conditions might matter
in how individuals coped with trauma.[75]

Notably, as well, the Detroit conferences brought in psychiatrist Robert Jay Lifton, who was to become one of the key linking
figures in the subsequent development, in the course of the 1970s, of
growing cooperation between experts working with Holocaust survivors (among them, Niederland and Krystal) and those working with
antiwar Vietnam veterans in formulating the concept of PTSD that
entered the DSM-III in 1980. Lifton was in Detroit to report on his
work with survivors of the atomic blast at Hiroshima, but in the conversations, both formal and informal, he came to see similarities in
diverse survivor experiences.[76]

Ultimately it took Vietnam to bring the Holocaust fully into
focus.[77] As manifestly different as the cases of soldiers and survivors
were, the incontrovertible fact is that the growing public discussion surrounding Vietnam veterans and the pressure of antiwar groups helped
greatly to push PTSD into the DSM, with absolutely crucial positive
results for shifting the mainstream of medical opinion internationally.
Especially striking, among the dozens of examples by which the linkage
was established as medical and popular common sense, was an essay in
the *New York Post* in 1972 carrying the banner headline "Auschwitz &
Viet: – The Survivors." Indicatively, Niederland and Lifton were both
quoted under the subhead "Both Groups Feel Guilt" (see Figure 6).[78]
Interestingly, moreover, in his efforts to get the traumas experienced
by Holocaust survivors taken more seriously both by his professional
peers and by the wider US public, Krystal had initially called attention
not to the parallels between survivors and soldiers serving in Vietnam

Auschwitz & Viet:
—The Survivors

By ROBERT BAZELL

A survivor of Auschwitz, walking a New York street on a snowy day, is suddenly gripped with terror, believing he is once again on the forced death march he took through the German winter of 1945.

A young Vietnam combat veteran begins to glance around fearfully as he stands in Times Square. "These people all look alike," he says to himself. "How do I know who is friend and who is enemy?"

Both stories — based on actual case histories of people who confused the horror of their past with present reality — were offered as examples yesterday by a panel of psychiatrists and psychologists comparing the emotional problems of returning Vietnam veterans with those of the survivors of Nazi concentration camps.

Similarities Cited

"At first glance, the suffering of the two groups would hardly seem comparable. One is a warrior who perpetrated violence, while the other is a victim," said Dr. Chaim Shatam, a professor at New York University who led the panel.

"But both are groups of people who, because of their immersion in irrational killing, find themselves in a society which would prefer to ignore them."

And, he said, the similarities extend to the actual nature of the psychic disturbances.

Dr. William Niederland, professor of psychiatry at Downstate Medical Center, Brooklyn, who has examined more than 800 concentration camp survivors, described what he termed the "survivor syndrome."

According to Dr. Niederland, some 80 per cent of the camp survivors live in fear of renewed persecution and experience continuing depression which often leaves them unable to form normal human relationships. Often, he said, they have terrible nightmares in which, for example, they might find themselves buried under mounds of bodies.

Both Groups Feel Guilt

Much of this sort of disturbance, said Dr. Niederland, stems from the survivor's feeling guilty about "remaining alive while the rest of his family or his friends died in the camp."

Similarly, Dr. Robert Lifton, a professor at Yale who has worked closely with antiwar veterans' groups here, said the Vietnam veteran often comes to feel that "his own survival is tied to the death of others." And, Lifton said, this leads to guilt and anxiety.

Other panelists argued that Vietnam veterans face a situation different from soldiers in former wars because, as one put it, "society's sparse acceptance of the war and the vague nature of the Vietnam war have completely stripped away the glory of being a soldier, leaving only emptiness and guilt."

The panel discussion was part of the International Forum of Psychoanalysis, which ended yesterday at the Hilton.

Figure 6 "Auschwitz and Viet: – The Survivors" appeared in the *New York Post* in 1972. The growth of passionate activism against the USA's involvement in and escalation of the war in Vietnam turned out to be a decisive factor in bringing traumas experienced by survivors of Nazi persecution and concentration and death camps into both public consciousness and scientific legitimacy. From *New York Post*, October 3, 1972 © 1972 *New York Post*. All rights reserved. Used by permission and protected by the Copyright Laws of the United States. The printing, copying, redistribution, or retransmission of this Content without express written permission is prohibited.

in general, but rather to the possible parallels between the experiences of survivors and specifically those soldiers who had experienced imprisonment in POW camps.[79] The comparison with Vietnam also proved to be especially important for the perpetually nagging issue of the time lag. This issue that had so stumped sympathetic physicians and had given rejecters countless opportunities for mockery of survivors and their advocates was suddenly understood to be not only pervasive but also a key characteristic feature of human response in the aftermath of encounters with severely distressing events.[80]

Throughout it was not just a matter of echoes and analogies, however, but also of the concrete networking of individuals. In addition to Lifton, a further essential figure in the cooperation between doctors like Niederland working with Holocaust survivors and those working with Vietnam veterans was Chaim Shatan, a psychiatrist who joined with Lifton in "rap groups" of anti-Vietnam War veterans. Shatan demonstratively included a reference to "death camps" in his influential op-ed, "Post-Vietnam Syndrome," which appeared in the *New York Times* in 1972.[81] (In 1974, Shatan would also – and strikingly – win the "First Annual Holocaust Memorial Award of the New York Society of Clinical Psychologists" for his paper, subsequently published in the *Psychoanalytic Review*, on "Bogus Manhood, Bogus Honor," a devastating critique of the US Marine Corps' training program, its breaking of recruits' spirits, and its inculcation of brutality.)[82]

Finally, most important was Nancy Andreasen, the highly respected psychiatrist (and among other things specialist on psychiatric complications from traumatic burn injuries) who had been charged by Robert Spitzer, the lead editor for DSM-III, to head the workgroup that ushered PTSD into the DSM in 1980. Andreasen was familiar with Niederland's writings and determined to include concentration and death camp survivors into a definition of post-traumatic stress that went beyond what some veterans' advocates had called "Post-Vietnam Syndrome."[83] The 1976 draft memorandum by Nancy Andreasen to Robert Spitzer, Lyman Wynne, Chaim Shatan, Robert Lifton, Jack Smith, and Leonard Neff on "Post-traumatic disorder" listed at the outset the range of traumatic experiences that could cause this disorder. They included: rape, military combat trauma, natural disasters like floods and earthquakes, accidents like airplane crashes or large fires, and also, expressly, "mass catastrophes … of human origin (Hiroshima, torture, death camps)."[84]

In sum, and to put the overall point another way: initially the battle over reparations for survivors had forced advocates for survivors to articulate an early case for the uniqueness of the Holocaust, and the utter *non*comparability of racial persecutions and concentration and death camp experiences with the experiences of soldiers or even of civilians during wartime. Yet, by a twist of historical fate, it later took the catastrophic decline in the USA's moral authority internationally due to the war in Vietnam and the rise of a passionate antiwar movement to bring not just soldiers' but also survivors' traumas into Americans' public consciousness and into official medical nomenclature and professional policy. In this particular crucial strategic instance – and no matter how problematic the impulse to compare would also remain – the new emphasis on comparison and not just uniqueness provided an exceptional opportunity for an advance in moral, medical, and legal thinking.[85]

Conclusion

One great problem with the ascent of PTSD, however, and inevitably, was that it relativized and blurred the differences between victims and perpetrators – not just between survivors of concentration and death camps, on the one hand, and US soldiers returning from Vietnam, on the other, but also between a soldier who had been tortured as a prisoner of war and a soldier who had been a war criminal. (And at the same time, the possibility that the Vietnamese victims of US violence might be traumatized was not even taken into account.) Or as the German-born (but longtime Chilean-resident) psychoanalytic psychotherapist David Becker has put it, the effect was an "amoralization" of trauma.[86] In his book on the limitations of the PTSD concept, *Die Erfindung des Traumas – verflochtene Geschichten* (The Invention of Trauma – Entangled Histories, 2006), and in numerous articles in Spanish, German, and English, Becker has reported on his work in Chile with a team of mental health professionals striving to provide care for victims of torture and their families, as well as the families of those who were "disappeared" or executed for political reasons in the decades of the dictatorship.[87]

Already in the same years that the international movement against the Vietnam War was helping also to make Holocaust survivors' traumas a more frequent topic in US newspapers, the London-based organization Amnesty International had "appealed to the medical profession to combat torture worldwide and to help relieve its effects." The call was publicized in 1973, and by 1974 Amnesty International had established its first medical team to assess whether or not, in individual cases, torture had taken place. In the next years, the group studied Chilean exiles living in Denmark as well as victims of the Greek junta still living in Greece – establishing that the damaging sequelae of torture were similar and overrode in significance the problems of exile – and went on to study torture survivors also within Chile, in Argentina and Uruguay, in Spain, in Syria and Iraq, in Northern Ireland, and in Zanzibar.[88] By the later 1970s and early 1980s, the sequelae of torture were discussed at international gatherings of medical professionals and tentative concepts of treatment combining somatic and psychotherapeutic care were beginning to be developed.[89] The PTSD diagnosis was soon put to the test.[90] Within the USA, professionals working with such groups as Indochinese refugees, particularly survivors of the mass slaughters and concentration and forced labor camps of the Pol Pot government in Cambodia (1975–1979), as well as refugees from the Red Terror purges under the Marxist takeover in Ethiopia (1976–1978), the Khomeini regime in Iran (1979–1989), and exiles from Communist Eastern Europe, frequently found the new diagnostic option of PTSD to be useful, and certainly more suitable, given the symptoms they were seeing, than the alternative possible diagnoses of severe depression or psychosis.[91]

There was, however, something distinctive about the phenomenon of torture as it was being used in the 1970s.[92] As a Danish team working with Amnesty International noted, whereas torture had existed since time immemorial, the intention had generally been "to punish people, to beat out confessions, to obtain information, or to convert or reform people." Confession, conversion, and reform were still relevant purposes of torture in some instances. But a novelty particularly noticeable among the new Cold War dictatorships allied with the USA, especially though not exclusively in the Latin American countries of Chile, Argentina, and Uruguay, had as its main purpose "the breakdown of the individual" – the deliberate destruction of his or her identity. The point was both "to neutralize an active opponent of the regime and, second, to release this former active opponent in his or her broken down condition as a deterrent and warning to others who might be in opposition to the rulers."[93] Torture, moreover, as Becker observed, put victims into unbearable double binds: "Either one betrays one's political convictions and comrades or one's wish to survive and thereby one's self and one's family. However one chooses, one chooses wrongly. The technique of forcing a person into an existentially crucial choice among unacceptable options is the surest way to drive someone insane ... Nobody survives torture as a hero."[94]

The methods used in Chile as in other Latin American dictatorships involved the most wanton and grotesque cruelty, including relentless sexual abuse, electric shocks applied to the genitalia and other sensitive body parts, beatings, burns, threats to family members, mock executions, and imaginatively designed humiliations and degradations, such as coerced violence between prisoners, forced eating of feces, or exposure while naked to rodents and spiders. As the group affiliated with Amnesty International summarized, the sequelae of torture inevitably comprised both physical (headaches, gastrointestinal and muscular pains) *and* mental damages: "impairment of memory, impaired ability to concentrate, nightmares, sleep disturbances, sexual disturbances, fear, depression, fatigue, sense of guilt, feeling of isolation, loss of identity and very low self-perception."[95] But there was yet more.

As with that other distinctive innovation of the totalitarian regimes of Chile (1973–1990), Argentina (1976–1983), and Uruguay (1973–1985), in particular – the phenomenon of "disappearance" of political opponents of the dictatorships – so, too, with their use of torture, the governments, and, by extension, the majority of the populace, systematically denied that it was happening, disclaiming any knowledge of its existence and refusing any information to family members and loved ones. Torture and disappearances were not "speakable." Family members, too, were put into double binds. If "the family chooses to accept the death of the loved one, they 'kill' him; if they choose to maintain hope, they deny their everyday life experience." Often, survivors were upon release from prison forced to sign papers declaring that they had been treated well. This enforced rupture with veracity was of course also a calculated political tactic. And its effects eddied out into the society as a whole. As Becker's team summarily put it: "A division in social reality was generated."[96] There was thus no agreement on truth or facts, no space where loss or injury could be acknowledged.

Becker's team, based in Santiago, had been led since 1977 by the young Chilean psychologist Elizabeth Lira; other members were

María Isabel Castillo, Elena Gómez, and Juana Kovalskys.[97] Becker joined them from 1982 onwards, staying beyond the end of the dictatorship in 1990, ultimately returning to Berlin in 1999. Already in the 1990s, he additionally began providing training to mental health professionals amidst traumatized populations in such diverse locations as Zagreb, Luanda, and Gaza – most recently also in Tajikistan – and became regularly consulted as a specialist particularly on therapeutic care in areas of ongoing military strife and/or economic emergency. One of Becker's greatest preoccupations has been the horrendous fact that, although the trauma industry is booming internationally – indeed it has been growing exponentially since the 1980s – there are nonetheless every year ever more disaster zones with ever more traumatized people, and everywhere there is burnout, inadequate funding, and inadequate willpower actually to change the sociopolitical situations causing all the suffering.[98] And in all too many cases what is being offered by the self-styled experts is "the nonsense of cheap promises of salvation."[99] In places that have been in upheaval for years with no end in view – and with the inevitably ensuing corrosion of the fabric of familial and other support systems and with transgenerational transmission of trauma – the truth is that the most overwhelming feeling of the therapists on site is helplessness.[100]

Becker has also become the foremost interpreter and extender of the ideas first developed by the German-Dutch-Jewish psychoanalyst Hans Keilson, especially Keilson's book *Sequentielle Traumatisierung bei Kindern: Untersuchung zum Schicksal jüdischer Kriegswaisen* (first published in German in 1979 and subsequently published in English in Israel in 1992 as *Sequential Traumatization in Children: A Clinical and Statistical Follow-up Study on the Fate of the Jewish War Orphans in the Netherlands*). Keilson was in the anti-Nazi resistance and provided care for Jewish children in hiding during the Nazi occupation of the Netherlands, and then conducted a detailed longue-durée follow-up study focusing first on the postwar crisis situation in which decisions had to be made about whether to return children to a Jewish milieu or allow them to remain with the non-Jewish families that had protected them, and then also revisiting their cases when they had grown into adulthood.[101] The other influences on Becker are the postcolonial literary theorist Edward Said (for his insights into the mutual entanglements of colonizer and colonized) and the psychoanalyst Frantz Fanon (whom Becker reads – especially in his *Black Skin, White Masks*

[1952] – as a pioneering theorist of trauma in the colonial context), together with such tendentially nonpolitical but clinically innovative British psychoanalysts as Michael Balint (for his emphasis on the therapeutic relationship), Wilfred Bion (for his ideas on group process but also on how the analysis might serve as a "container" for the pain of the patient), Donald Winnicott (for his concept of creating a "holding" environment, his attention to the countertransference, but also his notion of therapy as a transitional space), and Masud Khan (for his idea of "cumulative traumatization").[102]

In addition to the "amoralization," another related problem with PTSD identified by Becker – here building on Keilson – is how the concept, even as it officially recognized external triggers of internal suffering, actually *decontextualized* the suffering by focusing on and measuring the level of ensuing pathology inside the individual rather than continuing to attend to the burdens of the experiences and environment. In short, it made what had been – and in many cases still was – a sociopolitical issue into a personal issue, and a medicalized one at that. As a psychoanalyst, Keilson – like Becker in his wake – was most definitely interested in intrapsychic processes. (Keilson had read not only the literature on post-Holocaust trauma, from both sides of the Atlantic, by Kolle, von Baeyer, Venzlaff, Krystal, and Niederland, among others, but also the work of Karl and William Menninger, Heinz Hartmann et al., Anna Freud, Melanie Klein, Donald Winnicott, and Masud Khan.)[103] But intrapsychic processes were always in imbrication with the sociopolitical environs. The way the PTSD diagnosis – and the checklist on which the diagnosis was based – was conceived placed the emphasis on an overwhelming event or at least on a circumscribed period of time in the past rather than on an ongoing process that might well be continuing into the present; thus there was little or no room for thinking about cumulative traumatization and "chronification." In Becker's view, there was no question that the *T* (for trauma) in PTSD was real. But he objected to the *P*, *S*, and *D*. All too often, there was no "post-", as crises continued; "stress" was far too mild a term for what traumatized people had gone through; and "disorder" localized the problem in the person rather than the situation.[104]

Two innovations from Keilson were thus crucial. One was his rejection of the measuring of symptoms (one simply could not, according to Keilson, express suffering in numerical terms). What *should* be catalogued, instead, were the experiences, the external contributory factors, "as measure of the burden" (*als Mass der Belastung*) that the individual was carrying.[105] Keilson's second main contribution was his insistence on seeing the trigger for trauma no longer as an *event*, or an experience restricted to a limited amount of time, but rather as a sequential *process*, one that absolutely needed to include the *before* and the *after* of the worst experiences – and also one that included Freud's concept of "deferred" effects. (It was not just that there was a time lag between experience and the emergence of symptoms; the relationship between past and present was far more intricate, as new experiences could transform what prior experiences had meant.)[106] One of the awful paradoxes of the post-Holocaust controversies over damages to mental health, after all, had been the way that physicians sympathetic to the survivors had been forced to focus all their attention on establishing causal connections between symptoms and experiences in the time of hiding or imprisonment. Specifically because the doctors intent on rejecting survivors' claims continually sought to redirect attention either to a patient's character structure preceding the entry into the concentration and death camps or to the patient's supposed desire for financial gain and/or difficulties adjusting to life after the war, doctors concerned to defend the reality of the damage done to survivors had to suppress the relevance of prehistory and aftermath. Keilson brought the prehistory and the aftermath back – as well as the recursive interrelationships between these. This made individuals' stories more complex and confounding, but it also made the mental health outcomes much more comprehensible.[107]

All of this was in the background to Becker's full-scale critique of PTSD. But so too were his years in Chile and his efforts, together with Lira and others, to develop adequate therapeutic models. Beginning in 1984, Lira and Becker and shifting constellations of their coworkers as well as collaborators from further teams of psychologists helping victims of the political repression under either medical or church auspices – including the Center for Mental Health and Human Rights (CINTRAS) and the Foundation for Social Assistance of the Christian Churches (FASIC) began openly publishing reflections on the challenges of therapeutic work with torture survivors and with the family members of those disappeared or politically executed. The initial result was *Psicoterapia y represión política* (Psychotherapy and Political Repression, 1984), published in Mexico City (see Figure 7).[108] In 1985, in post-dictatorship Buenos Aires, the first Latin American

Figure 7 *Psicoterapia y represión política* (Psychotherapy and Political Repression) was published with the authors' names on the cover in 1984, in the context of cautiously rising public protest against the repressive dictatorial government of Chile. A year earlier, members of this network of therapists providing essential but clandestine care for survivors of torture had dared to publish only under pseudonyms. The cover statement announces: "Here is a book that brings together the experiences of a work collective for mental health that, with its therapies, has shared in the pain of patients who were victims of the violence endured in Chile since Salvador Allende was overthrown and in the privilege of fighting against [that violence] with a psychotherapeutic approach."

Seminar on Torture was organized in collaboration with Argentinean mental health professionals; in 1986, another congress was held in the Uruguayan capital of Montevideo.[109] In 1988, psychotherapists working with the Argentinean group protesting the disappearances, the "Mothers of the Plaza de Mayo," published, in Spanish and English, an anthology on *Psychological Effects of Political Repression*. As the lead editor, Diana Kordon, remarked, "With the book we tried to break the phenomenon of social denial."[110] And after the plebiscite of 1988 calling for a return to democratic governance in Chile, it became safer there too to report in yet fuller detail on the nature of the work and its dozens of participants, work which had always involved legal and political efforts and social support for families as well as psychotherapeutic ones; a valuable and comprehensive anthology was based on a conference held in Santiago in 1989 and published under the title *Tortura: aspectos médicos, psicológicos y sociales* (Torture: Medical, Psychological and Social Aspects, 1989). Here the Chilean psychologist Adriana Maggi, who had worked with FASIC as well as with Becker and Lira, explained the political conditions of terror and confusion, the shattered state of the torture survivors and the "dissociation" evinced by family members of the disappeared. "For us as therapists, it was difficult to set up a chief complaint or make a diagnosis of people." They came "not because they were sick, but because of their situation." The regime had lasted sixteen years and "the damage to people has been continuous, it is cumulative and has become chronic." Maggi elucidated that therapists' efforts had been above all directed to helping victims "re-find" themselves, and to "put rationality in fact."[111] Or, as Lira had put it already in 1984, "Within the therapeutic space we tried to find a path to make it possible to re-acquire the present, one that made it possible to resist the radical process of dehumanization to which we were subjected. In this connection we understand psychotherapy as a process of profound interhuman obligation."[112]

The result was a rejection *both* of PTSD as a diagnostic category *and* of the classic psychoanalytic ideal of analyst "neutrality." Lira in particular called for "active non-neutrality" and advanced the notion of a "bond of commitment" (*vinculo comprometido*) that needed to be provided by the therapist, not least in view of what was after all an ongoing and, moreover, deliberate – albeit simultaneously continually disavowed – political repression. For a therapist to refuse to take a political position was to make it impossible for the patient to rebuild trust in human relationships or to recover the cognitive coherence that had been so intentionally destroyed both by the torturers' sadism and the government and communal denial surrounding it.[113]

Becker, in retrospect, found the idea of a "bond of commitment" both naive and overly idealistic – something that may have inadvertently facilitated therapists' acting out more than collaborative work with the patients in processing each one's unique agonies. While he concurred that in extreme political situations "only a therapist who consciously takes on non-neutrality can support the development of a therapeutically effective transference relationship," there were also dangers to externalizing all aggression onto the dictatorship. "There must be room for [the patient's] doubt about and hate of the therapist and for the therapist's hate of the patient." The approach also presumed some sort of "ideal traumatized patient" who had a "'normal' psychic structure" before the breakdown caused by torture, and "of course there is no such patient." The challenge was to maintain the right balance of empathy and abstinence, and to attend always to the interrelationships between past and present, and between the intra- and the extrapsychic.[114]

Over time, the combination of the years in Chile and subsequently in other crisis regions, together with his engagement with Keilson – whom he got to know – and his extensive reading in the literature produced by those psychoanalytically inclined physicians who had been at the forefront of the struggle to get post-Holocaust trauma recognized both medically and legally, in juxtaposition and connection with reflections on the writings of Said and Fanon, gave Becker a new vantage point for thinking about both Vietnam and PTSD. From a more global rather than narrowly US or European point of view, the ascent of PTSD could be understood as a side-effect of both the Cold War and of struggles over decolonization. From this perspective, Becker came to see Vietnam as "one of the last great imperial wars" and to rethink PTSD's emergence as a striking compromise, a compromise which, at one and the same time, managed both to acknowledge and to disavow its late colonial context: "The war was lost. The horrors of this war should somehow be recognized, but its political significance, its colonial destructive force should simultaneously be disavowed." This doubleness in the response to Vietnam in turn provided the key to the PTSD concept as it had been formulated in the DSM: "Suffering is acknowledged, but it is stripped of its (colonialist) contents. It is understood that social processes cause pathology, but the processes themselves are off limits for discussion."[115]

In fact, Becker argued, in view of the exponential proliferation of trauma projects in the early twenty-first century – all in the midst of ever-metastasizing wars, both large and small, each spawning more suffering and which no world leaders seemed able to bring to an end – that trauma work had indeed become a business, but that it also needed to be understood as a long-unfolding postcolonial process. In addition, he noted that it was apparent in hindsight that the theorization of survivor trauma post-Holocaust had actually marked the high point of professionals' understanding of the complexities of interaction between context and psyche. One of the many troubles with the pervasive application of PTSD, and the development of ever-new quick-fix treatment modalities, was that "the specific treatments are split off from awareness of the sociopolitical dimensions." In sum: the creation of PTSD had been, at once, a triumphant outcome of the battles over post-Holocaust trauma as they were fought through in the specific historical context of post-Holocaust resentment and antisemitic animus against survivors and, because it had mixed perpetrators together with victims and depoliticized the experiences of both, it was – as Becker expressly observed – already "a regression from the achievements and developments in the wake of the Holocaust."[116] The imperative to find more sensitive ways to conceptualize the continual imbrication of intrapsychic dynamics with sociopolitical contexts – and to seek better means to provide at least some amount of care and healing in the midst of ongoingly catastrophic situations – remained.

4 THE STRUGGLE BETWEEN EROS AND DEATH

"Aggression is a fundamental force of life."
Alexander Mitscherlich, 1969[1]

The postwar West German context of adamant enmity toward survivors of the Nazi onslaught created the conditions to prompt the international psychoanalytic and psychiatric communities to take notice of the brute facticity of adult trauma and its manifold possible adverse effects. This, in turn, and however grudgingly and slowly at first, ultimately led these communities quite zealously to adjust their scientific and conceptual frameworks and reference points accordingly. A few years after the trauma debates had been set in motion by controversies surrounding the West German restitution law of 1956, the psychoanalytic community would once more, and however unexpectedly, be caught up in a second internecine conflict – again at the intersection of popular culture and scholarly discussion. Here, too, the controversy would serve as the stimulus to reconsider another critical element of human experience: aggression. Crucially, and consequentially, the arguments over whether or not humans were innately aggressive – and what to conclude from that fact, if indeed it was a fact – became intricately intertwined with another drama: an effort to return psychoanalysis to post-Nazi Germany, a society that remained not only still residually antisemitic but also highly dubious about psychoanalysis as an intellectual thought-system.

Aggression, this second great vital force beside libido, had been identified by Freud variously – at least since the topic pressed itself upon his attention with the events of World War I – as an equally powerful and parallel drive to libido, *or* one at odds with libido and providing a countervailing pressure, *or* one which got peculiarly mixed up with and fused with libido (or vice versa, as libido got fused with aggression), *or* a phenomenon which grew in proportion as libidinal aims were thwarted.[2] But was it a "drive" – in German, *Trieb* (early on often mistranslated into English as "instinct")? At times, particularly in his 1920 essay, "Beyond the Pleasure Principle," and again in 1923 in "The Ego and the Id," Freud referred to this impulse as the "death-drive," or "destruction-drive," in contrast to the libidinal "life-drive."[3] And, as of 1930, he wrote in a letter to Ernest Jones, with respect to "the problem of the aggressive or death drive," that "I can no longer manage without assuming this basic drive, either psychologically or biologically."[4] In *Civilization and its Discontents* (also 1930) he referred to "the struggle between Eros and Death."[5] But Freud never settled the issue, even to his own satisfaction. Subsequent to Freud's death in 1939, the topic had gone in and out of focus in the bitter debates roiling the global psychoanalytic diaspora that had been set in motion by Nazism's brutal ascent. Often it became relegated to the margins. But when the topic showed up at all, it did so mainly in the interstices of discussions of early childhood – prompted not least by the controversial emphases of (by that point Britain-based) Melanie Klein on greed, rage, and envy in babies.[6] It also appeared, albeit in a stringently depoliticized form, in American ego psychologists Heinz Hartmann and Ernst Kris's efforts, together with Anna Freud, to systematize Freudian ideas about normative stages of development in *Psychoanalytic Study of the Child*, the journal launched in the USA in 1945.[7] Yet the topic finally resurfaced with peculiar intensity in post-World War II West Germany.

In no other national context would the attempt to make sense of aggression become such a core preoccupation specifically for psychoanalysts and allied professionals. And, conversely – and in strong contradistinction especially to developments in the postwar United States – in no other postwar national context would the wider public reception of psychoanalysis as a whole, in its dual nature as a clinical and culturally critical enterprise, be so strongly shaped by debates not over sexual desire and behavior but rather over the vagaries and vicissitudes of human aggression. Although the topic of sex did ultimately reenter the West German debate about aggression as well, the main emphasis of the controversies remained on the subject of aggression itself.

This, in turn, had everything to do with the unanticipated but absolutely tremendous excitement with which the work of a non-analyst, the Austrian-German specialist on animal behavior – zoologist, ethologist, and ornithologist – Konrad Lorenz was received by the West German media and public. Lorenz was a specialist particularly on parental "imprinting" in graylag geese, but also devoted observer-reporter of the vast repertoire of behaviors of other animals, from monkeys to rats to fish to dogs. From quite early on in the postwar years Lorenz was a household name in West Germany due to his beguilingly folksy tales of animal doings, published as *Er redete mit dem Vieh, den Vögeln und den Fischen* (He Spoke with the Cattle, the Birds, and the Fish, 1949) and *So kam der Mensch auf den Hund* (Man Meets Dog, 1950). And he was well known among research professionals, including among psychoanalysts on both sides of the Atlantic, for numerous scholarly essays on instincts, evolution, and behavior. British and American analysts were particularly fascinated by what they saw as the implications of his research for demonstrating the importance of early mother-child bonding. But psychoanalysts followed many other aspects of Lorenz's work as well, and he was footnoted in a tremendous number of postwar psychoanalytic texts.[8] Yet it was the book appearing in 1963, *Das sogenannte Böse: zur Naturgeschichte der Aggression* (The So-Called Evil: On the Natural History of Aggression, published in the USA and UK in 1966 as *On Aggression*) that was the truly blockbuster hit which secured Lorenz's international reputation.

Both in the Anglo-American and in the West German context, Lorenz's book on aggression would often be read in conjunction with two further books exploring the animal origins of human behavior published a few years later: the American playwright (and student of behavioral science) Robert Ardrey's *The Territorial Imperative* (1966) and the British zoologist Desmond Morris' *The Naked Ape* (1967).[9] One strand of public fascination with these texts clearly had to do with a wave of interest in biological as opposed to sociological explanations of human nature – and not least with a desire to re-secure traditional notions of gender in an era of rapidly changing social roles for men and women.[10] However, there was something distinctively post-Nazi German about the glowing appreciation and fervor with which Lorenz's specific contribution to the wider project of analogizing from animals to humans was embraced.

On Aggression, after all, as the original German title indicated, was a vigorous defense of aggression as by no means always a force for evil. The short take-home message – amidst all the witty, cheerfully chatty accounts of animal conduct – was welcome indeed. It had two main components: aggression was ubiquitous in animals and in people (i.e., it was not just a German specialty). And more importantly: aggression was a force for *good*. All cultural progress and effective activity, as well as, and however counterintuitively, the treasured bonds of deep friendship and marital love, had roots in the aggressive instinct.

It was also Lorenz who did more than anyone else to introduce Freud into the national conversation on aggression. Lorenz had situated himself, at the very opening of *On Aggression*, as someone who had long been resistant to psychoanalysis, not least because he could not agree with "the concept of a death drive, which according to a theory of Freud's is a destructive principle which exists as an opposite pole to all instincts of self-preservation."[11] But then, as Lorenz reported, he had been delighted to find, in his travels across the USA (these included, in 1960–1961, a longer-term visit at the Menninger Clinic in Topeka, Kansas, but also time in New York), that many American analysts did not agree with the idea of its existence, either. What Lorenz did find useful, however, was Freud's belatedly found conviction that aggression, like libido, *was* a drive. The difference was that Lorenz was eager to see the aggressive drive as life-preserving and life-enhancing ("in natural conditions it helps just as much as any other to ensure the survival of the individual and the species").[12]

However unintentionally, what the publication of *On Aggression* set in motion was an outpouring of debate in 1960s-1970s West Germany over whether or not aggression was truly best understood as a drive, and also, more generally, whether Freud was a useful resource or a problem.[13] No other text caused more people to start wondering what Freud himself had actually argued. Not just Lorenz and his supporters, but also Lorenz's critics – and they were increasingly vociferous – contributed to the reformulation of what Freud was thought to stand for.

By the later 1960s and early 1970s, at least three new versions of Freud were circulating in the West German media and wider public discussion. One was a sex-radical version, which restored to public attention Freud's own erstwhile commitment to seeing libido as the force that explained almost everything in life. Another was the far more conservative Freud who had insisted that humans were not by nature good; this version, however paradoxically, was a co-production of Lorenz's supporters with those of his critics who could not accept the idea of aggression as a drive at all and instead proposed alternate models of human behavior which more strongly emphasized social and political factors. And the third was the complex effort at compromise that the physician and psychoanalyst Alexander Mitscherlich formulated.

In 1967, Alexander Mitscherlich, with his wife Margarete, also an analyst, published what is still the most influential and internationally known product of West German psychoanalysis: *Die Unfähigkeit zu trauern* (translated in 1975 as *The Inability to Mourn*). In the coauthored title essay, the Mitscherlichs argued that what Germans had proven themselves unable to mourn was *not* the multiple millions of murdered Jews of Europe that had been killed in their name and in all too many cases with their assistance, but rather their own erstwhile passionate love for Adolf Hitler. Yet, while this has not generally been noted, another persistent theme in the book – there were seven other chapters, only one other of which was coauthored, while the rest were written solely by Alexander – was the question of how best to understand the phenomenon of human aggression.[14] This included the need to develop a more complex theoretical framework than Freud had managed to produce – not least in view of the massive empirical evidence provided by Germans themselves, but also in light of the many further demonstrations of its ubiquity throughout human history. Mitscherlich never did succeed in developing a fully satisfactory theoretical framework, and his writings showed the strain of the effort to find middle ground. And yet ultimately Mitscherlich's strategic genius lay not least precisely in an ability to leave the theoretical questions open.

Henceforth, the public and professional arguments about Freud in West Germany would no longer be about whether or not to take him seriously. Rather, the question became *which* Freud would be promoted and invoked in order to advance a variety of political agendas. At the same time, all the previously assumed alignments between theoretical framework and political implications got scrambled. The controversies, in short, sparked both a repositioning of psychoanalysis within West German culture and a reconsideration of what exactly the content of psychoanalysis might be.

Mitscherlich, Psychoanalysis, and Aggression

Alexander Mitscherlich witnessed in his lifetime the return of psycho-analysis to post-Nazi Central Europe. He was instrumental in securing for psychoanalysis a far greater social prestige than it ever had in Freud's own day, and he did so primarily by advancing a highly idiosyncratic version of psychoanalysis as a secular moral-political language. Mitscherlich became, on the one hand, *the* main West German representative of the psychoanalytic enterprise, through his editorship of the journal *Psyche*; his clinical and theoretical work especially in psychosomatics (psychosomatics in fact became the major pathway by which psychoanalysis eventually became integrated into German medicine); his ongoing activism in bringing emigrated psychoanalytic celebrities back to address the West German public; and, after an early postwar stint in Heidelberg, his directorship of the Sigmund-Freud-Institut in Frankfurt am Main. On the other hand, Mitscherlich would also serve as "the conscience of the nation," a "gentle repentance-preacher."[15]

Mitscherlich managed to finesse this double role not least by amalgamating creatively elements of a Heinz Hartmann-inspired American ego psychology with frankly left-liberal political commentary on current events with (what in hindsight may seem rather unanalytic and conceptually clunky) persistent enjoinders to West Germans to develop what he variously referred to as "ego-strength" (*Ichstärke*), "self-control," "capacity for critical thinking," or "the critical thinking-capacity of the ego."[16] The contrast with someone like his French counterpart Jacques Lacan, whose baseline assumption was that there could be no such thing as a stable ego, could not have been starker.[17] But, for West German conditions, Mitscherlich's approach proved ideal. This was, after all, a culture in which contempt for psychoanalysis in the wider public and among medical professionals had been intensively fostered under the Nazis. Freud was said to have a "dirty fantasy" and an "Asiatic world view," and psychoanalysis was deemed both to contain "nothing original" – for to claim otherwise would be "to give too much honor to the unproductivity of the Jewish race" – and to be "nothing other than the Jewish nation's rape of Western culture."[18] These attitudes hardly disappeared overnight in the war's aftermath. But despite this Mitscherlich succeeded spectacularly in convincing West Germans to think about psychoanalysis differently, not least through a distinctive style which mixed declared empathy for – and identification with – his fellow citizens with encouragement and coaxing injunction.

Yet it remains also crucial to register how much Mitscherlich's work was profoundly shaped by an irritated, albeit sporadic, engagement with the astonishing public success of Konrad Lorenz. In correspondence with mentors and friends, Mitscherlich declared his disdain for Lorenz and his sense of intellectual superiority to him. And in 1964, Mitscherlich organized a workshop – to which he invited Lorenz – whose express aim was to repudiate Lorenz's conclusions about aggression.[19] The book resulting from this workshop eventually appeared in 1969 as *Bis hierher und nicht weiter: ist die menschliche Aggression unbefriedbar?* (Up to Here and no Further: Can Human Aggression not be Pacified?) But actually his relationship to Lorenz's oeuvre was more complicated. It is not just that already in his earliest published writing on aggression (a two-part meditation, "Aggression und Anpassung" [Aggression and Adaptation], in *Psyche* in 1956 and 1958) Mitscherlich had cited Lorenz favorably. In addition, Alexander's essays in the magnum opus of 1967, *The Inability to Mourn*, return recurrently to the puzzle of human aggression and the book most certainly needs to be read not only as a repudiation but also as a partial incorporation of Lorenz's theses. So too Mitscherlich's marvelous speech in 1969 on the occasion of his winning the Peace Prize of the Frankfurt Book Trade – "Über Feindseligkeit und hergestellte Dummheit" (On Hostility and Man-made Stupidity) – remained in conversation with Lorenz's theses (and was indisputably understood that way by the media). The preeminent liberal news magazine *Der Spiegel*, for instance, in a reprint of the full text, plucked from the speech and chose as its headline the Mitscherlich remark that "Aggression is a fundamental force of life," clearly positioning the speech within the ongoing national fracas over how to feel about the existence and value of an aggressive drive.[20]

Aggression thus became one of the central themes of Mitscherlich's public life (see Figure 8a&b). In addition to *The Inability to Mourn* and *Bis hierher und nicht weiter*, he published or co-published three further books on the topic: *Aggression und Anpassung in der Industriegesellschaft* (Aggression and Adaptation in Industrial Society, 1968, with Herbert Marcuse and others); *Die Idee des Friedens und die menschliche Aggressivität* (The Idea of Peace and Human Aggressivity, 1969); and *Toleranz – Überprüfung eines Begriffs* (Tolerance – Verification

Figure 8a Alexander Mitscherlich (seated center, with glasses) talking with the American psychoanalyst and developer of self psychology Heinz Kohut, a close friend, at the Sigmund-Freud-Institut in Frankfurt am Main in the late 1960s. In the background are coworkers from the institute, from left to right: Klaus Horn, Rolf Klüwer, Johann-Gottfried Appy, Doris Mayer, and Tobias Brocher.

Figure 8b Alexander Mitscherlich in 1973 at the Sigmund-Freud-Institut in Frankfurt am Main at the celebration for his sixty-fifth birthday. A year earlier, *Der Spiegel* had once again reported on the ongoing heated debates between New Leftists, ethologists, and psychoanalysts and had captioned a photo of Mitscherlich with the words "Psychoanalyst Mitscherlich: Aggressivity is a drive."

of a Concept, 1974), which contained multiple essays on aggression, cruelty, and war, including a reprint of the Peace Prize speech. The timing was crucial. Mitscherlich was just – barely – succeeding in getting psychoanalysis to be taken seriously in West Germany when Lorenz's *On Aggression* burst on the scene.[21]

In the West German context, Nazism and the Holocaust lurked behind nearly all the ensuing arguments. At the same time, the debates would be filled with multilayered subtlety and innuendo, as within seemingly innocuous remarks there could be worlds of meaning. A new spate of violence and wars around the globe in the 1960s and after added a cacophonous diversity of possible resonances to what Alexander Mitscherlich had, in *The Inability to Mourn*, summarized succinctly as "the aggression problems of our time" or what he a few years later would refer to as "the enormous amount of aggression erupting everywhere."[22] The USA's escalation of the war in Vietnam from 1965 on, the renewed outbreak of war in the Middle East in 1967, and eventually also the rise of violent leftist movements within the West whose actions were, in turn, met by state violence, provided countless occasions both to evade *and* to engage the actual intricacies of what had happened during the Third Reich. Current events complexly refracted the attempts to make sense of the national past. Nonetheless, it bears remembering that the debates also went international – as, among other things, the International Psychoanalytical Meeting in Vienna in 1971 would focus the entirety of its discussions around the question of an aggressive drive. Here Anna Freud referenced the debates between Lorenz and his critics and conceded – in a speech that garnered wide media attention – that her father's theories of aggression remained unproven.[23]

Lorenz's Critics

Although the New Left student movement that reshaped the political landscape of West Germany after the mid-1960s liked to describe itself as antifascist, it is better understood as an "anti*post*fascist" movement – in other words, a movement developed in opposition to the more conservative early postfascist settlement in West Germany.[24] Certainly, there was something distinctively "antipostfascist" about the fury with which members of the West German New Left – and those of their elders who sympathized with them – would attack Lorenz from the later 1960s on. In the process, Lorenz and Mitscherlich were intermittently lumped together. Even though they disliked each other, they were treated by their critics as similar. In the pages of the venerable weekly *Die Zeit*, for example, the progressive poet and journalist Hans Krieger opined in 1969:

> One really has to call it tragic: Mitscherlich is the sole German psychoanalyst who is determined to pursue the sociopolitical responsibility of his discipline with full earnestness and whose voice carries weight with the public ... But he hardly ever gets concrete ... Mitscherlich's thinking is paralyzed by the unresolved contradictions of Freud's drive-dualism. In the final analysis, then, the decisive evils are after all only secondarily caused by society, because 'evil,' hate, and pleasure in destruction are ineradicably biologically anchored in human nature.[25]

In sum, what Krieger as well as younger New Left-affiliated authors hated was the idea that aggression was inborn and inevitable. They were determined to emphasize that it was society that encouraged violence, and that human beings could be changed if only society was changed. In the process, some – convinced that Freud stood for the idea of innate aggression – rejected psychoanalysis entirely. In this spirit, the editor of an anthology entitled *Zur Aggression Verdammt?* (Condemned to Aggression?, 1971) blasted both Lorenz and Mitscherlich, but pointedly urged "above all the psychoanalysts to spend the next decades on research and otherwise – remain silent. Whoever reads psychoanalytic texts, always again runs into the same, old hypotheses (of Oedipus-, of castration-complex, of the death drive, etc.), that get passed on in a kind of ignorant 'inbreeding,' without a single convincing bit of empirical proof being provided."[26] The escalation of the conflicts over the value and causes of aggression, however, had another effect as well, for they inadvertently triggered a sarcastic backlash in the mainstream media against what rapidly came to seem like the New Left's severe naiveté about the dark sides of human nature.

    The evolving debate also drew in new advocates for Lorenz, including Lorenz's student, the ethologist-anthropologist Irenäus Eibl-Eibesfeldt, the author of *Liebe und Hass* (Love and Hate, 1970), which asserted early on in passing that *both* ethology and psychoanalysis "have established that man has an innate aggressive drive," took side swipes at Lorenz's left-wing opponents, and later in the book mocked the New Left's sex-radical communal experiments.[27] In subsequent writings, Eibl-Eibesfeldt took aim at the gullibility of the New Left's "educational optimism" and expressed doubt "that one can prevent the development of undesirable tendencies simply through appropriate childrearing and somehow thereby create a society without pecking order and without aggression."[28]

Strikingly, some of Lorenz's critics fussed a great deal over whether or not Freud had really been committed to the notion of a death drive, with some pointing out that Freud had conceded the idea was speculative, others that Freud had, after all, resisted it for twenty years, and yet others noting the incoherencies that had ensued for Freud as he explored the idea and how he had subsequently contradicted or modified the notion once more.[29] Others, like the historian Hermann Glaser, author of the widely acclaimed *Eros in der Politik* (Eros in Politics, 1967), simply sidestepped the problem by accepting without complaint a dualist drive theory that saw aggression as a drive comparable to libido, while nonetheless spending the bulk of his text accumulating evidence that a culture based in sexual repression exponentially fueled the prevalence of aggression. Precisely *because* Freud had been alert to "the dark pull of evil," Glaser ventured, it was all the more important to attend to what Freud had said about the damage done by sexual repression and to work toward an "eroticized" society in which human beings lived "in freedom," and in which "reason is no longer oppressive, but open to sensuality." "Mass murderers," those who engaged in "tormenting and slaughtering innocent people, for example in concentration and extermination camps, in 'cleansings,' in expulsions," were, in Glaser's view, "product[s] of a repressed society."[30] But many who were unsettled or disgusted by Lorenz – and even more alarmed by "what great popularity is enjoyed in Germany by the aggression-drive hypothesis" – actively sought substitute models to explain human behavior and were adamant that there could be no such thing as a nonlibidinal drive; they emphasized instead that aggression was above all a *learned* behavior, and that there was much that could practically be done to discourage its spread.[31]

Among the most ardent critics of Lorenz were also those who strove to combine a recovery of the work of the Freudian Marxist Wilhelm Reich (who had famously contended in the 1920s and 1930s, in numerous variations, that aggression was the result of a lack of sexual satisfaction) with an updated version of the "frustration-aggression" theories of inter- and intragroup violence and scapegoating developed by psychologist John Dollard and his team at Yale, which had grown out of Dollard's fieldwork on race relations in the US South. The philosopher Arno Plack, for example, was outraged by what he diagnosed as Lorenz's feat in making not sex but aggression "the *Ur*-drive, the drive of all drives, that moves everything that is living."[32] Plack's book, *Die Gesellschaft und das Böse: Eine Kritik der herrschenden Moral* (Society and Evil: A Critique of the Dominant Morality, 1967) was meant – as was made clear by both the title and the cover format (which had the words "DAS BÖSE" repeated over and over in huge black letters against a hot pink background) – as a definitive rebuttal to Lorenz. For Plack, the enthusiasm for Lorenz and the public skepticism about the New Left's efforts at sexual liberation were all part of one big package of misconceived morality. It was the dominant morality, in Plack's view, that repressed and thereby perverted the sexual drive and made pleasure in brutality and killing pervasive. As Plack reductively but fervently declared: "It would be wrong to hold the view that all of what happened in Auschwitz was typically German. It was typical for a society that suppresses sexuality."[33]

Yet another variation, meanwhile, involved the reflections of Herbert Marcuse. He remained an unapologetic advocate, as he had been since the 1950s, for a radical and utopian understanding of the Freudian inheritance. However, simultaneously he continued to mull over a puzzle that had long preoccupied many members of the Frankfurt School (including its erstwhile member Erich Fromm, who had been one of the first to theorize the impact of feelings of powerlessness): how the increasing vulnerability experienced by individuals in a competitive-technological society exacerbated aggression and diminished individuals' capacity for political resistance.[34] Mitscherlich's younger associate Klaus Horn also repeatedly built on Marcuse, Mitscherlich, *and* Freud in order to push beyond the stalemated terms of debate. Horn persistently challenged the Lorenzians' instrumental concept of "the biological," referring to their "ideological," "ontologized," or "reified" approach, as they strove to trump the New Left. He regarded it as no coincidence that in the USA as well, under the impact of the "Nixon restoration," there was an increasing backlash against Cold War liberal social engineering projects – a backlash based upon the pretext that there was, as an article in *Fortune* magazine had put it, a "basic intractability of human nature."[35] Horn had given a lot of thought to just how extraordinarily tractable human nature had proven to be under Nazism, and found this argumentative appeal to intractable "human nature" repellent. The whole point of sophisticated psychoanalysis, he contended, was to understand not just the continual interaction of the biological and the cultural, but also, quite literally, their mutual constitutiveness.[36]

Nonetheless, already by the early 1970s, a new version of Freud gained ascendancy in the West German media and among a wider public, finally securing his status as august authority. It did so, however, by portraying Freud as a conservative and a pessimist. As late as 1968, the inventor of psychoanalysis had been celebrated in *Der Spiegel*, at least, as one of the great liberators of humankind from centuries of hypocrisy around and hostility to sexuality. (Here Freud was placed, rather startlingly, in a lineage with the actively anti-psychoanalytic but certainly pro-sexual Alfred Kinsey and William Masters.)[37] By 1971, however, the very same periodical was explaining that Freud was increasingly being understood to lend gravitas to the downbeat idea that human nature irretrievably tended toward mutual unkindness: "Freud's teaching about aggression and the behavior research of Lorenz are ever more frequently being enlisted for the development of a conservative theory of society."[38] Again in 1972, *Der Spiegel* published an interview with the psychoanalyst Friedrich Hacker focused upon his tome *Aggression: die Brutalisierung der modernen Welt* (Aggression: The Brutalization of the Modern World, 1971) that addressed him as "a Freudian [*als Freudianer*]" and in the same breath invoked "Freud's view, delivered in the wake of the First World War, that a potential for aggression resides in the human being, that has to find expression, one way or another."[39] While Hacker considered himself as rather more balanced, *Der Spiegel* placed his volume, along with a new one by Robert Ardrey (*The Social Contract*, 1970), among "the recently constantly swelling ranks of books in which the conservative conception of a hierarchically organized society is being defended against the New Left."[40] Perhaps this was not surprising, since Hacker's volume was graced with a foreword by none other than Lorenz. Here and elsewhere, Lorenz was blatant in his disdain for the young rebels.[41]

To twenty-first-century eyes, the idea of accepting the existence of a drive for aggression might seem uncontroversial and banally, if sadly, obvious – or it could seem wrong but inconsequentially so. The pivotal point here is that under the very specific circumstances of a culture only a quarter-century away from (what had been at the time an exceedingly popular) mass-murderous dictatorship, the claim seemed, to many people, not just wrong, but emphatically and menacingly so – even if not all commentators critical of Lorenz invoked the Holocaust, but rather pointed to current events unfolding in their present. *Der Spiegel* surmised at one point in 1972 that "The heatedness of the debate about this is most likely explained by the fact that people use the Freudian teaching of an inborn drive-potential in order to deduce a kind of legitimation of war."[42] Indeed, some of Lorenz's fiercest critics put their case in these terms: "The talk of an aggression-drive is perilous; it encourages the further spread of aggressive behavioral tendencies and heightens the danger of war in international relations.[43] Critics also took issue with what was perceived as Lorenz's endorsement of a society based on constant competition and striving for higher status in the social pecking order.[44] Meanwhile, Erich Fromm joined the conversation from abroad in his *The Anatomy of Human Destructiveness* (1973) to explain the appeal of Lorenz's "simplistic" "instinctivism" by suggesting it must be "welcome to people who are frightened and feel impotent to change the course leading to destruction." He added that a more "serious study of the causes of destructiveness" would force a "questioning of the basic premises of current ideology." In other words, it would force an analysis of "the irrationality of our social system and … the taboos hiding behind dignified words, such as 'defense,' 'honor,' and 'patriotism.'" Nothing short of an analysis in depth of our social system can disclose the reasons for the increase in destructiveness, or suggest ways and means of reducing it. The instinctivist theory offers to relieve us of the hard task of making such an analysis." As perceptive as these observations are about the possible political implications of Lorenz's work, it is nonetheless telling with regard to Lorenz's role in bringing Freud more fully into international conversation that Fromm, early on in the book, in tracing a history of "instinctivist" theories (all the way back to William James and William McDougall), expressly paired with each other the "'neo-instinctivists' Sigmund Freud and Konrad Lorenz."[45]

In fact, however, there was even more to it. Many of Lorenz's critics on the left were convinced his entire purpose was to provide exoneration for the elder generation of Germans. A group around the young psychologist Herbert Selg explained – as *Der Spiegel* summarized it – the "great public resonance" of Lorenz's book in West Germany by the way it "seems to exculpate all those 'whose slate did not stay completely clean,' in accordance with the motto: 'If we have an aggression drive and this drive must be expressed, then we actually can't really help ourselves, that ...' " (the ellipsis was in the original).[46] This was a clear gesture back to the past of the Third Reich. Already in 1966, the philosopher Rolf Denker had bluntly proposed as a reason for Lorenz's "bestseller" status "no doubt, for one thing, the ongoing discussion of the gruesome deeds of the Third Reich ... One looks for an answer to the question, how something like that was possible." However,

> the way the book has been discussed until now will not galvanize people to actions against aggression or for its more sensible channeling, but rather is more likely to lead to disposing of the topic in a trivializing and affirmative way. For many the expositions will have a reassuring effect ... Who knows how many aging, publicly unknown fascists who received this book as a Christmas present have acquired a relieved conscience from reading it.[47]

Along related lines – summing up the tone of the debates retrospectively in 1978 – the New Left literary and cultural critic Klaus Theweleit, in his massive two-volume work on proto-fascist and fascist patterns in German history, *Männerphantasien* (Male Fantasies), meditated on "the immense popularity of theories of human beings as intrinsically aggressive." Theweleit strove to discredit those theories further by deliberately associating them with the self-exculpatory maneuvers of the high-ranking Nazi Hermann Göring, who from his Nuremberg prison cell in 1946 had fatuously and self-servingly informed the American psychologist G. M. Gilbert that "there is a curse on humanity. It is dominated by the hunger for power and the pleasure of aggression."[48] Psychoanalyst Paula Heimann was more careful, and made no presumptions about Lorenz's motivations. But she was at pains to emphasize the profound noncomparability of Lorenz's findings about animals, in which intraspecies aggression could serve "the preservation of the species, for which the preconditions are the possession of territory, food, mating, brood-behavior, and which is limited in its ferocity by innate inhibitory mechanisms," and the kind of brutalities that were unique to humans. What distinguished the human from the animal was twofold: on the one hand, "the feeling of pleasure that is derived from the tormenting and destruction *per se*" and, on the other, the human being's tendency to *rationalize* that pleasure in cruelty and "to invent noble goals with whose help he disguises and implements his delight in destruction." As she pointedly added: "Our memory of the human concept of '*Lebensraum*' is still fresh; and with it the sluices to unlimited and calculated cruelty were opened wide."[49] It was precisely the example of the Third Reich that provided the clearest evidence of the difference between human and other animals.

Cruelty as Work

One of Mitscherlich's most characteristic moves was to declare the insolubility of the puzzle of whether or not aggression was innate. Already in *The Inability to Mourn*, the Mitscherlichs announced that "we do not know for certain whether there is such a thing as primary destructivity (a genuine 'death drive') or whether the natural pleasure of aggression is transformed into the pleasure of inflicting pain only by experiences of impotence, humiliation, and loss of self-esteem."[50] Similarly, in 1969, in *Die Idee des Friedens*, Mitscherlich included a footnote repeating a point he had already made in his earliest *Psyche* essays on aggression (reprinted here with slight modifications), which summarily remarked that "the difficult drive-theoretical question about a primary drive-pair (Eros-Destrudo) or a reactive origin of aggressivity can hardly be answered on the basis of our current knowledge."[51] Nonetheless, Mitscherlich undermined this agnostic stance at other points, frankly expressing his commitment to Freud's concept of a "death drive," acting dismissively toward what he (interchangeably) referred to as the "behaviorist counter-theory" or "frustration theory," voicing objection to "the doctrine that man's hostility is simply a reaction to the disappointments and the suffering which society has meted out to him," and distancing himself specifically from the idea he ascribed to Wilhelm Reich – that aggression and destruction derived from "inhibited urges."[52]

At other moments, however, Mitscherlich also freely incorporated ideas that sounded a great deal as though they came from Wilhelm Reich. Already in his first major book, *Auf dem Weg zur vaterlosen*

Gesellschaft (1963, On the Way to a Fatherless Society, translated in 1970 as *Society Without the Father: A Contribution to Social Psychology*), Mitscherlich had written about the phenomenon of "substituting persecution of sex for sex."[53] In *The Inability to Mourn*, Mitscherlich noted: "The conclusion can hardly be avoided that aggression has to make up for missing and unattainable libidinal satisfaction." And later in the book, meditating on how the phenomena of "brutal excesses – such as torture to promote morality – contain an element of perverted libidinal gratification," he remarked that "the fact that throughout long periods of Christian history sexual lust was damned, forced the individual to repress sexuality and to find partial substitute satisfaction in acts of destruction."[54] Similarly, in the title essay from his anthology on "Tolerance," Mitscherlich entered into the Reichian spirit when he wrote about the possible causal relationships between sexual frustration and misdirected violence. He noted at one point: "The role of pleasure in cruel acts – or more precisely: the libidinization of cruelty – is often chosen as an escape in the attempt to satisfy inner tensions wherever pleasure as such is treated by the superego and from the heights of the civilized value-world as sinful, culture-less, animalistic and thereby is soured and ruined for the individual." Or at another moment, but with the causation reversed, he argued: "Tolerance contributes to the strengthening – the development and differentiation – of the libidinous side of world events. It relaxes and thereby subdues aggressive inclinations."[55] And in yet another essay from 1970, this one on "sexual enlightenment for grown-ups," Mitscherlich, in his inimitably awkward but moving phrasing, channeled a combination of Marcuse and Hartmann when he reminded readers that "Eros" could only do its needed work in "generating compassion… in countless interpersonal as well as global-political matters" if it was permitted "access to the ego, to its shaping in conscious insight."[56]

Ultimately, Mitscherlich found the language he was looking for. In 1974, in an essay entitled "Zwei Arten der Grausamkeit" (Two Kinds of Cruelty), Mitscherlich – perhaps taking his cue from Paula Heimann, who had been his own training analyst (in 1958–1959 in London) – expressed what had been missing, and tellingly so, from the ethologists in their obsession with proving the evolutionary origins of human aggression. The human animal differed from the others because it was not just aggressive but *cruel*. At the same time, Mitscherlich held fast to his conviction that "the only psychological theory that, neither moralistic nor anxious, keeps in focus the time-transcending phenomenon of cruelty, is Freud's death-drive thesis."[57]

"Cruelty as work" – so Mitscherlich's new formulation – was cruelty that was approved by a collectivity, rather than arising from a private predilection; cruelty as work was characterized by an absence of subsequent remorse; cruelty as work almost always depended on the absolute helplessness of the victims; and cruelty as work was "asexually destructive." As Mitscherlich put it: "Cruelty as *work* knows no orgasm; instead it is about piece-rate labor, about managing one's daily allotment of tormenting and murdering ... The destruction-worker goes home in the evening like others do with the feeling of having had a busy day." Yes, this "destruction-worker" might well experience pleasure, but it was in very few cases a sexual pleasure. Instead – and here Mitscherlich borrowed both from the survivor of Gestapo torture Jean Améry and from the narcissism theories of the Austrian-American analyst Heinz Kohut – it was an "unhindered omnipotence-experience" – "the realization of fantasies of a 'grandiose self.'" These were the dynamics, Mitscherlich believed, that had been most in evidence at Treblinka and Auschwitz, but also in the forest at Katyn (where in 1940 the Soviet secret police had massacred more than 14,000 members of the Polish intelligentsia and officer corps), among the Brazilian death squads (paramilitary forces employed by the dictatorship), at Con-Son (the penal colony at which US soldiers tortured Communists), and at My Lai (where in 1968 US soldiers murdered hundreds of unarmed Vietnamese villagers). The Marquis de Sade's elaborate fantasies had attracted at best a handful of followers through the centuries. "Eichmann, by contrast, was of a different sort. He provided the killings the way one provides a supermarket with wares."[58] Here Mitscherlich had offered his most thoughtful comments yet on "cruelty as pleasure" versus "cruelty as work." Both were uniquely human. But "cruelty as work" was the far more prevalent problem – and, in his view, the strongest evidence that the death drive was real.

The Klein Revival

Eventually, there was to be yet a fourth way to conceptualize aggression in West German debates about psychoanalysis and human nature. It emerged predominantly out of a perceived need, especially among younger analysts and trainees, for improved approaches to their most recalcitrant patients – whether they were manifestly self-destructive, or bewildering and challenging because of their aggression toward or wily manipulation of the analyst, or overtly psychotic or on the emotionally unstable "borderline" to psychosis. But ultimately this fourth conceptualization was also applied for political analyses – along multiple, albeit somewhat mutually contradictory, lines. For some, it offered a potentially more generally applicable model of human nature; for others it was thought to provide insight into the sinister appeal of Nazism specifically for the broad sectors of the German population. But conversely, and paradoxically, the essence of the model – its not merely somber but downright threatening assessment of human nature – seemed simultaneously to explain why there had been such a demonstrable time lag in the model's acceptance in West Germany in the postwar decades.[59]

The three preeminent figures in the return of this darker vision were all, in some manner, either directly or indirectly, influenced by the work of Melanie Klein. The first was the Chilean-American Otto Kernberg, whose family had fled from Nazi-occupied Austria when he was a child. The other two, like Klein, were British: Hanna Segal and Herbert Rosenfeld. Both were, as was Kernberg, émigrés from Nazism: Segal had fled from Poland in 1939, Rosenfeld from Germany already in 1935.

Klein had arrived in England in 1926 at the invitation of Ernest Jones and was already well situated there long before Sigmund and Anna Freud came in flight from the Nazi annexation of Austria in 1938. The rivalry between Klein and Anna Freud would be fierce and permanent. It was to be fought through by the British psychoanalytic community, whilst World War II was raging, in the so-called "Controversial Discussions" which pitted the principals and their followers on both sides against each other. But it led as well to an important compromise by which not only the Kleinians and the "Annafreudians," but also a self-designated "Independent" or "Middle Group" encompassing Donald Winnicott, Masud Khan, Ronald Fairbairn, and Michael Balint, among others, were able to train candidates each in their own way without interference from the other groups. (Members of the Middle Group blended and integrated ideas from both of Freud's "daughters" with clinical innovations of their own. Some emphasized the formative influence of early object relations and thereby deemphasized or changed their views on the source or existence of drives (in many cases arguing expressly that humans were, already in infancy, primarily object-seeking rather than drive gratifying beings); some – especially Balint – returned to Freud's erstwhile associate Sándor Ferenczi's suggestions that the analyst of deeply troubled patients might be required to be far more maternal and empathetic than paternal and stern if any healing of a "basic fault" acquired in early mother-child relations were to occur.)[60]

Klein maintained a belief in the value of a drive-based model of human nature, although she placed the Oedipal crisis far earlier in a child's development than had Freud. While Freud assumed that children worked through their triangular relationship with both parents between the ages of three and five, Klein assumed that Oedipal predicaments and fears (including desires for both parents and envy of and fantasies about their relationship with other) existed already in the first two years of life. In the Controversial Discussions, Kleinians insisted that not only was the "death drive" real, but – contra Freud – it was *primary*. Freud had assumed that libido drove early infant development, and he had remained uncertain how to make sense of both other-destructive and self-destructive impulses. For Freud, as Paula Heimann (during the war still a Kleinian) had put it, "The libido is the first-born and privileged child, the destructive instinct is the late-comer, the stepchild. Libido was recognized as such from the first; the other instinct, its adversary, went under various disguises, and had several names before its true identity was established."[61] Klein and her followers, by contrast, believed that early infanthood was dominated by unconscious phantasies (spelled with a "ph" to distinguish them from conscious fantasies) – including terror of parental punishment, and that only gradually did good experiences and libidinal impulses like gratitude and the desire to repair relations with needed objects help the infant to mature into a more integrated being.[62] Anna Freud's focus on young children's ego development seemed much less scary than Klein's ideas about projective identifications, primitive internal objects (and part-objects), fears, defensive mechanisms, and the paranoid-schizoid and depressive positions Klein saw as the two universal models of human development.[63]

It has been argued – by the Stuttgart-based psychoanalyst Ruth Cycon, in the 1990s a main advocate for Klein and editor of the German translation of Klein's collected works – that the postwar years in

West Germany were marked by "denial and manic 'self-reparation'" as well as "psychotic defense mechanisms" (interestingly, this replicated fairly conventionally the Mitscherlichs' argument in *The Inability to Mourn*). But Cycon also asserted that German psychoanalysis had been badly damaged by having been cut off from the most important developments in other lands, and she proposed:

> The end of the war and the liberation from Hitler's terror-regime left behind a people that had for many years lived in a social world of insanity. Melanie Klein's discovery of gruesome-destructive, psychotic fantasies of dismembering, rupturing, robbing and emptying, burning (through urine), poisoning (through excrements), gassing (through gastrointestinal gases) and the total annihilation of the object that has through excessive projection become absolutely evil, the description of which has prompted horror, repudiation, and hostile defense, had become reality in Germany. Psychotic phantasies, which we all at times encounter in our dreams and in the analysis of profoundly disturbed patients, had become merciless actions.[64]

Thus Cycon had unabashedly sought to enlist Kleinian concepts to address entanglement with the Nazi past.

It was Otto Kernberg who became the first Kleinian to come to broad public notice in West Germany. This was not least due to American historian Christopher Lasch's bestselling diagnosis-*cum*-diatribe, *The Culture of Narcissism* (1979), which had included a chapter explicating the theories of the new psychoanalytic stars and experts on character disorders Heinz Kohut and Otto Kernberg. Lasch's book appeared in German as *Das Zeitalter des Narzissmus* (The Era of Narcissism, 1980).[65] And even though Lasch's application of Kohut's and Kernberg's theories in his sourly intemperate assessment of Americans as vacuous, shallow, needy, and grasping represented a misapplication and a gross distortion of both men's work, what did come across to West German audiences – as both Kohut's and Kernberg's works were translated into German and both men visited West Germany and were interviewed and profiled in the West German media – was that Kohut and Kernberg were in competition with each other, and that although (or because) both were specialists on character disorders, they had put forward mutually incompatible therapeutic frameworks.[66] Initially Kohut received the most attention in

West Germany. This was likely not only the result of his close friendship with Mitscherlich but also due to the way his work seemed to give support to the Lasch-promoted pop-cultural opinion about what was ailing human beings in the 1970s more generally. This sense of immediate cultural relevance earned Kohut honorable mention in such a philosophically and sociopolitically high-impact site as Jürgen Habermas' *Theory of Communicative Action* (1981).[67] And it was a connection Kohut was not averse to fostering.[68]

But it was to be Kernberg's Kleinian view of human nature that came to appear far more true to the post-Nazi German experience. Kernberg's *Borderline Conditions and Pathological Narcissism* (1975) had already been making the rounds in German translation in 1978.[69] By 1980, a West German analyst reported on how Kernberg and Kohut as well as Winnicott and Mahler were being received in Germany and, albeit hesitantly, being integrated into the prior frameworks, and how their arrival marked a slow transition away from a presumption of the centrality of the Oedipus complex to an interest in earlier forms of damage – so that some people were already so damaged and "beleaguered" by the time they arrived at the Oedipal moment that they had very few reserves for coping with it.[70] By 1985, *Die Zeit* commented that also literature scholars had learned to slip the words "narcissism" and "borderline" into their conversations, and "it has become *de rigueur* to invoke Kernberg and Kohut."[71] Again in 1986, *Die Zeit* used Kernberg to critique Kohut, noting that "in the final analysis, he [Kohut] has called into question the entire concept of the drive [*den ganzen Triebbegriff*] … He neglects the negative transference, he has a supportive, reeducative approach." Citing Kernberg's darker vision of human nature, the newspaper affirmatively quoted his critical jab: "Kohut sees aggression only as a reaction to frustrating experiences and does not see that cruelty and sadism can also give pleasure."[72] By the later 1980s, Kernberg had emerged as one of the most significant figures in German-speaking psychoanalytic circles.

As for Hanna Segal, the introduction of her work on Klein had been available in German translation as early as 1974 (though notably this was already a delay in comparison with its translations into Spanish, Portuguese, Italian, and French, all in the 1960s). But it was the Fischer paperback edition of 1983 that became the most relied-upon text.[73] In addition, however, in the retrospective view of contemporaries, one of the most significant developments were the visits to

London to receive supervision from Kleinians and neo-Kleinians and, moving in the other direction, the visits from Londoners to Germany. "I believe that it was even more these 'personal encounters' that were for many German analysts far more important than any text."[74] Or, as another put it: "Even though I was 'familiar' clinically and theoretically with ... Kleinian figures of thought in some way, it is in hindsight not surprising that it was the living contact with some of the London representatives that allowed me to experience the potential of this approach."[75] Two analysts remembered: "Despite having completed our training at the Sigmund-Freud-Institut in Frankfurt we had hardly an inkling of the theories of Melanie Klein."[76] And no one became more important as a supervisor to West German analysts than Herbert Rosenfeld, whose work on the "destructive narcissism" and "pathological narcissistic organization" of severely damaged patients seemed to these young analysts to offer both clinical and political perspectives that had been missing in the extant approaches available to them. As an analyst who had not met Rosenfeld but learned a great deal from his exponents expressed the point appreciatively in 2015, the impact of Rosenfeld "cannot be overestimated": "Rosenfeld conveyed as a German-speaking (Kleinian) supervisor from London in the beginning and middle of the 1980s ... a concrete clinical access to the patient, one that also incorporated an awareness and a taking-seriously of the (self-)destructive elements in transference and countertransference – in place of an application of inflexible 'knowledge' that denies the manifestations of the death-drive and in so doing partially enacts it" – as he additionally offered an opportunity for "reflections on elements of National Socialist mass psychology."[77] As the West German psychoanalyst Sophinette Becker remembered with regard to the early 1980s, "It manifested itself not so much in a reading of the writings of Melanie Klein, but rather a consulting of Kleinians or post-Kleinians in London. There arose lots of supervision groups and corresponding travel."[78] Supervision groups with British Kleinian guests were started over the course of the 1980s and into the early 1990s in Heidelberg, Stuttgart, Munich, Frankfurt, Darmstadt, Hamburg, and Berlin.[79] Already at the time, however, Becker was concerned that the new enthusiasm for Klein in West Germany might have (unacknowledged) mixed motives. As she wrote in an essay coauthored with Hans Becker (no relation), one of her colleagues in Heidelberg: "What is noticeable is that for a couple of years now we can see a practically inflationary use of Kleinian terminology like 'splitting,' 'projection,' 'projective identification,' etc., after the work of Melanie Klein was for a long time frowned upon in the Federal Republic of Germany. This late discovery of Melanie Klein coincides in time with the discussion of psychoanalysts about the National Socialist era." Yet Becker and Becker were a bit skeptical about the newly pervasive injunctions for everyone to get in "touch with their own psychotic kernels" – as obvious as it was that these often had to do with "the un-worked-through NS-past" – and worried that "faddish developments can after all be a form of collective defense." Becker and Becker noted that it was all too easy to take up new psychoanalytic approaches, but still ignore power relations and looming dangers in the real-world present.[80]

Nonetheless, it is clear that the revival of Kleinian psychoanalysis in West Germany was part of a far broader transnational phenomenon – and that at least part of the impetus lay in real-world events. For instance, as the British writer Jacqueline Rose pessimistically observed in 1993, Klein mattered again not least because

> the new brutalism of Thatcherism in the 1980s and the [First] Gulf War [of 1991], with its renewed and absolute moral antinomies for the West, are just two instances where some seemingly irreducible negativity, bearer of a violence sanctioned – if only momentarily – by State and subjects, appears to rise up to the surface of political consciousness, ... confronting us with something at the limits of psyche and social alike.[81]

The evolving geopolitics of the 1980s and 1990s made a return to Klein's work seem freshly significant. It was surely no coincidence that it was in connection with the IPA congress in Hamburg in 1985 – the first time since the Third Reich that the IPA was permitted to be held again on German soil – that Hanna Segal delivered her much-debated speech on the insanity of the renewed escalation of the nuclear arms race triggered not least by Ronald Reagan's Star Wars program.[82]

Conclusion

It could be argued, looking back, that Lorenz's provocation pushed some rather productive theorizing into view that was unlikely to have happened otherwise. Mitscherlich, at least, had found himself in a continual double argument – on the one side with the market competitor Lorenz, but on the other with the often overly simplistic but indisputably morally passionate anti-Lorenz New Left. All through the postwar decades, Mitscherlich had worked on multiple fronts at once: striving to shore up psychoanalysis' cultural authority; channeling directly or creatively repurposing potentially interesting ideas from other disciplines; continually finding common ground between warring factions while with disarming graciousness appreciating insights from each; and endlessly circling around knotty, insoluble puzzles of human behavior while coaxing his fellow citizens to think along with him.

But there was to be yet another unexpected turn to this particular chapter in the history of psychoanalysis. Although rumors had circulated in professional circles in the 1960s that Lorenz had been a Nazi, the height of the debates about Lorenz's ideas about aggression (1963–1973) occurred without any public mention of the possibility. Not until 1973, when it was announced that Lorenz would be winning the Nobel Prize jointly with his fellow Austrian Karl von Frisch and the Dutch-British Nikolaas Tinbergen for "their discoveries concerning 'organization and elicitation of individual and social behavior patterns'" in animals – were journalists spurred to investigate, and find, Lorenz's (initially vehemently denied) Nazi party affiliation, as well as nasty eugenicist remarks he had put in print in 1940 about the degeneration purportedly caused by domestication (of humans as well as of animals), and in which he had unabashedly called for "a sharper eradication of the less ethically valuable [*eine noch schärfere Ausmerzung ethisch Minderwertiger*]."[83] Lorenz subsequently declared his own phrasing unfortunate and claimed that his use of the word "eradication" had never meant murder, and he made semi-apologetic remarks in the autobiography produced for his Nobel acceptance (1973).

Scholars in the 1970s and into the present disagree about the significance of Lorenz's Nazi sympathies, some seeing him as at worst a badly naive opportunist, while others are convinced not only of his malice but of the corrupting influence of racist and eugenicist perspectives on the quality of his science; further eugenicist writings produced between 1938 and 1943 were found later.[84] Lorenz, however, remained uninhibited in his views. At the occasion of his eighty-fifth birthday in 1988, for instance, he remarked in an interview about his annoyance that "Humanity has done nothing sensible about overpopulation.

One could for this reason develop a certain sympathy for AIDS [*Man könnte daher eine gewisse Sympathie für Aids bekommen*]." And once again he invoked the peculiar language he had used in 1940, explaining that "ethical" people had fewer children, but "criminals" were breeding uncontrollably (see Figure 9).[85] In short, and however counterintuitive this may seem, despite the best efforts of Alexander Mitscherlich, through a complex set of circumstances, it was – irony of ironies – an ex-Nazi who succeeded in provoking the conversation that initially brought psychoanalysis back to post-Nazi Germany.

Meanwhile, there was to be a delay before English-language reception of Mitscherlich started in earnest – and, when it did start, it was not what anyone might have expected. In part, this had to do with the core take-away ideas, the title concepts, as it were – in the one case too vague and universal, and in the other too narrowly specific – put

Figure 9 Konrad Lorenz in 1988, being interviewed by the West German journal *Natur* at the occasion of his eighty-fifth birthday. The caption, remarkably, reads: "A life in research riding the waves of success. Just as Sigmund Freud demystified sexuality, so Konrad Lorenz elucidated another existence-determining drive: Aggression."

forward by Mitscherlich in his two translated books. *Society Without the Father*, although published in the USA in 1970, was concerned not so much with the absence of literal fathers as with the difficulty of individuality in modernity and with the loss of the "father image" – by which he meant an orienting connection to traditional authorities.[86] As anyone raised in the postwar USA with constant injunctions to avoid being "other-directed" and instead become properly "inner-directed" would recall, Mitscherlich was drawing on points made by sociologist David Riesman in *The Lonely Crowd* (1950).[87] There was, one can surmise, no felt need to reimport Riesman home.[88]

The Inability to Mourn, by contrast, had above all been addressed to post-Nazi German conditions. Robert Jay Lifton, in his preface to the 1975 American edition, had ambitiously tried to elaborate a comparison with "post-Vietnam and post-Nixon America" and to explain the disturbing intensity of discovering the presence of evil in what one had once loved: in the US case, "faith in American national virtue" turned into brutal killing and meaningless death in Southeast Asia – and Lifton invoked the Mitscherlichs' insights into "the defense against collective responsibility and guilt – guilt whether of action or of toleration."[89] (Mitscherlich had become friends with Lifton not least through their shared interests in antiwar activism but also due to Lifton's need for Mitscherlich's help in developing the project that was to become *The Nazi Doctors*.)[90] Arguably, however, precisely the dynamics of denial and defense that Lifton was naming also blocked any immediate uptake or sense that the lessons could be applied domestically within the USA.

Mitscherlich died in 1982, after a several-year struggle with Parkinson's. In a transition rich with – however unintentional, nonetheless telling – symbolism, the foremost West German exponent of the borderline syndrome, the psychoanalyst Christa Rohde-Dachser, in 1986 became Mitscherlich's successor as a professor in the Institute for Psychoanalysis at the University of Frankfurt am Main. Her pioneering *Habilitation* text of 1981 synthesizing the then-extant scholarship – replete with references to the works of Klein, Kernberg, Segal, and Rosenfeld – appeared in print in 1983 as *Das Borderline-Syndrom* (The Borderline Syndrome); it has been continually updated and is now in its seventh edition.[91] In 1991, she published *Expedition in den dunklen Kontinent: Weiblichkeit im Diskurs der Psychoanalyse* (The Expedition to the Dark Continent: Femininity in the Discourse of Psychoanalysis).[92] There she explored the patriarchal socialization and unconscious fantasies – as well as repressions, primitive defenses, and disavowals – shaping Freud's own and subsequent psychoanalysts' understandings not only of ideas about gender but also of a broad variety of core psychoanalytic concepts.[93]

After his death, the presence of Mitscherlich in German society effectively vanished for the next quarter-century. When attention returned, the assessment of his legacy would be differentiated if not openly critical. Two historians, Tobias Freimüller and Martin Dehli, published impressively well researched and argued biographies in 2007, with Freimüller shedding fresh light on developments in the background to Mitscherlich's highest-profile years in the 1960s (and seeing the crucial turning point in Mitscherlich's life to be his dismay at Germans' disinterest, in 1945, in confronting the horrors of the immediate past in which they had been complicit), while Dehli's biography repositioned Mitscherlich as having had rather more right-wing nationalist sympathies in his young adulthood in the Weimar Republic than he subsequently would acknowledge, and as having either misunderstood or deliberately misrepresented psychoanalysis as having been completely destroyed during the Third Reich (and thus having been able to portray himself as rebuilding it from a complete void, rather than within a contaminated and ambiguous mess). In 2008, yet a third tremendously source-rich biography, by Timo Hoyer, a scholar affiliated with the Sigmund-Freud-Institut, appeared. In 2008, in *Die Zeit*, a reviewer of all three books headlined his review with the observation that to Mitscherlich's enduring credit, he had "given ostracized psychoanalysis once again a home in Germany."[94] Yet, as late as 2009, a reviewer of Dehli was able summarily to declare that, although Mitscherlich was "one of the most influential psychoanalysts after 1945," "nowadays Alexander Mitscherlich (1908–1982) is almost entirely forgotten," and to wonder whether that forgetting was caused by the fact that his book titles had become slogans – for which no one remembered the actual content – or whether his erstwhile ubiquity and influence had depended on his personal charisma and public presence far more than on his writings.[95]

Part III

RADICAL FREUD

5 EXPLODING OEDIPUS

"For the disjointed fragments of Oedipus remain stuck to all the corners of the historical field, as a battlefield and not a scene from bourgeois theater. Too bad if the psychoanalysts roar their disapproval at this point."
                                  Gilles Deleuze and Félix Guattari, 1972[1]

In 1972, the French psychoanalyst Félix Guattari – student and analysand of Jacques Lacan's, independent Left political militant, and passionate advocate for the rights of the mentally ill – coauthored, with the philosopher Gilles Deleuze, a book which turned out to be an instant cult classic: *L'Anti-Œdipe* (translated into English as *Anti-Oedipus* [1977]), the first volume of what would become, with *Mille Plateaux* (A Thousand Plateaus, 1980), a two-volume work with the umbrella title *Capitalisme et schizophrénie* (Capitalism and Schizophrenia). *Anti-Oedipus* was a frontal assault on reductionist versions of Freudianism and Marxism both. That assault was embedded in a chaotically joyful remix of idiosyncratic original ideas with concepts lifted not only from Baruch Spinoza, Immanuel Kant, and Friedrich Nietzsche but also from psychoanalysts Wilhelm Reich, Melanie Klein, and Frantz Fanon as well as Lacan, and leavened all through with quotes from (and riffs on) literary notables from D. H. Lawrence and Henry Miller to Antonin Artaud. It first appeared with Les Éditions de Minuit, a legendary press with its roots in the French resistance to Nazi occupation. It was repudiated almost immediately, and apoplectically, by prominent psychoanalysts, psychiatrists, and philosophers in France – repudiations to which both men responded, singly and together, with amplifications and clarifications, in a welter of short texts, talks, and interviews.[2] Among the complaints put forward by French psychoanalysts was that the authors had confused social reality with psychic reality – and in so doing had committed nothing less than a "murder" of psychic reality.[3]

Subsequently, the volume would be disparaged yet further in other lands by guardians of Marxist rectitude or of general common sense. (English commentators seemed to have taken special offense, with Terry Eagleton retrospectively summarizing the content of *Anti-Oedipus* as "the most banal anarchist rhetoric," a book in whose "apodicticism of desire ... there can be no place for political discourse proper," while Perry Anderson found in it nothing but "saturnalian subjectivism.")[4] Yet the volume had, nonetheless or as a result, within less than a year become one of the enduring touchstone texts for the European New Left and counterculture.[5] As a reviewer of a recent dual biography of Deleuze and Guattari noted, *Anti-Oedipus* turned the two men into "the Rolling Stones of radical theory" (see Figure 10).[6]

Figure 10 Gilles Deleuze and Félix Guattari in France in 1980. In interviews and public presentations, they consistently expressed how close and mutually meaningful their collaboration was and frequently explicated each other's ideas.

By the first decades of the twenty-first century, enormous amounts of ink have been spilled – and even more space taken up in the ether – on Deleuze and Guattari, separately and as a duo, and on *Anti-Oedipus* and *A Thousand Plateaus* in particular. It is striking and indicative that the volumes have been experiencing a renaissance in more recent years, conspicuously within the realms of queer studies and disability rights work, but also in activism around ecological issues, in antiracist and postcolonial analyses, and in reflections on the expansion of virtual reality through the Internet.[7] Especially noteworthy, moreover, is the increasing range of affirmative invocations of Deleuze and Guattari in both clinical and theoretical writings of turn-of-the-millennium psychoanalysts – across a global expanse, from Dublin to Johannesburg to São Paulo and from San Francisco to Toronto, Tel Aviv, and Tehran.[8] To research the uses to which the books' core ideas are currently being put is in fact to enter a maelstrom of mutually incompatible assertions, ranging in tone from the ostentatiously erudite to the archly ironic to the achingly earnest.[9]

The very best critical scholarship so far has, appropriately, located *Anti-Oedipus* historically (especially, and most clearly, as a book written in the early aftermath of the upheavals of May 1968), but it has contextualized the book and its authors primarily in the specifics of the French national intellectual milieu.[10] Scholars have rooted Guattari's development as a thinker and activist in relationship mainly to his early political militancy in and around Communist and Trotskyist groups concerned about the Algerian war, in his longstanding closeness to Lacan (Guattari had been for a while considered Lacan's heir apparent, until displaced by Jacques-Alain Miller, Lacan's son-in-law), and – most importantly – in the alternative-experimental therapies for persons with schizophrenia called "institutional psychotherapy" co-developed by Guattari's mentor Jean Oury at the innovative asylum La Borde in the Loire valley where Guattari was employed from 1955 on.[11]

A great deal of the academic scholarship, however, has lifted *Anti-Oedipus* out of space and time entirely, treating it as principally a contribution to philosophy (whether wacky-elusive, spurious-problematic, or canonical-impressive). As Peter Osborne pointed out in 2011 in *New Left Review*, much of this is fetishization and rehash.[12] Nonetheless, snarkiness, especially toward Guattari, also appears to remain an ever-tempting option – and whether this should be read as a sign of more general prissiness toward the wild abandon supposedly characterizing the 1970s or of an incapacity to identify the deep humaneness evident in *Anti-Oedipus*, and in all Guattari's writings on madness and politics from the mid-1950s through to his death in 1992, remains an open question.[13] A recurrent phenomenon, moreover, has involved treating Guattari as the *enfant terrible* sidekick contaminating the purportedly superior, more serious academic work of Deleuze.[14] In view of this situation, others have avidly worked to pull Guattari out of Deleuze's shadow.[15] And, although there is yet to be a journal titled *Guattari Studies* to parallel the *Deleuze Studies* launched in 2007, one can sense an incipient shift underway from the standardly used shorthand adjective "Deleuzoguattarian" to the possible coinage "Guattareuze."[16] Most recently, Guattari has begun to be restored to historiography as, actually, the first drafter of much of the original text of *Anti-Oedipus* – and as an intellectual in his own right, indeed one who continued to lecture, write both independently and, together with others besides Deleuze (and on a wide range of cultural and socioeconomic issues), to be a practicing analyst, and to continue to be involved in psychiatric reform initiatives.[17]

One crucial point has, nonetheless, and strangely, been missing in the voluminous scholarship on *Anti-Oedipus*. It should not really be so surprising that psychoanalysts in the twenty-first century are finding Deleuze and Guattari to be orienting and relevant to them. For – and this is my contention – *Anti-Oedipus* needs to be understood also *as a psychoanalytic text*, not just an attack on psychoanalysis.[18] This becomes clearer when we look at the text's unusual uses of Reich, Klein, Fanon, and Lacan, but also when the publication of *Anti-Oedipus* is placed within international psychoanalytic trends of its moment. Doing so reveals as well that the book needs to be understood as initiating a conceptual paradigm shift, particularly in its fresh take on the problem of ideology – and the puzzle of what attracts human beings to particular political stances. Specifically in drawing on psychoanalytic concepts, the book reconceives how psyches and politics might be thought to interrelate.

Anti-Oedipus was being written at (what turned out to be) the switch-point to the second half of the Cold War. It was at the height of the sexual revolution and the concomitant ascent of gay rights and feminist movements. It was also in the midst of massive global economic reconfigurations (in which the Soviet Union – Guattari was to argue – functioned more as a welcome frenemy to Western capitalism than as its opposite), and, not least, in the context of violent efforts by the West to put down postcolonial insurgencies even as new Cold War dictatorships with US support were arising – from Chile to Greece to Indonesia.[19] For overdetermined reasons, many of the leading figures in the international psychoanalytic movement in the first twenty years of the Cold War had fled not just from critical political engagement of any kind (perceived to be risky not least because of the experience of Nazism so recently left behind and because of the strong anticommunism prevailing in the refugees' new homelands). They fled as well from any attention whatsoever to extrapsychic conditions (as Ernest Jones had, at the very first postwar meeting of the International Psychoanalytical Association in 1949, enjoined them with "unceasing vigilance" to do).[20] Psychoanalysis had succeeded so brilliantly in the first half of the Cold War, especially in the USA but by extension also internationally, precisely by shedding whatever socially subversive potential it had once had. Concomitantly, many leading figures in the psychoanalytic community had lost interest in seriously theorizing the complex interconnections between the self and the wider society.[21] As Guattari was to remark in a 1985 interview: "The most singular and personal factors have to do with social and collective dimensions. It is stupid to imagine a psychogenesis independent of contextual dimensions, but that's what psychologists and psychoanalysts do."[22]

For Guattari, in his daily interactions at La Borde with individuals diagnosed with schizophrenia and other psychoses as well as in his clinical activity as an analyst in Paris, and in his critical reflections on local and global politics alike, nothing could have been further off the mark than this stubborn refusal of psychoanalysts to theorize the multiplicity of interconnections between selves and social structures and processes. Guattari traced the problem back to a blindness in Freud himself – in the same breath in which he also averred that Freud might still be the surest guide to insight.[23] Yet it took some time for him to find the words he had been looking for to express a different vision, one that was at once psychoanalytically informed whilst critical of the deformations psychoanalysis had accrued. In the writings Guattari produced in the run-up to the collaborative effort that was *Anti-Oedipus*, in *Anti-Oedipus* itself, and in the many further texts generated by him in its long unwinding aftermath, there was a continual searching for a language that could communicate effectively his conviction of the unremitting mutual imbrication of selves and society. The work with Deleuze would be utterly transformative for them both.

Ultimately, prime among the ideas put forward in *Anti-Oedipus* would be the notion of the unconscious as more of a "factory" than a "theater" – continually churning and producing rather than symbolically representing – and of a world in which human beings are best understood as "desiring-machines" (*machines désirantes*). Or rather, more accurately, human beings are conceived as composed of multiple, endlessly shifting, connecting and disconnecting desiring-machines, which are in turn continually connecting and disconnecting to all other life (both human and non-human), in flows interrupted and changed by stoppages, surges, and redirections. As it turns out, this concept was born of a confluence of numerous streams of thinking. But, as will be discussed below, underacknowledged by scholars but especially significant would be Deleuze and Guattari's unorthodox redeployment of psychoanalytic ideas.

Some scholars have contended that the machinic imagery grew not just out of Guattari's concern with "*economic machines*" (and "the relations of production and of contradiction ... something that happens between Moscow, Washington, Peking, Leopoldville") but also with the increasing rationalization of subjectivity in what was then (as we can now see, overly optimistically) referred to as "late capitalism" (or what Guattari himself would come to call "Integrated World Capitalism" – in which, as Guattari would repeatedly put it, "subjectivity is manufactured just as energy, electricity, and aluminum are").[24] And some have suggested that this made for an initially odd fit with Deleuze's Bergsonian vitalism.[25] Others have noted that the idea of the human as a machine was already to be found in Lacan's seminars from the 1950s – and indeed Lacan (correctly) gave the credit straight back to Freud.[26] But the seemingly disconcerting merger of mechanical and natural imagery had a long history in French social thought reaching back into the nineteenth century.[27] And certainly, Deleuze and Guattari were quite unapologetic about their blending of "mechanism and vitalism" – *and* both of these with psychoanalysis – at one point invoking the Nobel Prize-winning geneticist and virologist Jacques Monod and his idea of "microscopic cybernetics" to buttress their argument that "it is not a matter of biologizing human history, nor of anthropologizing natural history. It is a matter of showing the common participation of the social machines and the organic machines in the desiring-machines. At man's most basic stratum, the Id."[28]

Reinterpreting Reich, Klein, and Lacan

In the world of *Anti-Oedipus*, desire – which is sexual, yes, but also far more than sexual – is invested directly in the social field, with no need of sublimation or mediation of any kind. Perhaps the term chosen for the German translation – *Wunschmaschinen* ("wishing-machines" – a reversion to Freud's original term *Wunsch*, which Lacan and all subsequent French Freudians had translated as *désir*, and which thus in turn in the English translation showed up as "desire") – can convey more redolently to English-language readers the more-than-sexual, reality-constituting nature of the interconnected machines that Deleuze and Guattari insisted were not meant as metaphors but rather as more suitable descriptions of how reality actually worked (in contrast to a conventional, but in their view highly misleading, notion of societies composed of internally coherent and bounded autonomous individuals). On the other hand, as Deleuze put it in his preface to Guattari's 1972 essay collection: "What is at stake is the libido as such, as the very essence of desire and sexuality: it invests and disinvests the flows of all kinds that run through the social body."[29] Deleuze and Guattari did literally mean that also economics was a sexual matter.

Deleuze and Guattari's wager was that their potentially elusive – or perhaps to many even implausible or preposterous – abstract ideas (such as: desire is directly invested in the social field; it is impossible to distinguish cleanly between the rational and irrational aspects of human nature; sexual desire needs to be thought of in far more expansive terms; and there is "no distinction in nature between political economy and libidinal economy") could be understood by readers pretty immediately in statements like these:

> The truth is that sexuality is everywhere: the way a bureaucrat fondles his records, a judge administers justice, a businessman causes money to circulate; the way the bourgeoisie fucks the proletariat; and so on. And there is no need to resort to metaphors, any more than for the libido to go by way of metamorphoses. Hitler got the fascists sexually aroused. Flags, nations, armies, banks get a lot of people aroused.[30]

What was Hitler doing in this story? The answer had everything to do with the historical moment and mood in which *Anti-Oedipus* was being written – both post-1945 but also post-1968. The book was very much concerned with the emotional damages caused by a particular formation of capitalism – in everyone. It consistently searched for a language to articulate how economic conditions and processes shaped individual selves. But simultaneously, Deleuze and Guattari were continually rethinking how to talk about selves in the first place. The last time these questions had been pondered seriously by psychoanalytically informed authors had been in connection with the puzzle of the massive popular appeal of the fascisms of the 1930s and 1940s.[31] The stages of postfascist theorizing about fascism would play out very differently in France than in post-Nazi West Germany, or, for that matter, in post-Mussolini Italy. But in every Western nation, individuals empathetic with the New Left, exhilarated in 1968 and searingly depressed soon after, sought better ways to understand and articulate just how exactly economic and political conditions shaped subjectivities – and vice versa. And everywhere politically searching individuals – in this way no different from their 1930s and 1940s predecessors – would run into difficulties, especially in theorizing the problem of *ideology*.

The iconoclast Marxist Freudian Wilhelm Reich had first proposed, in his *The Mass Psychology of Fascism* (1933), that an answer to the question of why human beings submitted to political arrangements that were not in their economic interest might lie not just in the intellectual content or even the emotional appeal of the ideological "befogging" to which they were subjected by the powers that be, but literally in the *corporeal* impact of ideology, especially an ideology that enforced sexual fear and self-restriction.[32] "What has to be explained," Reich wrote, "is not the fact that the man who is hungry steals or the fact that the man who is exploited strikes, but why the majority of those who are hungry *don't* steal and why the majority of those who are exploited *don't* strike."[33] This was of course an old question – very old, in fact, going back at least to the 1550s, when the young French jurist and writer Étienne de La Boétie inquired into the puzzle of what he called "voluntary servitude" – and indeed called for what we would now term civil disobedience, and a question posed most famously again by Spinoza in 1670 (as Deleuze and Guattari too noted) when he asked, "Why do men fight *for* their servitude as stubbornly as though it were their salvation?"[34] Or, in Deleuze and Guattari's elaboration: "After centuries of exploitation, why do people still tolerate being humiliated and enslaved, to such a point, indeed, that they *actually want* humiliation and slavery not only for others but for themselves?"[35] Most pressing to Reich was the question why the Right in the 1930s had seemed to be so much better at attracting people than the Left.[36] Over and over, Reich asked: "*Why do the masses allow themselves to be politically swindled?*"[37] Or, at another point: "*What was going on in the masses that they followed a party whose leadership was objectively as well as subjectively in diametrical opposition to the interests of the working masses?*"[38] These were perfectly legitimate political-philosophical questions – and quite evidently still time- and place-transcending ones (more typically shorthanded in the twenty-first century USA as "What's the matter with Kansas?") – but twentieth-century fascism had posed the problem in unique terms.[39]

Reich was in many ways a loyal Freudian. He emphasized that "consciousness is only a small part of psychic life," that "*libido* … is the prime motor of psychic life," and that fear of parental punishment in childhood (for perceived sexual transgression) could ensue in an unconscious but consequential conflictedness anchored "in deep layers of the personality."[40] (Inevitably he was both wrong and right, silly for example in his conviction that it was above all parental prevention of child masturbation that prepared people for being obedient citizens and workers, yet lucidly articulate about the way voices in one's head could inflect the most intimate reflexes of the body.) Reich also ventured that anyone seeking to understand Nazism's appeal needed a model of human selfhood as *inevitably riven*. In his terms:

> A realistic appraisal would have had to point out that the average worker bears a contradiction in himself; that he, in other words, is neither a clear-cut revolutionary nor a clear-cut conservative, but stands divided. His psychic structure derives on the one hand from the social situation (which prepares the ground for revolutionary attitudes) and on the other hand from the entire atmosphere of authoritarian society – the two being at odds with one another.[41]

Or, as he phrased the matter in a new preface written in 1946, fascism was "not, as is commonly believed, a purely reactionary movement – it represents an amalgam between *rebellious* emotions and reactionary social ideas."[42] The thing Reich grasped best, in short, was that fascism addressed antiauthoritarian and not just authoritarian longings.

Reich would provide rich inspiration for Deleuze and Guattari. But for many reasons – not just the charmingly overweening hopes he had pinned on sexual liberation, but more so his persistent perplexity over the paths by which ideologies entered psyches, and the apparent undecidability surrounding whether the content of fascist ideas was "hogwash," irrelevant in comparison with its emotional effect, or whether in fact that hogwash should be scrutinized for clues to its hidden meanings – it was evident that his ideas required updating for the era of Cold War consumer capitalism, sexual revolution, and violent struggles over decolonization.[43] And Deleuze and Guattari set to this task with great energy. Above all, they suggested, the very idea of "ideology" had been the main stumbling block to understanding.

As late as 1967, in an anguished essay about French public passivity and insouciance in the face of the US war in Vietnam, Guattari had still relied on the concept of ideology, using it *both* in the generic sense, as a belief system ("With the Vietnam War what is being reinforced in the United States is an ideology of a master race, with its correlates of puritanism, its exterminatory myths of a 'bad object': all that is other, all that pretends to escape or literally escapes from the American way of life"), *and* in the sense that media manipulation and spin could and did explain why the public was quiescent in the face of this "nightmare" of "American aggression": "The worst acts of barbarism committed daily by the American expeditionary corps, the puppet troops of Saigon and their allies are methodically turned back from the awareness of a public opinion shaped by the 'information machinery.' One starts to think of fascism." Guattari did hasten to add to that last comment: "Certainly, Hitlerism developed in a totally different historical context. But this should not prevent us from reflecting on the process of moral degeneration now displayed by the most powerful nation in the world – apart from those active minorities struggling against the tide without up to now, however, obtaining decisive results." And this thought led directly into additional mulling about what ideology was and how it worked: "Freud, after Marx, gave us the means to approach that function of misrecognition and defense that is ideology [*nous a donné le moyen de mieux approcher cette fonction de méconnaisance et de défense de l'idéologie*]." And further, the encouragement to "misrecognition" was something done to people rather than emerging out of them. In a clear nod to Marx's famous dictum from the

1840s – "The ideas of the ruling class are in every epoch the ruling ideas" – Guattari remarked:

> The relations of production in the so-called consumer societies are arranged such that the dominant classes will have an increasing hold on the unconscious determinations of individuals. Lifestyles and modes of information, institutions, everything predisposes us to accept wholesale systems of coercion of all kinds and near-absolute subjection to economic dynamics. In return, we are witnessing the fact that these consumer societies are increasingly generators of collective perversions of the kind we have experienced before yesterday with Nazism, yesterday with the war in Algeria, and now with the war in Vietnam.[44]

At this juncture, Guattari could not see the active participation of the dominated classes in the situation.

But by the time they co-wrote *Anti-Oedipus*, Deleuze and Guattari had figured out that the concept of ideology blocked insight more than facilitated it. Their innovation was to shift attention from ideology to what they identified as the prior question of *desire*. As Deleuze put it in an interview given shortly after the publication of the book:

> We're not contrasting desire, as some romantic luxury, with interests that are merely economic and political. We think, rather, that interests are always found and articulated at points predetermined by desire ... Because however you look at it, desire is part of the infrastructure (we don't have any time for concepts like ideology, which are really no help at all: *there are no such things as ideologies*).[45]

And a year later, in another interview, Deleuze returned to this point: "Ideology has no importance whatsoever: what matters is not ideology, ... but the organisation of power." And: "We do not say: ideology is a trompe l'oeil (or a concept that refers to certain illusions). We say: there is no ideology, it is an illusion. That's why," Deleuze continued, "it [the idea of ideology] suits orthodox Marxism and the Communist Party so well. Marxism has put so much emphasis on the theme of ideology to better conceal what was happening in the USSR: a new organization of repressive power."[46] To rely on the concept of ideology was to misrecognize what was going on.[47]

164 / Cold War Freud

Reich, moreover – like so many other theorists of fascism who followed in his wake – had also stumbled over how to explain the emotional-physiological mechanisms of connection between the sexual and the political-economic categories of existence. For Deleuze and Guattari, the conceptual mistake lay in assuming a divide between these realms in the first place – not least because that then led to the endlessly awkward use of such terminological inventions of psychoanalysis (to describe phenomena that might in any event be non-existent) as "sublimation," "desexualization," and "resexualization."[48] Or perhaps Deleuze put it most clearly in his preface to Guattari's essay collection in 1972:

> We can see how this orientation differs from Reich's; there is not a libidinal economy that would subjectively prolong through other means political economy; there is not a sexual repression that would interiorize economic exploitation and political subjugation. Rather, for Guattari, desire as libido is already everywhere, sexuality surveys and espouses the whole social field, coinciding with the flows that pass underneath the objects.[49]

Such comments no doubt sounded ridiculous to anyone schooled in demarcating categories of existence: money and political arrangements to one side, more intimate longings to the other. But experimenting with thinking of these fields in perpetually flowing interaction had the potential to clarify what was otherwise endlessly mystifying.

The contention put forward in *Anti-Oedipus*, then, was that desire was roiling continuously, in everyone, beyond and below all ideology. Yet, as Deleuze and Guattari also noted – and here again they were building on Reich's idea that people could be both rebellious *and* conformist – that roiling desire could, at any moment, go in *either* revolutionary-"schizophrenizing" *or* fascistic-paranoid directions (or both at the same time). This was, as it happened, a really original use of Reich; completely different, for example, from the way he had been deployed in and around 1968 in West Germany in sexual liberationist movements (although also in West Germany the simplistic optimism that sexual emancipation would bring about political revolution had given way already by the early 1970s to a more Herbert Marcuse-inspired melancholy that emphasized the "repressive desublimation" at work in consumer capitalism).[50] What Guattari had picked up on was Reich's intuitive grasp of fascism's "libidinal energy."[51] And Reich would continue to be used imaginatively by Guattari in his efforts to grapple both with the lessons of German fascism for his present, and with what he increasingly came to feel was a symbiosis and complicity between the Cold War superpowers.[52]

Deleuze and Guattari's canniest and most original move in *Anti-Oedipus*, however, was to blend the obviously politicized Reich with ideas taken not just from the (generally politically disinterested) Lacan – but also from the stringently apolitical (but for them enormously useful) British child analyst Melanie Klein. Klein believed in the force of both libidinally possessive, incorporation-craving and lethally aggressive, even annihilating drives – already in infants. But she also insisted that these drives were always-already object-directed, in fact, and significantly, *part*-object-directed (as she called attention as well to the continual interchangeability, in the imagination, of fluids and body parts, sperm with milk, penis with nipple). Above all, she insisted on the consequentialness of projective identification and in general on the extraordinary role of unconscious phantasy in determining human behaviors. Her writings swirl with anarchic, and definitively socially inappropriate, urges – especially in children (though with adults by no means exempt). Girls serving up cakes made of feces, toddler boys attempting to enter their mothers to gobble up the babies imagined within, children of both sexes using toy trains or horses as they symbolize their parents' intercourse and their rage in the face of it: these are routine elements of Kleinian texts.[53] Moreover, Klein emphasized just how close to psychosis and self-disintegration almost all human beings often were, filled with persecutory-paranoid and benign or reparation-intending impulses jostling with each other for supremacy – a constant state of internal war.[54] Distinctions between inside and outside were continually collapsing; objects were regularly split; love and hate coexisted in the same instant.[55] The opening sentences of *Anti-Oedipus* made this apparent:

> It is at work everywhere, functioning smoothly at times, at other times in fits and starts. It breathes, it heats, it eats. It shits and fucks. What a mistake to have ever said *the* id. Everywhere *it* is machines – real ones, not figurative ones: machines driving other machines, machines being driven by other machines, with all the necessary couplings and connections. An organ-machine is plugged

into an energy-source-machine: the one produces a flow that the other interrupts. The breast is a machine that produces milk, and the mouth a machine coupled to it.[56]

It was Klein, not Reich, who gave Deleuze and Guattari the kind of imagery they needed for making vivid the constant natural-*cum*-mechanical flux they thought best described daily life.[57]

Lacan – whose work too had been informed by Klein's, but differently – was, inevitably, an interlocutor in *Anti-Oedipus* as well.[58] Both Deleuze and Guattari had been influenced by him (Guattari far more than Deleuze) – and the text, while searingly critical of his less imaginative rivals and minions, never once truly attacked him.[59] From Lacan – persuasively hostile as he consistently was to the assumptions about maturity and adaptation built into US ego psychology – Deleuze and Guattari got essential ideas about the instability of all persons, the potency of the unconscious, the metonymic slipping and sliding and substitutions in chains of meaning, the constant splitting or doubling of selves and objects, and the foundational importance of misrecognition and miscommunication between selves and others. Although disinterested in his distinctions between the registers of the Symbolic, the Imaginary, and the Real, and convinced that he too had not taken his own intuitions far enough, Deleuze and Guattari nonetheless took definite inspiration from the fact that Lacan had challenged the notion that psychic life could best be explained within the confines of the "daddy-mommy-me" Oedipal triangle.[60]

In general, Lacan had worked in the 1940s and 1950s to redefine the significance of the Oedipal story as lying not so much in erotic or homicidal impulses toward literal parents, but rather in the human toddler's entry into language and culture in general. But he also specifically stressed that actual, consequential familial dynamics – in their infinite individual variations – all too often involved *more* than three characters (whether the temporarily all-important "fourth" in this endlessly renewing "quaternary" or "quartet situation" was a declassé father's enigmatic creditor, an adored love-object's conniving sister, or the generous lady at the post office). The bottom line was that Lacan was inclined to question the traditionally assumed Oedipal scenario as the all-encompassing explanation for human woes. So many individuals' stories, Lacan wrote, had "a structure quite different from the one traditionally given – the incestuous desire for the mother, the father's prohibition, its obstructive effects, and, all around that, the more or less luxuriant proliferation of symptoms," in short "the general anthropology derived from analytic doctrine as it has been taught up to the present." Lacan was blunt: "The whole oedipal schema needs to be re-examined."[61] This, then, was the background against which Deleuze and Guattari declared that it was not enough to expand the "daddy-mommy-me" triangle to a quadrangle, moving a few additional bit players – a grandmother, a father's boss – into view.

The point was, first, to see through the absurdity of much of what had been said over the decades about the presumed importance of the familial triangle, with its pretend-transgressive prescribed roles and its glum, restrictive outcome – but also to see both the personal and the political damages the presumption of the Oedipal complex's importance caused. In short, and in notable contrast to Reich, Deleuze and Guattari were not hostile to families at all. Rather, they criticized what they perceived as a willful and appalling myopia in familialist thinking.[62]

The Inextricability of the Personal and the Political

For Deleuze and Guattari, psychoanalysts' persistent insistence on the verity and existential significance of Oedipal dynamics grotesquely curtailed any grasp of how the immense complexity of the real world was always already impinging on, cross-cutting, and infinitely complicating every possible individual story. As *Anti-Oedipus* announced: "There is no Oedipal triangle: Oedipus is always open in an open social field. Oedipus opens to the four winds, to the four corners of the social field (not even 3+1, but 4+n)." And nothing made the impoverishment of the traditional triadic psychoanalytic story clearer than a glance over the rim of the French hexagon: "It is strange that we had to wait for the dreams of colonized peoples in order to see that, on the vertices of the pseudo triangle, mommy was dancing with the missionary, daddy was being fucked by the tax collector, while the self was being beaten by a white man."[63] The footnote that followed was to Fanon.

It was not enough, then, to supplement Reich by questioning, with Klein and Lacan, the stability, boundedness, and coherence of the individual. The challenge was to find ways to express not only the inner multiplicity/fragmentation/dispersion of individual psyches (in Guattari's terms: "we are all little groups" [*nous sommes tous des groupuscules*]) but also their many *interconnections with* the wider social and political field.[64] Psychoanalysis thus far had too often privatized everyone's grasp of social reality, perpetually redirecting attention away from the actual profusion of flows between unconsciouses, rerouting all explanations for human dilemmas into a narrowly intrafamilial set of stories. This version of psychoanalysis, Deleuze and Guattari averred, was intensely complicit not just in producing continual misapprehension of reality, but in repressing desire directly.[65]

Certainly, Deleuze and Guattari were not the first or only thinkers to find it ludicrous – factually wrong, emotionally pernicious, and politically debilitating all at once – for psychoanalysis to ignore the extrapsychic and wider social and political dimensions of life. Radical Freudians like Otto Fenichel in the 1930s and 1940s had vigorously made this point.[66] And precisely the moment of the early 1970s saw a revival of this demand also in the neighboring countries of West Germany, Switzerland, and Italy.[67] The kind of analysis Deleuze and Guattari were asking for (they called it "schizoanalysis" *not* because they romanticized madness – a misunderstanding they continually had to refute – but in order to call attention to the craziness in the world that required assessment as much as or more than individual craziness) took its sense of ethical clarity not least from a consideration of the lessons of colonialism and anticolonial struggles.[68]

The colonial experience showed the limits of traditional psychoanalytic theorizing.[69] But Deleuze and Guattari were confident that the phenomena of interconnection and intersection between the intra- and the extrapsychic were ubiquitous: "It could always be said that these extreme situations of war trauma, of colonization, of dire poverty, and so on, are unfavorable to the construction of the Oedipal apparatus – and that it is precisely because of this that these situations favor a psychotic development or explosion." But Deleuze and Guattari disagreed: "We have a strong feeling that the problem lies elsewhere":

> The family is by nature eccentric, decentered ... There is always an uncle from America; a brother who went bad; an aunt who took off with a military man; a cousin out of work, bankrupt, or a victim of the Crash; an anarchist grandfather; a grandmother in the hospital, crazy or senile. The family does not engender its own

ruptures. Families are filled with gaps and transected by breaks that are not familial: the Commune, the Dreyfus Affair, religion and atheism, the Spanish Civil War, the rise of fascism, Stalinism, the Vietnam war, May '68 – all these things form complexes of the unconscious, more effective than everlasting Oedipus.[70]

In countless variations, Deleuze and Guattari tried to find adequately evocative language for conveying their points about interconnection and intersection.

Already in the 1967 essay on Vietnam, Guattari had tried to say why the French public *should* care – for in his view the "drama" of Vietnam had "unconscious repercussions" for "the existence of one and all" – and in this context he noted that "at the level of the unconscious subject, truth is indivisible: the distinction between private life and different levels of social life does not hold." The tragedy of Vietnam; the defeat of the "spirit of Bandung" and with it of the early postwar hopes for global "peaceful coexistence"; "the secret and paradoxical despair of western revolutionaries, their sense of powerlessness in the face of that growing economic hold on workers which causes them to accept their fate without flinching and perhaps even to love it in its sickening banality": *all* of this was intricately interrelated.[71] When Deleuze in his 1972 preface to Guattari's essays asked rhetorically, "What do we not make love and death with?" what he meant, among other things, was that "our loves and our sexual choices are less derivatives of a mythical Daddy-Mommy than they are of a social reality, interferences and effects of flows cathected by the libido" – flows that were also economic, racial, political. The "enormous *Spaltung* cutting through the Communist world of today" (a reference to the Sino-Soviet split) was surely more important in innumerable daily lives than whatever (supposedly) happened to Oedipus in classical Greece. But he meant in addition that in the language of psychotics one could often hear the psychoses of entire societies, "the voices of the mad, who speak to us essentially of politics, economy, order and revolution." Quoting Guattari, Deleuze wrote: "'delirium speaks foreign languages, hallucinates history, and class conflicts or wars become the instruments of self-expression.'" And once more: "'The distinctions between private life and the various levels of social life are no longer valid.'"[72]

A Collective Generosity

In the years that followed the publication of *Anti-Oedipus*, Guattari would return again and again to a number of interlocking themes. On the one hand, he remained concerned about the extraordinary success of "Integrated World Capitalism" (or as he frequently shorthanded it: IWC) in spreading its tentacles around the globe, including into the Third World, and into people's innermost selves – into "the very hearts of individuals."[73] ("A certain type of subjectivity, which I would call capitalistic, is overtaking the whole planet, ... with standardized fantasies and massive consumption of infantilizing reassurances. It causes every kind of passivity, degeneration of democratic values, collective racist impulses.")[74] On the other hand, he remained strongly committed to his radicalized Lacanian-*cum*-Kleinian conviction that selves were never coherent.

Thus, for instance, on a month-long visit to Brazil in 1982, in the final years of the dictatorship, as democratic life was just beginning again to stir, and in which Guattari had the opportunity to meet – in roundtables and public discussions – with Afro-Brazilian and other antiracist activists, gay, lesbian, and feminist groups, psychoanalysts and other mental health workers, academics and members of local branches of the newly founded Partido dos Trabalhadores (PT, or Workers' Party), Guattari repeatedly made remarks to the effect that:

> The capitalistic order produces modes of human relations even in their unconscious representations: the ways in which people work, are educated, love, have sex, and talk. And that's not all. It manufactures people's relations with production, nature, events, movement, the body, eating, the present, the past, and the future – in short, it manufactures people's relations with the world and with themselves. And we accept all this because we assume that this is "the" world order, an order that cannot be touched without endangering the very idea of organized social life.

It was precisely in this context, moreover, that Guattari returned to the idea first developed in *Anti-Oedipus* to the effect that ideology itself was a misconstrued concept. "Rather than speak of *ideology*, I always prefer to speak of *subjectivation*, or the *production of subjectivity*." For: "The notion of ideology does not allow us to understand this *productive* function of subjectivity. Ideology remains in the sphere of representation, whereas the essential production of IWC does not simply concern representation, but also a modelization of behavior, sensibility, perception, memory, social relations, sexual relations, imaginary phantoms, etc." Yet at the same time, Guattari missed few opportunities to state not only that "*subjectivity is ... essentially social*," but also that "in my view, there is no clear unity of the person," that it was necessary always to be "radically questioning these notions of the individual," and indeed that "Freud was the first to show how precarious the notion of the totality of an ego is."[75] Once again, to believe in the existence of autonomous bounded individuals, unimpinged on by their surroundings, was simply mistaken.

In addition, Guattari continued at the turn from the 1970s to the 1980s to pursue his intuitive (indeed, as it turns out, prescient) sense that there would soon be "closer and closer relations between East and West, not only in economic terms, but also in policing the world: greater and greater cooperation between the technocrats, bureaucrats, armed forces etc. of the Eastern- and Western-bloc countries" – and that he did not "believe the current phase of American capitalism and Soviet antagonisms is anything else but transitory." On the contrary, he predicted: "We'll end up with a new distribution of zones of influence, meant to force the planet into a North-South axis ... American capitalism and Soviet bureaucracy have too much to gain by getting along and by compromising."[76] Yet simultaneously, and ever the anarcho-utopian, Guattari also always sought the countervailing openings and possibilities, the cracks in the social streamlining that would allow "*processes of singularization*" to emerge. While there was no such thing as a delimited and coherent individual, there was absolutely idiosyncrasy – and it was much to be cherished. For Guattari, moreover, desire ever remained a potentially transformative force, one which for him included "*all forms of the will to live, the will to create, the will to love, the will to invent another society.*"[77] Maintaining hope against hope, Guattari asked in 1985: "How does one go about producing, on a large scale, a desire to create a collective generosity with ... tenacity ... intelligence and ... sensibility?" For, as he mused, "perhaps I am a naïve and incorrigible optimist, but I am convinced that one day there will be a return to collective judgment, and these last few years will be considered the most stupid and barbaric in a long time."[78]

Multiple generations of readers, in by now a dizzying array of countries, have found in both *Anti-Oedipus* and in its even more jazz-riff-like successor *A Thousand Plateaus* pointers for a different way of living a dissenting-dissident life.[79] Among other things, *Anti-Oedipus* was published right at the cusp of the transition between an older left politics organized around class conflict and the newer left movements soon to be referred to collectively as "identity politics." Guattari was acutely aware of the shift, but also of the ways in which the (ever-shape-shifting) IWC was immediately finding ways to insinuate itself into these new sensibilities and social movements.[80] And as a result, and even more importantly, Deleuze and Guattari both, already in *Anti-Oedipus*, and recurrently thereafter, consistently emphasized the problems – strategic and existential both – inherent in any movement that presumed a coherence of identity, in individuals or in groups. Deleuze and Guattari were always more attuned to fluidity of boundaries. To their critique of the concept of ideology, they thus added a critique of the idea of identities.

Especially noteworthy, as they were writing in the midst of the sexual revolution, was Deleuze and Guattari's insistence that any movement basing itself in presumptions of inherent and bounded sexual identities was just as "Oedipalized" and wrong-headed as the normative heterosexism it claimed to be opposing: "It is a lie to claim to liberate sexuality, and to demand its rights to objects, aims, and sources, all the while maintaining the corresponding flows within the limits of an Oedipal code (conflict, regression, resolution, sublimation of Oedipus), and while continuing to impose a familialist and masturbatory form or motivation on it that makes any perspective of liberation futile in advance." Moreover, and "for example," they went on to argue: "No 'gay liberation movement' is possible as long as homosexuality is caught up in a relation of exclusive disjunction with heterosexuality ... instead of bringing to light their reciprocal inclusion and their transverse communication." In general, all the figurative roles available within sexual relations as they were conventionally conceived – and here they invoked D. H. Lawrence – were just "so many tourniquets cutting off the flows of sexuality": "'fiancée, mistress, wife, mother' – one could just as easily add 'homosexuals, heterosexuals,' etc. – all these roles are distributed by the Oedipal triangle, father-mother-me, a representative ego thought to be defined in terms of the father-mother representations, by fixation, regression, assumption, sublimation – and all of that according to what rule?" For finally, they concluded: "Making love is not just becoming as one, or even two, but becoming as a hundred thousand ... not one or even two sexes, but *n* sexes."[81] Deleuze and Guattari unabashedly recommended that *everyone* could benefit from "becoming-homosexual" or "becoming-woman."[82] This was a much more radical – or, simply, queerer – conceptualization of sexuality than was being envisioned by some of the sex rights movements emerging at the time.

However, it was not just a matter of breaking down the boundaries between sexual or gender identity categories; the aim, as throughout *Anti-Oedipus*, was to question the whole inherited and inevitably false demarcation between "the sexual" and other realms. As Guattari put it in 1973 in Milan in response to an audience question about whether it might not be better, instead of theorizing at length about fascism, to be inspired by the anti-psychiatrist David Cooper to "make love everywhere": "Of course, I am in agreement!" But immediately Guattari went on, with his characteristic mix of sly humor and sincerity, to say that "making love" did not need to be reduced to something inter-individual. "There are all sorts of ways of making love! One can do it with flowers, with science, with art, with machines, with social groups." For, "as soon as one breaks the personalogical framework of Oedipal sexuality, ... a transsexuality is established in connection with the social field, that is to say with a multiplicity of material flows and semiotic flows. The entire individual libidinal economy, closed in on itself, is put in question."[83] It makes sense that in the era of the Occupy movement and fierce protests worldwide over austerity and global warming, *Anti-Oedipus* the book – and Guattari the thinker and activist – would be experiencing a renaissance. Michel Foucault was not wrong when he remarked, in his preface to the English translation of 1977, that *Anti-Oedipus* could be read as a guide to "this art of living counter to all forms of fascism." Scholars have not only tended to be puzzled by Deleuze and Guattari's frontloaded, but nonetheless rather brief, discussion of fascism in *Anti-Oedipus* – but also have wondered how Foucault could have used his preface to the English translation of *Anti-Oedipus* to make a case for the book as "*An Introduction to the Non-Fascist Life*" and then to go on to enumerate as central among the book's lessons such recommendations as:

• Free political action from all unitary and totalizing paranoia.
• Develop action, thought, and desires by proliferation, juxtaposition, and disjunction, and not by subdivision and pyramidal hierarchization.

- ... Prefer what is positive and multiple, difference over uniformity, flows over unities, mobile arrangements over systems ...
- Do not think that one has to be sad in order to be militant, even though the thing one is fighting is abominable ...
- Do not become enamored of power.[84]

But in fact the re-theorizing of fascism and the workings of desire were core concerns of *Anti-Oedipus* and one of the prime reasons for the book's deep appeal to successive cohorts of leftists – and also now feminist, queer, and disability activists (see Figures 11a&b and 12).

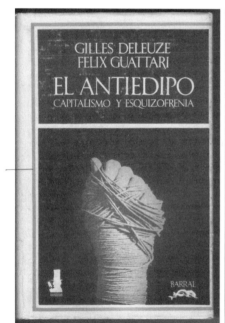 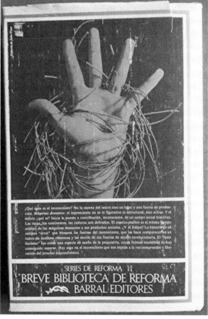

Figures 11a&b Front and back covers of the Spanish translation of *Anti-Oedipus*, *El Antiedipo* (published by the Barcelona-based press Seix Barral in 1974). The book had quickly become an international sensation, appearing already in 1974 also in West Germany (as a pirated edition with the imaginary press Suhrbier and officially with the major press Suhrkamp) and in 1975 in Italy (with the prestigious publishing house Einaudi) – notably countries which were just in those years seeing wrenching intergenerational struggles over the legacies of fascism. The text arrived in the USA with the English translation of 1977 (with Viking), and in post-*junta* Greece in 1981 (with Ekdoseis Rappa, which had also translated Michel Foucault).

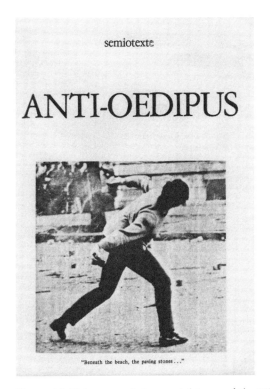

semiotext(e)

ANTI-OEDIPUS

"Beneath the beach, the paving stones . . ."

Figure 12 Title page of the special issue of the US-based journal *Semiotext(e)* in 1977 dedicated to Deleuze and Guattari's *Anti-Oedipus*, linking the book to the uprisings of May 1968 in Paris and containing interviews and translations of short supplemental texts by Deleuze and Guattari, as well as riffs on the book's significance by such prominent French intellectuals as Jean-François Lyotard, Jacques Donzelot, and Guy Hocquenghem.

Conclusion

All through, in the immediate wake of its publication and since, *Anti-Oedipus* – due no doubt not least to its title, and to the brilliantly savage fun it made of a certain kind of ossified psychoanalysis – has often been represented as a withering critique of psychoanalysis in its entirety.[85] In fact, some scholars have seen the book's writing and publication as marking Guattari's definitive turn away from psychoanalytic thinking – although they are then hard pressed to explain how he continued to see patients in analysis and why he remained a member of the École Freudienne.[86] And of course the book did represent a relentless attack. As Deleuze and Guattari themselves had put it: "Psychoanalysis is like the Russian Revolution; we don't know when it started going bad. We have to keep going back further. To the Americans? To the First International? To the secret Committee?"[87]

But, as noted, the book was not just an assault on psychoanalysis. It was also a work *of* psychoanalysis. It was as much a work of psychoanalysis as Viennese émigré to New York Ernst Kris's conceptualization of danger as an "invigorant" (whether emanating from antisemitic thugs on the street or the encounter with the German Luftwaffe during the evacuation from Dunkirk), or Berlin émigré to Los Angeles Ernst Simmel's theorizations of antisemitism (1946), or British analyst Donald Winnicott's essay on the Berlin Wall (1969), or German analysts Alexander and Margarete Mitscherlich's *The Inability to Mourn* (1975 [1967]), or Cyprus-born Turkish Muslim American Vamik Volkan's dozens of writings on interethnic conflict worldwide from the 1970s to the present, or the Czech-born New York analyst Martin Bergmann's *Generations of the Holocaust* (1982) or his "Psychoanalytical Reflections on September 11, 2001" (2004).[88] Or, for that matter, as Sigmund Freud's *Civilization and its Discontents* (1930).[89]

Interestingly, moreover, with their commitment to the idea of internally chaotic selves as well as their insistence on attention to extra-psychic contexts, Deleuze and Guattari had rather more in common with (the often conservative) Volkan than with the others, all of whom remained in one way or another, with the possible exception of the object relations-oriented Winnicott, attached to a Freud-based model of drives and their vicissitudes – once again demonstrating that there is no intrinsically necessary relationship between a particular psychoanalytic concept and the uses to which it can be put. Even more specifically, however, *Anti-Oedipus*, along with the many auxiliary texts that Guattari and Deleuze produced around and after it, was a work which explored prospects for the renewal of a psychoanalytic project that was in any event running into conceptual problems *both* clinically-therapeutically *and* when it turned its attention to broader questions of politics and culture.

It is not just – though also – that the icon of Oedipus had been under plenty of attack already. Deleuze and Guattari's mocking of Oedipus was taken as a huge affront by a French psychoanalytic community that felt incredulous that anyone could doubt the verity of this master trope.[90] But within and around the psychoanalytic movement worldwide, Oedipus had, needless to say, hardly remained sacrosanct. In the USA, widely read and influential neo-Freudians like Karen Horney and Erich Fromm had already in the 1930s and 1940s dismissed the Oedipus complex as a figment of Freud's imagination, while simultaneously pushing the idea that social anxiety and the search for safety in an overwhelming and disempowering world were stronger motivational forces than sexual desire could ever be.[91] But also someone as passionately invested in a drive-based model of psychoanalysis (and as generally opposed to Horney and Fromm) as the Frankfurt School philosopher-sociologist Max Horkheimer had in 1948 suggested that the story of Oedipus might need to be modified under changing economic conditions. Horkheimer noted that the assumptions about "the father-relationship so central to Freudian theory" were based on an outdated premise that sons had reasons to identify with and aspire to the position of strength and responsibility which fathers had once represented. This model, Horkheimer observed, had "disappeared long ago." Not only were fathers being steadily replaced as orientation points by "collectives such as the children's sport club, the fraternity, and the like," but the constant "detached adjustability" that the ever more insecure economic situation demanded of young adults meant that "it is no longer the son's fear of the father that is the typical psychological fact but the father's secret fear of the son."[92] This thread in turn would be taken up by none other than the West German analyst Alexander Mitscherlich, who, in the course of the 1960s, and especially in his book about the emergence of "a fatherless society," stressed the declining role of paternal authority in the development of a child's subjectivity and the growing role of sibling rivalry (in the broadest, metaphorical sense of individual disorientation in mass society).[93] Tellingly, one reviewer in 1966 had summed up Mitscherlich's findings as "Replacing Oedipus by Cain."[94] And, perhaps even more to the point, the Chicago-based former ego psychologist and subsequent inventor of self psychology Heinz Kohut would be understood, over the course of the 1960s and 1970s, to be moving not just himself but many of his colleagues, in the USA and in Europe as well, "from Oedipus to Narcissus."[95] The IPA meetings of 1973 in Paris and 1975 in London would be consumed with debates about character disorders which had (or were thought to have) their source in pre-Oedipal difficulties.[96] By 1979 – and while, of course, there was a mighty difference between redirecting attention to pre-Oedipal issues and exploding Oedipus entirely – nonetheless the "waning" or "decline of psychoanalytic interest in the oedipal phase and oedipal conflicts" could fairly be taken as established fact.[97]

In addition, and more generally, the postwar psychoanalytic settlement was in considerable trouble. The US American dominance of the International Psychoanalytical Association and its authoritarian structures had been vigorously challenged already in 1969 at the IPA Congress in Rome. But US American psychoanalysis was in the greatest difficulties at home. After all, only two years before *Anti-Oedipus* was published, gay rights activists were storming the American Psychiatric Association meeting and criticizing the most homophobic analysts. And only one year before *Anti-Oedipus*, the *New York Times Magazine* had run an essay explaining "The FemLib Case Against Sigmund Freud."[98] At the turn to the 1970s, leading analysts routinely admitted that the field, which only a few years earlier had seemed glowingly secure, was in crisis.[99]

Guattari, then, can be usefully understood as a crucial figure in the far larger transnational wave of Left-politically engaged revitalization of psychoanalysis that swept Western Europe and Latin America at the turn from the 1960s to the 1970s – and that he continued to develop all through the 1980s and early 1990s. Among the many fascinating features of this revitalization was the recurrent phenomenon by which ideas taken from other analysts were repurposed or developed further in unexpected ways. Sometimes the inspirational sources had been leftists themselves; no surprise that Wilhelm Reich and Frantz Fanon were of interest to Guattari, although what he did with Reich in particular was highly innovative. However, there was also a broader – and to our contemporary eyes more startling – propensity to use tendentially nonpolitical analysts' conceptual approaches for inventive purposes. The resolutely apolitical Melanie Klein, for instance, was mixed directly with Karl Marx in Latin America – from Argentina to Mexico.[100] And she had been made an unexpected bedfellow with Reich in *Anti-Oedipus*. Another good example was the use made of US ego psychologist Heinz Hartmann's ideas about adaptation and maturity and US self psychologist Heinz Kohut's ideas about a "grandiose self" – positions already considered incompatible with each other, but mixed together and given a left-liberal twist – in Mitscherlich's moral-clinical writings in West Germany. And, as the next chapter will show, Hartmann's ideas about ego development and Kohut's ideas about narcissism could be blended in other ways as well, as they would be taken up and put to use for expressly antihomophobic purposes in the work of the Swiss analyst Fritz Morgenthaler.

6 ETHNOPSYCHOANALYSIS IN THE ERA OF DECOLONIZATION

"The whites think too much, and then they do a lot of things; and the more they do, the more they think. And then they earn a lot of money, and when they have a lot of money, they are worried that the money might get lost. Then they think even more and make more money and they never have enough money. Then they're not settled any longer. That's why they're not happy."

Dogon village chief in conversation with Paul Parin, 1963[1]

In 1952, a trio of radical psychoanalysts, bound to each other by love, friendship, and shared curiosities, opened a joint practice in Switzerland: Paul Parin, Goldy Parin-Matthèy, and Fritz Morgenthaler (see Figure 13). Starting in 1954, the three, together with Fritz's wife Ruth, repeatedly left their practices and their patients in Zurich to embark on several-months-long journeys to West Africa, becoming enthralled by the people and, eventually, undertaking anthropological fieldwork. Beginning in 1960, among the Dogon in Mali (emerging just then from French colonial rule – a process with complex contradictory consequences for the Dogon themselves), the Parins and Morgenthaler first experimented with a combination of modified psychoanalytic and ethnographic methods to explore issues of the relationship between selfhood and society; a later trip also brought them to work among the Anyi in Ivory Coast.[2] In these settings the three were developing a hybrid project which came to be called "ethnopsychoanalysis," a project which they, both on their own initiative and then also in dialogue with their good acquaintance, the Romanian-French-American

Figure 13 Fritz Morgenthaler, Paul Parin, and Goldy Parin-Matthèy in 1954, upon return from their first trip to Africa, gathered in the atelier of Fritz's father, the painter Ernst Morgenthaler, in Zurich-Höngg. Two years earlier, the three had opened their shared medical and psychoanalytic practice at the Utoquai in the city center of Zurich.

anthropologist and analyst George Devereux (the coiner of the term), are co-credited with him as founding. Subsequently, in 1972–1973 and again in 1979–1980, Morgenthaler also visited among the Yatmul along the Sepik River in Papua New Guinea, observing the work of ethnologists engaged in fieldwork there, Florence Weiss and Milan Stanek, and, on the second trip, exploring with them and with his ethnologist son Marco Morgenthaler how also non-psychoanalysts might adapt ethnopsychoanalytic approaches in their conversations and interactions with informants.[3]

Numerous publications emerged from these collaborations. Among the most significant are the books coauthored by the Parins with Fritz Morgenthaler, *Die Weissen denken zuviel* (Whites Think Too Much, 1963), translated into French in 1966 as *Les Blancs pensent trop*, and, in 1971, *Fürchte deinen Nächsten wie Dich selbst*, translated into English in 1980 as *Fear Thy Neighbor as Thyself*.[4] There were in addition an abundance of articles, in German, French, English, and Italian, with titles such as: "The Oedipus Complex among the Dogon of West Africa," "Typical Forms of Transference Among West Africans," "Ego and Orality in the Analysis of West Africans," and "Is the Internalization of Aggression Necessary for Social Adaptation?"[5] Also important is the book about the Yatmul coauthored by Morgenthaler father and son with Florence Weiss, *Gespräche am sterbenden Fluss* (Conversations by a Dying River, 1984), translated into French in 1987 (with a foreword by the sociologist-anthropologist Georges Balandier) as *Conversations au bord du fleuve mourante*.[6] In between and alongside these ethnopsychoanalytic publications, the Parins and Fritz Morgenthaler – singly, all together, or in different combinations of two – published further books and scores of essays, in psychoanalytic journals and in mainstream and alternative media, about the politics of their era and about psychoanalytic theory and technique. Eventually, Paul Parin also turned to fiction and memoir.[7]

There are many ways we could tell the story of this trio and its significance.[8] Of interest for us is not just the prolific work the three produced from the early 1960s on, within psychoanalysis, within anthropology, and at the intersection of those two fields – their innovative mash-up of different clinical and theoretical approaches, or the ways their cross-cultural experiments in the so-called Third World deeply informed the stands they took on the politics of the First (including, and crucially, the sexual politics) – but very much also its delayed-reaction and then ardently enthusiastic reception. This is the thread that this chapter pursues.

For the case of the Parins and Morgenthaler shows once more, with uncommon clarity and richness, how in the history of psychoanalysis ideas can often take hold and accrue import in the oddest of sequences, not all at once, but selectively in some instances, cumulatively in others – and with lines of connection between concepts and their consequences running backwards and forwards and sideways in time. This proposition pertains to the Parins and Morgenthaler in at least three ways. One involves the reception of their work by New Left youth in the 1970s and 1980s, a reception which literally co-constructed the meaning of the writings they had produced in the 1960s and also – significantly, and directly – pushed them, dialogically,

even further than they were going on their own. Another way the proposition applies involves the ideas they took up from psychoanalytic
predecessors and contemporaries – often, as it happens, ideas developed in quite stringently apolitical clinical settings – and how those
ideas were repurposed in their work, giving them whole new uses and
audiences. And a third relevance lies in what is visible in their writings
to us now, in the 2010s, when we can see things that they could not
have known. This includes the ways the texts from the 1960s did not
only anticipate, by two decades, a model of self-reflexive anthropology
that was to become de rigueur since the 1980s, but also a two-person,
relational model of psychoanalysis. This two-person model had always
had a contrapuntal – albeit often denigrated – presence within the psychoanalytic movement (a lineage for instance that is traceable from
the Budapest-based Sándor Ferenczi through Harry Stack Sullivan in
the USA or, again, from Ferenczi through John Rickman and Michael
Balint in the UK), but which only gradually gained ground in the wider
psychoanalytic community from the 1980s on. (And for complex reasons, both bad and good, it has remained contested.) Nonetheless, and
for us today within our inherited categories at first glance contradictorily, the Parins and Morgenthaler, despite their commitment to a two-
person model, and despite their political engagements, also retained a
strong investment in ego psychology (more typically associated with
the one-person model), in *intra*psychic dynamics (more typically associated with apolitical practitioners), and in the idea of instinctual drives
(a notion anathema to most relationally oriented analysts today).

While the delayed-reaction reception was vital, the concrete
historical context of original production does also matter greatly to
our comprehension of their significance. Parin, Parin-Matthèy, and
Morgenthaler were central figures in a complicated process whose history has not yet been comprehensively written, but which might be
described as a mutual rescue operation of psychoanalysis and politics,
specifically a kind of independent moral Left politics emerging in Central Europe in the aftermath of Nazism. Indisputably, psychoanalytic
concepts proved essential in the formulation of new moral-political
understandings in the wake of fascism (as important, for example, as
progressive Christian theological reformulations – and often overlapping with them).[9] But in addition a case can, in fact needs to, be made
that the infusion of moral-political earnestness saved psychoanalysis as
an enterprise as well, and gave it a longer and richer life within Central

Europe than it would have had if it stayed solely within a medical-therapeutic remit. For Switzerland, the key figures were the Parins and Morgenthaler, but their influence was broadly transnational.

Becoming a *Mini-Ethnie*

Before becoming psychoanalysts, the Parins and Morgenthaler all had medical backgrounds and all had worked in zones of war or postwar devastation. Goldy Parin-Matthèy (born 1911, in the Austrian city of Graz, into a Swiss-heritage Huguenot family) trained at the University of Graz as a medical laboratory assistant. Paul Parin (born in 1916 and raised in Polzela, then also part of the Austro-Hungarian empire, now in Slovenia, into a Swiss-heritage Jewish-and-assimilated family) studied in Zagreb, Graz, and Zurich and became a medical doctor, initially working as a surgeon and later specializing in neurology. Morgenthaler (born 1919 in Oberhofen near Bern, into a family of artists – his father Ernst Morgenthaler was a prominent impressionist painter, his mother the famous doll designer Sasha Morgenthaler) went to school in Paris and Zurich, studied medicine in Zurich, and after a residency in Paris returned to Zurich to work in neurology. Morgenthaler subsequently became an accomplished painter in his own right.

As a young woman in Graz, in the artistic and intellectual circles in which Goldy Matthèy moved (her best friend was the artist Maria Biljan-Bilger), she first got to know antifascist activists, anarchists, socialists, and communists. One friend from those days, Herbert Eichholzer, would later be murdered by the Nazis for his work in the anti-Nazi resistance, including protest against the so-called "euthanasia" program. Initially she had studied ceramics, but by 1933–1934 Matthèy was working for August Aichhorn, the founder of psychoanalytic pedagogy, in an alternative institution for "difficult" delinquent youth in Vienna; thereafter she returned to Graz and worked in a laboratory at the university hospital. But in 1937 she went with her cousin (also Maria's husband) Ferdinand Bilger to become one of approximately 1400 Austrians who joined the International Brigades on the anti-Franco side in the Spanish Civil War. There she worked with the left-wing medical organization Centrale Sanitaire Suisse (CSS) as an X-ray technician under the pseudonym "Liselot" first in Albacete and then in Vic. The CSS had been founded in Zurich in 1937 as a section of the

Centrale Sanitaire Internationale, whose purpose was to support the Republican forces in Spain; in 1939 she left Spain for France with other members of the CSS, only to be interned for two months in a camp in St. Zacharie near Marseille. It was upon her release that she moved to Switzerland and took up a position as director of a hematological lab in Zurich. This is where she met Parin, then a young medical student.

From September 1944 to October 1945, again in connection with CSS, the pair was in Yugoslavia, together with five other surgeons, in order to provide humanitarian medical aid – first to Tito's partisans battling the Nazis and the Italian fascist army until the war there ended in mid-May, and then to assist in the aftermath.[10] Matthèy would return to Yugoslavia with CSS once more in 1946 and, this time with Morgenthaler, helped to build a hospital in Prijedor (now Bosnia). Parin visited her there, and his friendship with Morgenthaler began. (Morgenthaler had fallen ill; Parin treated him, giving his first-ever penicillin shot.) The three became inseparable from that time on.

Upon their return to Zurich, all three would undertake analyses with the neurologist and psychoanalyst Rudolf Brun, and in 1952 they opened their shared practice and began to take patients. They founded, with Jacques Berna, the left-leaning Psychoanalytic Seminar Zurich, and – through its many upheavals – trained, mentored, and/ or inspired the two next generations of progressive analysts in Switzerland, Austria, and West Germany. In addition, Morgenthaler had a strong reputation and following in Italy, traveling there frequently for teaching. All three were affiliated with the International Psychoanalytical Association, Parin also serving in an official capacity. They nurtured close and collegial relationships with a far-flung international network of the leading psychoanalysts of their day, including many Americans. Their influence on the New Left, within and outside of psychoanalysis, would be substantial. And it is no less indicative that the Parins and Morgenthaler not only argued within the IPA on behalf of lay analysts (supporting Anna Freud in this), as well as for less controlling treatment of analytic candidates, but also split off from the Swiss Psychoanalytic Society in solidarity with the European-Latin American Plataforma movement of young left-leaning analysts-in-training.[11]

Morgenthaler died in 1984 at age 65 (on a trip, of a heart attack, in Addis Ababa, Ethiopia), but Parin-Matthèy would live until 1997 and Parin until 2009. From the 1970s through to the 1990s the Parins were well known in Switzerland and West (and then united)

Germany as influential public intellectuals writing on all the crucial Cold War and post-Cold War issues – from the student protests of the 1960s and the USA's involvement in Vietnam and the Latin American dictatorships to the danger of the nuclear arms race and the right-wing turn in the West in the 1980s, but also on the limitations of Marxism and the catastrophe that was Soviet socialism. They were consistently more anarchist than socialist. Celebrated in their later years as "the dream couple of the European Left," their 58-year love affair was as much a part of their aura as their antifascist credentials.[12] But throughout their long lives, what the couple worked on and what they stood for – politically and existentially – would remain inextricable from their threesomeness with Morgenthaler.[13] When Paul Parin died in 2009, the Swiss psychoanalyst Ralf Binswanger (one of Morgenthaler's former analysands, who had also been close to both of the Parins), in his obituary-*cum*-homage tribute to the trio dubbed them a *Mini-Ethnie* (a mini-ethnicity of three).[14]

Looking for Oedipus Elsewhere

In their first longer stay among the Dogon in Mali in 1960, as the three experimented with shifting away from ethnographic methods based in participant-observation life or direct questioning of informants toward conducting psychoanalyses, one main aim was simply to see if psychoanalysis could be used – sensitively, self-critically, respectfully – also to understand non-Western selves. The idea was to employ the cross-cultural comparative findings to test the validity as well as the limits of the psychoanalytic theories of psychosexual stages, ego structure, Oedipal conflicts, defenses and resistances that had been developed in a Western context. Riffing on Freud's comment that "where id was there ego shall be," they emphasized that in Africa they were not trying to help to develop ego where id had been but rather to recognize *as* ego what had emerged out of id in such a different way there.[15]

However, in some ways more like ethnographers, the Parins and Morgenthaler paid their informants (obviously a direct – and some critics thought scandalous – inversion of the usual relationship between patient and doctor). The reasoning of the Parins and Morgenthaler was that it was only fair and just to reimburse their conversation-partners for time lost from the work they would be otherwise doing; depending on the season, this would be farming millet, sorghum, and onions, or preparing the harvested materials for collective use or for market. (In discussion with the village elders, they settled on the typical hourly wage of 50 Central African francs for adults; half of that for adolescents.) Moreover, the informant-clients were in no distress and were emotionally normal by their cultures' standards. Yet these were, nonetheless, daily hour-long sessions, sessions in which the analysts encouraged intimate disclosure and free association, provided interpretations (in fact one could say that their distinctive style was to interpret early and often), and remained, especially as the relationships deepened, continuously attentive to issues of transference and countertransference (see Figure 14).[16]

One relevant context for the Parins' and Morgenthaler's experiments was the decades-old phenomenon, going back to the 1920s, of merger and mutual borrowing as well as heated disputation between psychoanalysis and anthropology. The Polish anthropologist Bronisław Malinowski set off a firestorm in the 1920s when he said that his research among the Trobrianders of Papua New Guinea had proven that the Oedipus complex was *not* universal. (The Trobrianders had no concept of the father's role in reproduction; it was the maternal uncles that served as authority figures for children coming of age.) Psychoanalysts were incensed at this attack on one of their most deeply held convictions. ("They reacted," as one psychologist put it a few years ago, "comparably to the reaction of traditional Catholics when one expresses skepticism about Mary's immaculate conception.")[17] One analyst, however, failed to be distressed. In his 1931 manifesto, *Der Einbruch der Sexualmoral* (published in English translation much later – in 1971, indicatively in the midst of a new sexual revolution – as *The Invasion of Compulsory Sex-Morality*, in 1972 also in French and Italian), the sex-radical Marxist Freudian Wilhelm Reich was delighted at what he took to be Malinowski's findings that sexual freedom correlated with marvelously peaceable social relations.[18]

Some of the prior efforts at the intersection of psychoanalysis and anthropology were definitely concerned to critique modernity and seek inspiration from supposedly nonmodern peoples, specifically around issues of sexual freedom.[19] One notable early example – in addition to Reich's channeling of his own interpretation of Malinowski – was Margaret Mead's *Coming of Age in Samoa* (1928). Mead contended that young girls in Samoa were free to enjoy casual sex with a variety

Figure 14 Paul Parin in conversation with his informant-analysand, Abinu, a Dogon, in 1960 in the village of Bongo in Mali. Abinu, who was approximately fifty years old, had excellent French, having gone to school in colonial times and having served for several months in the French army during World War II; he had also worked in the Gold Coast (now Ghana). When Parin first came to Bongo, the villagers were accustomed to tourists who would want to be shown around for a fee. Parin explained that "I am a tourist, but one who wants to get to know the land with his ears and not with his eyes" and he asks if Abinu will speak with him one hour daily for 50 Central African francs per hour (to compensate for the time Abinu will lose from his work as a planter). Abinu agrees. In a marvelous reversal of ethnographic relationships, Abinu asks Parin whether he comes "from the same tribe as Professor Griaule?" – a reference to the well-known anthropologist that had studied the Dogon since the early 1930s. Parin explains that no, Switzerland is a neighboring country to France. They end up having extraordinarily rich conversations, among other things about the intricacies of gender relations among the Dogon.

of partners before settling into marriage and contrasted this with the restrictiveness of US gender and sexual relations; the book was a much-discussed bestseller and earned headlines such as "Samoa is the Place for Women – Economically Independent, Don't Have to Cook and go Home to Dad When Husbands Get Tiresome" and "Where Neuroses Cease from Troubling and Complexes are at Rest."[20] Meanwhile, as texts like Malinowski's challenged the universality of psychoanalytic theories, and Mead's ongoing work emphasized how profoundly different cultures shaped the selves that people developed within them,

other scholars insisted on universal commonalities in human nature
across cultural divides, and particularly insisted on the universality of
Oedipus. The ever-loopy Géza Róheim, indignant critic of Malinowski, was the classic instance of a psychoanalyst-anthropologist who
spent his life eagerly (one might say overeagerly) identifying penises
and patricidal wishes in every culture he could visit in person or read
about from his armchair.[21] The biggest trend at the intersection of the
two fields, however, involved applying psychoanalytic concepts to an
interpretation of so-called "primitive" myths, symbols, and rituals.[22]
In a way, it made sense that the two fields were reciprocally interested.
Both sought insight into primal issues, even grotesque ones: murderous
wishes, unclean desires of all kinds, the dark magic phantasms of the
human mind. Greek mythology, from which Freud had borrowed the
concept of Oedipus in the first place, concerned these themes as well.

Yet rare was the effort actually to conduct psychoanalysis with non-Western peoples.[23] Even when psychoanalytic concepts
were employed, it was only, as it were, after the fact, either to interpret retrospectively material that had been gathered in fieldwork or to
attempt to adjudicate, as Malinowski and Róheim each in their own
way had done, the universal applicability (or not) of psychoanalytic
theories. Prior ethnographic work ranged widely in approach. Some
scholars focused strictly on being a participant-observer in communal
life (while also being aware of the impact of their presence on the interactions they were documenting). Others – perhaps most famously the
French anthropologist Marcel Griaule – expressed more concern with
trying to outwit informants into revealing secrets of their culture even
when the informants were striving to hide those secrets (thereby of
course acknowledging the complex power differentials and the tensions
between observer and observed).[24] Meanwhile, the preponderance of
psychiatric work in the colonial context, whether psychoanalytically
inflected or not, had been deeply imbued with racism.[25] The evidence
on this point is overwhelming – though it is noteworthy that there have
recently been efforts to rescue from the taint of racism some of the
canonical authors, both British and French. In particular, the French
Lacanian (but also Adlerian) psychoanalyst Octave Mannoni, author
of *Psychologie de la colonisation* (1950, translated in 1956 as *Prospero
and Caliban: The Psychology of Colonization*) based on his work in
Madagascar – sharply criticized by Frantz Fanon for his assumptions
of an "inferiority complex" among the colonized – has of late been

revived not least for the insights he provided into the psychological problems also of the colonizers.[26] And recent research has uncovered British psychologists (as opposed to psychiatrists) whose work among colonized peoples turned up such compelling data of the colonized's intelligence, emotional independence, and imagination that the scholars self-censored so as not to undermine the rationale of imperial rule. Among these, there were analysts and others informed by psychoanalytic ideas who undertook such projects as gathering accounts of the dreams of colonized individuals.[27]

The Parins' and Morgenthaler's work may best be compared with the one well-known prior effort to conduct psychoanalysis with an African individual, the South African Wulf Sachs' 1930s study of a Manyika healer-diviner named John Chavafambira and that man's struggles to come to terms with Western culture. The resulting book was entitled *Black Hamlet* (1937), later retitled *Black Anger*.[28] Certainly the Parins and Morgenthaler understood themselves, in 1960, as the first to conduct psychoanalytic conversations with Africans since Sachs' project. Almost coterminous with them was the work of the French psychologist and psychoanalyst Marie-Cécile Ortigues with Wolof, Lebou, and Serrer patients at the Fann Hospital in Senegal from 1962 to 1966, which resulted in the book *Œdipe africain* (African Oedipus, 1966), cowritten with her philosopher husband Edmond Ortigues.[29] As both titles – *Black Hamlet* and *Œdipe africain* – suggest, Sachs and the Ortigues were serious believers in the universality of Oedipus. Sachs largely imposed a Western model on Chavafambira (and found him deficient by comparison – even as Sachs intended his work as a robust indictment of South African racism).[30] The (strongly Lacanian) Ortigues were particularly interested in cultural variation and the different ways Oedipal conflicts would be experienced and expressed in a society that was not only polygamous but also one in which children were often shared among relatives.

Around the time the Parins and Morgenthaler went into the field, there were already six or seven (if not more) ways circulating among psychoanalysts and anthropologists to think about the existence and nature of an Oedipus complex. Malinowski in the 1920s had simply declared the complex non-universal, and explored the different complex (one in which the major taboo concerned not mother-son but rather brother-sister incest) he claimed to have found among the matrilineally organized Trobrianders; the British psychoanalyst Ernest

Jones, representing Freud, had retorted that whatever configurations Malinowski had found were a variant on, and hence a confirmation of, the ubiquity of Oedipus.[31] (Indeed, some later anthropologists, notably Melvin Spiro, contended that the more forcefully a culture appeared to deny the existence of a child's sexual and aggressive wishes toward its parents or parental figures, the *more* true, the more powerfully, the Oedipal complex was at work.)[32] But by the 1930s and 1940s there were quite a few analysts – notably the neo-Freudian émigrés Karen Horney and Erich Fromm in the USA – who declared that the Oedipus complex had never existed in any culture, that the whole idea was best seen as Freud's own fantasy or as an unwarranted extrapolation from limited evidence.[33] Melanie Klein in England, for her part, insisted on the complex's reality, but located the ferocious and desirous wishes at an earlier moment in infant development, placing its timing at around 18 months, rather than 3–5 or 4–6 years of age.[34] Jacques Lacan in France in the 1940s and 1950s also took the view that Oedipus was universal, but he redefined its significance as lying not so much in desirous or lethal impulses toward literal parents, but rather in the human toddler's entry into language and culture in general – an emergence that involved distinguishing among, and understanding relations between, the conceptual triumvirate of me, you, and he or she – even as Lacan also, as noted in the prior chapter, stressed that actual, consequential familial dynamics all too often involved more than three characters.[35]

George Devereux, meanwhile, who was later to be in recurrent friendly exchange especially with Paul Parin, already in the 1950s stayed with the story Freud had taken from Greek mythology. However, Devereux flipped it to emphasize that both the brutally murderous and the taboo-breaking sexually covetous impulses originated from the *parents*, not the children – and wondered aloud what it was about other analysts that had caused them to disavow (or, as he put it, "scotomize," that is, erase from consciousness) this insight; Devereux also questioned the heterosexual framing Freud had given the story, recovering violent same-sex desires in earlier versions of the myth.[36] And, in the early 1960s, anthropologist Anne Parsons (daughter of the sociologist Talcott Parsons) was concerned to argue that also within the West – her example was the culture of southern Italy, around Naples – there could be considerable variation in the forms taken by the Oedipus complex. Parsons emphasized strong mother-son ties in a culture which combined reverence for the figure of the Madonna with frank secular joking about sexual matters, a combination she saw as fostering a situation in which the son's respect for the mother was stronger than his respect for his father, even while the son remained orally dependent on his mother's solace well into adulthood – as the mother also was permissive toward her son's masculinity and sexual activity.[37] (It would take into the 1980s and 1990s for psychoanalysts to explore how Oedipal developments could be redescribed to account affirmatively, rather than hostilely, also for homosexually oriented outcomes.[38] And it was also the mid-1990s when scholars began to explore how "the invention of Oedipus" may have involved Sigmund Freud's very own efforts to "heterosexualize" himself in a vehemently antisemitic culture which feminized Jewish men.[39] Efforts to reconceive the Oedipal story in a family situation with same-sex parents are only getting underway now.)[40]

The Parins and Morgenthaler, for their parts, took the universality of some kind of Oedipal conflicts for granted, and published repeatedly on the variations of Oedipal constellations and outcomes that they saw among the "tradition-directed" but in colonial-postcolonial-evolution tribal groups they encountered.[41] However, they were more interested in exploring what they saw as the different kinds of egos (for example, among the patrilineally organized Dogon: oral, flexible, group-dependent) that – they contended – emerged in a culture where children's physical needs were consistently and immediately met by mothers, other adults, and peers, and anxiety over abandonment by the group proved to be more elemental and determinative than the castration anxiety more typical among individual autonomy-oriented Europeans.[42] (The psychoanalytic psychotherapist Vera Saller, who had known the Parins and Morgenthaler well, perceptively pointed out decades later that they had no doubt underestimated the dependency wishes and fears of abandonment manifest also among *Europeans*.)[43] Among the matrilineal Anyi, the Parins and Morgenthaler found yet another constellation. In contrast to the tendentially generous, curious, reliably responsible, mutually supportive, and hospitable-to-outsiders manner prevalent among the Dogon, the Anyi displayed far more suspicion and fear, not only toward visitors but also amongst themselves. In addition, the Parins and Morgenthaler found among the Anyi a self-protective tendency to drop relationships before one was rejected oneself, to treat individuals as interchangeable and replaceable, to be aggressive in manner (albeit not violent), and to be completely unconcerned with demonstrating a dependable work ethic. The Parins and Morgenthaler thought there must be a relationship between these regularly appearing characteristics and the fact that, although nursing infants were in constant sensuous and caring contact with their mothers' bodies, as toddlers they were confronted – as a group – with the daily administration of painful chili-pepper enemas; the mothers' behaviors could only seem like repeated anal rapes.[44]

Without question, the Parins and Morgenthaler found, in what Parin had once generically referred to as "the comparative study of peoples" (*vergleichende Völkerkunde*), relevance also for making better critical sense of dynamics within European culture.[45] They expressly saw themselves as turning the methods they had developed in their visits to Africa – and especially their attunement to the impact of cultural context on psyches – also onto what they referred to as "our own ethnicity" (*unsere eigene Ethnie*).[46] A good example was the essay that Parin and Morgenthaler co-wrote for Alexander Mitscherlich's 1969 anthology on aggression, *Bis hierher und nicht weiter* (Up to Here and No Further); the universal fact of human aggression, they noted there, did *not* mean that all societies were inevitably violent – on the contrary, some cultures were clearly better able than Europeans to preempt violence.[47] All three felt sure more generally that their encounters in Africa had made them "freer and braver" in their interactions with their European analysands – and indeed also "less inclined to treat a behavior different from our own as pathological; that has also affected our theoretical perspectives."[48]

One of the conclusions from their work about which the Parins and Morgenthaler felt most strongly was the point that societies do indeed shape selves at the most elemental levels. This they took as essential evidence against the trend so prevalent in postwar psychoanalytic circles, predominant especially in the USA and UK, though also apparent in France, to refuse to entertain extrapsychic considerations. As far as the Parins and Morgenthaler were concerned, to ignore extrapsychic contexts was not just politically ignorant but also, quite simply, scientifically wrong.

Yet – in this way again more like Mitscherlich and less like the Melanie Klein-inspired Félix Guattari – the Parins and Morgenthaler remained, for a long time, attached to an ego psychological framework drawn substantially from Anna Freud (and from Sigmund Freud directly), replete with a belief that psychic life involved drives and defenses above all (indeed, it would be only Morgenthaler who would subsequently evince interest also in the less drive-centered self psychological work of Heinz Kohut). For instance, in the introduction to *Die Weissen denken zuviel*, the Parins and Morgenthaler expressed their distinctive combination of radical universalism with interest in the differential impact of cultures like this: "Theoretically it is to be expected that the drive-resources of all human beings are the same, and that the drive-forces that express themselves in the course of an analysis obey the same laws everywhere." Yet they went on to say: "It is also necessary to know well the environment of the analysand in order to understand the counter-forces that defend against the drives, for these counter-forces have been formed by the environment."[49] At the same time, and all through, the Parins and Morgenthaler were perfectly self-aware as well that no psychoanalysts anywhere, also those operating within their own cultures, ever got the "truth" from their analysands; rather, what psychoanalysts got were free associations which – they argued – "will be organized [by the analyst] more in accordance with the defenses that have influenced them than by their reality-content."[50]

Whites Think Too Much

The Parins and Morgenthaler were not just concerned to use their ethnopsychoanalytic explorations to gain some intermittent critical leverage on European society. In addition, they clearly sought to challenge themselves, and gain greater flexibility and range in their own work as psychoanalysts, by allowing themselves to be in mutually transformative relationship in their daily conversations with their informants. Two dimensions at least are important here. One of these is the sensibility that they so evidently shared with the manifestly eccentric but magnificently creative George Devereux: the willingness to go outside one's comfort zone. Devereux, who had been analyzed by Róheim, had gained fame as the author of *Reality and Dream: Psychotherapy of a Plains Indian* (1951) – a book which in its sequential editions garnered prefaces from *both* (the otherwise mutually opposed) Margaret Mead and Karl Menninger – but his most self-reflexive works were his methodological ones, most notably *From Anxiety to Method in the Behavioral Sciences* (1967) and *Ethnopsychoanalysis: Psychoanalysis and Anthropology as*

Complementary Frames of Reference (1978). Whatever one thinks of Devereux's dogged insistence that psychoanalytic and anthropological toolkits could never be used simultaneously – that the more one understood about a phenomenon in cultural contextual terms, for example, the less one understood it in terms of the specificity of an individual patient's or informant's psychology (an emphatic conviction that might have been rooted more in his self-awareness that he could all too easily be tempted, when treating psychotherapeutically a patient from another culture, to go off track in the therapy in order to collect anthropologically fascinating data) – there is no question that Devereux was acutely insightful not just about the impossibility, but the very undesirability, of neutrality and objectivity on the part of anthropologists.[51] Devereux's wager was that the only real data produced in the anthropological encounter were the anthropologist's own subjective countertransferential reactions to the transference his or her presence had triggered.[52]

The other dimension involved the respectful treatment of their informants as co-producers of the conceptual conclusions about culture and selfhood that the Parins and Morgenthaler were evolving. The heart of *Die Weissen denken zuviel* comprised thirteen case studies of individuals with whom Parin and Morgenthaler had formed analytic-conversational relationships. (Parin-Matthèy took lessons in the local language and certainly participated in interaction with the villagers. But she did not, during the 1960 trip, conduct analytic conversations.)[53] The men developed strong attachments with their analysand-informants, mostly male but also female, and did so with a high degree of mutuality of disclosure and obviously genuine affection. And, although they were learning much about cultural difference in the conversations, they also did regularly provide interpretations, often of their analysand-informants' transferential dynamics toward themselves, and/or of the analysand-informants' psychic conflicts – over such matters as familial or village hierarchies, rivalries, inclusions and exclusions, or over childhood or adolescent losses, fears, or humiliations that had not been consciously processed – in such a way that the analysand-informants evidently experienced as helpful. Years later, Parin, for instance, would be told by a former analysand-informant how he still appreciated that he learned that his stomach ailments were due to "swallowed-down anger," and he had learned to manage subsequent incidents by imagining himself talking with Parin.[54]

They had approached potential informants with a simple over-
ture: "We would like to get to know [the Dogon] and understand how
they think and feel." [55] The chief in the village they chose as their home
base (Sanga), a man named Ogobara, had volunteered himself spon-
taneously as the first analysand; soon the news got around that these
were "tourists of a special kind" – they did not want to observe any
traditional rites like mask dances, but rather wanted to get to know
the locals "with their ears." Other villagers joined in not least in order
to be understood as gracious toward the chief's guests. Morgenthaler
ventured further to villages that were approximately twenty kilometers
away – and there he was received as a visitor from Sanga; one of the
villages was Andiumbolo and there again it was a respected representative of the village chief – in this case the chief's nephew, Dommo – who
presented himself as the "manager of public opinion" in the village and
facilitated contacts. [56]

It could certainly be argued that the trio was ethnographically
naive. [57] They had deliberately chosen as their base a village where ethnographers had been before – and had been positively received. Yet, at
the same time, they did not consider what kind of syncretistic effect
this prior contact might have had and instead asserted that their interest lay precisely in the fact that the culture of the Dogon had remained
traditional. [58] In addition, the Parins and Morgenthaler had chosen
villages in which many inhabitants spoke French because they had
attended French colonial schools – as they also relied on translators
for conversations with individuals less fluent in French. On the one
hand, then, there was no pure tradition to be observed. The Dogon of
Sanga, already in the 1960s, were hardly unworldly; one of their own,
Dolo Sominé, was the Minister of Health in the newborn Republic of
Mali. [59] Others had traveled to Niger, Ivory Coast, Ghana, or Algeria;
some had served in the French military. [60] Moreover, they were well
accustomed to European visitors. As a later anthropologist once joked
about the Dogon, nearly every village group had an "anthropologist
in residence." [61] On the other hand, the Parins and Morgenthaler were
continually impressed, not just on their first visit but also upon their
subsequent return in 1966, at how supply their hosts managed to
adapt to the demands of the new young state, just as they had managed to adapt to the colonizers, while maintaining many aspects of
their inherited ways (however inevitably modified); it would only be
in the early 1980s that tourists and beggars became dominant fixtures

of the economy.[62] Meanwhile, there was also no way that the Parins and Morgenthaler could have known that the literature they had studied in preparation for their first visit could not be relied on; it was years before it was revealed that Marcel Griaule, author of the much-admired *Dieu d'Eau* (God of Water, 1948 – translated as *Conversations with Ogotemmêli*), had been fooled by his imaginative tall-tale-telling informant when he thought he was learning the intricacies of Dogon cosmology.[63]

Arguably they were also psychoanalytically naive, not least as they stressed just how rapidly they were able to notice the arising of resistances within their analysands and the quick establishment of transferences.[64] There is no question that their efforts to complicate the universalism they had set out both to challenge and to confirm repeatedly ran up against their desire to have empathic contact with individuals from another culture.[65] But that was not the criticism leveled at the time. Instead, Griaule's daughter and sometime collaborator, the ethnologist Geneviève Calame-Griaule, as well as the Ortigues, criticized them not just for paying their informants but, more than that, for being the importunate ones, the ones asking for something, rather than waiting for a suffering individual to address them for help.[66] And another French commentator was snide about the evident polemicism of the title, declaring that "in its demagogy it is certainly no guarantee of the value of the ideas which the authors bring us."[67]

Yet the title was not so much a comment on race or color, as rather on the miseries produced by capitalism. The original quote came from a Dogon village chief – translated into French by the analysand-impresario Dommo – who had remarked that Europeans were always so stressed and unable to enjoy daily life:

> The whites think too much, and then they do a lot of things; and the more they do, the more they think. And then they earn a lot of money, and when they have a lot of money, they are worried that the money might get lost. Then they think even more and make more money and they never have enough money. Then they're not settled any longer. That's why they're not happy.[68]

It is also noteworthy that, when a number of their former hosts in Sanga had read the French translation of the book, they told the authors that they were "very satisfied with your book. You have not lied. We are like the way our ancestors made us and how we have spoken with you." Interestingly, moreover, when another ethnographer visited Sanga in later years and told the story of the Dommo-translated village chief's remarks about capitalism and unhappiness to his local tour guide, the tour guide responded by saying: "Now I feel the same way. My head is dizzy. I can no longer sleep. I am always asking myself: How can I make more money?"[69]

Whatever its authors' lack of sophistication and ensuing conceptual shortcomings, *Die Weissen denken zuviel* included tremendous amounts of ethnographic observation.[70] Reading the book now, what stands out above all are its portraits of sassy, self-assured women and sensitive, conflicted men. Without much flagging or fanfare, the Parins and Morgenthaler described the subtleties and dynamics of gender relations in a bigamous culture.[71] Dogon women were exceedingly independent – valued highly not least for their reproductive capacities; sexual relations were by any standards liberated. Although matches were made by families – who promised their offspring to each other when the children were still little – individuals who did not like their family's choice were free to seek other partners and, in general, there was substantial flexibility in personal arrangements. Children engaged in experimental sex-play without any adult remonstrations; teenagers spoke frankly within their peer groups about best sexual techniques and vetted and helped individuals approach their first objects of desire; adult women and men alike took lovers (and there were complicated rules about with whom a potential shared child would live, should an affair last longer than the permitted three years and thus begin more closely to approximate a marriage); sometimes two wives would get fed up with their shared husband and both threaten to leave him; much humor surrounded men's efforts to hold their wives and keep them satisfied, demonstrating kindness and good work habits. Not all men were able to achieve the ideal of two wives; much of the diffidence or insecurity in men involved an intra-male pecking order.[72]

Another revelatory area concerned the coexistence of pagan and Muslim cultures. A shift to increasing adherence to Islam had been tentatively fostered in the colonial era, but the results were uneven at best. It was, of all things, decolonization and the national independence just being achieved in 1960 that would, in the years following, force the trend toward Islamic observance far more strongly, and encourage the building of more mosques; at the same time, the new state's trend toward a celebration of negritude allowed individuals to blend, in their own practices and self-presentations, traditional Dogon rites like mask dances with the perceived-to-be-more-modern identification as Muslim.[73] Both before and after independence, many who had formally converted to Islam explicitly continued pagan rites as well. Meanwhile, the women encountered by the Parins and Morgenthaler joked that men found Islam appealing because they hoped it would make their women more subservient; some also laughingly declared that the happiest combination might well be a Muslim man with a pagan woman.[74]

Later, Parin would remark that the second big book project, *Fear Thy Neighbor as Thyself*, was actually the more rigorously conceptually developed book – as he also noted that it was never to achieve the wide readership that *Die Weissen denken zuviel* ultimately did.[75] But there was to be a time lag between the publication of the earlier book in 1963 and its subsequent cult status. Certainly there were younger ethnographers, among them the Swiss ethnopsychoanalysts Florence Weiss (who Morgenthaler, with his son, would visit in Papua New Guinea in the 1970s) and Maya Nadig and Mario Erdheim (who worked in Mexico), as well as the American anthropologist Vincent Crapanzano (who worked in Morocco), who did not just rely on psychoanalysis for thinking about myths, rituals, or symbols, but also drew direct inspiration from Devereux and from the Parins and Morgenthaler above all to reflect on the dynamics of their interactions with their subjects.[76] The psychoanalytically informed American anthropologists L. Bryce Boyer and Daniel Freeman became close friends with the Parins and Morgenthaler as well, and Parin recurrently participated in the "Workshop for Psychoanalytic Anthropology" at the annual fall session of the American Psychoanalytic Association, and was cofounder and coeditor of the *Journal for Psychoanalytic Anthropology*.[77] And there were ethnographically inclined young New Left-affiliated psychoanalysts inspired directly by the Parins and Morgenthaler, like the Austrian Johannes Reichmayr (later author of the major primer for the field of ethnopsychoanalysis, *Einführung in die Ethnopsychoanalyse – Geschichte, Theorien und Methoden* [Introduction to Ethnopsychoanalysis – History, Theories, Method, 1995], subsequently updated and expanded as *Ethnopsychoanalyse: Geschichte, Konzepte, Anwendungen* [Ethnopsychoanalysis: History, Concepts, Uses, 2013], and coeditor of the *Ethnologie und Psychoanalyse: Biographisches Lexikon der psychoanalytischen Ethnologie, Ethnopsychoanalyse und interkulturellen psychoanalytischen Therapie* [Psychoanalysis and Ethnology: Biographical Lexicon of Psychoanalytic Ethnology, Ethnopsychoanalysis and Intercultural Psychoanalytic Therapy, 2003]) and the Swiss-born Ursula Hauser, who would develop ethnographically sensitive group psychotherapy and psychodrama in Costa Rica, Mexico, Cuba, and El Salvador.[78] But the Parins and Morgenthaler took somewhat more time to reach a popular audience.

Sales of *Die Weissen denken zuviel* lagged despite early reviewer attention, but interest was revived not least in the context of the student rebellions of 1968.[79] By 1969, the first edition of the book had sold out.[80] An article that Parin published in the West German New Left journal *Kursbuch* in 1972 – comparing formations of the Oedipal complex in Dogon, Anyi, and European cultures – drew even more attention to the trio's work among left-leaning students.[81] So too did an article citing them appreciatively in the same issue of *Kursbuch* by the psychoanalyst (and respected former head of the West German Socialist German Students' Association) Reimut Reiche. Reiche praised Anne Parsons and the Parins and Morgenthaler as he merged the insights from *Die Weissen denken zuviel* and *Fear Thy Neighbor as Thyself* to argue that they had proven that conventional ego psychologists' version of the Oedipus complex was *not* universally applicable but rather a capitalist-culture-bound, genital-primacy-obsessed one.[82] The biggest turnaround in the reception, however, was to be quite unexpected. It had everything to do with sexual politics and with postfascist intergenerational dynamics in West Germany.

The Position of the Perversions

In 1974, in the pages of *Psyche*, the prestigious West German journal of psychoanalysis, Fritz Morgenthaler – for a change writing only under his own name – published an utterly chaotic but soon to be extraordinarily influential essay. Entitled "Die Stellung der Perversionen in Metapsychologie und Technik" (The Position of the Perversions in Metapsychology and Technique), the essay had five unevenly balanced parts. Starting out from a brief account of a bisexual, suicidal arsonist, it then moved on without transition to introduce an original theory of perversions. Morgenthaler proposed seeing perversions as "creative ego-achievements" evolved in response to disruptions or chronic inter-ference in the development of the self in early childhood.[83]

Morgenthaler unselfconsciously blended aspects of the (at that time newly popular revisionist) work on narcissism of self psychologist Heinz Kohut with more classic Heinz Hartmann-esque ego psychologi-cal reflections (albeit selectively plucked), while also borrowing from Phyllis Greenacre's theories of the fetish. The bit taken from Hartmann was the idea that a symptom – in Hartmann's words – "which when viewed laterally is pathological and can be attributed to certain defi-ciencies at particular stages of development, may present the best solu-tion for an optimal interaction between the mental systems and the self when viewed longitudinally, i.e., in terms of the total development of the personality."[84] The concept drawn from Greenacre's work of the early to mid-1950s was that a fetish often had developed in response to a traumatic incident in early childhood (a key example she gave was of a man with a foot and buckled shoe fetish who had been deeply dis-turbed by overhearing and partially observing at least three abortions performed on his mother).[85] Both Hartmann and Greenacre, in short, although with distinct valences – as Hartmann was genially optimis-tic, while his close associate Greenacre's tone about her patients could come off as condescending – implied that symptoms could also be the products of an individual's efforts at self-healing.

It was in these passages that Morgenthaler floated what was to become one of his signature concepts: the idea of a perversion or a preferred orientation as a *Plombe*, literally a "filling" (as in a dental fill-ing for a cavity, something that is an alchemical mixture of substances that plugs an awkward fissure but does so perfectly), something closing and holding together a "terrible gap" within the self.[86] Morgenthaler saw such a phenomenon literally as an achievement of the ego, i.e., as itself a creative solution to a particular psychological difficulty in early development. At some points in the essay, Morgenthaler additionally floated the metaphors of a "plug" or a "bridging structure." What he meant was that what might seem at first glance to be a sexual matter was actually better understood as a sexualized attempt to solve a more primal existential issue. (This was an idea that had also, albeit with different emphases, been put forward in Kohut's work.)[87] The perver-sion or orientation, Morgenthaler averred, like any symptom, fulfilled a function – indeed *was* a function. The analyst's task was to honor and work with and around it.

But then suddenly the essay led the reader to Papua New Guinea (with an insert of two full-page photographs portraying a woman dressed as a man and a man dressed as a woman, participating in a tribal ritual). Here Morgenthaler recounted his own experience (during his initial sojourn there with Florence Weiss and Milan Stanek in 1972–1973) observing Yatmul initiation rights. When the young boys came of age, they had their backs scarified to look like the tribal totem – a crocodile – and the women of the community dressed as men and danced "hectically-phallically," while the brothers of the mothers of the initiates cross-dressed as women. An elaborate sensual dance ensued, in which the men dressed as women offered food to the boys, feeding them by hand. These cross-dressed maternal uncles, through their seductive caressing and offering of food to the boys, were, Morgenthaler proposed (or: projected or fantasized), collectively reenacting the solicitously yearning as well as threatening "early pregenital mother," "penisless" and "phallic" at once, but *also*, simultaneously, and ingeniously, in his view, represented the by turns "castrated" and "castrating" father. (Morgenthaler clearly brought his own assumptions about the universality of Oedipus into his observation.) In Morgenthaler's summary view: "The point of the whole ritual is to perform and to represent how the young man, after the completed initiation, has been fully incorporated into the community of men, the mythical crocodile community, and in this way made immune to the temptation of incest." And Morgenthaler mused further about the "stunning emotional force with which the events are communicated to and engraved in every individual member of the crocodile village collective," noting the visceral impact also on him as an outside observer, and he stressed that the effect of the ritual would be much less powerful if done by the real mothers; the transvestism was essential, he thought, to its emotional impact. The transvestite ritual, in his view, was a creative invention of the community, a kind of "sociocultural *Plombe*," a collective perverse filling, a supple but potent process that dramatized, and thereby sought to resolve preemptively, what could otherwise have become a potential communal problem (see Figure 15a&b).[88]

And then the essay abruptly shifted once more: to two final sections on effective analytic technique in response to perverse patients. The penultimate section was the most relevant. Here we encountered a new patient, an immigrant to Switzerland of (undisclosed) foreign

Figure 15a Photographs taken by Fritz Morgenthaler during a trip to the Sepik district of Papua New Guinea in 1972–1973. During the *naven* ritual observed by Morgenthaler, the Yatmul woman (left) is dressed as a man and the Yatmul man (right) is dressed as a woman. Morgenthaler chose these images to accompany the article he published in *Psyche* in 1974 on "The Position of the Perversions in Metapsychology and Technique."

ethnicity, a lonely owner of a small business, a man who suffered in unacknowledgeable resentment from the oppressive hypochondria and panic attacks of his aging mother, and struggled with the fact that he was "a manifest homosexual" and – as it happened, like the young arsonist with whom the essay began – also a masochistic one, someone who chose to have sex with strangers who would provide aggressively performed, indeed physically painful, anal penetration. But perhaps the most noteworthy element of the discussion was Morgenthaler's description of a mistake he felt he made in the course of the analysis and then his successive efforts to correct that mistake, as Morgenthaler explicitly blamed the mistake on his own defensive anxiety about being provoked, by the patient, to acknowledge homosexual feelings *within himself*. (The outcome was quite tender: the patient ultimately retained his homosexuality but lost his masochism – in other words, he became unproblematic to himself.) Morgenthaler's main concluding notion, inspired by Kohut, was that in cases of perversion the analyst needed precisely *not* to become a transferential *object* for the patient, but rather should serve as a *function* for the patient (just as the perversion

Figure 15b Another photograph taken by Morgenthaler. While the women dressed as men carry spears, the cross-dressed brothers of the mothers of the initiates stimulate appreciative collective laughter as they stumble awkwardly around in their female garb. But then they get more overtly seductive, gently circling around and caressing the initiates, finally offering the pubescent boys bits of food carried on palm leaves, attempting to feed the youngsters by placing the bits in their mouths. In Morgenthaler's summary reflections, the maternal uncles' dancing and other behaviors could be interpreted as ritualistically enacting – and thereby preemptively inoculating the community against – "the incest temptation and seducement."

itself was a function), helping the patient develop a more flexible and – in Kohut's terms – "expanded self."[89]

As noted, the essay was chaotic. But its publication set in motion an unexpected sequence of events.[90] The first significant event involved a young sociologist named Martin Dannecker, doctoral student of Theodor Adorno and arguably *the* intellectual leader of the West German gay rights movement – among other things screenwriter for the movement-kickstarting film *Nicht der Homosexuelle ist pervers, sondern die Situation, in der er lebt* (It is Not the Homosexual Who is Perverse, but the Situation in Which He Lives, 1971) – who found the essay useful as he was preparing a theoretical book, *Der Homosexuelle und die Homosexualität* (The Homosexual and Homosexuality), which appeared in German in 1978. Dannecker was strongly interested in psychoanalysis, very alert to the antihomophobic impulses in Freud's own work, and committed to pushing back against the authority of such prominent antihomosexual psychoanalysts as the American Charles Socarides, whose work had also appeared in West Germany and had been positively received by professionals there and whose views set the terms to which activists needed to respond.[91] (It is relevant that the confidently clever American antihomophobic psychoanalytic theories of Robert Stoller – who cheerfully announced that *everyone* was a pervert in some way, heterosexuals by no means exempt – would not come to West Germans' attention until a couple of years later.) Thus, as Dannecker was searching for support and new ways of thinking, Morgenthaler's peculiar essay proved productive. The only other antihomophobic pushback text readily available at that moment was the French gay rights activist Guy Hocquenghem's *Le Désir homosexuel* (Homosexual Desire, 1972), which, building on Deleuze and Guattari's *Anti-Oedipus*, celebrated what Hocquenghem called the "'superior' homosexual," the promiscuous homosexual "who mechanically 'plugs in and out' of other men" (in the spirt of Deleuze and Guattari's "desiring machine"). Dannecker objected strenuously.[92] Although not hostile to promiscuity, Dannecker was concerned to understand what he found to be the unsatisfying parts of the cruising culture, and to make sense of what psychological factors were at work in warding off the possibility of longterm same-sex attachments. What Dannecker found intriguing in Morgenthaler – as he deemed the "essay [about 'The Position of the Perversions'] of great importance for the theory of homosexuality" – were multiple points, among them the repudiation of Socarides' conversion aims as by definition "unanalytic," as well as the idea of a preference or a perversion as an "ego-achievement," a *Plombe*. In addition, he was moved by Morgenthaler's suggestion that sexual activity could also serve *non*sexual, ego-stabilizing aims (an interesting, if at the time unacknowledged, echo with the work of Karen Horney), and above all by Morgenthaler's commitment to facilitating not his patients' heterosexuality, but rather their capacity for durable and passionate (though not necessarily sexually exclusive) love.[93]

And Morgenthaler's 1974 essay also caught the attention of Volkmar Sigusch, West Germany's most prominent sexologist. Sigusch was in 1977 just starting to solicit updated contributions for the second, revised edition of his enormously successful handbook on the therapeutic treatment of sexual disturbances – and Sigusch deliberately wanted to make the collection *more* psychoanalytic.[94] (An important side story here involved how, just as gay rights activists in the USA had been working to remove homosexuality from the DSM and in this way helped US psychiatry marginalize its – in the USA tendentially more homophobic – psychoanalytic community in favor of a supposedly more objective approach based on checklists of measurable symptoms, the radical sexuality researchers in Germany were demanding *more* Freud, rather than less.)[95] Sigusch wrote to Morgenthaler to ask if he would contribute the entry on "Homosexualität" (Homosexuality), expressly because Morgenthaler's 1974 *Psyche* essay had "profoundly impressed" him.[96] And Morgenthaler was glad to oblige.[97] The essay on "Homosexuality" which then did appear in the 1980 edition of Sigusch's volume (again typical: it was vintage Morgenthaler in its blithely unconcerned mixing of schools, in this case Hartmann, Anna Freud, and Greenacre together with Kohut, Margaret Mahler, Otto Kernberg, and René Spitz), along with overlapping pieces Morgenthaler published in 1979–1980 in the mainstream and influential *Neue Zürcher Zeitung* and the *Berliner Schwulenzeitung*, a gay newspaper, secured Morgenthaler's status – and one can still read this on Wikipedia today, both in German and in English – as *the* first European analyst, of any nationality, to declare that homosexuality was not in and of itself pathological (see Figure 16).[98]

A few Morgenthaler statements from the "Homosexuality" essay have become legendary: "The assumption that a same-sex partner choice is already in itself a symptom ... is an insulting insinuation." "Sexuality, in whatever form it shows itself, can never be a neurosis, a psychosis, a morbidity." The notion that there is "a polar opposition between heterosexuality and homosexuality ... is 'by definition false consciousness,'... an error in thinking." And once again there was the crucial *ethno*psychoanalytic gesture to what could be learned from "foreign cultures": *both* that homosexuality can appear as one form of human sexual life in all times and places *and* that homosexuality, as well as fetishism or transvestism, could not possibly be intrinsically psychopathological, since cultures handled them so distinctly.[99]

Suddenly, Morgenthaler was in demand in West Germany – and fascination developed also with his innovations in analytic technique. His dream seminars in particular (which he had offered for years in Italy and Switzerland) became legendary. (A main point was that the analyst and the analytic setting were always already present in the dreams, as were the associations, and that the telling of the dream was an event which structured the emotional interaction in the psychoanalytic situation – and that the sequencing of the telling of the dream

Neue Zürcher Zeitung — **LITERATUR UND KUNST**

Karl Geiser: Unveröffentlichte Federzeichnung aus dem Jahre 1929.

Innere und äussere Autonomie

Von Fritz Morgenthaler

Sexualität, in welcher Form sie sich auch immer zeigt, kann niemals eine Neurose, eine Psychose, eine Morbidität sein. Das Krankhafte kann stets nur als Ausdruck einer disharmonischen Entwicklung im gesamten psychischen Haushalt verstanden werden. Die Annahme, dass eine gleichgeschlechtliche Partnerwahl bereits ein Symptom darstellt, dass Homosexualität an sich ein Individuum psychisch krank macht, ist eine Unterstellung. Die Erfahrung der Menschen aller Kulturen zeigt, dass Homosexualität eine der Möglichkeiten ist, wie sich normalerweise menschliches Sexualleben ausformt.

sende Erfahrung der Körperbeherrschung, bei der Entwicklung der autonomen Funktionen die Entdeckung lustbetonter Körpergefühle an einem abgerundeten Bild des Selbst beteiligt. Ausnahmslos spielt dabei die Autoerotik eine wichtige Rolle. Wenn das Kleinkind onaniert, experimentiert es damit, sich selbständig und ohne äussere Hilfe, also meist unabhängig von der Mutter, Befriedigungen zu verschaffen. Man kann auch sagen, dass die autoerotischen Befriedigungen des Kindes Triebhandlungen darstellen, die die späteren autonomen Funktionen des Ich vorausplanen.

Im klassischen Griechenland hung zwischen Männern von gro Bedeutung, und dennoch ist dies bisher wenig Beachtung gesch Dass Jacob Burckhardts vierbän sche Kulturgeschichte» kaum au tigen Aspekt des griechischen L mag allenfalls als Prüderie des 1 entschuldigt werden. Aber sogar lage des «Oxford Classical Di 1970 gibt keine Auskunft über — selbst wenn der Mythos von Z med behandelt wird.

Das Buch von K. J. Dover ist das diesem Thema gewidmet ist in unserem Jahrhundert veröf deutsche Gelehrte Paul Brandt ges, reich illustriertes Werk «Se Griechenlands» (1925/26). Natü dabei nicht seinen wirklichen und benutzte deshalb das Pse Licht. Thomas Mann bewunderte pries vor allem das Kapitel über tät. Und dennoch ist Lichts Buch Publikum kaum zugänglich.

Aber was sind denn die schoc sachen über das griechische Lebe den Gelehrten ignoriert und von ken unter Verschluss gehalten w kend von Gerichtsreden und Ko zwei wichtigen Quellen der öff nung, berichtet Dover objektiv schönigungen.

Die Basis des klassischen gri terrichtssystems war die erotisc von Lehrer (Erastes) und Zöglin Oder mit Dover zu sprechen: «l Tendenz, homosexuelle Liebe a von pädagogischer und geschlec hung zu betrachten.» Es war die l geren, seinen Lehrer durch sein l hen zu inspirieren. Der Aeltere st sich seines Geliebten als würdi indem er im Stadion und auf de

Figure 16 Drawing by the sculptor and photographer Karl Geiser, 1929, a close friend of the Morgenthaler family, printed as an illustration in the *Neue Zürcher Zeitung* in July 1979 to accompany an abbreviated version of the essay by Fritz Morgenthaler declaring that homosexuality is not a pathology.

mattered as well; in general, Morgenthaler was often more interested in the *direction* of a dream, its trajectory, than in attempting to decode symbols.)[100]

Morgenthaler also, among other things, took the view that one should treat the patient as an equal, and this included: as someone who could handle a not correct interpretation. (Donald Winnicott in the UK had emphasized that one's interpretation should not be too "correct" – it was not only acceptable but actually good to be slightly off, so that more productive work with the patient could ensue.)[101] Morgenthaler, by contrast, meant the idea of not being correct somewhat differently. He explicitly believed in taking a strong standpoint early on, thereby as it were forcing a transference, and then working "dialectically" (his term) with whatever emerged. And in what turned out to be, along with the *Plombe*, another oft-invoked turn of phrase: Morgenthaler saw the unconscious of the analysand as a theater director, motivating the analysand to various scene-stagings, which facilitated the progression of the analysis; he definitively believed that, in analysis, two unconsciouses were in communication with one another. (If the analyst remained blind to what the analysand was trying to show him, despite all the strenuous efforts of the analysand's unconscious, then the analysand might become resigned and depressed – and then this would be another sign to the analyst to notice and diagnose his *own* resistances to understanding.) Or, in another metaphor, Morgenthaler saw the analysand as taking the analyst by the hand, leading him through but also sometimes directly *into* obstacles – and then this would cause the analyst to stumble so that the scales would fall from his eyes. [102] In general, Morgenthaler understood analysis to involve the emotional movement produced in both partners to the ongoing conversation; analysis was mutually transformative or it was no good at all.

On the other hand, Morgenthaler was given to saying to his trainees: "You can't change people, you can only seduce them." [103] This was a kind of life credo for him. Again, the reference to "seduction" was meant as a metaphor – a way of expressing the reciprocal risk of an analytic relationship, but also a way of emphasizing that it would be impertinent for an analyst to see him- or herself as the one above the fray, neutrally and objectively leading another human being into health. What Morgenthaler meant was that intensive emotional involvement and setting-in-motion of mutual knowing between people was the only way that any healing could ever happen. [104]

Conclusion

There are conflicting memories as to what year it began – 1979? 1980? 1981? – but the Parins and Morgenthaler started to become heroes for the counterculture in West Germany. (In some accounts, it was first Morgenthaler who was invited to present his thoughts on "Homosexuality" in West German New Left bookstores – with his young associate and sometime coauthor and editor Hans Jürgen Heinrichs coordinating the visit to Frankfurt, and soon thereafter Parin and Parin-Matthèy were invited as well; Parin's own version has it that he came first, to

speak about "Politics and Psychoanalysis.")[105] And, not least, growing numbers of young progressive West Germans found their way to
Zurich, to go into analysis with one of the three.[106] *Die Weissen denken zuviel* became mandatory reading in West German New Left circles, indisputably a cult book – and it has remained legendary into our
new millennium.[107] A love story in the New Left journal *Pflasterstrand*
turned on the drama of a young Marxist man eager to impress a girl
he meets in Mexico en route to the Sandinistas in Nicaragua by quoting from *Die Weissen denken zuviel*. A bookstore (in Cologne) painted
the book title in huge letters on the windows.[108] A bookstore owner
(in Frankfurt) reminisced that "Paul Parin changed everything," giving the depressed post-1968 counterculture a new sense of engaged
direction.[109] And one memoir reported that, within the counterculture, West Germans began to divide their acquaintances into "Dogon"
vs. "Anyi" – the Dogon being generous and happy, the Anyi fearful
and defensive.[110] As late as the 1990s, a Swiss development organization was advertising for donors using the slogan "Die Weissen denken zuviel" – apparently experiencing the slogan as meaningful and
evocative rather than romantically primitivizing.[111] The book was still
being recommended as great travel reading in the venerable weekly
newspaper *Die Zeit* as recently as 2007.[112] And Morgenthaler's concept of the *Plombe* – despite critical sexologists' subsequent realization that Morgenthaler had not only unhelpfully lumped mild fetishes
together with murderous perversions but had also not distinguished
sexual orientations from narcissistic disturbances – would continue to
prove immensely generative. Into the later twentieth and early twenty-
first century, analysts and other therapists interested in the sexualization of actually pre- or nonsexual (regressive or aggressive) wishes too
threatening to be acknowledged have continued to find the idea of the
Plombe highly useful.[113]

    Many members of the New Left, as they were themselves aging
at the turn from the 1970s to the 1980s, although powerfully interested in Freud (for overdetermined reasons – concerned to understand
their parents' attraction to fascism, working to recover the radical Jewish inheritance of the early twentieth century that had been destroyed
by the Nazis, but also trying to make sense of their own unhappiness,
as the political revolution they hoped to make was defeated), did not
care especially about the details of debates about the universality of
Oedipus. But *Die Weissen denken zuviel* mattered because it seemed to

offer another model for how human community could be organized – with less competitiveness and more solidarity. Furthermore, the very idea that *different cultures produce different kinds of selves* turned out to be extraordinarily important.[114]

Indeed, it is no coincidence that the only other anthropologist read as ardently at that time was Bronisław Malinowski. The late 1970s and early 1980s saw a veritable Malinowski revival in West Germany, unmatched in any other European nation. Malinowski's *The Sexual Life of Savages* (1929) was invoked endlessly in debates about childrearing and sex education.[115] For there is no question that the dream of sexual liberation was about more, in postfascist West Germany, than the pursuit of pleasure *per se*. It was very much about major hopes for the total remaking of human nature as less aggressive and more free – not least at a moment when the sexual revolution seemed not to have fulfilled the initial promise of also transforming political conditions.

As it turned out, then, what was at stake in the merger of anthropology and psychoanalysis in the decades after Freud's death was quite different from what was argued over during Freud's lifetime. For the post-Freud era was, above all, additionally the postfascist, post-Holocaust, and wars-of-decolonization era. The war in Vietnam in particular, coming together, as it did, with intergenerational tensions over the legacies of the mass murder of European Jewry, posed the problems of the relationships between sex and aggression in wholly new ways (as did the rise of animal experts like Konrad Lorenz, who praised aggression as necessary and were celebrated for doing so).

And, meanwhile, the nature of the questions about sex had changed. The sexual repressions of Freud's era had been lifted, but many people still did not feel as free as they had hoped. Sexual liberationist aspirations had to be formulated in wholly new terms.

Morgenthaler in his writings after 1980 continued to theorize sexual desire – in an era when so many other analysts had lost interest in the topic. His collected and updated essays on desires and their vicissitudes were published in 1984, the year of his death, under the title *Homosexualität, Heterosexualität, Perversion* (in 1988, they appeared in English as well, as *Homosexuality, Heterosexuality, Perversion*). Here Morgenthaler, among other things, distinguished sharply between what he named "the sexual" (*das Sexuelle*) – a vital capacity, if not *the* vital capacity – and "sexuality" (*die Sexualität*) – that dreadful grid of the socially acceptable into which life in its complexity all too often got stuffed.[116] As Parin summarized it in the earliest postmortem tribute to his lifelong friend (Parin had stepped in to deliver a conference paper that Morgenthaler had been scheduled to present), "the sexual," for Morgenthaler, was that which "arises from the id, is unconscious, is movement, without goal, without direction, without an object; the sexual strives for pleasure, but it is not yet a wish. As an emotional happening, it addresses the emotion of the analyst directly, as emotion it lends its power to creativity, to love, to liberation from restrictions and from repression." By contrast, Parin went on, "sexuality" for Morgenthaler was that which "the sexual" turned into once it met the ego and its defenses, and – in numerous further developmental steps – the world and culture. "Sexuality is the already-having-become [*das Gewordene*] ... whether heterosexual, homosexual or perverse, sexuality is already the limitation of the sexual."[117] Or again – in yet another of his famous metaphors – Morgenthaler had thought of "the sexual" as a guerilla force, battling creatively in an ever-uneven match with the dictatorship that was socially formed "sexuality."[118]

In the years after Morgenthaler's death, Parin too took up the cause of sexual rights. Parin wrote several essays in the mid-1980s critically analyzing the psychic damage done to the victims of antihomosexual prejudice, exposing and repudiating the homophobia within West German analytic institutes, and providing a searing critique of the domestication of and/or increasing disinterest in "the sexual" in US ego and self psychology as well as British and French Annafreudian, Kleinian, and Lacanian schools.[119] However romantically naive this may appear in hindsight, and however explicitly aware Parin was also of Frankfurt School philosopher Herbert Marcuse's insight into consumer capitalism's "repressively tolerant" acceptance of greater sexual diversity as long as people were otherwise politically and socially conformist, Parin unapologetically placed himself on the side of "the subversive potential, the pleasure-giving and social convention-exploding power of sexual drives" – believing that tapping this potential was one of the best ways to help human beings stop adapting to the political repression, once again, as of the mid-1980s (e.g., Ronald Reagan, Margaret Thatcher, Helmut Kohl), rising all around them.[120]

In addition, then, to their radical-universalist humanism and their conviction that the critique of what Parin (quoting Freud) called "the hypocrisy in culture" (*Kulturheuchelei*) was – or at least should be – obligatory and intrinsic to psychoanalysis, what made Morgenthaler's and the Parins' writings stand out was precisely this defiant liberationist impulse that they all three traced back to Freud himself.[121] Meanwhile, the ethnopsychoanalytic impulse to attend more closely to the reciprocally destabilizing dynamics between observer and observed became absorbed into the anthropological mainstream, even as skepticism about the value of psychoanalytic concepts among anthropologists turned ethnopsychoanalysis into at best a niche venture. But the lessons learned in ethnopsychoanalytic explorations turned out to have clinical value as well.[122]

Ethnopsychoanalysis can be said to form one crucial tributary precursor to the approaches now more familiarly labeled – in our twenty-first-century moment of massive global migrations, multiethnic societies also within the West, and countless public mental health initiatives in both the developed and the developing world – as "transcultural psychiatry" or "intercultural therapy."[123] Devereux's student, Egyptian-born, Paris-based Tobie Nathan, is one of the most influential and innovative current practitioners of transcultural psychiatry, but there are also many who were influenced by *Œdipe africain* author Marie-Cécile Ortigues.[124] And many others continue to find inspiration specifically in the examples set by the Parins and Morgenthaler.[125] In the year 2016, a major conference was held in Vienna, dedicated to recovering and honoring the work of Paul Parin.[126]

AFTERWORD

"Psychoanalysis is not possible without an attack on the status quo; the critique of society is intrinsic to it. I know that many colleagues are of a different opinion."

Paul Parin, 1989[1]

In 1969, at the International Psychoanalytical Association congress in Rome, the Los Angeles-based analyst Leo Rangell was elected to the presidency in an upset victory over the Chicago-based analyst Heinz Kohut (soon to become famous as the creator of self psychology as an alternative to ego psychology).[2] Whether Kohut – who had learned in advance that his fortunes looked unexpectedly bleak and had formally withdrawn his candidacy – lost because he was already breaking from the (at that moment still powerful) ego psychological consensus in the USA, or whether it was this defeat at the hands of colleagues that spurred him into developing an alternative framework with even more ardor and sense of purpose, and what role Anna Freud had played in either favoring or undermining his chances, exercised the psychoanalytic rumor mill and later the historians of psychoanalysis for quite some time. Did Anna Freud promote Kohut because she believed him to be loyal to the ego psychological cause or because she above all wanted to prevent a presidency by Rangell because he, like several other Los Angeleans, had (some) support from the British Kleinians, her persistent nemeses?[3] Both were probably true.

Years later, at the occasion of the centenary of the IPA in 2010, Rangell recalled his version of these intricacies, but also went on to offer his retrospective take on what he had come to see as "a peak and a turn" within the international psychoanalytic movement between 1969 and 1975 across four crucial IPA congresses in Rome, Vienna, Paris, and London. About Rome in particular, Rangell remembered that "the world was in turmoil, and psychoanalysis was at its peak." And although he contended that "once the drama of the election had settled down" he was "acutely intent about the nature of the moment at which it had come," he also acknowledged that he had been

> unaware of the strength of the gathering students' revolution until I saw their parades in Rome. The day before I was to be elected president at the Business Meeting, as I walked in the street with my adolescent son, marchers carrying banners "Down with the AP$A" [a reference to the American Psychoanalytic Association, perceived to be disproportionately dominant in the IPA] invited me to join them. I told my son that tomorrow they will point at me as the enemy. Deconstruction, of every intellectual discipline, was in the air; psychoanalysis was not to be exempt.[4]

And at another moment in his retrospection, reflecting on the significance of the preeminent American ego psychologist Heinz Hartmann's death in 1970 coinciding with the excitement of preparing for the first time in the postwar era to return the IPA congress to the city of Vienna, where psychoanalysis had been born and from whence Freud had escaped from mortal danger only three decades earlier, Rangell remarked again that "the post-War era of exuberance and reparation had reached a high point – we hardly knew that a decline was next."[5] But the remainder of his memories revolved mainly around intra-IPA dramas and jostlings for power. And it included as well a restatement of his oft-declared concern that the sense of coherence that had marked the theoretical edifice of the first two postwar decades of psychoanalysis had come, at the turn from the 1960s to the early 1970s, to a lamentable end as an increasing "pluralism of theories" proliferated "at the expense of a steady growth of the Freudian theoretical tree."[6] Rangell firmly believed that "theoretical fragmentation" was responsible for the decline of psychoanalysis.[7]

Rangell appeared unaware both that the "student protesters" about whom he grumbled would become notable revitalizers of the Freudian project in their respective countries – some within and

many outside of the IPA – or that the years he saw as the end of the
movement he loved were in fact the beginning of a second golden age
for psychoanalysis within the West, one in which the insurgent young
analysts' search for more effective clinical approaches were inseparable from their awareness that social and political contexts inevitably impinge on psyches. For instance, precisely the individuals that
had coordinated the protest and counter-congress in Rome in 1969 –
among them the Italians Elvio Fachinelli and Marianna Bolko and the
Swiss Berthold Rothschild – would become preeminent and widely
respected leaders in their psychoanalytic communities. Fachinelli, who
died prematurely of cancer in 1989, was an extraordinarily creative
and generous analyst, an important translator of Freud into Italian
but also the first to bring Lacan's work to Italy, an activist on behalf
of alternative preschool education, and, like Guattari or the Parins
and Morgenthaler, an energetic and joyful utopian and antiauthoritarian. He called – as one associate remembered – "for letting go of a
kind of psychoanalysis which has the answers (*'una psicoanalisi delle
risposte'*) and for moving toward a psychoanalysis which questions
(*'una psicoanalisi delle domande'*)."[8] Bolko and Rothschild are both
still active to this day.[9]

These three, and the dozens of further individuals with whom
they were allied and networked also in Austria, France, the UK, West Germany, and Latin America, all took seriously the puzzle of the relationships between political conditions and psychic interiority. They ascribed
to a view expressed perhaps most succinctly by Morgenthaler at the IPA
congress in Paris in 1973 (and subsequently appreciatively reiterated by
Alexander Mitscherlich's young associate and later editor of the West German journal *Psyche*, Helmut Dahmer) to the effect that "Psychoanalysts
[today] seem not to notice that in their ignoring of the meaning of their
own social role they become ever more similar to those medical professionals at the turn of the century that were hostile to psychoanalysis – just
with the difference that those physicians in the past wanted to disregard
the unconscious while present-day analysts want to pay no attention
to societal problems."[10] Or, as another essential mentor to the younger
generation, the brilliant Freiburg-based West German analyst Johannes
Cremerius (proponent of the clinical innovations of Ferenczi and Balint,
close associate of Mitscherlich and also the Parins and Morgenthaler, as
well as frequent collaborator with the revered radical Sullivanian Italian
schizophrenia expert Gaetano Benedetti), would remark a decade later

in an essay on the psychoanalytic "abstinence rule": the "refusal of psychoanalysts to take a stand on social problems" was based on a complete "misjudgment of reality." Moreover, this misjudgment all too often hid from view, even from analysts themselves, the way they used the ideals of self-withholding and of political discretion to satisfy inappropriate but unacknowledged needs of their own within the analytic setting.[11] This bequest was a burdensome heritage for later generations. Among other things, then, it apparently had not occurred to Rangell that the main trouble with international psychoanalysis at the turn to the 1970s may have lain precisely in the earlier postwar US psychoanalytic settlement he had sought so determinedly to defend.[12]

None of the strong interest they took in the interrelationships between psychic dynamics and "societal problems" meant that the insurgent generation and its sympathetic elders did not take fantasies or intrapsychic processes seriously. On the contrary. Especially in the 1980s, the final decade of the Cold War, issues of catastrophe – from Ronald Reagan's Star Wars missile defense system to the nuclear facility explosion at Chernobyl, the arrival of the HIV/AIDS epidemic, and the ongoing disappearances and tortures marking Latin American dictatorships – all demanded that the constant intricate interplay between inside and outside, fantasy and reality, be theorized anew.[13] Moreover – and as the protractedly postponed but then growing engagement of analysts on both sides of the Atlantic in the 1980s with the longue-durée legacies of the Holocaust (for the children of survivors but also of perpetrators, as for the psychoanalytic movement itself) made all too painfully clear, ignoring the extrapsychic reality of the Holocaust in particular had been a major mistake, empirically-scientifically as well as, and most importantly, therapeutically.[14] The Tel Aviv-born but West German-trained Frankfurt-based psychoanalyst Sammy Speier put the problem perhaps most bluntly. Writing around the time that the IPA was finally going to be meeting on German soil, in Hamburg in 1985, a time filled with raging inter- and intragenerational struggles not just over German psychoanalysis' complicities during the Third Reich but also over the rigidities and silences in too many postwar training analyses, Speier observed caustically: "That we have an unacknowledged and un-worked-through history of mass murder behind us, is a state of affairs that we like to ignore." Pointedly, he continued: "Since 'Auschwitz,' a traditional concept of classical psychoanalysis in accordance with which fantasy trumps reality is no longer valid; since then it has been established that reality is frequently far worse than the most ferocious unconscious fantasies." More personally, he added: "Gradually it became clear to me, that behind my fear, and the fear of colleagues and patients, of asking questions of the psychoanalyst, of psychoanalysis, was not the fear of opening the door to the parents' bedroom, and being confronted by the 'primal scene,' but rather, more likely, the fear of opening the door to the gas chambers."[15] Notably, among the analysts whose work Speier found relevant to cite affirmatively were the Dutch-German sequential traumatization expert Hans Keilson and the British Kleinian psychosis specialist Herbert Rosenfeld, as well as Cremerius, the Parins, and the Mitscherlichs.

One contribution I hope this book will make is to redirect the conversation about the history of psychoanalysis and the political Left within the West. Numerous scholars have rehearsed the defeat of left-leaning psychoanalysis in the 1940s, including not just the expulsion of Reich from the official fold but also the plethora of inducements to self-censorship – in the USA, the UK, France, and Latin America – that help to explain why so much of the profession remained politically quiescent, if not, on many issues, reactionary. But rereading the work of individuals like Mitscherlich and Guattari and Parin and Morgenthaler – and the dozens they and others like them inspired – should change the way we write the history of psychoanalysis and the Left. That history was not over in the 1940s. Nor were, as of the 1950s and 1960s, such non-analysts as the Frankfurt School sociologist-philosopher Herbert Marcuse in *Eros and Civilization* and *One-Dimensional Man* or the American scholar Norman O. Brown in *Life Against Death* the only writers trying to revive it. There was a whole other wave taking shape in the later 1960s and through the 1970s and 1980s.

One reason we have missed it is that so much of the master narrative of psychoanalysis as a whole – aside from the work on Freud himself – has hinged on the American story. That emphasis has its good reasons, since nowhere was psychoanalysis more popularly and professionally successful than in the USA in the first two decades after World War II. But the effect has been to occlude from view much work done elsewhere. So many of the fruitless – and oft-recycled – debates between those appalled by what they see as either the enragingly offensive or loopily ludicrous aspects of psychoanalysis, and those who respond by mounting energetic defenses of psychoanalysis, whether on the grounds of intrinsic merit or breadth of cultural influence, turn on a rather limited set of characters. Thus the increasing marginalization of psychoanalysis that occurred in the USA from the 1970s on, as biomedical approaches regained the upper hand within psychiatry and as talk therapy was outsourced to less pricey professionals, is hailed as triumph for good sense by those who find (what they think is) psychoanalysis repellent, and seen as a terrible shame by those who wish to preserve a body of thought they find precious and endangered.[16] Both sides lose a chance to treat the history of psychoanalysis much as one would any other kind of intellectual or cultural history.[17] Yet the vital and serious questions posed by such individuals, including such exceptional postwar American individuals, as Stoller and Eissler, or those posed by key Europeans, from Keilson and Mitscherlich to Guattari to Parin and Morgenthaler, have, it bears pointing out, not lost any of their pertinence for our twenty-first-century present. And significantly, all of the answers they found utilized aspects of the Freudian inheritance.

The "massif central" of psychoanalysis, as the longtime Chilean-resident psychoanalytic psychotherapist David Becker observed with solemn candor in his book on torture and trauma, "remained internationally and also in Latin America that which it had become already so long ago: a professional association of therapists that did their best to stay clean."[18] This made the individuals who risked themselves and who put forward alternative visions all the more remarkable. Thus, one aim of *Cold War Freud* has been to recover those singular individuals that have either been forgotten or whose contributions have been generally misunderstood or misconstrued, in the hopes that they and their reflections and perceptions might be restored to the canon – not least because the ideas they put forward can still speak to us today.

The British biologist and Nobel Prize-winner Peter Medawar once referred to psychoanalysis as the "most stupendous intellectual confidence trick of the twentieth century."[19] The American literary critic Frederick Crews famously declared Freud to be "the most overrated figure in the entire history of science and medicine," someone "who wrought immense harm through the propagation of false etiologies, mistaken diagnoses, and fruitless lines of enquiry."[20] The mainstream media consensus in the USA, from at least the late 1980s – not coincidentally in the wake of the Food and Drug Administration's approval, in 1987, of Prozac (fluoxetine) for use as an antidepressant but also in the context of a wave of debates about whether Freud had failed his female patients when he (purportedly) gave up on the idea that many of their symptoms may have been the result of sexual abuse when they were children – was that Freud was not only long since literally dead, but that his ideas had become profoundly irrelevant in the fields of psychiatry and psychology. Freudian ideas might, at best, be found in departments of comparative literature or cultural studies. As the feminist activist Gloria Steinem said in the early 1990s at the height of the controversies over Freud's shifting views on the reality of child sexual abuse: "Sending a woman to a Freudian therapist ... is not so far distant from sending a Jew to a Nazi."[21] (Steinem soon enough modified her position, seeing value in feminist psychotherapy.)[22]

Nonetheless, there seemed to remain a great urgency about stating this irrelevance of Freud – or was it the danger of Freud? – again and again. As the *New York Times* asked in 1995, at the occasion of the major kerfuffle over whether or not to stage a Freud exhibit at the Library of Congress: if the wrongness of psychoanalysis had long since been so definitively proven, and psychiatry had already for quite some time been moving on to a more biochemical conceptualization of selfhood, why were the critics of the exhibit so determined to sabotage it entirely? Why keep beating this dead horse?[23] Or – as the journalist Ellen Willis asked ten years thereafter, in 2005 – what on earth might explain that "jocular uneasiness that afflicts the press when it contemplates the fact that Freud, buried so many times, refuses to die"?[24] Similarly, when *Newsweek* brought out a cover story at the occasion of the 150th anniversary of Freud's birth in 2006, the author noted that the for-so-long-delayed opening of the archives at the Library of Congress was leading "debunkers [to find] much to confirm what they've said all along, that his canonical 'cures' were the product of wishful thinking and conscious fudging, and his theories founded on a sinkhole of circular logic." Or as psychiatrist Peter D. Kramer put it to *Newsweek*, when asked whether Freud's ideas had any validity in light of the most up-to-date scientific knowledge: "I'm afraid he doesn't hold up very well at all ... It almost feels like a personal betrayal to say that. But every particular is wrong: the universality of the Oedipus complex, penis envy, infantile sexuality."[25] More recently yet, in 2011, when historian Joan Wallach Scott published *The Fantasy of Feminist History* – a book whose central conceptual argument, made in a scrupulously careful, at once empirically and theoretically grounded set of case studies, was that historians could benefit greatly from utilizing psychoanalytically informed interpretive methods – she was at pains to emphasize that there was a certain kind of psychoanalysis which was indeed appalling and which was not to be confused with the approach for which she was advocating. The psychoanalysis that Scott found productive "as a critical reading practice for history" was one attentive to the instability of all meanings. It was "not the psychoanalysis associated with normative prescription, not the psychoanalysis invoked to pathologize homosexuality, not the psychoanalysis that assigns individuals to categories."[26]

The psychoanalysis that was being referred to by these – variously – vituperatively dismissive, righteously indignant, inquisitively curious, self-distancing, or cautiously clarifying declarations – *the* psychoanalysis that everyone loves to hate – was, as it happens, only *one* kind of psychoanalysis. It was internationally influential, from the 1940s to the 1970s. But it was above all a product of the first half of the Cold War, particularly in the USA. And, as this book has aimed to show, there were numerous other forms and uses of psychoanalysis – many of them profoundly politically creative and morally engaged – that evolved in the postwar years.

As it turned out, in the postwar period there was an astonishing array of – often mutually incompatible – psychoanalytic concepts of human selfhood in circulation. Did healthy ego development depend on "sublimation" or "neutralization" – or, in another variant, on "desexualization" and "deaggressivization" – of the libidinal and destructive drives?[27] Or was the term "drive" – in Freud's definition of 1915, "the demand made upon the mind for work in consequence of its connection with the body" – not even the right way to think about the interrelationship between soma and psyche in the first place?[28] Maybe there was not only no such thing as a "death drive," but no such thing as a "sexual drive" either. Were humans, for example, far more powerfully motivated by anxiety and the search for security in a frequently threatening world?[29] Or was there, alternatively, another impulse just as, if not more, strongly motivating human beings – an impulse toward developing a coherence of self? Or maybe, within what looked like sex, they were also working through other kinds of traumas and longings entirely? How much did different cultures shape the egos that, for better or worse, eventually developed out of the inchoate muck of their residents' ids? Were human beings best understood as messes of unconscious terrors and the most bizarre fantasies, all too often on the edge of psychosis – in their quotidian interactions as in their geopolitics? There was, as it turned out, an extraordinary plasticity to the thought-system that evolved under the aegis of the name of Freud.

ACKNOWLEDGMENTS

I came to the writing of this book as a complete outsider to psychoanalysis. Five years in, it is a privilege to thank the numerous individuals that have entered my life because of it. The list of my debts is long.

Psychoanalysts, psychiatrists, and psychologists on both sides of the Atlantic were enormously generous interlocutors. I thank Gerald Adler, Salman Akhtar, Roberta Apfel, Sophinette Becker, Alexander Behringer, Ralf Binswanger, Marco Conci, James Dalsimer, John Frank, the late Sanford Gifford, Ulrich Gooss, Henry Greenspan, Herbert Gschwind, the late James Hansell, Lawrence Hartmann, Robert Krell, Nathan Kravis, Anton Kris, the late Henry Krystal, Kenneth Lewes, Joseph Lichtenberg, Paolo Migone, Warren Poland, Ilka Quindeau, Reimut Reiche, Johannes Reichmayr, Bennett Simon, and Falk Stakelbeck. Extra-special thanks go to Ayelet Barkai and John Barnhill for the durability of their friendships, for their patience with my many questions, and for facilitating ethnographic immersion in psychoanalytic worlds.

The staff at the Sigmund Freud Archives at the Library of Congress was unfailingly gracious and helpful during my many visits; so too were Marisa Shaari at the Oskar Diethelm Library at Weill Cornell, Olga Umansky at the Boston Psychoanalytic Society and Institute, Michael Simonson and Frank Mecklenburg at the Leo Baeck Institute, Agnes Katzenbach at the archive of the journal *Psyche: Zeitschrift für Psychoanalyse und ihre Anwendungen* in Frankfurt am Main, and Stephan Steiner at the Archiv der Sigmund Freud Privatuniversität Wien. Nellie Thompson reoriented me beautifully in one supremely efficient day at the New York Psychoanalytic Society and Institute.

Nancy Andreasen, Thomas Kohut, Esther Krystal, Marco and Jan Morgenthaler, Mark Seem, and Volkmar Sigusch shared unstintingly material from their personal archives.

Financial support, precious time, and marvelous environments for thinking and writing were provided by the John Simon Guggenheim Memorial Foundation, the School of Social Science at the Institute for Advanced Study, and the Shelby Cullom Davis Center for Historical Studies at Princeton University. At the Davis Center, I especially appreciated the intellectual engagement of David Bell, Philip Nord, Moshe Sluhovsky, and Keith Wailoo. The two first talks out of this project were delivered at Harvard, at the invitations of Nancy Cott and Peter Gordon, respectively. I thank them both not just for creating these occasions but also for long-running conversations about intellectual history from which I have learned much. I benefited greatly as well from the judicious counsel of Elizabeth Lunbeck. Subsequently, audiences at Brandeis, Columbia, Goucher, Illinois, Minnesota, New York University, Northwestern, Pacific Lutheran, Rutgers, Sewanee-University of the South, and the University of North Carolina, the Center for Jewish History, the Lessons and Legacies conference of the Holocaust Educational Foundation, the University of Basel, the European University Institute in Florence, the Institute for Queer Theory in Berlin, as well as psychiatric and psychoanalytic audiences at the Boston Psychoanalytic Society and Institute, the conference of the Deutsche Gesellschaft für Analytische Psychologie in Berlin, the Frankfurter Psychoanalytisches Institut, the Psychiatrische Universitätsklinik in Munich, Montefiore Medical Center, Weill Cornell Medicine, and the University Hospital of Psychiatry in Zurich transformed my understanding about matters large and small.

My students at the Graduate Center have been magnificent; I could not be luckier. For their indefatigable research assistance, I thank especially Lukasz Chelminski, Christopher Ewing, T. Scott Johnson, Julián González de León Heiblum, Nicholas Evangelos Levis, Chelsea Schields, Andrew Shield, Francesca Vassalle, and Ran Zwigenberg. No less gratitude goes to Helena Rosenblatt, Thomas Kessner, David Nasaw, James Oakes, and Gary Wilder for spectacular collegiality.

Earlier versions of chapters were previously published; permission to reprint is gratefully acknowledged here. A prior version of Chapter 2 appeared as "What Happened to Psychoanalysis in the Wake of the Sexual Revolution? A Story about the Durability of

Homophobia and the Dream of Love, 1950s–2010s," in Alessandra Lemma and Paul Lynch, eds., *Sexualities: Contemporary Psychoanalytic Perspectives* (New York: Routledge, 2015), 19–40. Another version of Chapter 3 appeared as "The Obscenity of Objectivity: Post-Holocaust Antisemitism and the Invention of Post-Traumatic Stress Disorder," in Nitzan Lebovic and Andreas Killen, eds., *Catastrophes: A History and Theory of an Operative Concept* (Boston: De Gruyter, 2014), 128–155. A shorter version of Chapter 4 was published as "'The Aggression Problems of Our Time': Psychoanalysis as Moral Politics in Post-Nazi Germany," in Matt ffytche and Daniel Pick, eds., *Psychoanalysis and Totalitarianism* (New York: Routledge, 2016), 87–101. A previous version of Chapter 5 appeared as "Desire's Politics: Félix Guattari and the Renewal of the Psychoanalytic Left," in *Psychoanalysis and History* 18/1 (2016), 7–37. Warm thanks to all the editors for the opportunities to test ideas and for their critical feedback and support.

Extraordinarily helpful readings of drafts of chapters or of the entire manuscript were provided by Ralf Binswanger, Jeffrey Escoffier, Stefanos Geroulanos, Nathan Kravis, Johannes Reichmayr, Camille Robcis, Joan Scott, Todd Shepard, Judith Surkis, and Andrew Zimmerman. For essential relevant discussions and for their ever-inspirational mentorship and friendship, I also thank Omer Bartov, Deborah Cohen, Geoff Eley, the late John Forrester, Brad Prager, Anson Rabinbach, Detlef Siegfried, and Zev and Alice Weiss.

Close by in the neighborhood, the Kucich-Sadoff and Bilsky-Rollins homes were terrific havens for laughter and critical thinking alike. And, for recurrently providing the most wonderful homes away from home I thank, from the bottom of my heart, Gunter Schmidt and Karin Renter, Markus and Babette Borgert, Pascal Strupler and Cornelia Theler. I am grateful to all for many clarifying conversations about the politics of psychology and the psychology of politics alike.

The following individuals know, I trust, how steadfastly I love them. I would be lost without the sturdy friendships of Caroline Arni, Jonathan Fine, and William Kelly. During the time this book was being written, Brendan Hart and Anne Montgomery started a family of their own; I am so glad that, together with Isaiah, they continue to be connected to ours. Finally, deepest love and thanks go to Michael and Lucy Staub for making the adventure that is a shared life so endlessly interesting. You are the reasons for everything.

NOTES

Introduction

1 Ernest Jones, "Opening Address by the President, Dr. Ernest Jones," reprinted in Anna Freud, "Report on the Sixteenth International Psycho-Analytical Congress," *Bulletin of the International Psycho-Analytical Association* 30 (1949): 178–179.
2 Riccardo Steiner, "The (Ir)resistible Lightness of Our Past" (paper delivered November 28, 1998), available at: http://psychoanalysis.org.uk/articles/the-irresistible-lightness-of-our-past-riccardo-steiner (accessed January 29, 2016).
3 Jones, "Opening Address," 178–179; on the complex situation of the Freuds in relation to Reich, see Riccardo Steiner, *"It is a New Kind of Diaspora": Explorations in the Sociopolitical and Cultural Context of Psychoanalysis* (London: Karnac, 2000).
4 "Social Orientation Urged on Freudians," *New York Times* (July 28, 1971): 38; "Analyst Favors Expanding Base of Freud's Theories," *Kansas City Times* (July 28, 1971): 12; Alden Whitman, "Revision in Father's Theory is Proposed by Anna Freud," *International Herald Tribune* (July 31–August 1, 1971): 5. Also quoted in the Paris edition of the *Herald Tribune*, July 29–31, 1971, cited in Erich Fromm, *The Anatomy of Human Destructiveness* (New York: Henry Holt, 1973), 205fn22.
5 "Analyst Favors," 12.
6 See the text of Mitscherlich's formal presentation at the congress: Alexander Mitscherlich, "Psychoanalysis and the Aggression of Large Groups," *International Journal of Psycho-Analysis* 52 (1971): 161–167. The published text of the presentation does not include the "all our theories" remark that had been carried in the press.
7 "Analyst Favors," 12.
8 "Social Orientation," 38.
9 On American predominance at the IPA meeting in Rome in 1969, see the remark ("they [the Americans] made up almost half the participants")

in Marianna Bolko and Berthold Rothschild, "A 'flea in one's ear': An account of the Counter-Congress of the *International Psychoanalytic Association* of 1969 in Rome" (2006), available at: eupsycho.com/Volume_03/Numero_1/TM_2015-1_3-BolkoRothschild_pp13-26.pdf (accessed January 29, 2016), 21. There had been 1,500 registrants for the Rome conference. See Frances H. Gitelson, "Report of the 27th International Psycho-Analytical Congress," *Bulletin of the International Psychoanalytical Association* 53 (1972): 90. Even into the 1980s, the US contingent within the IPA membership was approximately one-third. See Judith M. Hughes, "American Exceptionalism: A Challenge to an International Movement," in Peter Loewenberg and Nellie L. Thompson, eds., *100 Years of the IPA: The Centenary History of the International Psychoanalytical Association 1910–2010* (London: International Psychoanalytical Association, 2011), 244–259, esp. 256.

10 See Gigi Ghirotti, "Si è aperto all'insegna della contestazione il Congresso internazionale di psico-analisi," *La Stampa* (July 29, 1969): 2; Gigi Ghirotti, "Psicanalisti, tutti 'da Carlino,'" *La Stampa* (July 30, 1969): 2; Marianna Bolko, "Psicoanalisi e psicoanalisti (1973)," *Psicoterapia e Scienze Umane* 9.4 (1975): 20–31; Berthold Rothschild, "'Plataforma' in den letzten zwanzig Jahren (Vortrag anlässlich des 20. Jubiläums ihrer Gründung, 10.–12. Nov. 1989 in Rom)," *Luzifer-Amor* (1993): 55–62; Paolo Migone, "I venti anni di 'Plataforma Internacional,'" *Il ruolo terapeutico* 53 (1990): 41–43; and the interview with Ursula Hauser by Mathias Morgenthaler, "'Ich verdiente nichts und lebte von Reis und Bohnen,'" *Tagesanzeiger* (August 3, 2013), available at: http://blog.tagesanzeiger.ch/berufung/index.php/2012/ich-verdiente-nichts-und-lebte-von-reis-und-bohnen/ (accessed January 29, 1969).

11 Bolko and Rothschild, "A 'flea,'" 22.

12 Alexander Mitscherlich, "Introduction to Panel on Protest and Revolution," *International Journal of Psycho-Analysis* 50 (1969): 103–108; see also Alexander Mitscherlich and John J. Francis, "Panel on 'Protest and Revolution,'" *International Journal of Psycho-Analysis* 51 (1970): 211–218.

13 See the comments by Arnaldo Rascovsky, Léon Grinberg, and others in Frances H. Gitelson, "Report of the 26th International Psycho-Analytical Congress," *Bulletin of the International Psychoanalytical Association* 51 (1970): 133–137.

14 The Argentineans that had been most active in the counter-congress were Armando Bauleo and Hernán Kesselman; later the venerable Austrian-Argentinean psychoanalyst Marie Langer (who had been Bauleo and Kesselman's own analyst) was another of the most active figures in Plataforma, and in her blending of Freud and Marx and in her personal manner she was adored by, and a huge inspiration for, also many younger Europeans. Eighteen Argentineans, led by Langer, joined Plataforma and, at the same time, formally cut their ties to both the IPA and its Argentine member association. See Marie Langer et al., "Psychoanalyse zwecks Sozialismus," *Neues Forum* (March 1972): 39–40. Langer is a complex and significant figure. In the 1950s, her work on motherhood and infertility was both problematic in its emphasis on psychogenic sources of infertility and could be considered more generally conservative; by 1971, at the Vienna IPA, she was a major proponent

of a left-wing renewal; in the 1980s, having fled the Argentinean dictatorship for Mexico in 1975 (a patient had revealed to her that she was on the
regime's "death list"), she worked on mental health projects for the Sandinistas in Nicaragua – and also provided long-distance support and "supervision"
for psychotherapists working with torture victims in Chile. For a sample of
her work on infertility, see Marie Langer, "Sterility and Envy," *International
Journal of Psycho-Analysis* 39 (1958): 139–143. For her own account of her
repoliticization in the context of the international youth revolt of the later
1960s, see Marie Langer, "Psychoanalyse – in wessen Dienst?" *Neues Forum*
(September–October 1971): 39–42. For an example of an interview in which
Langer is pushed to address her earlier conservatism with regard to women's
sexuality, see Carmen Lugo, "Marie Langer: Ideología y Psicoanálisis," *Fem*
1.1 (1976): 35–38. An enthusiastic portrait of Langer is provided in Nancy
Caro Hollander, *Love in a Time of Hate: Liberation Psychology in Latin
America* (New Brunswick: Rutgers University Press, 1997). On Langer's more
conservative earlier postwar work, and the threat to her life, see Mariano Ben
Plotkin, *Freud in the Pampas: The Emergence and Development of a Psychoanalytic Culture in Argentina* (Stanford: Stanford University Press, 2001), 76,
91, 94, 200, 218; and Rachel Greenspan's dissertation-in-progress at Duke
University. On her later meaning for left-leaning Europeans, see Johannes
Reichmayr, "Bilder aus unserem Lateinamerika-Album," *Werkblatt* 29/30
(1992): 7–25; and the obituary by Gertraud Migsch and Jutta Rainer, "Zum
Tod von Marie Langer," *Werkblatt* 14/15 (1988), 6–9. For a poignant reflec-
tion on the emotional sustenance provided by her support of the Chileans, see
David Becker, *Die Erfindung des Traumas – Verflochtene Geschichten* (Freiburg: Edition Freitag, 2006), 89–90, 225–227. For retrospective ambivalence
about Langer, see the interview with Ursula Hauser by Marta Vardynets and
Mariia Demianchuk, "An Attempt to Capture Goldy Parin-Matthey" (February 24, 2012), available at: http://media.wix.com/ugd/828439_6d43f9a475e-
16dd89063eecadf0c146c.pdf (accessed July 30, 2016).

15 See Aline Rubin, Belinda Mandelbaum, and Stephen Frosh, "'No Memory, No Desire': Psychoanalysis in Brazil During Repressive Times," *Psychoanalysis and History* 18.1 (2016): 93–118; Becker, *Die Erfindung*, 89;
Sergio Lewkowicz and Silvia Flechner, eds., *Truth, Reality, and the Psychoanalyst: Latin American Contributions to Psychoanalysis* (London: Karnac, 2005); Mariano Ben Plotkin and Joy Damousi, eds., *Psychoanalysis
and Politics: Histories of Psychoanalysis Under Conditions of Restricted
Political Freedom* (New York: Oxford University Press, 2012).

16 For example, see Sherry Turkle, *Psychoanalytic Politics: Freud's French
Revolution* (New York: Basic, 1978); Camille Robcis, *The Law of Kinship: Anthropology, Psychoanalysis, and the Family in France* (Ithaca: Cornell University Press, 2013); Marco Conci, "Gaetano Benedetti, Johannes
Cremerius, the Milan ASP, and the future of the IFPS," *International Forum
of Psychoanalysis* 23 (2014): 85–95

17 See the finding aid: http://rs5.loc.gov/service/mss/eadxmlmss/eadpdfmss/
2004/ms004017.pdf (accessed January 29, 2016).

18 John C. Burnham, "The 'New Freud Studies': A Historiographical Shift,"
Journal of the Historical Society 6.2 (2006): 213–233, here 213–214.

19 See in this context especially the eloquent and succinct account in Daniel Pick, *Psychoanalysis: A Very Short Introduction* (Oxford: Oxford University Press, 2015).

20 Dinitia Smith, "Freud May Be Dead, But His Critics Still Kick," *New York Times* (December 10, 1995), available at: www.nytimes.com/1995/12/10/weekinreview/idead-trends-freud-may-be-dead-but-his-critics-still-kick.html (accessed January 29, 2016); Michael S. Roth, *Freud: Conflict and Culture* (New York: Knopf, 1998); Mikkel Borch-Jacobsen and Sonu Shamdasani, *The Freud Files: An Inquiry into the History of Psychoanalysis* (Cambridge: Cambridge University Press, 2012).

21 Sander Gilman, *Freud, Race, and Gender* (Princeton: Princeton University Press, 1993). For one example among many following this thread, see Daniel Boyarin, "Freud's Baby, Fliess's Maybe: Homophobia, Anti-Semitism, and the Invention of Oedipus," in Diana Fuss, ed., *Pink Freud* (special issue of *GLQ*) 2.1–2 (1995): 115–147.

22 Mari Jo Buhle, *Feminism and Its Discontents: A Century of Struggle with Psychoanalysis* (Cambridge, MA: Harvard University Press, 1998); Eli Zaretsky, *Secrets of the Soul: A Social and Cultural History of Psychoanalysis* (New York: Knopf, 2004).

23 The example Burnham gave was of Freud's longtime and intimate but later denigrated associate Sándor Ferenczi, based in Budapest, whose role in the formulation of Freud's ideas, as well as in alternative but enormously generative innovations in clinical style all his own, had been systematically underacknowledged for much of the post-Freud era.

24 George Makari, *Revolution in Mind: The Creation of Psychoanalysis* (New York: Harper Perennial, 2008).

25 John C. Burnham, ed., *After Freud Left: A Century of Psychoanalysis in America* (Chicago: University of Chicago Press, 2012).

26 John Forrester, "Editorial," *Psychoanalysis and History* 16.1 (2014): 1–2.

27 Matt ffytche, "Editorial," *Psychoanalysis and History* 18.1 (2016): 1.

28 For these and additional signally important contributions, see: Stephen Frosh, *Hate and the "Jewish Science": Anti-Semitism, Nazism and Psychoanalysis* (New York: Palgrave Macmillan, 2005); Veronika Fuechtner, *Berlin Psychoanalytic: Psychoanalysis and Culture in Weimar Republic Germany and Beyond* (Berkeley: University of California Press, 2011); Daniel Pick, *In Pursuit of the Nazi Mind: Hitler, Hess, and the Analysts* (Oxford: Oxford University Press, 2012); Camille Robcis, *The Law of Kinship: Anthropology, Psychoanalysis, and the Family in France* (Ithaca: Cornell University Press, 2013); Michal Shapira, *The War Inside: Psychoanalysis, Total War and the Making of the Democratic Self in Postwar Britain* (Cambridge, UK: Cambridge University Press, 2013); Elizabeth Lunbeck, *The Americanization of Narcissism* (Cambridge, MA: Harvard University Press, 2014); Emily A. Kuriloff, *Contemporary Psychoanalysis and the Legacy of the Third Reich: History, Memory, Tradition* (New York: Routledge, 2014); Erik Linstrum, *Ruling Minds: Psychology in the British Empire* (Cambridge, MA: Harvard University Press, 2016); Mariano Ben Plotkin and Joy Damousi, eds., *The Transnational Unconscious: Essays in the History of Psychoanalysis and Transnationalism* (New York: Palgrave Macmillan, 2009); Plotkin and Damousi, *Psychoanalysis and Politics;* Warwick

Anderson, Deborah Jenson, and Richard C. Keller, eds., *Unconscious Dominions: Psychoanalysis, Colonial Trauma, and Global Sovereignties* (Durham: Duke University Press, 2011).

29 Omnia El Shakry, "The Arabic Freud: The Unconscious and the Modern Subject," *Modern Intellectual History* 11.1 (2014): 89–118.

30 Lewis Aron and Karen Starr, *A Psychotherapy for the People: Toward a Progressive Psychoanalysis* (London: Routledge, 2013): Eli Zaretsky, *Political Freud: A History* (New York: Columbia University Press, 2015).

31 Fuss, *Pink Freud*.

32 For example, see Christopher Lane and Tim Dean, eds., *Homosexuality and Psychoanalysis* (Chicago: University of Chicago Press, 2001); Ann Pellegrini, Daniel Boyarin, and Daniel Itzkovitz, eds., *Queer Theory and the Jewish Question* (New York: Columbia University Press, 2003); Jack Drescher and Vittorio Lingiardi, eds., *The Mental Health Professions and Homosexuality: International Perspectives* (New York: Haworth, 2003); Lee Edelman, *No Future: Queer Theory and the Death Drive* (Durham: Duke University Press, 2004); Jack Drescher and Joseph P. Merlino, eds., *American Psychiatry and Homosexuality: An Oral History* (New York: Harrington Park, 2007); Teresa de Lauretis, *Freud's Drive: Psychoanalysis, Literature, and Film* (New York: Palgrave Macmillan, 2008); Leo Bersani, *Is the Rectum a Grave? And Other Essays* (Chicago: University of Chicago Press, 2010); Alessandra Lemma and Paul E. Lynch, eds., *Sexualities: Contemporary Psychoanalytic Perspectives* (New York: Routledge, 2015).

33 Philip Rieff, *The Triumph of the Therapeutic: Uses of Faith after Freud* (New York: Harper & Row, 1966), 31.

34 See on this point Mitscherlich's recovery of an astute comment made by the overtly political Otto Fenichel in a critical review of Edward Glover's *War, Sadism, and Pacifism* (1933). As Mitscherlich summarizes: "Adducing Freud, Fenichel warns against an uncritical expansion of psychoanalytic interpretation into areas that are not open to direct psychoanalytic observation and in which the analyst may be insufficiently familiar with the relevant research methods and findings. The consequence is that 'even in areas where psychological inquiry as such would be legitimate, the wrong questions are asked.' Concerning collective aggressive behaviour, without which war is unthinkable, Fenichel writes: 'It may be that without an aggressive instinctual drive of the masses, warfare would be impossible. But the aggressive drive does not specifically aim at war. However, for its activity in a number of people to take the form of warfare, the "apparatus of society" must be functioning in certain specific ways. The aggressive drive would not lead to war if the realities were different. The single individual does not go to war because he has failed to sublimate his aggressive drive, but because – thanks to existing systems, for instance imperialism – he is forced either directly or by trickery into doing so.' " Mitscherlich, "Psychoanalysis and the Aggression of Large Groups," 164. Yet note also how the Turkish-American psychoanalyst Vamik Volkan, active in conflict resolution teams in many parts of the world, answers in the affirmative the rhetorical question in his subtitle, "Individual and Large-Group Identities: Does Working With Borderline Patients Teach Us

Anything about International Negotiations?" (2007), available at: www.
vamikvolkan.com/Ind%FDvidual-and-Large-group-Identities%3A-
Does-Working-with-Borderline-Patients-Teach-Us-Anything-About-
International-Negotiations-.php (accessed January 29, 2016).

35 For an especially interesting assessment, see Jan Abram, "DWW's Notes
for the Vienna Congress 1971: A Consideration of Winnicott's Theory of
Aggression and Interpretation of the Clinical Implications," in Jan Abram,
ed., *Donald Winnicott Today* (London & New York: Routledge, 2012),
302–330. For a defense of Winnicott as a political thinker, see Sally Alexander, "D. W. Winnicott and the Social Democratic Vision," in Matt fftyche
and Daniel Pick, eds., *Psychoanalysis in the Age of Totalitarianism* (London: Routledge, 2016), 114–130. For an example of French reception
of Winnicott, see André Green, *On Private Madness* (London: Hogarth,
1986); and André Green, *André Green at the Squiggle Foundation* (London: Karnac, 2000).

36 On historicizing moral reasoning, cf. Jan Goldstein, "Toward an Empirical
History of Moral Thinking: The Case of Racial Theory in Mid-Nineteenth-
Century France" (Presidential Address to the American Historical
Association, January 3, 2015), available at: www.historians.org/about-
aha-and-membership/aha-history-and-archives/presidential-addresses/jan-
e-goldstein (accessed January 29, 2016).

37 Janet Malcolm, *In the Freud Archives* (New York: Knopf, 1983).

38 Dagmar Herzog, *Sexuality in Europe: A Twentieth-Century History*
(Cambridge, UK: Cambridge University Press, 2011).

39 For example, see Franz Alexander, "Mental Hygiene in the Atomic Age"
(1946), in *The Scope of Psychoanalysis: 1921–1961* (New York: Basic
Books, 1961), 454; and Robert Jay Lifton, "The Sense of Immortality: On
Death and the Continuity of Life," *American Journal of Psychoanalysis* 33
(1973): 3–4.

40 On the absolutely essential role of conservative thinkers in promoting
Freudianism in the postwar USA, see Matt fftyche, "Freud and the Neo-
cons: The Narrative of a Political Encounter from 1949–2000," *Psychoanalysis and History* 15 (2013): 5–44.

1 The Libido Wars

1 Karen Horney, *The Neurotic Personality of Our Time* (New York: Norton,
1937), 157.

2 The classic text here is Will Herberg, *Protestant-Catholic-Jew: An Essay
in American Religious Sociology*, 2nd ed. (New York: Anchor Books,
1960). See also Kevin Kruse, *One Nation Under God: How Corporate
America Invented Christian America* (New York: Basic Books, 2015) –
as well as Norman Vincent Peale, *The Power of Positive Thinking*
(New York: Prentice-Hall, 1952).

3 Cf. Lewis Aron and Karen E. Starr, *A Psychotherapy for the People*
(New York: Routledge, 2013), as well as: David Hollinger, "Jewish Intellectuals and the De-Christianization of American Public Culture in the

Twentieth Century," in *Science, Jews, and Secular Culture: Studies in Mid-Twentieth-Century American Intellectual History* (Princeton: Princeton University Press, 1996); and Edward Shorter, "The Psychoanalytic Hiatus," in *A History of Psychiatry: From the Era of the Asylum to the Age of Prozac* (New York: John Wiley & Sons, Inc, 1997), 145–189. Psychoanalyst Lawrence Kubie refers to psychoanalysis as "the Jewish science" already in 1936, a point also noted in Franz Alexander's review of Kubie's book: Franz Alexander, "Practical Aspects of Psychoanalysis," *Psychoanalytic Quarterly*, 5 (1936): 283–289, here 288.

4   The relationship between psychoanalysis and religion in the postwar USA has been under-studied. It has mainly been approached from the perspective of scholars of Catholicism concerned with how Catholicism became "psychologized." The books by C. Kevin Gillespie, S.J. and Robert Kugelmann are most helpful for the US story; Agnès Desmazières has worked in the Vatican archives and, in addition to giving some attention to the USA, has done a superb job exploring the activism of psychoanalytically interested priests and laity in Belgium, France, the Netherlands, and Italy: C. Kevin Gillespie, S.J., *Psychology and American Catholicism: From Confession to Therapy?* (New York: Crossroad, 2001); Robert Kugelmann, *Psychology and Catholicism: Contested Boundaries* (New York: Cambridge University Press, 2011); and Agnès Desmazières, *L'Inconscient au paradis: comment les catholiques ont reçu la psychanalyse, 1920–1965* (Paris: Payot, 2011). Very useful points about the modernization of American Catholicism can be found in Abraham Nussbaum, "Profession and Faith: The National Guild of Catholic Psychiatrists, 1950–1968," *Catholic Historical Review* 93.4 (October 2007): 845–865.

5   One retrospective commentator noted: "Hartmann's influence on contemporary analysis seems at an all time low, and when cited, it is rarely for contributions, but as representative of all that was wrong with American psychoanalysis during its halcyon days – the 40s, 50s and 60s": Martin Schulman, review of Martin S. Bergmann, ed., *The Hartmann Era*, in *Division 39* (Summer 2002), available at: www.apadivisions.org/division-39/publications/reviews/hartmann.aspx (last accessed January 15, 2016). Yale Kramer cites the years 1945–1965 as the "golden age." Yale Kramer, "Freud and the Culture Wars," *Public Interest* 124 (1996): 44. See also Neil G. McLaughlin, "Why Do Schools of Thought Fail? Neo-Freudianism as a Case Study in the Sociology of Knowledge," *Journal of the History of the Behavioral Sciences* 34.2 (Spring 1998): 113–134.

6   On the cheekily (or crassly) pro-sex bohemian version of psychoanalysis promoted in the USA, and especially in Greenwich Village, in the 1910s–1920s and the debates associated with such names as André Tridon, Floyd Dell, V. F. Calverton, and Samuel D. Schmalhausen – including their ongoing ambivalence about female sexual agency, see Mari Jo Buhle, *Feminism and its Discontents: A Century of Struggle with Psychoanalysis* (Cambridge, MA: Harvard University Press, 1998), 93–98; Elizabeth Wilson, "Bohemian Love," *Theory, Culture & Society* 15.3 (1998): 111–127; and Nancy Cott, "Revisiting the Transatlantic 1920s: Vincent Sheean vs. Malcolm Cowley," *American Historical Review* 118 (February 2013): 65–67. Malcolm Cowley's spoof of 1930 already marks the end of the era

of enthusiasm: Malcolm Cowley, "Oedipus: The Future of Love," *New Republic* (August 20, 1930): 14–16.

7 Clara Thompson, "Ferenczi's Contribution to Psychoanalysis," *Psychiatry* 7.3 (August 1, 1944): 245–252; Kurt Eissler, "Remarks on the Psycho-Analysis of Schizophrenia," *International Journal of Psycho-Analysis* 32 (1951): 139–156; Gail A. Hornstein, *To Redeem One Person Is to Redeem the World: The Life of Frieda Fromm-Reichmann* (New York: Free Press, 2000).

8 Franz Alexander, "Mental Hygiene in the Atomic Age," in *The Scope of Psychoanalysis, 1921–1961: Selected Papers* (New York: Basic, 1961), 454.

9 See Harry Stack Sullivan, *Conceptions of Modern Psychiatry* (New York: Norton, 1940); Harry Stack Sullivan, *The Interpersonal Theory of Psychiatry* (New York: Norton, 1953); cf. Buhle, *Feminism and its Discontents*, 115; and Marco Conci, *Sullivan Revisited – Life and Work: Harry Stack Sullivan's Relevance for Contemporary Psychiatry, Psychotherapy and Psychoanalysis*, 2nd ed. (Trento: Tangram Edizioni Scientifiche, 2012).

10 For Fromm, the notion that personal agency and effort mattered was in most cases a pernicious lie. "The adult is told he can achieve anything that he wishes, if he only wants it enough and makes an effort, and he is as responsible for his success as for his failure. Life is presented as a great game in which first and foremost not coincidence but rather his own skill, own diligence and own energy are decisive. These ideologies are starkly contradicted by the factual situation. The average adult in our society is in reality extraordinarily powerless, and this powerlessness has the even more oppressive effect in that he is made to believe that things should actually be completely different and it is his fault if he is so weak." Moreover: "In authoritarian states the incapacity to have any influence is raised up to a conscious principle. But also in democracies there is an extraordinary discrepancy between the ideological notion that the individual member of society can help as a part of the whole to determine the fate of the whole and the actual gulf which separates the individual from the centers of political and economic power." In short, comprehension of causation within this actual state of affairs perpetually eluded the ordinary citizen. The average individual, also in the middle class, could not, Fromm averred, understand the "complicated economic and political processes" and "determinative forces in a market-based economy"; these processes and forces instead seemed "indecipherable," like "inscrutable powers of fate." Erich Fromm, "Zum Gefühl der Ohnmacht," *Zeitschrift für Sozialforschung* 6 (1937): 95–119, here 113–114.

11 Horney, *The Neurotic Personality*, 288, 284, 20. Horney's main argument had to do with the idea that everyone was walking around with repressed (and hence unconscious) hostilities and that it was these, in combination with the defenses against them, that were the source of constant anxiety; and "it remains one of Freud's great achievements to have seen the role of rivalry in the family, as expressed in his concept of the Oedipus complex and in other hypotheses. It must be added, however, that this rivalry itself is not biologically conditioned but is a result of given cultural conditions and, furthermore, that the family situation is not the only one to

stir up rivalry, but that the competitive stimuli are active from the cradle to the grave" (285). Moreover: "All these factors together – competitiveness and its potential hostilities between fellow-beings, fears, diminished self-esteem – result psychologically in the individual feeling that he is isolated ... It is this situation which provokes, in the normal individual of our time, an intensified need for affection as a remedy ... Because it corresponds to a vital need, love is overvalued in our culture ... And the ideological emphasis that we place on love serves to cover up the factors which create our exaggerated need for it. Hence the individual – and I still mean the normal individual – is in the dilemma of needing a great deal of affection but finding difficulty in obtaining it" (286–287).

12 Karen Horney, *New Ways in Psychoanalysis* (New York: Norton, 1939), 9–10, 48, 52.

13 Karen Horney, "The Flight from Womanhood: The Masculinity-Complex in Women, as Viewed by Men and by Women," *International Journal of Psycho-Analysis* 7 (1926): 324–339, here 331. See also her daughter's retrospective reflections: Marianne Horney Eckardt, "Feminine Psychology Revisited: A Historical Perspective," *American Journal of Psychoanalysis*, 51 (1991): 235–243.

14 Karen Horney, "The Problem of the Monogamous Ideal," *International Journal of Psycho-Analysis* 9 (1928): 318–331.

15 Horney, "The Problem of the Monogamous Ideal." Horney described the "desire for monopoly" of the partner as a "derivative of the oral phase, when it takes the form of the desire to incorporate the object in order to have sole possession of it. Often, even to ordinary observation, it betrays its origin in the greed of possession which not only grudges the partner any other erotic experience, but is also jealous of his or her friends, work or interests." (Here too, as was so often her wont, she managed to slide in a tiny feminist dig in a speculative aside to the effect that this unconscious oral origin might explain even better than consciously articulated reasons could why it was that "men have not only actually succeeded in enforcing the naïve and complete demand for monogamous fidelity upon their wives more energetically than women have upon their husbands, but that the instinct to claim monopoly is stronger in men.")

16 Horney, *The Neurotic Personality*, 157–158.

17 Horney, *The Neurotic Personality*, x, 61, 63, 75.

18 For example, Sigmund Freud, "Inhibitions, Symptoms and Anxiety" (1926), in *The Standard Edition of the Complete Psychological Works of Sigmund Freud*, vol. xx (1925–1926), 75–176.

19 Horney, *The Neurotic Personality*, 15.

20 Horney, *New Ways in Psychoanalysis*, 10.

21 Horney, *The Neurotic Personality*, 149. For example, in her chapter on "The Role of Sexuality in the Neurotic Need for Affection," she says "Moreover, if we accept Freud's assumption that dissatisfied libido is the driving force for seeking affection, it would scarcely be understandable why we find the same craving for affection, with all the complications described – possessiveness, unconditional love, not feeling wanted, etc. – in persons whose sexual life from the physical point of view is entirely satisfactory." And then Horney adds the acerbic footnote: "Cases like these,

with definite disturbances in the emotional sphere coexisting with a capacity for full sexual satisfaction, have always been a puzzle to some analysts, but the fact that they do not fit into the libido theory does not keep them from existing" (149).

22 Horney, *The Neurotic Personality*, 159.

23 Erich Fromm, *Escape from Freedom* (New York: Avon, 1969 [orig. 1941]), 318, 24, 32–33, 172, 319, 200, 269.

24 The Association for the Advancement of Psychoanalysis [Karen Horney], "Understanding of Individual Panic," *American Journal of Psychoanalysis*, 2 (1942): 40–41; Susan Tyler Hitchcock, *Karen Horney: Pioneer of Feminine Psychology* (New York: Chelsea House, 2005), 83.

25 John Dollard, *Caste and Class in a Southern Town* (New York: Harper, 1937).

26 Leonard S. Cottrell, Jr., "Review of Horney, *New Ways in Psychoanalysis*," *American Journal of Sociology* 44.6 (May 1939): 997–999; Joseph K. Folsom, "Review of *New Ways in Psychoanalysis* (and eight other books)," *American Sociological Review* 4.6 (December 1939): 876–879, here 876–877.

27 Initially, Kubie had been torn and more moderate on Horney – in fact, Kubie could be seen as himself an intermittent dissenter – but especially Fritz Wittels pushed him to turn on her. Wittels complained that because Horney's work was so "avidly read by social workers, politically minded laymen and by critics of the *New York Times* ... forty years of patient scientific work were thrown to the dogs." See Susan Quinn, *A Mind of Her Own: The Life of Karen Horney* (New York: Simon and Schuster, 1987); and Nathan G. Hale, *The Rise and Crisis of Psychoanalysis in the United States: Freud and the Americans, 1917–1985* (New York: Oxford University Press, 1995), 142–143. Intriguingly, in a letter nearly a decade later, Kubie expressed his ongoing sense of "muddle" about whether there were such distinct entities as id, ego, and superego at all. Kubie to Karl Menninger, June 27, 1950, reprinted in *The Selected Correspondence of Karl A. Menninger, 1945–1965*, ed. Howard J. Faulkner and Virginia D. Pruitt (Columbia: University of Missouri Press, 1995), 97–98.

28 "Statement on Behalf of the New York Psychoanalytic Society and Institute," *Psychoanalytic Review* 29 (1942): 222–232.

29 Karl Menninger quoted in Hitchcock, *Karen Horney*, 89. As Hitchcock notes: "He meant Karen Horney." Hitchcock also explains the immense consequences of the Horney group's exclusion from the American Psychoanalytic Association's approbation: "Without acceptance at the national level, their training did not qualify students for official positions as analysts, their research would not be accepted by major journals, and their members would not be invited to meetings and conventions" (90).

30 "For the Psyche," *Time* (September 2, 1946), 73–74, here 73.

31 An interesting early affirmative appropriation of Horney by Karl Menninger can be found in Karl A. Menninger, "Polysurgery and Polysurgical Addiction," *Psychoanalytic Quarterly* 3 (1934): 173–199. Here he described her 1933 essay "The Denial of the Vagina" as "clearly expounded" (181–182). He also cited her paper "Female Masochism" – which he had hear her deliver and which he discussed with her in person

in 1933 – as he contended that "The theme developed by Horney, referred to above, may make it necessary to exalt this masochistic element of the wish to be castrated to the dignity of a separate category, for it is certainly true that to be driven to surgery for the purpose of suffering, to suffering for the purpose of obtaining pity and to the seeking of pity as a substitute for love is a psychological trend quite different from secondary (masochistic) erotization of punitive suffering as a device for making the best of a bad bargain" (198). Zilboorg's patronizing of Horney as seriously naive in her dismissal of the instincts ("the denial of the totality of the biological forces"), her "voluntaristic, sociological philosophy" and "exclusivistic culturalism," as well as the "anthropocentric idealism" he found intrinsic to her belief in free will, can be found in Gregory Zilboorg, "The Fundamental Conflict with Psycho-Analysis," *International Journal of Psycho-Analysis* 20 (1939): 480–492, here 488–489, 491; and Gregory Zilboorg, "The Sense of Reality," *Psychoanalytic Quarterly* 10 (1941): 183–210, here 209.

32 Russell Jacoby, *The Repression of Psychoanalysis: Otto Fenichel and the Political Freudians* (New York: Basic, 1983); Eli Zaretsky, *Secrets of the Soul: A Social and Cultural History of Psychoanalysis* (New York: Knopf, 2004). Psychoanalyst Judith Hughes observed recently that "Years later, Americans would pay a heavy price for the gender bias that hostility to lay analysis entailed. For where lay analysis flourished, so too did female analysts ... By the 1970s American psychoanalysis found itself, thanks to its continued insistence on a medical degree ... in a professional cul-de-sac; it found itself in an intellectual cul-de-sac as well." Judith M. Hughes, "American Exceptionalism: A Challenge to an International Movement," in Peter Loewenberg and Nellie L. Thompson, eds., *100 Years of the IPA: The Centenary History of the International Psychoanalytical Association 1910–2010* (London: International Psychoanalytical Association, 2011), 244–259, here 249–250.

33 Russell Jacoby, "The Lost Freudian Left," *The Nation* (October 15, 1983), 344.

34 Louis Menand, "Freud, Anxiety, and the Cold War," in John Burnham, ed., *After Freud Left: A Century of Psychoanalysis in America* (Chicago: University of Chicago Press, 2012); Elizabeth Ann Danto, "'Have You No Shame?' – American Redbaiting of Europe's Psychoanalysts," in Joy Damousi and Mariano Ben Plotkin, eds., *Psychoanalysis and Politics: Histories of Psychoanalysis under Conditions of Restricted Political Freedom* (New York: Oxford University Press), 213–231.

35 Emily Kuriloff, "Revelations in Psychoanalytic History," review of George Makari, *Revolution in Mind: The Creation of Psychoanalysis*, *Contemporary Psychoanalysis* 45 (2009): 577–580, here 580; Aron and Starr, *A Psychotherapy for the People*, 111.

36 See in this context also the devastating assessment of prominent American psychoanalysts' views on female adolescence in Rachel Devlin, *Relative Intimacy: Fathers, Adolescent Daughters, and Postwar American Culture* (Chapel Hill: University of North Carolina Press, 2005).

37 Herbert Marcuse, *Eros and Civilization: A Philosophical Inquiry into Freud* (New York: Vintage, 1955); Norman O. Brown, *Life Against Death: The Psychoanalytical Meaning of History* (New York: Vintage, 1959).

38 Another variant on this trend involved the reinterpretation of the classic developmental stages of the libido (oral, anal, phallic, etc.) in far less sexualized terms – albeit combined, again, with conservative notions of gender and with an ongoing celebration of genital maturity – in Erik H. Erikson, *Childhood and Society* (New York: Norton, 1950, 1963).

39 Edward Bibring, "The Development and Problems of the Theory of the Instincts," *International Journal of Psycho-Analysis* 22 (1941): 102–130; Heinz Hartmann, "Comments on the Psychoanalytic Theory of Instinctual Drives," *Psychoanalytic Quarterly* 17 (1948): 368–388; David Rapaport, "The Autonomy of the Ego," *Bulletin of the Menninger Clinic* 15.4 (July 1951): 113–123. Also see Martin S. Bergmann, ed., *The Hartmann Era* (New York: Other Press, 2000); and Robert S. Wallerstein, "The Crystallization of the Majority Consensus: 1954," *The Talking Cures: The Psychoanalyses and the Psychotherapies* (New Haven: Yale University Press, 1995), 71–87; as well as the scathing critique by Jacques Lacan of "the American troika, Hartmann, Loewenstein and Kris. These writings are sometimes quite disconcerting in the way they disengage concepts. They are always referring to the *desexualised* libido – they almost get to the point of saying *delibidinised* – or of deaggressivated aggression." Jacques Lacan, *The Seminar of Jacques Lacan, Book 1: Freud's Papers on Technique 1953–1954* (New York: Norton, 1988), 164.

40 Hartmann, "Comments on the Psychoanalytic Theory of Instinctual Drives," 371; see also Heinz Hartmann, "Comments on the Psychoanalytic Theory of the Ego," *Psychoanalytic Study of the Child* 5 (1950): 74–96.

41 For example, Karl A. Menninger with the collaboration of Jeanetta Lyle Menninger, *Love Against Hate* (New York: Harcourt Brace, 1942); Robert Knight, "Functional Disturbances in the Sexual Life of Women: Frigidity and Related Disorders," *Bulletin of the Menninger Clinic* 7.1 (January 1, 1943): 25–35; Phyllis Greenacre, "A Contribution to the Study of Screen Memories," *Psychoanalytic Study of the Child* 3 (1949): 73–84; Phyllis Greenacre, "The Prepuberty Trauma in Girls," *Psychoanalytic Quarterly* 19 (1950): 298–317; Ralph R. Greenson, "On Moods and Introjects," *Bulletin of the Menninger Clinic* 18.1 (January 1954): 1–11; Leo Rangell, "The Role of the Parent in the Oedipus Complex," *Bulletin of the Menninger Clinic* 19.1 (January 1955): 9–15.

42 Herbert Marcuse, "Critique of Neo-Freudian Revisionism," *Eros and Civilization*, 238–274; Herbert Marcuse, "A Reply to Erich Fromm," *Dissent* 3.1 (1956): 79–81; Erich Fromm, "A Counter-Rebuttal to Herbert Marcuse," *Dissent* 3.1 (1956): 81–83.

43 Adorno first presented his critique of Horney at the San Francisco Psychoanalytic Society on April 27, 1946; the paper was translated by Rainer Koehne and first published in 1952, as Theodor W. Adorno, "Zum Verhältnis von Psychoanalyse und Gesellschaftstheorie," *Psyche* 6 (1952): 1–18; later as "Die revidierte Psychoanalyse," in Max Horkheimer and Theodor W. Adorno, *Sociologica II. Reden und Vorträge* (Frankfurt: Suhrkamp, 1962). The English-language original typescript is held at the archive of the Akademie der Künste in Berlin.

44 UCLA philosophy professor Hans Meyerhoff astutely observed in 1964 that "The rise of ego-psychology corresponds to a decline of libido theory. The libido theory tends to be modified or reduced; in fact, it may be

whittled down to a point where the literature of ego-psychology becomes indistinguishable from anti-Freudian revisionism." Hans Meyerhoff, "Psychiatry after Freud," *New York Review of Books* (June 25, 1964).

45 For example, see Alexander Reid Martin, "Karen Horney's Theory in Today's World," *American Journal of Psychoanalysis* 35.4 (1975): 300. As Martin explained: "Freud gave sexuality a primary role. Growing out of respect for the whole individual, the Horney philosophy gives sexuality a secondary role. We now see the sexual life as a kind of barometer, as the most sensitive indicator of the individual's emotional difficulties and not as the basic source of those difficulties. Out of this whole approach comes the finding that most so-called sexual problems and anomalies have a non-sexual basis."

46 Precursor squabbles between believers in psychoanalysis and defenders of religion had existed in Austria-Hungary, Germany, and Switzerland since Freud first start propounding his ideas and gaining adherents. But it was only in the immediate post-World War II years in the USA that the battle became heated and consequential. As Gregory Zilboorg put it in 1949: "Before World War II the problem of psychoanalysis versus religion seemed to be – to put it in psychoanalytic terminology – repressed or partially repressed." Gregory Zilboorg, "Psychoanalysis and Religion," *Atlantic Monthly* (January 1949): 47–50. Also in 1949, the prominent future neoconservative (at that point still a liberal) Irving Kristol noted that back in fin-de-siècle Central Europe, where psychoanalysis was born, religion had seemed "a patient ripe for the grave." While certainly some religious spokesmen had protested against the fledgling upstart movement of psychoanalysis, "the contest was not exactly an exciting one, if only because few people could get enthusiastic about God, one way or the other." Suddenly, however, "transplanted to the melting pot of America," the terms of debate had shifted dramatically and the consequences, in Kristol's view, were nothing short of "astonishing." Irving Kristol, "God and the Psychoanalysts: Can Freud and Religion Be Reconciled?" *Commentary* (November 1, 1949).

47 Joshua Loth Liebman, *Peace of Mind* (New York: Simon and Schuster, 1946), 19; on Liebman "borrow[ing] his concepts from both Freud and Horney," see Herbert Holt, "Review of Liebman, *Peace of Mind*," *American Journal of Psychoanalysis* 6 (1946): 51.

48 David Davidson and Hilde Abel, "How America Lives: Meet an American Rabbi and His Family," *Ladies Home Journal* 65 (January 1948): 123–131.

49 Andrew Heinze, *Jews and the American Soul: Human Nature in the Twentieth Century* (Princeton: Princeton University Press, 2004), 213–214. See also Cheryl Oestreicher, "Readers of Joshua Loth Liebman's *Peace of Mind*," *Reception* 6 (2014): 38–51.

50 "Radio Religion," *Time* (January 21, 1946).

51 Thomas C. Reeves, *America's Bishop: The Life and Times of Fulton J. Sheen* (San Francisco: Encounter Books, 2001). See also Irvin D. S. Winsboro and Michael Epple, "Religion, Culture, and the Cold War: Bishop Fulton J. Sheen and America's Anti-Communist Crusade of the 1950s," *Historian* 71.2 (2009): 209–233.

52 "Sheen Denounces Psychoanalysis," *New York Times* (March 10, 1947): 18.
53 Clare Boothe Luce, "The 'Real' Reason," *McCall's* (February 1947): 135.
54 Luce, "The 'Real' Reason," 156, 160.
55 The classic passage is in Augustine's *The City of God*, Book 13, Chapter 13.
56 Lawrence S. Kubie, "Psychoanalysis – Costly Fad or Boon to Mankind?" *New York Herald Tribune* (April 20, 1947), A7.
57 William Menninger, "An Analysis of Psychoanalysis," *New York Times Sunday Magazine* (May 18, 1947): 12, 48–50.
58 "Psychiatrist Quits in Catholic Clash," *New York Times* (July 20, 1947): 5.
59 Statement reported on in "Msgr. Sheen's Attack Hit by Psychiatrists," *New York Times* (July 2, 1947) 17, and reprinted in full in H. S. S., "Psychiatry and the Need for Religion," *Psychiatry* 10.3 (August 1, 1947): 336.
60 It would perhaps be no coincidence that when the press release of the four Catholic psychiatrists and the resolution of the Menninger-led Group for the Advancement of Psychiatry were both republished in the major journal *Psychiatry* (incidentally under the initials of Harry Stack Sullivan, a sign not only of his editorship of the journal but also of the Menningers' need for him in this hour of adversity and a sign that the attacks were perceived as dangerous to the entire profession) the overarching title chosen was strategically mollifying: "Psychiatry and the Need for Religion." (Unmistakably, the intended message was that religion also needed psychiatry – as well as psychoanalysis.) H. S. S., "Psychiatry," 335–336.
61 Erich Fromm, *Psychoanalysis and Religion* (New Haven: Yale University Press, 1950).
62 Gregory Zilboorg, "A Response," *Psychoanalytic Quarterly*, 13 (1944): 93–100; Gregory Zilboorg, *Psychoanalysis and Religion*, ed. Margaret Stone Zilboorg (New York: Farrar, Straus and Cudahy, 1962). Zilboorg has become notorious of late for his malfeasance as an analyst – and not just for analyzing, all at the same time, the composer George Gershwin, Gershwin's lover Kay Swift, Swift's husband, and numerous other relatives and friends (Swift once marveled in a letter to a friend about what "a lot of unadulterated bull" she had masochistically taken from Zilboorg). See Katharine Weber, *The Memory of All That* (New York: Crown, 2014). Zilboorg also (mis)interpreted George Gershwin's severe headaches and sudden falls – which turned out to be due to a brain tumor – as the results of neurosis. See Mark Leffert, "The Psychoanalysis and Death of George Gershwin: An American Tragedy," *Journal of the American Academy of Psychoanalysis and Dynamic Psychiatry* 39.3 (2011): 420–451. In his lifetime, however, he was seriously respected, as a great hope for their cause, by many Catholic clergy and by other church leaders who were eager to find reconciliation between Catholicism and psychoanalysis. The widely revered Catholic psychiatrist Thomas Verner Moore, for instance, had hoped that Zilboorg would succeed him as teacher at the Catholic University in 1944 (a plan dropped only because at the last minute the university discovered to its displeasure that Zilboorg had just divorced his wife of thirty-seven years and married his secretary). Benedict Neenan, *Thomas Verner Moore: Psychiatrist, Educator and Monk* (Mahwah, NJ: Paulist

Press, 2000), 199. The incident had no further bearing on his solid reputation at the time. When the Guild of Catholic Psychiatrists was founded in 1951, Zilboorg would be invited to address its first conference in Atlantic City in 1952.

63 Zilboorg, *Psychoanalysis and Religion.*
64 John C. Ford, "May Catholics be Analyzed?" *Linacre Quarterly* 20 (1953): 57–66.
65 Thomas P. Neill, "Freud and the Modern Mind," *Catholic World* 165 (April 1947): 11–17.
66 Kathleen Norris, "The Cure-All: Psychoanalysis," *Catholic World* 167 (June 1948): 218–222.
67 Fritz Kunkel, "How Much Truth Is There in Freud?" *Christian Century* (October 1948): 1106–1107.
68 "Are You Always Worrying?" *Time* 52.17 (October 25, 1948).
69 Zaretsky, *Secrets of the Soul*, 276.
70 Harold Blum in Bergmann, *The Hartmann Era.*
71 M. Ralph Kaufman, "The Role of Psychoanalysis in American Psychiatry," *Bulletin of the American Psychoanalytic Association* 6A (1950): 1.
72 William C. Menninger, *Psychiatry in a Troubled World: Yesterday's War and Today's Challenge* (New York: MacMillan, 1948); Harold B. Clemenko, "How the Menningers Fight Mental Disease," *Look* (August 15, 1950): 44, 48–51. By 1954, Karl was able to report that approximately 1,000 candidates were in analytic training across the country, and almost 1,000 doctors were getting "basic psychiatric training. This does not mean that all residents are undergoing basic psychoanalytic training although many are; many of those receiving psychoanalytic training have completed their psychiatric residency." Karl Menninger, "The Contribution of Psychoanalysis to American Psychiatry," *Bulletin of the Menninger Clinic* 18.3 (May 1954).
73 On how William Menninger "essentially constructed and supervised the army's psychiatry program during the last two years of the war," see Lawrence J. Friedman, *Menninger: The Family and the Clinic* (Lawrence: University Press of Kansas, 1990), 174; cf. 416.
74 "Are You Always Worrying?"
75 Zilboorg, "The Fundamental Conflict," 482.
76 Hale, *The Rise and Crisis*, 222–224. Another sign of just how auspicious the times were is how selective American psychoanalytic institutes could be. "Of the 4,096 applications for psychoanalytic training between 1944 and 1957, some 43 percent were rejected." Moreover, "of the 888 students in training in 1960 nearly half had decided to become analysts before medical school … Some 60 percent of this group had become interested while in the Armed Forces, where they had met psychoanalytic specialists whom they wished to emulate" (224).
77 Certainly, Karl Menninger was preoccupied with vigorous protection of the reputations of psychoanalysis and psychiatry already before the attacks from religious spokespeople. For example, see the discussions of his efforts to intervene in the representation of the psychiatrist-psychoanalyst in Alfred Hitchcock's *Spellbound* (1945), in Stephen Farber and Marc Green, *Hollywood on the Couch: A Candid Look at the Overheated Love Affair*

Between Psychiatrists and Moviemakers (New York: William Morrow & Co, 1993); and Veronika Rall, *Kinoanalyse: Plädoyer für eine Re-Vision von Kino und Psychoanalyse* (Marburg: Schüren, 2011), 274–275.

78 Gerald N. Grob, "Psychiatry and Social Activism: The Politics of a Specialty in Postwar America," *Bulletin of the History of Medicine* 60.4 (Winter 1986): 478, 483; Friedman, *Menninger*, 121.

79 Thus, while in 1946 he had made an attempt at balance in a brief review of Horney's most recent book (*Our Inner Conflicts*, 1945), and was able to say that he found "much excellent material" in her chapters on "sadistic trends" and on "resolution of neurotic conflicts," he also said that the style was "duller" albeit "more gracious" than the prior works, that the first part was "superficial and of little practical value," and that he did "not agree with many of the assumptions." "Book Notices," *Bulletin of the Menninger Clinic* 10.2 (March 1, 1946): 62. In 1950, he would make a point of writing to Diana Trilling to commend her for her critical comments about Margaret Mead's *Male and Female* in *Partisan Review*: "I feel you hit the nail exactly on the head. I am particularly glad that you exposed the Horneyism which Margaret Mead continues to get away with right under the noses of some good psychoanalysts who out to know better." (Trilling had expressly snarked about how much Mead's feminism sounded like Horney's – and about Mead's neglect of libido.) In a later letter he upbraided a friend who had deemed Horney "one of the ablest expositors of psychoanalysis" and complained that Horney, "whom I helped to bring to this country, abandoned psychoanalysis." About Sullivan he was more ambivalent, expressing some retrospective affection after Sullivan's death in 1949, but also envious and angry when Sullivan's views turned out to be more appreciated by clergymen than his own. See Menninger, *The Selected Correspondence of Karl A. Menninger, 1945–1965*, 96, 124, 153.

80 In 1954, Karl Menninger would explicitly write to his friend Seward Hiltner of the Federal Council of Churches about the book of a Methodist clergyman, Albert Outler, entitled *Psychotherapy and the Christian Message* (which Hiltner had also reviewed), and how much it annoyed him that Outler "seems to think well of Sullivan, Fromm and Horney. In other words, like the Pope and Bishop Sheen, especially the latter, he thinks well of the boys and girls that leave sex alone." Karl took the occasion to go on a further rampage against the neo-Freudians: "These folk repudiated the rest of us in the name of their more righteous, more truthful, more unique vision which was so different that they could no longer associate with us but had to proclaim their message in the individualistic and Messianic manner in the hope of getting a following, and followings they have, too … So I have this OTHER reason, you see, to dislike Dr. Outler. I just feel nervous about having to stand up in a meeting of psychoanalysts and admit that I have an interest in the field of religion when I know that this is going to mean to them Outler, Horney, Fromm and Sullivan." Menninger, *The Selected Correspondence of Karl A. Menninger, 1945–1965*, 152–53.

81 This concern runs from his very first book in 1930, *The Human Mind*, where he affirms the psychoanalytic discovery of the role of the sexual instinct but discusses at length his annoyance at psychoanalysis' overly sexual reputation, through to the 1950s. See Karl A. Menninger, *The*

Human Mind (New York: Literary Guild of America, 1930), 352–353. In 1956, in an ongoing argument he was having with his friend, the Philadelphia psychiatrist O. Spurgeon English, Menninger once more mentioned directly: "I have just been listening again to accusations that psychoanalysts don't consider the ethics of human life and feel that it is only necessary for a person to feel happy and non-conflictual, and so forth. One lawyer who has been analyzed and who is well-acquainted with many analysts told me recently that he was convinced that many analysts because of their own needs were encouraging patients to solve their protests against things as they are by as much sexual promiscuity as they could expeditiously manage. Now I want such accusations kept in the family." Menninger, *The Selected Correspondence of Karl A. Menninger, 1945–1965*, 175–176.

82 One of the things Karl would find most enervating was the fact that all too often, self-identified Christians who stepped forward to embrace psychoanalysis had the tendency to praise neo-Freudians as the most impressive exemplars of the Freudian tradition. Thus, for instance, the prominent University of Michigan psychologist Wilbert McKeachie, writing a long letter to the *Christian Century* in reaction against the Lutheran Fritz Kunkel's take-down of Freud, did defend Freud directly. In McKeachie's genial Liebmanesque view, "the aim of psychoanalysis is to give patients the ability to face their drives and temptations and deal with them on a rational, conscious level." Indeed, McKeachie found that "Freudian theory is surprisingly in accord with Christianity," and that psychoanalysis could help a man "to become a better Christian." Yet notably, when describing what great advances had been recently made in Freudian theory, the individuals McKeachie named were Fromm and Sullivan. W. J. McKeachie, "A Freudian Rejoinder," *Christian Century* (November 24, 1948): 1275. The neo-Freudian criticism of the Oedipus complex also made sense to some Christian commentators – as shown in an otherwise cheerful defense of Freud in the Catholic journal *Commonweal* by the psychologist Harry McNeill. McNeill suggested that Catholics could learn much from "the Moses of modern psychiatry [i.e., Freud] and his followers," and should not be overly worried about "the basic Freudian method," as it simply involved "throwing the light of reason on obscure impulses operating in the patient and bringing them eventually under conscious control." Nonetheless, McNeill maintained that there was no need to "accept ... the universality of the Oedipus complex, that invariable pattern of incestuous urges which Freud finds present in all children (and which, scientifically, has nothing like the painstaking studies of a Gesell or a Piaget to support it)." Harry McNeill, "Freudians and Catholics," *Commonweal* (July 25, 1947): 350–353.

83 Fulton Sheen, *Peace of Soul* (New York: McGraw-Hill, 1949), 70.

84 Sheen, *Peace of Soul*, 47, 94, 134, 136, 148fn5, 151–152, 158–159.

85 Sol W. Ginsburg, "Religion: Man's Place in God's World," in Hans Herma and Gertrud M. Kurti, eds., *Elements of Psychoanalysis* (Cleveland: The World Publishing Company, 1950). The Foreword is written by Oberndorf, and Ginsburg is listed as an "Advisory Editor."

86 "Some Common Misunderstandings of Psychoanalysis," in Herma and Kurti, *Elements of Psychoanalysis*, 313.

87 "Psychiatry and Religion," *Time* 57.16 (April 16, 1951): 65–66.

88 See Roland Dalbiez, *Psychoanalytical Method and the Doctrine of Freud* (London: Longmans, Green and Company, 1941); Maryse Choisy, *Psychanalyse et Catholicisme* (Paris: L'Arche, 1950); Joseph Nuttin, *Psychanalyse et Conception Spiritualiste de L'Homme* (Louvain: Publications Universitaire de Louvain, 1950); and Louis Beirnaert, S.J., "L'Eglise et la psychanalyse," *Etudes* 275 (1952): 229–237; as well as the discussions in Desmazières, *L'Inconscient au paradis*; and Elisabeth Roudinesco, *Jacques Lacan & Co: A History of Psychoanalysis in France, 1925–1985* (Chicago: University of Chicago Press, 1990), 196–205.

89 Although first accepting multiple reprimands from the Vatican, Oraison would eventually become a well-known proponent of greater sexual liberality – always, however, within a theological framework. Thus, for instance, in 1968 the jacket blurb for the English-language translation of his *Une Morale pour notre temps* (1964) declared: "A noted psychologist and theologian considers the precepts of conventional morality in the light of the legitimate findings of contemporary psychology. He finds the norms of traditional morality inadequate for modern man, and proposes a morality in tune with contemporary life. After careful consideration and deep study, the author concludes that a rigid, legalistic standard of morality which would apply to all men regardless of personal circumstances and subjective situations is not only unhealthy, it is un-Christian. He advocates a personal relationship with God – a God of love, not a moral scorekeeper in the sky. He condemns the legalism, the confusing abstractions, the impersonal codes, and in their place he offers a relevant, living Christian morality based on freedom and responsibility." Marc Oraison, *Morality for Our Time* (Garden City, NY: Doubleday, 1968). In due course, Oraison earned a place on the cover of the French porn magazine *Emmanuelle* with his authoritative assurance that "no, pleasure is not a sin." See the cover of *Emmanuelle* 2 (November 1974).

90 Francis J. Braceland and Peter A. Martin, "Leo H. Bartemeier, M.D., 1895–1982," *American Journal of Psychiatry* 140.5 (May 1983): 628–630; Leo H. Bartemeier, "An Autobiography of My Religion," in Paul E. Johnson, ed., *Healer of the Mind: A Psychiatrist's Search for Faith* (Nashville: Abingdon Press, 1972).

91 Felici in 1952 quoted in "Pius on Psychoanalysis," *Newsweek* (April 27, 1953): 101; and "Rota Judge Attacks Psychoanalysis," *Catholic Herald* (April 18, 1952), available at: http://archive.catholicherald.co.uk/article/18th-april-1952/6/rota-judge-attacks-psychoanalysis (accessed February 11, 2013).

92 See Percy Winner, "The Pope on Psychoanalysis," *New Republic* (October 20, 1952): 8.

93 Gordon F. George, S.J., "The Pope on Psychoanalysis," *America* (October 4, 1952): 12.

94 "The Moral Limits of Medical Research and Treatment: An Address Given September 14, 1952 by His Holiness Pope Pius XII to the First International Congress on the Histopathology of the Nervous System," available at: www.papalencyclicals.net/Pius12/P12PSYCH.HTM (accessed August 24, 2015).

95 "Pius on Psychoanalysis," 101.
96 "On Psychotherapy and Religion: An Address of His Holiness Pope Pius XII to the Fifth International Congress on Psychotherapy and Clinical Psychology Given on April 13, 1953," available at: www.papalencyclicals.net/Pius12/P12PSYRE.HTM (accessed August 24, 2015).
97 *La Dépêche de Toulouse*, June 1953, quoted in Serge Moskovici, *Psychoanalysis: Its Image and its Public* (Cambridge, UK: Polity Press, 2008), 274.
98 "On Psychotherapy and Religion: An Address of His Holiness Pope Pius XII to the Fifth International Congress on Psychotherapy and Clinical Psychology Given on April 13, 1953," available at: www.papalencyclicals.net/Pius12/P12PSYRE.HTM (accessed August 24, 2015).
99 Stephen Mitchell, *Relational Concepts in Psychoanalysis: An Integration* (Cambridge, MA: Harvard University Press, 1988); Glen O. Gabbard, "Relational Psychoanalysis: The Emergence of a Tradition," *Journal of the American Psychoanalytic Association* 48 (2000): 315–316; Emily Kuriloff, "A Two-Body Psychology," review of Lewis Aron and Fran Anderson, *Relational Perspectives on the Body* (1998), *Contemporary Psychoanalysis* 36 (2000): 537–543; Adrienne E. Harris, "The Relational Tradition: Landscape and Canon," *Journal of the American Psychoanalytic Association* 59 (2011): 701–735.
100 McLaughlin, "Why Do Schools of Thought Fail?"
101 Paris credits Susan Quinn's earlier biography with identifying Horney's perdurable troubles with the male members of the species and remarks that many of Quinn's readers were "dismayed by the inability of the physician [Horney] to cure herself," even as he styles his own contribution as reversing the valuation and finding that Horney's difficulties were "a source of her insight." Bernard J. Paris, *Karen Horney: A Psychoanalyst's Search for Self-Understanding* (New Haven: Yale University Press, 1994), xxv.
102 Heinz Kohut, *The Restoration of the Self* (Chicago: University of Chicago Press, 1977); Robert Stoller, *Perversion: The Erotic Form of Hatred* (New York: Pantheon, 1975).
103 It is actually quite interesting that the idea of nonsexual motives for sexual behavior can be used for both sexually conventional-normative and sexually transgression-affirming aims. A creative recent example of the latter can be found in Avgi Saketopoulou, "To Suffer Pleasure: The Shattering of the Ego as the Psychic Labor of Perverse Sexuality," *Studies in Gender and Sexuality* 15.4 (2014): 254–268.
104 See on this point Kristol, "God"; Kugelmann, *Psychology and Catholicism*; Nussbaum, "Profession and Faith." On Sheen's own eventual mellowing, see Eugene Kennedy, "Foreword," in Gillespie, *Psychology and American Catholicism*.
105 Francis J. Braceland, "Clinical Psychiatry," in Braceland, ed., *Faith, Reason and Modern Psychiatry: Sources for a Synthesis* (New York: P. J. Kenedy & Sons, 1955), 27. Relaxation of sexual vigilance and purity, even in thought, remained an area of contention. John C. Ford enumerated that not only was it "immoral deliberately to indulge the desire of unchaste sexual acts," but it was also "immoral deliberately to acquiesce,

as it were complacently, in unchaste sexual fantasies" and immoral as well "deliberately to excite within oneself, or to acquiesce in, unchaste sexual feeling and emotions" – "even for therapeutic purposes." On the other hand, however, "it is not at all clear … that the method of free association or the phenomenon of abreaction in themselves, or necessarily, involve any of these immoral activities." Meanwhile, "the neurotic patient may find the psychoanalytic interview, the process of free association, and the necessity of expressing the sexual content of consciousness a source of temptation and excitement. When this is merely incidental to the treatment, and not a means to an end, it is not necessarily immoral. Somewhere here a delicate line needs to be drawn." Ford, "May Catholics Be Psychoanalyzed?" quoted in Francis P. Furlong, S.J., S.T.D., "Peaceful Coexistence of Religion and Psychiatry," *Bulletin of the Menninger Clinic* 19.6 (November 1, 1955): 210–216.

106 Furlong, "Peaceful." Furlong disagreed with the Zilboorgian argument that psychiatry was only a form of medicine and here, too, he quoted John Ford's "May Catholics Be Psychoanalyzed?" to the effect that conflict was inevitable since both psychoanalysis and theology concerned themselves with human behavior.

107 Beirnaert, "L'Eglise et la psychanalyse," quoted in Furlong, "Peaceful," 213.

108 Beirnaert quoted in John LaFarge, S.J., "Foreword," in Braceland, *Faith, Reason and Modern Psychiatry*, xiv. Braceland's own essay is a plea for nationwide expansion of mental health care and willingness of the populace to seek that care. His argument was that Jesus too sought assistance when he needed it: "When Christ's burden was too heavy, he accepted the help of Simon of Cyrene" (10).

109 Karl Menninger to Ada McCormick, in *Selected Correspondence of Karl A. Menninger*, 61–62.

2 Homophobia's Durability and the Reinvention of Psychoanalysis

1 Robert Stoller in "A Symposium: Should Homosexuality Be in the APA Nomenclature? Robert Stoller, M.D., Judd Marmor, M.D., Irving Bieber, M.D., Ronald Gold, Charles Socarides, M.D., Richard Green, M.D., and Robert Spitzer, M.D." *American Journal of Psychiatry* 130 (November 1973): 1207–1216, here 1208.

2 Elizabeth Roudinesco, *Why Psychoanalysis?* (New York: Columbia University Press, 2001), 116.

3 Alfred C. Kinsey, Wardell Baxter Pomeroy, and Clyde E. Martin, *Sexual Behavior in the Human Male* (Philadelphia: Saunders, 1948); Alfred C. Kinsey et al., *Sexual Behavior in the Human Female* (Philadelphia: Saunders, 1953). For what is still the best essay on the impact of the Kinsey reports on American understandings of sexuality, see Regina Markell Morantz, "The Scientist as Sex Crusader: Alfred C. Kinsey and American Culture," *American Quarterly* 29.5 (Winter 1977): 563–589. On how Kinsey's "style of thinking" introduced a "completely different 'ontology'

of sexuality" in comparison with anything that had gone before, see Jeffrey Escoffier, "The Kinsey Effect: How the Kinsey Reports Killed Off Psychoanalytic Theories of Sexuality and Prepared the Ground for Social Construction," paper delivered at the Social Science History Association, Annual Conference, Chicago, November 20, 2016; and Escoffier's book in progress, *Sex O'Clock in America: The Long Sexual Revolution of the Twentieth-Century.*

4 Lionel Trilling, "Sex and Science: The Kinsey Report," *Partisan Review* 15 (April 1948): 475.

5 Martin Gumpert, "The Kinsey Report," *The Nation* 166 (May 1, 1948): 471.

6 Lawrence Kubie, "Psychiatric Implications of the Kinsey Report," *Psychosomatic Medicine* 10 (1948): 95–106; Robert Knight, "Psychiatric Issues in the Kinsey Report," in Albert Deutsch, ed., *Sex Habits of American Men: A Symposium on the Kinsey Report* (New York: Grosset and Dunlap, 1948).

7 Erich Fromm, "Sex and Character: The Kinsey Report Viewed from the Standpoint of Psychoanalysis" (1948), reprinted in Jerome Himelhoch and Sylvia Fleis Fava, eds., *Sexual Behavior in American Society* (New York: Norton, 1955), 301–311.

8 Sigmund Freud, *Three Essays on the Theory of Sexuality* (New York: Basic Books, 1962), 73.

9 Useful overviews of Freud's prohomosexual attitudes can be found in Richard Green, "Navigating the Straits of Oedipus," *New York Times* (December 11, 1988); Diana Fuss, ed., *Pink Freud.* Special issue of *GLQ* 2 (1995); Thomas Domenici and Ronnie C. Lesser, eds., *Disorienting Sexuality: Psychoanalytic Reappraisals of Sexual Identities* (New York: Routledge, 1995); and Tim Dean and Christopher Lane, *Homosexuality and Psychoanalysis* (Chicago: University of Chicago Press, 2001).

10 Freud, *Three Essays on the Theory of Sexuality*, 11.

11 Elizabeth Roudinesco, "'Other' Sexualities – I/Psychoanalysis and Homosexuality: Reflections on the Perverse, Desire, Insult and the Paternal Function" (an interview with François Pommier), *European Journal of Psychoanalysis* 15 (Fall–Winter 2002), available at: www.psychomedia.it/jep/number15/roudinesco.htm (accessed January 16, 2016).

12 Elizabeth Lunbeck, "Self-Love," *The Americanization of Narcissism* (Cambridge, MA: Harvard University Press, 2014), 83–112.

13 As Freud put it, in annoyance: "Magnus Hirschfeld has left our ranks in Berlin. No great loss, he is a flabby, unappetizing fellow, absolutely incapable of learning anything. Of course he takes your remark at the Congress as a pretext; homosexual touchiness. Not worth a tear." Letter from Sigmund Freud to C. G. Jung, November 2, 1911, in William McGuire, ed., *The Freud/Jung Letters: The Correspondence Between Sigmund Freud and C. G. Jung* (Princeton: Princeton University Press, 1974), 453–454. See the discussion in Herbert Gschwind, "'Manif[est] Homos[exuelle] wären – einstweilen – grundsätzlich abzuweisen. Sie sind ja meist zu abnorm': zum Verhältnis von Psychoanalyse und Homosexualität," *Psyche* 69.7 (July 2015), 632–647.

14 Sándor Ferenczi, "Letter from Sándor Ferenczi to Sigmund Freud, December 18, 1914," in Ernst Falzeder and Eva Brabant, eds., *The Correspondence*

of Sigmund Freud and Sándor Ferenczi Volume 2, 1914–1919 (Cambridge, MA: Belknap, 1996), 39; Sándor Ferenczi, "The Nosology of Male Homosexuality (Homoerotism)" [1914], in *First Contributions to Psycho-Analysis (International Psycho-Analytic Library* 45 [1952]), 43; Sándor Ferenczi, "Letter from Sándor Ferenczi to Sigmund Freud, February 21, 1926," in Ernst Falzeder and Eva Brabant, eds., *The Correspondence of Sigmund Freud and Sándor Ferenczi Volume 3, 1920–1933* (Cambridge, MA: Belknap, 2000), 250; Sándor Ferenczi, "Thalassa: A Theory of Genitality," *Psychoanalytic Quarterly*, 3 (1934): 5; and Sándor Ferenczi, "Notes and Fragments [1930–32]," *International Journal of Psycho-Analysis*, 30 (1949): 233.

15 Ferenczi, "The Nosology," 300, 303.

16 Ferenczi, "Introjection and Transference," in *First Contributions to Psycho-Analysis*, 43.

17 Helene Deutsch, "On Female Homosexuality," *Psychoanalytic Quarterly* 1 (1932): 484–510.

18 Karen Horney, "On the Genesis of the Castration Complex in Women," *International Journal of Psycho-Analysis* 5 (1924): 60–61; and Karen Horney, *New Ways in Psychoanalysis* (New York: W. W. Norton, 1939), 80–81.

19 Karen Horney, "Observations on a Specific Difference in the Dread Felt by Men and by Women Respectively for the Opposite Sex," *International Journal of Psycho-Analysis* 13 (1932): 352.

20 Marie Bonaparte, "The Male's Constructive Role in Female Sexuality," in Bonaparte, *Female Sexuality* (London: Imago, 1953), 130–131.

21 Jones quoted in Roudinesco, "'Other' Sexualities." Roudinesco observes further: "It was Ernest Jones and Anna Freud who, in contrast to Freud, held the most regressive attitudes towards homosexuality."

22 Edward Glover, in *Psycho-Analysis* (London and New York: Staples, 1939), 257; Edward Glover, "The Problem of Male Homosexuality," in *The Roots of Crime* (New York: International Universities Press, 1960).

23 Melanie Klein, *The Psycho-Analysis of Children (International Psycho-Analytic Library*, 22 [1932]), 78.

24 Klein, *The Psycho-Analysis of Children*, 46.

25 W. R. D. Fairbairn, "The Treatment and Rehabilitation of Sexual Offenders (1946)," in *Psychoanalytic Studies of the Personality* (London: Tavistock, 1952), 291–293; Robert Royston, "Sexuality and Object Relations," in Celia Harding, ed., *Sexuality: Psychoanalytic Perspectives* (Philadelphia: Taylor and Francis, 2001), 43.

26 H. F. Waldhorn, "Meetings of the New York Psychoanalytic Society," *Psychoanalytic Quarterly* 20 (1951), 337; and Anna Freud, "Report on the Sixteenth International Psychoanalytical Congress," *Bulletin of the International Psychoanalytical Association* 30 (1949): 195.

27 Roudinesco, "'Other' Sexualities."

28 Hans Herma and Gertrud M. Kurti, eds., *Elements of Psychoanalysis* (Cleveland: The World Publishing Company, 1950), inside cover.

29 For uncritical and affirmative summaries of prominent analysts' starkly antihomosexual views, see H. F. Waldhorn, "Meetings of the New York Psychoanalytic Society," *Psychoanalytic Quarterly* 20 (1951): 337–338; Irving

Bieber et al., *Homosexuality: A Psychoanalytic Study* (New York: Basic, 1962); and Harry Gershman, "The Effect of Group Therapy on Compulsive Homosexuality in Men and Women," *American Journal of Psychoanalysis* 35 (1975): 303–312. For further – but critically assessed – examples of hostile views on male homosexuality, see Kenneth Lewes, *The Psychoanalytic Theory of Male Homosexuality* (New York: Simon and Schuster, 1988); and Ralph E. Roughton, "Rethinking Homosexuality: What it Teaches Us About Psychoanalysis," *Journal of the American Psychoanalytic Association* 50 (Summer 2002): 733–763. For a homophobic Horneyan, see Fred Weiss, "The Meaning of Homosexual Trends in Therapy," *American Journal of Psychoanalysis* 24 (1964): 70–76. On Sullivan, see Naoko Wake, *Private Practices: Harry Stack Sullivan, the Science of Homosexuality, and American Liberalism* (New Brunswick: Rutgers University Press, 2011), 4, 132. For a sampling of the work on perversions, see Robert C. Bak, "The Phallic Woman – The Ubiquitous Fantasy in Perversions," *Psychoanalytic Study of the Child* 23 (1968): 15–36.

30 Edmund Bergler, *Homosexuality: Disease or Way of Life?* (New York: Hill and Wang, 1956), 28–29.

31 On lesbianism, see Judith M. Glassgold and Suzanne Iasenza, *Lesbians and Psychoanalysis: Revolutions in Theory and Practice* (New York: Free Press, 2000); Noreen O'Connor and Joanna Ryan, *Wild Desires and Mistaken Identities: Lesbianism and Psychoanalysis* (London: Karnac, 2004).

32 Sol W. Ginsburg, "Atomism of Behavior," in Donald P. Geddes, ed., *An Analysis of the Kinsey Reports on Sexual Behavior in the Human Male and Female* (New York: Mentor Books, 1954), 39.

33 Karl Menninger, "One View of the Kinsey Report," *GP* 8 (December 1953): 70.

34 Karl Menninger, "What the Girls Told," *Saturday Review* (September 26, 1953): 30. The anonymous author quoted in *GP* turns out to be the show business biographer Maurice Zolotow.

35 Menninger to Alexander, March 17, 1954, in Karl A. Menninger, *The Selected Correspondence of Karl A. Menninger, 1945–1965*, ed. Howard J. Faulkner and Virginia D. Pruitt (Columbia: University of Missouri Press).

36 "'Can You Measure Love?'" *Time*, May 17, 1954: 75.

37 Iago Galdston, "So Noble an Effort Corrupted," in Geddes, *An Analysis*, 46–47.

38 Edward S. Tauber, "The Reading of Kinsey as a Meaningful Experience," in Geddes, *An Analysis*, 184, 188.

39 Sigmund Freud, "A Special Type of Choice of Object Made by Men (Contributions to the Psychology of Love I)," in *The Standard Edition of the Complete Psychological Works of Sigmund Freud, vol. XI (1910): Five Lectures on Psycho-Analysis, Leonardo da Vinci and Other Works* (163–176); Sigmund Freud, "On the Universal Tendency to Debasement in the Sphere of Love (Contributions to the Psychology of Love II)," in *The Standard Edition of the Complete Psychological Works of Sigmund Freud, vol. XI (1910): Five Lectures on Psycho-Analysis, Leonardo da Vinci and Other Works* (177–190).

40 Dagmar Herzog, "Fear and Loathing," *Lapham's Quarterly* 2 (Winter 2009): 187–191.

41 For example, see Herbert Rosenfeld, "Remarks on the Relation of Male Homosexuality to Paranoia, Paranoid Anxiety and Narcissism," *International Journal of Psycho-Analysis* 30 (1949): 36–47; Daniel Lagache, "Homosexuality and Jealousy," *International Journal of Psycho-Analysis* 31 (1950): 24–31.

42 Andrew Heinze, *Jews and the American Soul: Human Nature in the Twentieth Century* (Princeton: Princeton University Press, 2004).

43 Kenneth Lewes, "Homosexuality, Homophobia, and Gay-Friendly Psychoanalysis," *Fort Da* 11A (2005): 13–34; and Michael E. Staub, "Person Envy," in Michael E. Staub, ed., *Madness Is Civilization: When the Diagnosis Was Social, 1948–1980* (Chicago: University Chicago Press, 2011), 139–165.

44 William Masters and Virginia Johnson, *Human Sexual Response* (Boston: Little, Brown, 1966).

45 William Masters and Virginia Johnson, *Human Sexual Inadequacy* (Boston: Little, Brown, 1970).

46 Mary Jane Sherfey, "The Evolution and Nature of Female Sexuality in Relation to Psychoanalytic Theory," *Journal of the American Psychoanalytic Association* 14 (1966): 28–125.

47 A panel on Masters and Johnson and Sherfey was held at the American Psychoanalytic Association meeting in Detroit, May 1967, and the papers were subsequently published, all in the *Journal of the American Psychoanalytic Association*: Marcel Heiman, "Discussion," *Journal of the American Psychoanalytic Association* 16 (1968): 406–416; Judith S. Kestenberg, "Discussion," *Journal of the American Psychoanalytic Association* 16 (1968): 417–423; Therese Benedek, "Discussion," *Journal of the American Psychoanalytic Association* 16 (1968): 424–448; and Sylvan Keiser, "Discussion," *Journal of the American Psychoanalytic Association* 16 (1968): 449–456. See also the further discussions in: Warren J. Barker, "Female Sexuality," *Journal of the American Psychoanalytic Association* 16 (1968): 123–145; and Judith S. Kestenberg, "Outside and Inside, Male and Female," *Journal of the American Psychoanalytic Association* 16 (1968): 457–520.

48 Mari Jo Buhle, *Feminism and its Discontents: A Century of Struggle with Psychoanalysis* (Cambridge, MA: Harvard University Press, 1998).

49 Ronald Bayer, *Homosexuality and American Psychiatry: The Politics of Diagnosis* (Princeton: Princeton University Press, 1987), 103–105; David L. Scasta, "John E. Fryer, M.D., and the Dr. H. Anonymous Episode," *Journal of Gay & Lesbian Psychotherapy* 6.4 (2002); Jack Drescher and J. P. Merlino, eds., *American Psychiatry and Homosexuality: An Oral History* (Binghamton, NY: Haworth, 2007).

50 For example, see Heinz Hartmann, Ernst Kris, and Rudolph M. Loewenstein, "Notes on the Theory of Aggression," *Psychoanalytic Study of the Child* 3 (1949): 9–36; Ernst Kris et al., "Problems of Infantile Neurosis – A Discussion," *Psychoanalytic Study of the Child* 9 (1954): 16–71.

51 The sense that analysts were all too often autocratic was not just an outside perspective. An articulate and moving challenge to analytic authoritarianism had already come from within: Hans W. Loewald, "On the Therapeutic Action of Psycho-Analysis," *International Journal of Psycho-Analysis* 41 (1960): 16–33.

52 Carl Elliott, *Better Than Well: American Medicine Meets the American Dream* (New York: Norton, 2003), 131, 155.

53 Bayer, *Homosexuality and American Psychiatry*, 116–118.

54 Evelyn Hooker, "The Adjustment of the Male Overt Homosexual," *Journal of Projective Techniques* 21 (1957): 18–31.

55 "81 Words," This American Life, National Public Radio, January 18, 2002, available at: www.thisamericanlife.org/radio-archives/episode/204/transcript (accessed January 22, 2016).

56 "Sick Again?" *Time* (February 20, 1978).

57 Elizabeth Lunbeck, "Borderline Histories: Psychoanalysis Inside and Out," *Science in Context* 19 (2006): 151–173.

58 Edward M. Weinshel, "Concluding Comments on the Congress Topic," *International Journal of Psycho-Analysis* 57 (1976): 456–457.

59 Roudinesco, *Why Psychoanalysis?* 116. See also: Kenneth L. Woodward and Rachel Mark, "The New Narcissism," *Newsweek* (January 30, 1978), 70–72; Susan Quinn, "Oedipus vs. Narcissus," *New York Times* (June 30, 1981).

60 Cf. Otto Kernberg, "Position Statement" (1975) prepared for the International Psychoanalytical Association meeting in London (IPA Archive, London). Kernberg was here very clear that "characterological problems continue to increase in the psychoanalysts' caseload" (31). Note also Kernberg's retrospective fury at what he took to be Heinz Hartmann's bland and serene unconcern in face of the phenomenon. In Kernberg's view, Hartmann's approach "superficialized the technique, ignored the theory, the drives, and made timidity the technical approach to patients. While we saw sicker and sicker patients with the most primitive sadomasochistic, aggressive things going on, the optimism of Hartmann regarding drives and adaptation ignored that clinical reality." Kernberg in Martin S. Bergmann, ed., *The Hartmann Era* (New York: Other Press, 2000), 231.

61 Elizabeth L. Auchincloss and Robert Glick, "The Psychoanalytic Model of the Mind," in Robert Michels et al., eds., *Psychiatry* (Philadelphia and New York: Lippincott-Raven, 1996/1997), 25. See also Kohut's annoyed/clarifying letter to the editor of *Newsweek*, January 25, 1978, reprinted in Heinz Kohut, *The Search for the Self: Selected Writings of Heinz Kohut*, vol. IV: 1978–1981 (London: Karnac, 2011), 569.

62 Orna Ophir, "The Paradox of Madness in American Psychoanalysis 1960–2000: Liberating Ethos, Praxis under Siege" (Ph.D. thesis, Tel Aviv University, 2008), 13–14.

63 Kohut himself, as late as 1980, told an interviewer with pride that he was able to cure a homosexual patient, not least by recommending strongly that he stay away from cruising areas. (Audiofile of Susan Quinn interview with Kohut, 3/29-3/30, 1980, Oral History Interviews, Boston Psychoanalytic Society and Institute.) This moment stands in peculiarly disconnected relation to Kohut's delighted – albeit possibly only strategic (private) – response to the radical Swiss psychoanalyst Fritz Morgenthaler's suggestion that there might be expanded – including antihomophobic – uses to his ideas about narcissism. Kohut to Morgenthaler, October 3, 1977, reprinted in Heinz Kohut, *The Curve of Life: Correspondence of*

Heinz Kohut 1923–1981, ed. Geoffrey Cocks (Chicago: University of Chicago Press, 1994), 358; cf. Dagmar Herzog, "Die Politisierung des Narzissmus: Kohut mit und durch Morgenthaler lesen," *Luzifer-Amor* 29.1 (2016), 67–97.

64 Green, "Navigating the Straits of Oedipus."

65 See the astute and highly critical summary of Socarides' innovations in Reimut Reiche, "Diskussion über Socarides' Theorie der Homosexualität," *Psyche* 26.6 (1972), 476–488.

66 Gershman, "The Effect of Group Therapy on Compulsive Homosexuality in Men and Women," 303, 310.

67 Charles W. Socarides, "Perversion: The Erotic Form of Hatred," *Psychoanalytic Quarterly* 46 (1977): 330–333, here 331. See also Charles W. Socarides, *Homosexuality* (New York: J. Aronson, 1978).

68 Charles W. Socarides, "Psychodynamics and Sexual Object Choice. II – A Reply to Dr. Richard C. Friedman's Paper," *Contemporary Psychoanalysis* 12 (1976): 375. Cf. Margaret S. Mahler, "On Human Symbiosis and the Vicissitudes of Individuation," *Journal of the American Psychoanalytic Association* 15 (1967): 756.

69 Charles Socarides, "Alienation in Perversions," *Psychoanalytic Quarterly* 51 (1982): 135.

70 Charles W. Socarides, "The Nature and Evolution of Female Sexuality," *Psychoanalytic Quarterly* 44 (1975): 153–156, here 155.

71 Kurt R. Eissler, "Comments on Penis Envy and Orgasm in Women," *Psychoanalytic Study of the Child* 32 (1977): 29–83.

72 Roughton, "Rethinking Homosexuality"; and Ralph E. Roughton, "The International Psychoanalytical Association and Homosexuality," *Journal of Gay and Lesbian Psychotherapy* 7 (2003): 189–196.

73 Christopher Lasch, *The Culture of Narcissism: American Life in an Age of Diminishing Expectations* (New York: Norton, 1979), 15, 33, 40, 50, 193, 203.

74 Reimut Reiche, "Haben frühe Störungen zugenommen?" in *Triebschicksal der Gesellschaft: Über den Strukturwandel der Psyche* (Frankfurt am Main: Campus, 2004), 41–62.

75 "A Symposium: Should Homosexuality Be in the APA Nomenclature?" *American Journal of Psychiatry* 130 (1973): 1209, 1213–1214.

76 "A Symposium," 1210.

77 "A Symposium," 1212–1213.

78 "A Symposium," 1208.

79 John Gagnon and William Simon, *Sexual Conduct: The Social Sources of Human Sexuality* (Chicago: Aldine, 1973).

80 Phyllis Greenacre, "Certain Relationships between Fetishism and Faulty Development of the Body Image," *Psychoanalytic Study of the Child* 8 (1953): 79–98; Phyllis Greenacre, "Further Notes on Fetishism," *Psychoanalytic Study of the Child* 15 (1960): 191–207; Masud Khan, *Alienation in Perversions* (London: Hogarth, 1979).

81 Robert J. Stoller, "Sexual Excitement," *Archives of General Psychiatry* 33 (August 1976): 899, 905; Nancy Friday, *My Secret Garden: Women's Sexual Fantasies* (New York: Pocket, 1974).

82 Stoller, "Sexual Excitement," 908.

83 Robert J. Stoller, *Observing the Erotic Imagination* (New Haven: Yale University Press, 1985), 175–177. A further point made by Stoller was that there was no such thing as a singular homosexuality, but rather a wealth of homosexualities – "as many different homosexualities as there are heterosexualities" (97, cf. 102, 107).

84 Stoller, *Observing the Erotic Imagination*, 176–177.

85 Stoller, *Observing the Erotic Imagination*, 178.

86 Only a historian, John Forrester, in his marvelous – at once appreciative and perceptively critical – essay on voyeurism and ethics in Stoller's clinical work is the exception to the more general rule of inattention or misreading. John Forrester, "The Psychoanalytic Case: Voyeurism, Ethics, and Epistemology in Robert Stoller's *Sexual Excitement*," in Angela Creager, Elizabeth Lunbeck, and M. Norton Wise, eds., *Science without Laws: Model Systems, Cases, Exemplary Narratives* (Durham: Duke University Press, 2007), 189–211.

87 Otto F. Kernberg, *Love Relations: Normality and Pathology* (New Haven: Yale University Press, 1995); Elizabeth L. Auchincloss and Susan C. Vaughan, "Psychoanalysis and Homosexuality: Do We Need a New Theory?" *Journal of the American Psychoanalytic Association* 49 (2001): 1168.

88 Vittorio Lingiardi and Jack Drescher, eds., *The Mental Health Professions and Homosexuality: International Perspectives* (Binghamton, NY: The Haworth Medical Press, 2003); and Camille Robcis, *The Law of Kinship: Anthropology, Psychoanalysis, and the Family in France* (Ithaca: Cornell University Press, 2013).

89 Mary Ballou, Marcia Hill, and Carolyn West, eds., *Feminist Theory and Practice: A Contemporary Perspective* (New York: Springer, 2008), xv–xvi.

90 Despite the esteem in which individual American analysts held Winnicott, his reception in the USA was delayed for a long time. See Paul Roazen, "A Meeting with Donald Winnicott in 1965," in Brett Kahr, ed., *Legacy of Winnicott: Essays on Infant and Child Mental Health* (London: Karnac, 2002), 33–34; and Nellie L. Thompson, "A Measure of Agreement: An Exploration of the Relationship of D. W. Winnicott and Phyllis Greenacre," *Psychoanalytic Quarterly* 77.1 (January 2008), 251–281.

91 Stephen Mitchell, "Psychodynamics, Homosexuality, and the Question of Pathology," *Psychiatry* 41 (1978), 254–263; Stephen Mitchell, "The Psychoanalytic Treatment of Homosexuality: Some Technical Considerations," *International Review of Psycho-Analysis* 8 (1981): 63–80; Nancy J. Chodorow, "Heterosexuality as a Compromise Formation: Reflections on the Psychoanalytic Theory of Sexual Development," *Psychoanalysis and Contemporary Thought* 15.3 (1992): 267–304; Ronnie C. Lesser, "A Reconsideration of Homosexual Themes: Commentary on Trop and Stolorow's 'Defense Analysis in Self Psychology,'" *Psychoanalytic Dialogues* 3 (1993): 639–641.

92 Robert C. Lane and Murray Meisels, eds., *A History of the Division of Psychoanalysis of the American Psychological Association* (Hillsdale, NJ: Lawrence Erlbaum Associates, 1994); and History Panel, *Division 39 Insight*, September 30, 2013, available at: http://division39blog.org/2013/09/history-panel/ (accessed May 8, 2015). The History Panel of Division

251 / Notes to pages 83–89

39 (the division of the American Psychological Association that brings together members interested in psychoanalysis) observed that "the outcome of the lawsuit was a victory for the litigants ... In many respects, however, the outcome of the lawsuit probably benefited APsaA [the American Psychoanalytic Association] the most, opening up a wider field of potential candidates as the pool of physician candidates dried up."

93 Chodorow, "Heterosexuality as a Compromise Formation."

94 Cf. Mitchell, "Psychodynamics, Homosexuality, and the Question of Pathology"; Mitchell, "The Psychoanalytic Treatment of Homosexuality"; Nancy J. Chodorow, "Prejudice Exposed: On Stephen Mitchell's Pioneering Investigations of the Psychoanalytic Treatment and Mistreatment of Homosexuality," *Studies in Gender and Sexuality* 3 (2002): 61–72; and Nancy J. Chodorow, *Individualizing Gender and Sexuality: Theory and Practice* (New York: Routledge, 2012).

95 Lewes, "Homosexuality, Homophobia, and Gay-Friendly Psychoanalysis," 17.

96 Auchincloss and Vaughan, "Psychoanalysis and Homosexuality," 1158.

97 On the desexualization of object relations-oriented psychoanalysis in Britain, see Robert Royston, "Sexuality and Object Relations," in Celia Harding, ed., *Sexuality: Psychoanalytic Perspectives* (Philadelphia, Taylor and Francis, 2001), 35–51. See also David Mann, *Psychotherapy: An Erotic Relationship: Transference and Countertransference Passions* (London: Routledge, 1997), 27; Joseph Schwartz, *Cassandra's Daughter: A History of Psychoanalysis* (London: Karnac, 1999).

98 Lewes, "Homosexuality, Homophobia, and Gay-Friendly Psychoanalysis," 17–19, 22.

99 Lewes, "Homosexuality, Homophobia, and Gay-Friendly Psychoanalysis," 31–32.

100 Kenneth Lewes, "A Special Oedipal Mechanism in the Development of Male Homosexuality," *Psychoanalytic Psychology* 15.3 (1998): 359.

101 Lewes, "Homosexuality, Homophobia, and Gay-Friendly Psychoanalysis," 16.

102 Lewes, "Homosexuality, Homophobia, and Gay-Friendly Psychoanalysis," 29–30.

3 Post-Holocaust Antisemitism and the Ascent of PTSD

1 Kurt R. Eissler, "Die Ermordung von wievielen seiner Kinder muss ein Mensch symptomfrei ertragen können, um eine normale Konstitution zu haben?" *Psyche* 17.5 (1963): 241.

2 So little known is this episode in the evolution of what became PTSD outside of Holocaust studies circles that in his critique of the now-extensive trauma industry, psychiatrist-historian Derek Summerfield singles out Holocaust survivors as *the* example of a group that recovered remarkably well without the benefit of a concept of post-traumatic stress. He sees

Vietnam-era concern with returning soldiers' troubles as the beginning of the (in his view deeply problematic) dissemination of the concept. Scc Derek Summerfield, "A Critique of Seven Assumptions Behind Psychological Trauma Programmes in War-Affected Areas," *Social Science and Medicine* 48 (1999), 1449–1462; and Derek Summerfield, "The Invention of Post-Traumatic Stress Disorder and the Social Usefulness of a Psychiatric Category," *British Medical Journal* 322 (January 13, 2001): 95–98. For a pro-PTSD but also Holocaust aftermath-minimizing account, see David J. Morris, *The Evil Hours: A Biography of Post-Traumatic Stress Disorder* (New York: Houghton Mifflin Harcourt, 2015). Morris estimates that PTSD afflicts as many as 30 percent of the post 9/11 generation of veterans of the USA's "war on terror," and 27 million US citizens in all – including survivors of rape, child abuse, car accidents, and natural disasters. See book jacket and promotional material, available at: www.theevilhours.com/David_Morris___The_Evil_Hours___The_Book.html (accessed January 17, 2016).

3 The felicitous coinage "invention-discovery" (to describe how a category of knowledge comes to acquire density and legitimacy and staying power over time) comes from Bruno Latour, *We Have Never Been Modern* (Cambridge, MA: Harvard University Press, 1993), 5.

4 On the evolution of ideas about trauma from late nineteenth-century industrial accidents and/or World War I shell shock to PTSD, see especially: Allan Young *The Harmony of Illusions: Inventing Post-Traumatic Stress Disorder* (Princeton: Princeton University Press, 1997); Paul Lerner and Mark S. Micale, eds., *Traumatic Pasts: History, Psychiatry and Trauma in the Modern Age* (Cambridge, UK: Cambridge University Press, 2001); Ben Shephard, *A War of Nerves: Soldiers and Psychiatrists in the Twentieth Century* (Cambridge, MA: Harvard University Press, 2003); Edgar Jones and Simon Wessely, *Shell Shock to PTSD: Military Psychiatry from 1900 to the Gulf War* (New York: Psychology Press, 2006); and Didier Fassin and Richard Rechtmann, *The Empire of Trauma: An Inquiry Into the Condition of Victimhood* (Princeton: Princeton University Press, 2009). For significant studies centered on Holocaust trauma and the battle over reparations for health damages, see the valuable bibliography in Robert Krell and Marc I. Sherman, *Medical and Psychological Effects of Concentration Camps on Holocaust Survivors* (New Brunswick: Transaction, 1997), as well as: Ruth Leys, *From Guilt to Shame: Auschwitz and After* (Princeton: Princeton University Press, 2007); Svenja Goltermann, *Die Gesellschaft der Überlebenden: Deutsche Kriegsheimkehrer und ihre Gewalterfahrungen im Zweiten Weltkrieg* (Munich: Deutsche Verlags-Anstalt, 2009); Norbert Frei, José Brunner, and Constantin Goschler, eds., *Die Praxis der Wiedergutmachung: Geschichte, Erfahrung und Wirkung in Deutschland und Israel* (Göttingen: Wallstein, 2009); and the foundational work, Christian Pross, *Paying for the Past: The Struggle over Reparations for Surviving Victims of the Nazi Terror* (Baltimore: Johns Hopkins University Press, 1998).

5 This symptom-checklist-based format still serves as the foundation for DSM-5, the revision completed in 2013.

6 This is a prejudice that has lingered, in some quarters, into the twenty-first century. See the discussion in Vamik Volkan, Gabriele Ast, and William F. Greer, Jr., *The Third Reich in the Unconscious: Transgenerational Transmission and its Consequences* (New York: Routledge, 2002). Vamik et al. report that psychoanalysts often castigated each other, in discussing work with the children of survivors, for seeking details of survivor parents' actual experiences rather than focusing strictly on the second generation's intrapsychic life. Volkan proposed as a conciliatory compromise the idea of at least acknowledging the *general* fact of millionfold systematic mass murder.

7 See the informative overview in Goltermann, *Die Gesellschaft*, especially Part II: "Die Produktion des psychiatrischen Wissens."

8 See Frank Biess, *Homecomings: Returning POWs and the Legacies of Defeat in Postwar Germany* (Princeton: Princeton University Press, 2006); and Goltermann, *Die Gesellschaft*.

9 The comparison with Israel is relevant. Although also in Israel there were rejecting physicians basing themselves on the inherited medical opinion and displaying the reflex of suspicion toward survivors' requests for pensions – opinion and reflex in which they, too (after all, often themselves of German origin), had been trained, the terms of contestation were ultimately unlike those carried out in West Germany, Western European nations, and the USA. See especially Nadav Davidovitch and Rakefet Zalashik, "Recalling the Survivors: Between Memory and Forgetfulness of Hospitalized Holocaust Survivors in Israel," *Israel Studies* 12.2 (Summer 2007): 145–163. Zalashik's book on psychiatry in Israel is devastating in its assessment of the "eugenic" attitudes of Israeli psychiatrists and government authorities who were eager to prevent the arrival of "crushed" people into the society of the young state and who wanted reparations moneys to go not to individual sufferers but rather to the Israeli mental health system as a whole. Sympathetic doctors within Israel thus made quite different arguments from those put forward in the USA and West Germany and Western Europe. They suggested that participation in building the new state would be healing, therapeutic – or they simply emphasized that survivors were resilient, and would be a source of strength for the new state, rather than a burden. Rakefet Zalashik, *Ad Nafesh: Refugees, Immigrants, Newcomers and the Israeli Psychiatric Establishment* (Tel-Aviv: Hakibutz Hameukhad, 2008 [Hebrew]), additionally available in German: Rakefet Zalashik, *Das unselige Erbe: die Geschichte der Psychiatrie in Palästina und Israel* (Frankfurt am Main: Campus, 2012). See in this context also the pathbreaking study by Leo Eitinger, *Concentration Camp Survivors in Norway and Israel* (Oslo: Oslo University Press, 1964).

10 See the case of Herr W. in Pross, *Paying*, 124–125.

11 See Gustav Bodechtel et al.'s introduction to Der Bundesminister für Arbeit und Sozialordnung, ed., *Die "Neurose": ihre versorgungs- und sozialmedizinische Beurteilung* (Stuttgart: W. Kohlhammer, 1960), 6.

12 Samuel Gringauz, "Psychische Schäden und Besonderheiten des Verfahrens: Brückensymptome und spätere Anmeldungen," *Die Wiedergutmachung* 256 (July 21, 1967): 1.

13 Schäffer quoted in Frank Stern, *Im Anfang war Auschwitz: Antisemitismus und Philosemitismus im deutschen Nachkrieg* (Gerlingen: Bleicher, 1991), 336.
14 Ernst Féaux de la Croix and Helmut Rumpf, *Der Werdegang des Entschädigungsrechts unter national- und völkerrechtlichem und politologischem Aspekt* (Munich: C. H. Beck, 1985), 10–11, 151–152, 158–159.
15 Schäffer's pronouncement summarized in "Der neue Tatbestand," *Der Spiegel* (January 29, 1958): 13.
16 See Frank Bajohr, "'Arisierung' in Hamburg; 'Schnäppchen aus Judenkisten,'" *Der Spiegel* (January 26, 1998), available at: www.spiegel.de/spiegel/print/d-7809630.html (accessed January 17, 2016); Susanne Meinl and Jutta Zwilling, *Legalisierter Raub: die Ausplünderung der Juden im Nationalsozialismus durch die Reichsfinanzverwaltung in Hessen* (Frankfurt am Main: Campus, 2004); and Götz Aly, *Hitler's Beneficiaries: Plunder, Racial War, and the Nazi Welfare State* (New York: Henry Holt, 2006).
17 See "Der neue Tatbestand," 13: "*Keine deutsche Stelle wage etwas dagegen zu unternehmen, aus Furcht, sie könne deswegen der Judenfeindlichkeit bezichtigt werden.*"
18 Adenauer's comment reported in Kai von Jena, "Versöhnung mit Israel? Die Deutsch-Israelischen Verhandlungen bis zum Wiedergutmachungsabkommen von 1952," *Vierteljahreshefte für Zeitgeschichte* 34.4 (1986): 470.
19 Letter quoted in "Der neue Tatbestand," 13.
20 Wolfgang See, letter to the editor of *Der Spiegel* (January 8, 1958): 9.
21 Otto Schmöger, letter to the editor of *Der Spiegel* (January 8, 1958): 9. See also another commentator: "Pressure produces counter-pressure. The Jews should not imagine that the German *Volk* will pay 20 or 30 or 40 billion for damages for which Moses is responsible. [*Druck erzeugt Gegendruck. Die Juden sollen sich doch nicht einbilden, dass das deutsche Volk 20 oder 30 oder 40 Milliarden für Schäden zahlt, die Moses zu verantworten hat.*]" Wilhelm Müller, letter to the editor of *Der Spiegel* (February 12, 1958): 6.
22 Walter Armbrust, letter to the editor of *Der Spiegel* (February 12, 1958): 5. (This one and a few other letters were reprinted as "pro-Jewish" in the New York-based German-language paper *Aufbau*.)
23 Peter Krabiell, letter to the editor of *Der Spiegel* (February 12, 1958): 5.
24 Letter to the editor, *Der Spiegel* (January 29, 1958): 6–7.
25 For a perceptive explanation of the increase in everyday expressions of antisemitism two years after the war's end, due, however paradoxically, to Nazism's defeat (replete not just with cabaret jokes like "The Jews are eating chocolate now. Only six million were gassed. Too bad!" but also with random streetcar conversations in which "A German woman, talking about Auschwitz with a Jewish woman, was reviled by fellow passengers: 'What do you care about that Jewish sow? What the Allies are doing to the Germans today is much worse than anything that ever happened in Auschwitz'"), see Samuel Gringauz, "Our New German Policy and the DP's," *Commentary* (June 1948): 508–514. The essay includes mention of a May 1947 poll of the German population in which 61 percent of those questioned "openly avowed anti-Semitism." See as well the study of attitudes in the early 1950s undertaken by Friedrich Pollock and Theodor Adorno, published in German in 1955, and in English as

Theodor W. Adorno, *Guilt and Defense: On the Legacies of National Socialism in Postwar Germany* (Cambridge, MA: Harvard University Press, 2010).

26 There was far more opportunity for potential false claims around the category of "restriction of freedom" (*Freiheitsbeschränkung*) – especially among claims made by non-German individuals living in flight or hiding in areas of German occupation during World War II – than there were around claims for damages to health, and the scandals around overly entrepreneurial lawyers more typically involved these. For example, see "Der neue Tatbestand," 14–16. Between 1956 and 1965, 922,879 claims involved restriction of freedom (of which 536,251 had been settled by 1965) and 485,488 involved damages to health, of which only 186,870 had been settled (and in turn only just under half of which had been settled by being approved). See Pross, *Paying*, 212–214.

27 Diel quoted in "Ich bin der Motor," *Der Spiegel* (March 5, 1958): 23.

28 Diel memorandum to his fellow CDU members quoted in "Der neue Tatbestand," 14.

29 The attacks on Jews seeking to reclaim their own property often got viciously *personal* – as though the individual Jews asking for reclamation of their own furniture or business were greedy and outrageous. See Mark Roseman, "'It went on for years and years': der Wiedergutmachungsantrag der Marianne Ellenbogen," in Frei et al., *Die Praxis*; and Atina Grossmann, "Family Files: Emotions and Stories of (Non-)Restitution," *German Historical Institute London Bulletin* 34.1 (2012): 59–78. On the wider phenomenon of resentment and antisemitism over the outcome of the war (German defeat and partial Jewish survival and refusal to accept German theft without complaint), see as well Constantin Goschler, *Schuld und Schulden* (Göttingen: Wallstein, 2005).

30 Among other things the paper argued that "world Zionism is pushing for World World III." See "Hier die Beweise: Weltzionismus hetzt zum dritten Weltkrieg," *Die Anklage*, 5 (January 1957): 2.

31 See Pross, *Paying*, 79. As late as 1975, the sympathizer doctor William Niederland was summarized as declaring that the problem was *not* in the law courts, the problem was with the other doctors. See Katharina Zimmer, "Ich hätte lieber sterben sollen: viele ehemaligen KZ-Häftlinge leiden heute an Verfolgungsangst und Schuldgefühlen," *Die Zeit* 44 (October 24, 1975): 54.

32 This case is discussed in Ulrich Venzlaff, "Erlebnishintergrund und Dynamik seelischer Verfolgungsschäden," in Hans-Joachim Herberg and Helmut Paul, eds., *Psychische Spätschäden nach politischer Verfolgung*, 2nd, rev. ed. (Basel and New York: Karger, 1967), 157–173, here 171.

33 One of the evaluators in this latter case expressed his regret: "It is unfortunately not possible adequately to connect this faulty attitude, which lies in the realm of the voluntaristic, with the emotional burdens of racial persecution." See the discussion of the cases in Kurt R. Eissler, "Perverted Psychiatry?" *American Journal of Psychiatry* 123.11 (May 1967): 1354–1356; and in the case of the woman labeled hysterical see also his account of her evaluators in Eissler, "Die Ermordung," 276–277.

34 Case discussed in Eissler, "Die Ermordung," 269. See in sympathizing German psychiatrist Kurt Kolle's work a related case about sleep disturbances

in a Jewish woman academic being dismissed as simply "neurotic" rather than the result of trauma. Kurt Kolle, "Die Opfer der nationalsozialistischen Verfolgung in psychiatrischer Sicht," *Der Nervenarzt* 29.4 (1958): 149.

35 *Anlagebedingt* means "caused by constitutional factors" – it can either be translated as "hereditary" or as referring to something to which one is predisposed – in other words, the "anxiety neurosis" was caused by a prior instability endogenous to the individual, not by the external experiences in the camps, and thus also not amenable to the granting of a pension. See esp. the discussion of the label in Eissler, "Perverted Psychiatry?" 1354–1356. Another indicative moment is documented in Göran Rosenberg's memoir of his Auschwitz survivor father David Rosenberg's struggles with the reparations offices. A doctor evaluating David Rosenberg writes: "Without a doubt the patient is exaggerating." And: "The symptoms of psychoneurosis that the patient alleges he has can no longer necessarily be linked to possible harm inflicted in the concentration camps." As the journalist Roger Cohen remarks in his review: "This bureaucratic letter is of a singular obscenity. Possible harm! ... [Rosenberg's book] is the most powerful account I have read of the other death – the death after the camps, the death from damage that proves insuperable." Roger Cohen, "Where the Road from Auschwitz Ends," *New York Times* (March 10, 2015), available at: www.nytimes.com/2015/03/11/opinion/roger-cohen-where-the-road-from-auschwitz-ends.html?_r=0 (accessed January 17, 2016).

36 Case evaluated by Niederland and discussed in Zimmer, "Ich hätte lieber sterben sollen," 54.

37 Hermann Witter, "Erlebnisbedingte Schädigung durch Verfolgung," *Der Nervenarzt* 33 (1962): 510. For insight into the von Baeyer clinic's work, see Walter von Baeyer, *Psychiatrie der Verfolgten; psychopathologische und gutachtliche Erfahrungen an Opfern der nationalsozialistischen Verfolgung und vergleichbarer Extrembelastungen* (Bern: Springer, 1964).

38 Helmuth Lotz, "'Psychische Spätschäden nach politischer Verfolgung': eine Stellungnahme zu dem Buch von H. Paul und H. J. Herberg," *Rechtsprechung zum Wiedergutmachungsrecht* 15.8/9 (1964): 351.

39 Hermann Ammermüller and Hans Wilden, *Gesundheitliche Schäden in der Wiedergutmachung* (Stuttgart: Kohlhammer, 1953), 24–25. Kretschmer's quotes (as well as the fact of their inclusion in Ammermüller and Wilden's government-sponsored book can also be found in Richard Dyck, "Die Neurosen in der Wiedergutmachung," *Aufbau* 14 (March 7, 1958): 1. For a sample of Kretschmer's pre-Nazi-era views on "race and genius," see Ernst Kretschmer, "Genie und Rasse," in Franz Weidenreich, ed., *Rasse und Geist* (Leipzig: Johann Ambrosius Barth, 1932).

40 Bodechtel et al., introduction to Bundesminister, *Die "Neurose,"* 4–5. Emphasis in the original.

41 Lotz, "'Psychische Spätschäden,'" 350–351.

42 Rainer Luthe, "'Erlebnisreaktiver Persönlichkeitswandel' als Begriff der Begutachtung im Entschädigungsrecht," *Monatsschrift für alle Gebiete nervenärztlicher Forschung und Praxis* 39.10 (1968): 465. Luthe was particularly obnoxious. In his essay – which was one extended attack on Ulrich Venzlaff's term "experience-reactive personality change" and which also harped on the puzzle of "the symptom-free interval or the paradoxical

intensification of symptoms" (i.e., the time lag between traumatic event and manifest illness) – he went so far as to suggest that suffering might ennoble and turn survivors "wise" and "holy" in the manner sought by some Eastern religions; he also suggested that it was the challenges of post-camp life and the come-down, i.e., the felt discrepancy in social status between pre- and post-camp life, that was more difficult for survivors than whatever had occurred in the camps themselves.

43 Witter, "Erlebnisbedingte Schädigung," 509.

44 Coiners of these terms were, respectively: René Targowla; Paul Freedman and V. A. Kral independently of each other; Ernst Kluge; Walter von Baeyer; Ulrich Venzlaff.

45 For example, see Lotz, "Psychische Spätschäden," 349–350; and Luthe, " 'Erlebnisreaktiver Persönlichkeitswandel,' " 465.

46 Luthe, " 'Erlebnisreaktiver Persönlichkeitswandel,' " 465.

47 Ammermüller and Wilden, *Gesundheitliche Schäden in der Wiedergutmachung*, 24.

48 For a fuller discussion of this phenomenon, see Dagmar Herzog, *Sex after Fascism: Memory and Morality in Twentieth-Century Germany* (Princeton: Princeton University Press, 2005), 22, 277.

49 Bodechtel et al., introduction to Bundesminister, *Die "Neurose,"* 6.

50 Wolfgang Lederer, "Persecution and Compensation: Theoretical and Practical Implications of the 'Persecution Syndrome,' " *Archives of General Psychiatry* 12 (May 1965): 467. The Vienna-born Lederer worked extensively with survivors in the San Francisco Bay area. See the obituary for Wolfgang Lederer from the *San Francisco Chronicle*, January 11, 2015, available at: www.legacy.com/obituaries/sfgate/obituary.aspx?pid=173720343 (accessed January 17, 2016).

51 See Pross, *Paying*, 125.

52 Hilel Klein, "Wiedergutmachung – ein Akt der Retraumatisierung," in Evangelische Akademie Bad Boll, ed., *Die Bundesrepublik Deutschland und die Opfer des Nationalsozialismus: Tagung vom 25.-27. November 1983 in Bad Boll* (Bad Boll: Evangelische Akademie, 1984), 51–52. On Klein, see Carl Nedelmann, "No Reconciliation, but Self-Searching in the Sense of Rapprochement," *International Journal of Psycho-Analysis* 86 (2005): 1133–1142.

53 See on these points Martin Leonhardt, "Die Begutachtung von Holocaust-Überlebenden: Ein Exkurs zu den Sollbruchstellen in der Identität des forensischen Psychiaters," *Forensische Psychiatrie und Psychotherapie* 9 (2002): 67; as well as Pross, *Paying*, 76–77, 99.

54 Hans Strauss, "Besonderheiten der nichtpsychotischen seelischen Störungen," *Der Nervenarzt* 28 (1957): 344; and Hans Strauss, "Psychiatric Disturbances in Victims of Racial Persecution," *Proceedings of the Third World Congress of Psychiatry* (Montreal, 1961): 1207. For a sense of the frequency with which a sympathetic doctor like William Niederland needed explicitly to counter Strauss's initial rejecting evaluations, see the case records in the William G. Niederland Collection 1903–1989, Leo Baeck Institute New York. For the complaints about Strauss discussed in the New York-based journal *Aufbau* and expressed by sympathetic doctors in an official petition and by distressed survivors in a letter to the West German consulate general, see Pross, *Paying*, 100–101.

55 Kolle, "Die Opfer," 148, 152–153.

56 Ernst Kluge, "Über die Folgen schwerer Haftzeiten," *Der Nervenarzt* 29 (1958): 462–465.

57 Eissler makes these points in 1963, as he also argues directly that "concentration camp trauma is something historically new." Eissler, "Die Ermordung," 286.

58 Kluge, "Über die Folgen," 464.

59 Kolle, "Die Opfer," 153–154.

60 Kolle, "Die Opfer," 153–154.

61 Paul Matussek, *Die Konzentrationslagerhaft und ihre Folgen* (Berlin: Springer, 1971).

62 Lotz, "'Psychische Spätschäden,'" 350.

63 The 75 percent comes from Strauss, "Psychiatric Disturbances"; Strauss means it positively. The fact that these good recovery rates confuse the arguments sympathizers want to make is raised both by Kluge, "Über die Folgen," 462, and by von Baeyer, *Psychiatrie der Verfolgten*, vi.

64 See Miriam Rieck and Gali Eshet, "Die Bürden der Experten: Gespräche mit deutschen und israelischen Psychiatern über ihre Rolle als Gutachter in Entschädigungsverfahren," in Frei et al., *Die Praxis*.

65 For example, see Lotz, "'Psychische Spätschäden,'" 350.

66 Ulrich Venzlaff, "Erlebnisreaktiver Persönlichkeitswandel: Fiktion oder Wirklichkeit?" *Der Nervenarzt* 40 (1969): 539–541.

67 Wolfgang Saxon, "Dr. William G. Niederland, 88; Formulated 'Survivor Syndrome,'" *New York Times*, August 5, 1993, available at: www.nytimes.com/1993/08/05/obituaries/dr-william-g-niederland-88-formulated-survivor-syndrome.html (accessed January 17, 2016). For an early articulation of Niederland's interest in the issue of survivor guilt, see his and Henry Krystal's comments (they were quoted together and summarized in the *New York Times*) in 1965: "'Of our patients, 92 per cent expressed self-reproach for failing to have their relatives,'" and "nine per cent expressed the wish that they had been killed instead of their relatives." Moreover, survivors were often beset by "a chronic tendency to worry, … fears about renewed persecutions and a general 'expectation of catastrophe,'" and "'many of our patients were not only unable to afford themselves some of the most innocent types of pleasure (for example, going to a movie, concert or social gathering with others) but even considered it outright immoral that they should enjoy themselves when most of their families had been killed.'" Raymond H. Anderson, "Study Confirms Survivor Guilt," *New York Times* (May 6, 1965): 21.

68 See Ulrich Venzlaff, *Die psychoreaktiven Störungen nach entschädigungspflichtigen Ereignissen: Die sogenannten Unfallneurosen* (New York: Springer, 1958); and the many case records available in the William G. Niederland Collection 1903–1989, Leo Baeck Institute New York.

69 Eissler, "Die Ermordung," 264–265, 286, 288, 291.

70 Nobody prior to Eissler had made these points. Consider the prehistory of countertransference theorizing from Freud through Winnicott, Heimann, Racker, Spitz, and Loewald. See Donald W. Winnicott, "Hate in the Counter-Transference," *International Journal of Psycho-Analysis* 30 (1949): 69–74; Paula Heimann, "On Counter-Transference," *International*

Journal of Psycho-Analysis 31 (1950): 81–84; Heinrich Racker, "A Contribution to the Problem of Counter-Transference," *International Journal of Psycho-Analysis* 34 (1953): 313–324; René Spitz, "Countertransference – Comments on its Varying Role in the Analytic Situation," *Journal of the American Psychoanalytic Association* 4 (1956): 256–265; Hans W. Loewald, "On the Therapeutic Action of Psycho-Analysis," *International Journal of Psycho-Analysis* 41 (1960): 16–33.

71 Eissler, "Perverted," 1358.

72 Eissler, "Perverted," 1357–1358.

73 Krystal estimated that there were approximately 4,000 survivors of the Nazi concentration camps living in the Detroit area and that "between 60 and 70 percent of the refugees living here have mental problems. They feel they are apart from other people. 'They cling together but they don't talk about the past ... They have feelings of guilt because they survived, while others perished.'" Quoted in Merle Oliver, "Nazi Survivors Can't Forget – Many Hit by Mental Ills," *Detroit News* (February 21, 1965): B. This news item also profiled Ulrich Venzlaff's participation in the Detroit conferences – and his insights into perpetrator psychology. Personal collection of Esther Krystal.

74 For example, the Los Angeles-based German-heritage gentile sympathizer psychoanalyst Klaus Hoppe, who had emigrated to the USA in the 1950s, was a key figure promoting the Eisslerian insights into contempt for the weak and the importance of attending to countertransference in all its complexities. See Klaus D. Hoppe, "Psychotherapy with Concentration-Camp Survivors," in Henry Krystal, ed., *Massive Psychic Trauma* (New York: International Universities Press, 1968), 204–219; Klaus D. Hoppe, "The Emotional Reactions of Psychiatrists when Confronting Survivors of Persecution" (and responses), in John A. Lindon, ed., *The Psychoanalytic Forum*, vol. III (New York: Science House, 1969), 187–211. See also the subsequent conference volume: William G. Niederland and Henry Krystal, eds., *Psychic Traumatization: Aftereffects in Individuals and Communities* (New York: Little, Brown, 1971).

75 An early and comprehensive overview of the pitfalls of attempts at analysis with Holocaust survivors is Eddy de Wind, "Psychotherapy after Traumatization caused by Persecution," in Niederland and Krystal, *Psychic Traumatization*, 93–114. On the initially unacknowledged problems within therapeutic efforts, see also Yael Danieli, "Therapists' Difficulties in Treating Survivors of the Nazi Holocaust and their Children" (Ph.D. dissertation, New York University, 1981); and Yael Danieli, "Countertransference in the Treatment and Study of Nazi Holocaust Survivors and Their Children," *Victimology: An International Journal* 5 (1981): 45–53. Looking back, psychologist Norman Solkoff noted summarily about those few Holocaust survivors who had experienced psychoanalytic treatment that "the going was rough and the results unpredictable." See Norman Solkoff, "The Holocaust: Survivors and Their Children," in Metin Başoğlu, ed., *Torture and its Consequences: Current Treatment Approaches* (Cambridge, UK: Cambridge University Press, 1992), 143. For a crushing example of a bad therapeutic experience, see Ruth Kluger, *Still Alive: A Holocaust Girlhood Remembered* (New York: Feminist Press, 2001), 185–191. Kluger

makes a direct connection between the offensive mishandling of her experience by the analyst (Lazi Fessler) and the active evasion of external realities of any kind in postwar US psychiatry: "The garden-variety psychiatry which flourished in New York in those days avoided all social criticism and any connection between individual suffering and historical evil – it was in full flight from the excess of history which we had just managed to put behind us. Hence all psychic suffering had to have its origin inside, in the mind of the patient. No cold winds from the outside could affect the hothouse of the psyche" (186).

76 Lifton interviewed by Ran Zwigenberg, June 9, 2011; and see also Robert Jay Lifton, *Witness to an Extreme Century: A Memoir* (New York: Free Press, 2011), 184–191, 241, 395–96.

77 See on this point also Rieck and Eshet, "Die Bürden," 459.

78 Robert Bazell, "Auschwitz & Viet: – The Survivors," *New York Post* (October 3, 1972): 26.

79 James A. Treloar, "The private hell of survivors: Years after death camps, they're tortured by feelings of guilt," *Detroit News* (November 7, 1971): 10B. Personal collection of Esther Krystal.

80 See Boyce Rensberger, "Delayed Trauma in Veterans Cited: Psychiatrists Find Vietnam Produces Guilt and Shame," *New York Times* (May 3, 1972): 19.

81 Chaim F. Shatan, "Post-Vietnam Syndrome," *New York Times* (May 6, 1972): 35.

82 Chaim F. Shatan, "Bogus Manhood, Bogus Honor: Surrender and Transfiguration in the United States Marine Corps," *Psychoanalytic Review* 64 (1977): 585–610. In the paper – which had much to say about the routineity, in the Marine Corps, of "'fag-bait[ing],'" "spurious virility" accompanied by actual "impotence" except when engaging in "violent aggression," and "the reversal of individual development to a stage when the person is only an appendage of an authority – regression and de-individuation" – Shatan observed also about US society as a whole: "We have become inured to official killing" (589, 596, 606, 608).

83 Personal communication from Nancy Andreasen, August 13, 2013.

84 1976 draft memorandum by Nancy Andreasen to Robert Spitzer, Lyman Wynne, Chaim Shatan, Robert Lifton, Jack Smith, and Leonard Neff on "Post-traumatic disorder" (personal collection of Nancy Andreasen, University of Iowa). See also Nancy C. Andreasen, "Posttraumatic Stress Disorder," in Harold I. Kaplan, Alfred M. Freedman, and Benjamin J. Sadock, eds., *Comprehensive Textbook of Psychiatry/III*, vol. II (Baltimore and London: Williams and Wilkins, 1980), 1517–1525.

85 It is instructive as well – not least because it reveals how reluctant psychiatrists and the public had once been to acknowledge Holocaust trauma, but also because it reveals how strategically necessary comparison was felt to be – to see how proactively Krystal, Niederland, and like-minded doctors sought to make comparisons between the experiences of survivors of Nazism with survivors of such much more mundane matters, however individually traumatizing, as car accidents. For example, see "Tragedy Survivors Studied for Traumas: Disorders Found," *San Diego Union* (December 31, 1967). Personal collection of Esther Krystal.

86 David Becker, "Zwischen Trauma und Traumadiskurs: Nachdenken über psychosoziale Arbeit im Gazastreifen," *Werkblatt* 27.65 (2010): 50–86, here 62.

87 David Becker, *Die Erfindung des Traumas – verflochtene Geschichten* (Freiburg: Edition Freitag, 2006).

88 Jørgen Ortmann et al., "Rehabilitation of Torture Victims: An Interdisciplinary Treatment Model," *American Journal of Social Psychiatry* 7.3 (Summer 1987): 161–167, here 161.

89 By 1978, a seminar on "Torture and the Medical Profession" had been held in Athens, resulting in the establishment of an international group tasked with developing treatment and rehabilitation proposals. *Report of an Amnesty International Medical Seminar: Violations of Human Rights: Torture and the Medical Profession, Athens 10–11 March 1978* (London: Amnesty International Publications, 1978). In 1979, another seminar, this time focused on treatment, was held in Copenhagen; also experts who had worked with survivors of concentration camps and of life in hiding during Nazi occupation were invited. Starting in 1979–1980, survivors of torture began to be treated at the University Hospital in Copenhagen and from 1980 to 1982 a treatment plan (combining social counseling, somatic health care and physiotherapy as well as massage, involvement of family members of the survivor, and psychotherapy – which included work with dreams, resistances, and efforts to reestablish the survivor's sense of identity and ability to trust) was formulated. By 1984, a first International Rehabilitation and Research Center for Torture Victims, partially funded by the Danish government and partially by donations, opened its doors in Copenhagen.

90 For a retrospective summary of the applicability as well as limitations of PTSD for torture victims, see also Ellen Gerrity, Terence M. Keane, and Farris Tuma, "Introduction," *The Mental Health Consequences of Torture* (New York: Springer, 2001).

91 See especially the publications of a team in Portland, Oregon led by the psychiatrist J. David Kinzie. Over time, as Kinzie's team worked to refine their psychotherapeutic approach to traumatized refugees, they increasingly familiarized themselves with and built on the writings of individuals who had worked with Holocaust survivors, including Leo Eitinger, William Niederland, and Hilel Klein – as well as Robert Jay Lifton. Through detailed reports on individual cases and elaborations of their own treatment approaches – including pharmaceutical interventions such as antidepressants and, in severe cases, antipsychotics, combined with alertness to stressors that might reexacerbate symptoms (for example, news from the home country) and supportive but cautious and deliberately nonintrusive psychotherapy adapted to the "traditional values" of the survivors' cultures of origin – they advanced the view that "posttraumatic stress disorder" specifically as it had been formulated in DSM-III was indeed the best descriptor and that medical professionals everywhere needed to learn to recognize its signs. J. David Kinzie et al., "An Indochinese Refugee Psychiatric Clinic: Culturally Accepted Treatment Approaches," *American Journal of Psychiatry* 137.11 (November 1980): 1429–1432; J. David Kinzie et al., "Posttraumatic Stress Disorder Among Survivors of

Cambodian Concentration Camps," *American Journal of Psychiatry* 141.5 (May 1984): 645–650; James K. Boehnlein et al., "One-Year Follow-Up Study of Posttraumatic Stress Disorder Among Survivors of Cambodian Concentration Camps," *American Journal of Psychiatry* 142.8 (August 1985): 956–959; J. David Kinzie and Jenelle Fleck, "Psychotherapy with Severely Traumatized Refugees," *American Journal of Psychotherapy* 41.1 (January 1987): 82–94.

92 The canonical statement of torture's effects, most devastatingly on victims, but also on family members of torture victims – and, crucially, also on perpetrators – is based on the pervasive use of torture in the French-Algerian war: Frantz Fanon, "Colonial War and Mental Disorders (1961)," in *The Wretched of the Earth* (New York: Grove, 2004), 181–219. Fanon expressly discusses the use of torture to extract information, and notes that the survivors who came to him for psychotherapeutic care were almost inevitably those who had actually known nothing (195, 198, 209).

93 Ortmann et al., "Rehabilitation." Or, as Becker phrased it, based on his work in Chile, where the dictatorship had been ruthless in its suppression of political opposition, the point of torture was "never just the acquisition of information, but always also the concrete and symbolic annihilation of the victim, that is the victim should be literally broken, so that he cannot go on fighting. Simultaneously the crushing of the victim is a sign for his friends, comrades and social milieu that a victory against the oppressor is impossible." Becker, *Die Erfindung*, 159.

94 Becker, *Die Erfindung*, 159.

95 Ortmann et al., "Rehabilitation."

96 Elizabeth Lira, David Becker, and María Isabel Castillo, "Psychotherapy with Victims of Political Repression in Chile: A Therapeutic and Political Challenge," in Janet Gruschow and Kari Hannibal, eds., *Health Services for the Treatment of Torture and Trauma survivors: From Symposia Sponsored by the AAAS Committee on Scientific Freedom and Responsibility at the AAAS Annual Meeting, Boston, Massachusetts, 14 February 1988, AAAS Annual Meeting, San Francisco, California, 16 January 1989* (Washington, DC: American Association for the Advancement of Science, 1989), 108, 101.

97 Initially two members of the team had published – in what turned out to be an oft-cited essay – under the protective pseudonyms Ana Julia Cienfuegos and Cristina Monelli: "The Testimony of Political Repression as a Therapeutic Instrument," *American Journal of Orthopsychiatry* 53.1 (January 1983): 43–51. This essay clearly states that the authors' names are pseudonyms. A year later, they dared to publish the essay – which they had originally written in 1981 – in Spanish under their own names: Elizabeth Lira and Eugenia Weinstein, "El Testimonio de Experiencias Políticas Traumáticas como Instrumento Terapéutico," in Elizabeth Lira, Eugenia Weinstein, Rosario Dominguez, Juana Kovalskys, Adriana Maggi, Eliana Morales, and Fanny Pollarolo, eds., *Psicoterapia y Represión Política* (Mexico City: Siglo Veintiuno Editores, 1984), 17–36. Lira would eventually become transnationally recognized for her brave work – among other things having slipped into prisons to provide therapeutic conversations by pretending to be a sister of a prisoner; she has since been appointed

member of three post-dictatorship national commissions on whether and how rehabilitation for survivors might be provided. See the remarks on video by Douglas Johnson, introducing Lira, at the conference "'As Full Rehabilitation as is Possible': Do Torture Survivors Have a Right to Care?" held at the Wilson Center's Latin American Program and Center for Victims of Torture in Washington, DC, 2011, as well as the text of Lira's presentation, both available at: www.wilsoncenter.org/event/full-rehabilitation-possible-do-torture-survivors-have-right-to-care (accessed January 22, 2016).

98 Becker, *Die Erfindung*, 9.
99 David Becker, "Hans Keilson und die Revolutionierung der Traumatheorie," *Neue Rundschau* 4 (2009): 71–83, here 82.
100 Becker, "Zwischen," 80–82.
101 Hans Keilson, *Sequentielle Traumatisierung bei Kindern: Untersuchung zum Schicksal jüdischer Kriegswaisen* (Giessen: Psychosozial-Verlag, 2005); Hans Keilson, *Sequential Traumatisation in Children: A Clinical and Statistical Follow-up Study on the Fate of the Jewish War Orphans in the Netherlands* (Jerusalem: Magnes, 1992).
102 Becker, *Die Erfindung*; Becker, "Zwischen." Becker was additionally impressed by the object relations-based theory of trauma developed by the British psychoanalysts Jonathan Cohen and Warren Kinston, especially their suggestions of how therapists might most sensitively deal with patients who had been, in Khan's terms, "cumulatively traumatized." See Jonathan Cohen and Warren Kinston, "Repression Theory: A New Look at the Cornerstone," *International Journal of Psycho-Analysis* 65 (1984): 411–422, esp. 419.
103 Keilson, *Sequentielle Traumatisierung*.
104 Becker, "Zwischen," 65.
105 Keilson cited in Becker, *Die Erfindung*, 166.
106 Becker invokes the useful explanation of Freud's notion of "deferred action" in Jean Laplanche and Jean-Bertrand Pontalis, *The Language of Psycho-Analysis* (London: Karnac, 1988).
107 In his book, *Sequential Traumatization*, Keilson had divided the experiences of hidden children into three traumatic phases. First was the enemy occupation of the Netherlands with the accompanying preliminary terror against the Jewish minority; second was the phase of deportation, forced separation of parents and children, hiding in improvised foster families, and time spent within camps; and third was the postwar period with the drama of guardianship allocation as the central theme. (As an example of how Keilson's findings, both statistical and qualitative, complicated whatever clarity of causation between camp experience and subsequent symptoms that sympathetic doctors had been at pains to prove, Keilson showed that a comparatively more favorable second phase followed by a comparatively unfavorable third phase led in adulthood to far more severe pathologies than a comparatively unfavorable second phase and a favorable third. This was the kind of empathetic accuracy that challenged well-meaning but problematic efforts to highlight simpler accounts of the relationship between cause and effect.) Based on his experiences in Chile, Becker ended up expanding

Keilson's three phases to six. The phase before traumatic processes had
even begun was the first (albeit with Becker's pointed accompanying
observation that all too often the before for one trauma was actually
the after of earlier ones); the second was the onset of direct persecution;
then the acute phase was divided into times of direct terror and times
of chronification – for example, stretches of time during a war or other
long times of waiting in which nothing concrete was happening but all
was filled with fearful anticipation; and then there were two stages of
aftermath, since many crises did not end all at once, and survivors often
went through a further difficult phase before finding anything resem-
bling existential safety.

108 Lira et al., *Psicoterapia y Represión Política*.
109 "Introduction," in Equipo de Salud Mental-DITT del Comite de Defensa
de los Derechos del Pueblo (CODEPU) and Organización Mundial contra la Tortura (OMCT) Ginebra – Suiza, *Tortura: Aspectos Médicos,
Psicológicos y Sociales* (Santiago, 1989), available at: www.blest.eu/bib-
lio/seminario/intro.html (accessed January 22, 2016); Nancy Caro Hollander, "Psychoanalysis Confronts the Politics of Repression: The Case of
Argentina," *Social Science and Medicine* 28.7 (1989): 757.
110 Diana R. Kordon, "Introduction," in Diana R. Kordon et al., eds., *Psychological Effects of Political Repression* (Buenos Aires: Sudamericana/
Planeta, 1988), 23.
111 Adriana Maggi, "Programa Terapéutico de Fasic: Una Experiencia de
Psicología Viva," in Equipo de Salud Mental-DITT del Comite de Defensa
de los Derechos del Pueblo (CODEPU) and Organización Mundial contra la Tortura (OMCT) Ginebra – Suiza, *Tortura*, available at: www.blest.
eu/biblio/seminario/index.html (accessed January 22, 2016).
112 Elizabeth Lira and Eugenia Weinstein in 1984, as translated from Spanish
into German, in Becker, *Die Erfindung*, 47.
113 "Principally, the therapeutic bond helps to facilitate and re-establish the
patient's capacity to trust others, establishing a genuine relationship built
on true facts, accepting love, hate, sadness, destruction, and many other
emotions, not only as part of the bond between therapist and patient,
but also the bond between human beings. In this context, painful, overwhelming, and fearful dimensions of a socially denied reality can be
reconstructed." Lira, Becker, and Castillo, "Psychotherapy," 109.
114 Becker, *Die Erfindung*, 50–51.
115 Becker, "Zwischen," 65.
116 Becker, "Zwischen," 83.

4 The Struggle between Eros and Death

1 Alexander Mitscherlich, "Aggression ist eine Grundmacht des Lebens,"
Spiegel 42 (October 13, 1969): 206.
2 Sigmund Freud, "Zeitgemässes über Krieg und Tod" (1915), *Gesammelte
Werke*, vol. X, 324–355; Sigmund Freud, "Jenseits des Lustprinzips"
(1920), *Gesammelte Werke*, vol. XIII, 3–69; Sigmund Freud, "Das

ökonomische Problem des Masochismus" (1924), *Gesammelte Werke*, XIII, 371–383; Sigmund Freud, "Das Unbehagen in der Kultur" (1930), *Gesammelte Werke*, vol. XIV, 421–506.

3 Freud, "Jenseits des Lustprinzips," 58, 60–61, 65–66, 69; Sigmund Freud, "Das Ich und das Es" (1923), *Gesammelte Werke*, vol. XIII, 237–289, here 269. For the best insight into Freud's recurrently recalibrated ideas about sexual, self-preserving, and destructive or death drives – as he evolved them in the revision process of "Beyond the Pleasure Principle," see Ulrike May, "The Third Step in Drive Theory: On the Genesis of *Beyond the Pleasure Principle*," *Psychoanalysis and History* 17 (2015): 205–272.

4 Letter from Sigmund Freud to Ernest Jones, January 26, 1930, in R. Andrew Paskauskas, ed., *The Complete Correspondence of Sigmund Freud and Ernest Jones 1908–1939* (Cambridge, MA: Belknap, 1993), 668.

5 Freud, "Das Unbehagen," 481.

6 Michal Shapira, "The Hitler Inside: Klein and her Patients," in *The War Inside: Psychoanalysis, Total War, and the Making of the Democratic Self in Postwar Britain* (Cambridge UK: Cambridge University Press, 2013), 87–111.

7 For example, see the mentions of aggression in Anna Freud, "Indications for Child Analysis," *Psychoanalytic Study of the Child* 1 (1945): 127–149; and Heinz Hartmann et al., "Comments on the Formation of Psychic Structure," *Psychoanalytic Study of the Child* 2 (1946): 11–38. Tellingly, the most extensive discussion of aggression in the journal's early years is in Edward Glover's overview of Melanie Klein's work: Edward Glover, "Examination of the Klein System of Child Psychology," *Psychoanalytic Study of the Child* 1 (1945): 75–118. See especially Glover's energetic demurral in footnote 23 on the final page (118).

8 C. W. Tidd, "Symposium on 'Psycho-Analysis and Ethology' I. Introduction," *International Journal of Psycho-Analysis* 41 (1960): 308–312; Marga Vicedo, *The Nature and Nurture of Love: From Imprinting to Attachment in Cold War America* (Chicago: University of Chicago Press, 2013).

9 Robert Ardrey, *The Territorial Imperative* (New York: Atheneum, 1966); and Desmond Morris, *The Naked Ape* (New York: McGraw-Hill, 1967).

10 Doris Bartlett and Francis Bartlett, "Social Implications of Biological Determinism," *Science and Society* 35 (Summer 1971): 209–219; Glendon Schubert, "Biopolitical Behavior: The Nature of the Political Animal," *Polity* 6 (Winter 1973): 240–275; Nadine Weidman, "Popularizing the Ancestry of Man: Robert Ardrey and the Killer Instinct," *Isis* 102 (June 2011): 269–299; and Erica Milam, *Looking for a Few Good Males: Female Choice in Evolutionary Biology* (Baltimore: Johns Hopkins University Press, 2010).

11 Konrad Lorenz, *Das sogenannte Böse: zur Naturgeschichte der Aggression* (Vienna: Borotha-Schoeler, 1963), ix–x. The English translation unhelpfully renders the German "Trieb" in this passage as "instinct" or "wish." See Konrad Lorenz, *On Aggression* (New York: Routledge, 2002 [1966]), x.

12 Lorenz, *On Aggression*, x.

13 Incidentally, within the USA Hartmann et al. had already pointed up the problems with the translation of *Trieb* as "instinct" as early

as 1949: Heinz Hartmann, Ernst Kris, and Rudolph M. Loewenstein, "Notes on the Theory of Aggression," *Psychoanalytic Study of the Child* 3 (1949): 9, 12–13.

14 On the Mitscherlichs' marriage as a *Denkgemeinschaft* (thinking-partnership) involving constant intellectual collaboration, see Tobias Freimüller, *Alexander Mitscherlich: Gesellschaftsdiagnosen und Psychoanalyse nach Hitler* (Göttingen: Wallstein, 2007), 252; on the process of deciding that *The Inability to Mourn* would be published under both of their names, although six of the eight essays included in the volume (all but chapters 1 and 4) had been singly authored by Alexander – though surely also produced in shared brainstorming and with Margarete's editing, see Timo Hoyer, *Im Getümmel der Welt: Alexander Mitscherlich* (Göttingen: Vandenhoeck & Ruprecht, 2008), 501–502.

15 Freimüller, *Alexander Mitscherlich*, 8; and Michael Rutschky, "Von Prof. Freud zu Dr. Caligari," *Cicero* (January 2006): 132.

16 Alexander Mitscherlich, "Toleranz – Überprüfung eines Begriffs," in Alexander Mitscherlich, ed., *Toleranz – Überprüfung eines Begriffs* (Frankfurt am Main: Suhrkamp, 1974): 10–17; cf. Alexander Mitscherlich and Margarete Mitscherlich, *Die Unfähigkeit zu trauern: Grundlagen kollektiven Verhaltens* (Munich: Piper, 1967), 171, 318; and Werner Bohleber, "Alexander Mitscherlich, die Psyche und die Entwicklung der Psychoanalyse in Deutschland nach 1945," *Psyche* 63 (2009): 99–128.

17 For example, see Jacques Lacan, "The Freudian Thing," in Jacques Lacan, ed., *Écrits*, trans. B. Fink (New York: W. W. Norton, 2002 [1966]).

18 Anon., "Die Rolle des Juden in der Medizin," *Deutsche Volksgesundheit aus Blut und Boden* (August–September 1933): 15; and Heinz Hunger, "Jüdische Psychoanalyse und deutsche Seelsorge," in Walter Grundmann, ed., *Germanentum, Judentum und Christentum*, vol. II (Leipzig: G. Wigand, 1943), 317.

19 Hoyer, *Im Getümmel der Welt*, 371–372; Alfred Krovoza, "Zum Verhältnis von Psychogenese und Soziogenese im Gewaltdiskurs," *Psyche* 55 (September 2001): 917.

20 Mitscherlich, "Aggression ist eine Grundmacht des Lebens," 206.

21 A felt sense of urgency in bringing psychoanalysis back to Germany was also a major concern of the Frankfurt School re-émigré sociologist-philosophers Theodor Adorno and Max Horkheimer. They were thus concretely instrumental in promoting and encouraging Mitscherlich (even as they were not consistently impressed with him and sometimes privately sniffed that they found his work to be derivative of their own ideas). See the discussion of both sides of Adorno and Horkheimer's attitudes toward Mitscherlich in Freimüller, *Alexander Mitscherlich*, 210–213. Horkheimer did cooperate closely with Mitscherlich – for example for a widely publicized lecture series in 1956 to celebrate the centenary of Sigmund Freud's birthday – in bringing prominent emigrated analysts back to West Germany to speak. (See Franz Alexander et al., *Freud in der Gegenwart: Ein Vortragszyklus der Universitäten Frankfurt und Heidelberg zum hundertsten Geburtstag* (Frankfurt amMain: Europäische Verlagsanstalt, 1956.) In addition to Alexander, other notable visitors were René Spitz, Erik Erikson, Michael Balint, and Herbert Marcuse.)

But, as late as 1965, Horkheimer was lamenting the West German public's ongoing disinterest in psychoanalysis. See Philip Shabecoff, "Germans Shunt Psychoanalysis to a Minor Role, Scholar Says: Professor Deplores Neglect of Practice in Region Where it Took Root," *New York Times* (February 22, 1965): 23. Not least due to the polemical stimulus provided by Lorenz and then to the rise of the New Left – and to the mediating efforts of Mitscherlich – that situation would soon change, and Freud would become nothing less than a national obsession. On the timing, see also: Alexander Mitscherlich, "Psychoanalyse heute," in *Gesammelte Schriften* VIII (Frankfurt am Main: Suhrkamp, 1964), 171–193; and Anthony D. Kauders, *Der Freud-Komplex: Eine Geschichte der Psychoanalyse in Deutschland* (Berlin: Berlin Verlag, 2014), 194–195, 207, 211.

22 Mitscherlich and Mitscherlich, *Die Unfähigkeit zu trauern*, 172; Alexander Mitscherlich, "Psychoanalysis and the Aggression of Large Groups," *International Journal of Psycho-Analysis* 52 (1971): 161–167, here 162.

23 For example, see the report on the IPA congress in Vienna in Alden Whitman, "Revision in Father's Theory is Proposed by Anna Freud," *International Herald Tribune* (July 31–August 1, 1971): 5; and see Anna Freud, "Comments on Aggression," *International Journal of Psycho-Analysis* 53 (1972): 163–171. In this talk Anna Freud also referenced the American psychoanalyst Kurt Eissler's declaration of belief in the existence of a death drive – in a paper which in turn had referenced both Hartmann and Mitscherlich: Kurt Eissler, "Death Drive, Ambivalence, and Narcissism," *Psychoanalytic Study of the Child* 26 (1971): 25–78. By contrast, note that Donald Winnicott – who had prepared to attend the congress in Vienna, but died six months earlier – did *not* concur that a "death instinct" existed, and spent years working to articulate an alternative to Freud's view. See Jan Abram, "DWW's Notes for the Vienna Congress 1971: A Consideration of Winnicott's Theory of Aggression and Interpretation of the Clinical Implications," in Jan Abram, ed., *Donald Winnicott Today* (London: New York: Routledge, 2012), 302–330.

24 Dagmar Herzog, *Sex after Fascism: Memory and Morality in Twentieth-Century Germany* (Princeton: Princeton University Press, 2005), 7, 139.

25 Hans Krieger, "Der Mensch – von Natur aus destruktiv?" *Zeit* 46 (November 14, 1969): 32–33.

26 Herbert Selg, ed., *Zur Aggression verdammt?* (Stuttgart: Kohlhammer, 1971), 147.

27 Irenäus Eibl-Eibesfeldt, *Liebe und Hass: zur Naturgeschichte elementarer Verhaltensweisen* (Munich: Piper, 1970), 13, 265–267.

28 Eibl-Eibesfeldt quoted in Klaus Horn, "Die humanwissenschaftliche Relevanz der Ethologie im Lichte einer sozialwissenschaftlich verstandenen Psychoanalyse," in Gerhard Roth et al., eds., *Kritik der Verhaltensforschung: Konrad Lorenz und seine Schule* (Munich: C. H. Beck, 1974), 192.

29 Rolf Denker, *Aufklärung über Aggression: Kant, Darwin, Freud, Lorenz* (Stuttgart and Berlin: W. Kohlhammer, 1966), 97; Krieger, "Der Mensch – von Natur aus destruktiv?" 32–33; Wolf Lepenies and Helmut Nolte, *Kritik der Anthropologie* (Munich: Carl Hanser, 1971), 104–105.

30 Hermann Glaser, *Eros in der Politik* (Köln: Verlag Wissenschaft und Politik, 1967), 28, 122, 258–259.
31 Selg, *Zur Aggression verdammt?* 9.
32 Arno Plack, *Die Gesellschaft und das Böse: eine Kritik der herrschenden Moral* (Munich: List, 1967), 249. Cf. Lepenies and Nolte, *Kritik der Anthropologie*, 117.
33 Plack, *Die Gesellschaft*, 309.
34 Herbert Marcuse, et al., *Aggression und Anpassung in der Industriegesellschaft* (Frankfurt am Main: Suhrkamp, 1968), 7–29.
35 Horn, "Die humanwissenschaftliche Relevanz," 190–191, 193; Klaus Horn, "Gesellschaftliche Produktion von Gewalt: Vorschläge zu ihrer politpsychologischen Untersuchung," in Otthein Rammstedt, ed., *Gewaltverhältnisse und die Ohnmacht der Kritik* (Frankfurt am Main: Suhrkamp, 1974), 62; and Tom Alexander, "The Social Engineers Retreat Under Fire," *Fortune* (October 1972): 132.
36 See also: Klaus Horn and Alfred Lorenzer, "Vorwort der Herausgeber," Alfred Lorenzer and Klaus Horn, "Vorbemerkung," and Klaus Horn, "Die theoretische Abschaffung des Subjekts in Form seiner selbstzerstörerischen Wiederkehr," all in Helmut Dahmer et al., *Das Elend der Psychoanalyse-Kritik Beispiel Kursbuch 29: Subjektverleugnung als politische Magie* (Frankfurt am Main: Athenäum, 1973), 1–2, 5–6, 77–128.
37 "Was für Zeiten," *Spiegel* 47 (November 18, 1968): 46–7.
38 "Der Wille zur Macht lebt," *Spiegel* 33 (August 9, 1971): 90.
39 "Was brutalisiert den Menschen?" *Spiegel* 24 (June 5, 1972): 124–128.
40 "Der Wille zur Macht lebt," 90; Robert Ardrey, *The Social Contract: A Personal Inquiry into the Evolutionary Sources of Order and Disorder* (New York: Atheneum, 1970).
41 Konrad Lorenz in Friedrich Hacker, *Aggression: Die Brutalisierung der modernen Welt* (Vienna: Molden, 1971), 11. Cf. H.-G. Rauch, "Der sogenannte Gute," *Zeit* 51 (December 14, 1973): 21.
42 "Was brutalisiert den Menschen?" 127.
43 Selg, *Zur Aggression verdammt?* 9.
44 Arno Plack, "Aggressivität als Frage an die Wissenschaften," in Arno Plack, ed., *Der Mythos vom Aggressionstrieb* (Munich: List, 1973), 10.
45 Erich Fromm, *The Anatomy of Human Destructiveness* (New York: Holt, Rinehart, 1973), 2–3, 35.
46 "Gefährliches Gerede," *Spiegel* 27 (June 26, 1971): 109.
47 Denker, *Aufklärung über Aggression*, 94–95.
48 Klaus Theweleit, *Male Fantasies*, vol. II, trans. Erica Carter (Minneapolis: University of Minnesota Press, 1978), 268.
49 Paula Heimann, "Entwicklungssprünge und das Auftreten der Grausamkeit," in Alexander Mitscherlich, ed., *Bis hierher und nicht weiter: ist die menschliche Aggression unbefriedbar?* (Munich: Piper, 1969), 105–107.
50 Mitscherlich and Mitscherlich, *Die Unfähigkeit zu trauern*, 197.
51 Alexander Mitscherlich, *Die Idee des Friedens und die menschliche Aggressivität* (Frankfurt am Main: Suhrkamp, 1969), 80.
52 Alexander Mitscherlich, "Aggression und Anpassung," *Psyche* 10 (1956): 183; Alexander Mitscherlich, "Vorwort," in Mitscherlich, *Bis hierher und*

nicht weiter, 8; Mitscherlich, "Aggression ist eine Grundmacht des Lebens," 209; and Mitscherlich, *Die Idee des Friedens*, 80.

53 Alexander Mitscherlich, *Auf dem Weg zur vaterlosen Gesellschaft* (Munich: Piper, 1963), 290.

54 Mitscherlich and Mitscherlich, *Die Unfähigkeit zu trauern*, 106, 198.

55 Mitscherlich, "Toleranz," 14, 30–31.

56 Alexander Mitscherlich, "Freuds Sexualtheorie und die notwendige Aufklärung der Erwachsenen," in Alexander Mitscherlich, ed., *Versuch, die Welt besser zu bestehen* (Frankfurt am Main: Suhrkamp, 1970), 146–147.

57 Alexander Mitscherlich, "Zwei Arten der Grausamkeit," in Mitscherlich, *Toleranz*, 168–189, here 175.

58 Mitscherlich, "Zwei Arten der Grausamkeit," 181–188.

59 The Stuttgart-based psychoanalyst Claudia Frank argued in 2015 that the decades-long delay in receiving Klein in West Germany is explicable: "in Germany the clinical usefulness of the death drive hypothesis could not be considered as long as destructive impulses were still an immediate social reality" (2015). Claudia Frank, "On the Reception of the Concept of the Death Drive in Germany: Expressing and Resisting an 'Evil Principle'?" *International Journal of Psycho-Analysis* 96 (2015): 425–444, here 425.

60 Michael Balint, *The Basic Fault: Therapeutic Aspects of Regression* (London: Tavistock, 1968).

61 Paula Heimann, "Some Aspects of the Role of Introjection and Projection in Early Development," in Pearl King and Riccardo Steiner, eds., *The Freud–Klein Controversies 1941–45* (London and New York: Tavistock/Routledge, 1991), 513. The paper was presented on June 23, 1943.

62 For example, see Melanie Klein and Joan Riviere, *Love, Hate and Reparation: Two Lectures* (London: Hogarth, 1937). Klein's ideas are accessibly explained in Hanna Segal, "The Early Stages of the Oedipus Complex," in *Introduction to the Work of Melanie Klein* (London: Karnac, 1988), 103–116.

63 As early as 1962, Donald Winnicott observed that Anna Freud was far more influential in the USA than she ever was in the UK – as he also explicated his great debt to Klein while simultaneously registering that he himself "simply cannot find value" in the "idea of a Death instinct." Donald Winnicott, "A Personal View of the Kleinian Contribution," in Abram, *Donald Winnicott Today*, 159–167, here 159, 165. For a more recent reaffirmation of the point that Anna Freud had more impact in the USA than in the UK, see the remarks by Clifford Yorke in "Conference Proceedings," in Martin S. Bergmann, ed., *The Hartmann Era* (New York: Other Press, 2000), 224.

64 Ruth Cycon, "Vorwort zur deutschen Ausgabe der gesammelten Schriften," in Cycon, ed., *Melanie Klein: Gesammelte Schriften*, vol. 1 (Stuttgart: Frommann-Holzboog, 1995), xii.

65 Christopher Lasch, *Das Zeitalter des Narzissmus* (Munich: Steinhausen, 1980).

66 Already in 1975, in the pages of *Psyche*, Kernberg had made his objections to and differences from Kohut clear. Otto Kernberg, "Zur Behandlung narzisstischer Persönlichkeitsstörungen," *Psyche* 29 (1975): 890–905.

67 Jürgen Habermas, *Theorie des kommunikativen Handelns*, vol. 1 (Frankfurt am Main: Suhrkamp, 1981), 569.

68 For example, see Heinz Kohut, *The Restoration of the Self* (New York: International Universities Press, 1977), 269, 277; and the German version of the same remarks in the translation: Heinz Kohut, *Die Heilung des Selbst* (Frankfurt am Main: Suhrkamp), 266, 273. See in this context also John Leo und Ruth Mehrtens Galvin, "The Preacher of Narcissism: Analyst Heinz Kohut's 'Self-Psychology' rewrites Freud," *Time* 116.22 (December 1980): 76–77; Kenneth L. Woodward and Rachel Mark, "The New Narcissism," *Newsweek* (January 30, 1978): 70; Heinz Kohut, letter to the editor of *Newsweek*, January 25, 1978, reprinted in Heinz Kohut, *The Search for the Self: Selected Writings of Heinz Kohut 1978–1981*, vol. IV (London: Karnac, 2011), 569.

69 Otto Kernberg, *Borderline-Störungen und pathologischer Narzissmus* (Frankfurt am Main: Suhrkamp, 1978).

70 Tilmann Moser, "Dörte von Drigalski: 'Blumen auf Granit,'" *Die Zeit*, November 14, 1980, available at: www.zeit.de/1980/47/zeit-des-jammerns (accessed January 25, 2016).

71 Joachim Dyck, "Stumm und ohne Hoffnung," *Die Zeit*, June 14, 1985, available at: www.zeit.de/1985/25/stumm-und-ohne-hoffnung/komplettansicht (accessed January 25, 2016).

72 Kernberg profiled in Edith Zundel, "Die ordnende Kraft," *Die Zeit*, November 21, 1986, available at: www.zeit.de/1986/48/die-ordnende-kraft (accessed January 25, 2016).

73 Hanna Segal, *Melanie Klein: eine Einführung in ihr Werk* (Frankfurt am Main: Fischer, 1983).

74 Sophinette Becker, personal communication, January 30, 2015.

75 Claudia Frank, "Herbert Rosenfeld in Deutschland: Zur Verführbarkeit/Korrumpierbarkeit durch die Idealisierung destruktiver Elemente damals und heute," *Luzifer-Amor* 28.56 (2015): 54–80, here 58.

76 Helen Schoenhals and Helga Wildberger, "Das Rosenfeldseminar in Heidelberg 1981 bis 1986: Ein Rückblick," *Luzifer-Amor* 28.56 (2015): 81–89, here 81.

77 Frank, " Herbert Rosenfeld," 55–56. In Frank's summary, as those who remembered encounters with him testified, Rosenfeld, in his supervisory role, encouraged analysts "to investigate things they did not understand, in order to glean new insights," had shown them "how to articulate interpretations in such a way that the patient would understand them," and helped above all simply by modeling how he took in material and thought about it (62).

78 Sophinette Becker, personal communication, January 30, 2015.

79 Frank, "Herbert Rosenfeld"; Schoenhals and Wildberger, "Das Rosenfeldseminar."

80 Sophinette Becker and Hans Becker, "Der Psychoanalytiker im Spannungsfeld zwischen innerer und äusserer Realität," *Psyche* 41 (1987): 289–306, here 293–294.

81 Jacqueline Rose, *Why War? – Psychoanalysis, Politics, and the Return to Melanie Klein* (Oxford: Blackwell, 1993), 143–144.

82 Hanna Segal, "Silence is the Real Crime," *International Review of Psycho-Analysis* 14 (1987): 3–12. The paper was delivered at the inaugural meeting of the "International Psychoanalysts Against Nuclear Weapons," held

in Hamburg in the immediate wake of the IPA congress. It was cited more than forty times by other analysts in subsequent years, and became a major reference point also for USA-based psychoanalysts and psychiatrists who organized in protest against the escalating nuclear arms race. Many of them – including Sanford Gifford, Bennett Simon, Howard B. Levine, Daniel Jacobs, and Lowell J. Rubin – made their home in Boston. See esp. Howard B. Levine et al., eds., *Psychoanalysis and the Nuclear Threat: Clinical and Theoretical Studies* (Hillsdale, NJ: The Analytic Press, 1988). In so doing, they were picking up a thread that had first been pursued by Franz Alexander and William Menninger. See Franz Alexander, "Mental Hygiene in the Atomic Age," in *The Scope of Psychoanalysis, 1921–1961: Selected Papers* (New York: Basic, 1961); and the mention of William Menninger's meeting with a group of psychiatrists in Topeka on "Our Children in the Atomic Age" in "Are You Always Worrying?" *Time* 52.17 (October 25, 1948). For the revival of concern about nuclear Armageddon in the 1980s, see also Riccardo Steiner, "Responsibility as a Way of Hope in the Nuclear Era: Some Notes on F. Fornari's 'Psycho-Analysis of War,'" *Psychoanalytic Psychotherapy* 2 (1986): 75–82; and Hans Becker, Sophinette Becker, and Helmut Lüdeke, "Wie unpolitisch darf ein Analytiker sein?" in Carl Nedelmann, ed., *Zur Psychoanalyse der nuklearen Drohung* (Göttingen: Vandenhoeck & Ruprecht, 1985). On the uneasy emotional climate at the Hamburg IPA, see Sophinette Becker, "Eine ganz normale Veranstaltung? Anmerkungen zum Hamburger Kongress," *Psyche* 40 (1986): 864–867.

83 Karolinska Institutet, press release (1973), available at: www.nobelprize.org/nobel_prizes/medicine/laureates/1973/press.html (accessed January 18, 2016); "Ausmurzung ethisch minderwertiger," *Spiegel* 43 (October 22, 1973): 22.

84 Katja Thimm, "Ruf nach dem Rassepfleger," *Spiegel* 41 (October 8, 2001): 209.

85 Konrad Lorenz, "Gespräch anlässlich seines 85. Geburtstags," *Natur* 11 (1988): 28–33.

86 As Harry Slochower, the editor of *American Imago*, reviewing the German original in 1966, articulately summarized Mitscherlich's views under the headline "Replacing Oedipus by Cain": "Man today attempts to gain individual autonomy while he must subordinate himself to the super-organization of a choking bureaucracy. This situation produces tensions in the relation between the individual and society providing the basis for neurotic modes, manifested in apathy and/or anxiety, aggression and destructiveness ... The oedipal father is replaced by competition with siblings – the Joneses. The single father is split into a vast army of neighbors who are envied ... An endless chain of Cain-Abel has replaced Oedipus-Laius." And further: "The parentless child grows up into a leaderless adult, directed by anonymous functionaries and engaging in anonymous functions. Here are the phylogenetic roots of narcissism and aggression. The alternative – adaptation by conformity – results in a regressive adaptation which can be observed on all social levels, and to a confusion of orientation. Harry Slochower, "Replacing Oedipus by Cain," *American Imago* 23 (1966): 84–86.

87 David Riesman, *The Lonely Crowd: A Study of the Changing American Character* (New Haven: Yale University Press, 1950).

272 / Notes to page 149

88 Intriguingly but peculiarly, it would take until the 1990s before "father-lessness" became an American obsession. As it happened, no one would do more to promote both the notion of a "fatherless society" and the name of Alexander Mitscherlich among Americans than the poet, antiwar activist, fairy tale and Jungian archetype scholar Robert Bly. Already in the opening pages of his blockbuster hit of 1990, *Iron John*, Bly referred to Mitscherlich as an important influence on his thinking. Free-associative and freewheeling as it was, the book inspired tens of thousands of men, in the USA and around the world, to seek stronger intergenerational familial relationships and to reclaim emotion in general, in reaction against, but also in imitation of, many aspects of second-wave feminism. Robert Bly, *Iron John: A Book about Men* (Reading, MA: Addison-Wesley, 1990). When Harper Perennial was motivated to publish the first American paperback edition of *Society without the Father* in 1993 (Tavistock in England and Harcourt Brace Jovanovich had published the English translation in hardcover in 1969 and then there had been twenty-plus years of disinterest), it was Bly who wrote the Foreword. This Foreword did a credible job summarizing Mitscher-lich's historical-cum-philosophical arguments – as it also with impressive vigor slammed George Bush, Sr. for the First Gulf War and lambasted the US press for its self-inflicted ineptitude and its increasing craven cowardice vis-à-vis the powerful. Robert Bly, "Foreword," in Alexander Mitscherlich, ed., *Society Without the Father: A Contribution to Social Psychology* (New York: Harper Perennial, 1993). By the mid-1990s, the political valences shifted again, as multiple authors invoked Mitscherlich while sounding the alarms about the purported disaster zone that was the American family or the pitiful wreck that was the American man, and by the second decade of the twenty-first century Mitscherlich's name is most frequently invoked in the context of the "fathers' rights" movement. For a sampling, see Andrew Kimbrell, *The Masculine Mystique: The Politics of Masculinity* (New York: Ballantine, 1995); David Blanken-horn, *Fatherless America: Confronting our Most Urgent Social Problem* (New York: Basic, 1995); Ray B. Williams, "The Decline of Fatherhood and the Male Identity Crisis," *Psychology Today*, June 19, 2011, available at: www.psychologytoday.com/blog/wired-success/201106/the-decline-fatherhood-and-the-male-identity-crisis (accessed January 25, 2016). In 2013, an author writing for the website of the organization Fathers4Jus-tice ("a publication for parents on the wrong side of the standard pos-session order") took the occasion of the shooting of children by Adam Lanza at Sandy Hook Elementary School in Connecticut to argue that the source of the rising "mindless violence afflicting our world today" was "Fatherlessness." Warwick Marsh, "Remember the Fatherless and Absent," *Fathers4Justice*, July 1, 2013, available at: www.f4joz.com/news/newspage.php?yr=13&id=6 (accessed January 25, 2016).

89 Robert Jay Lifton, "Preface," in Alexander Mitscherlich and Margarete Mitscherlich, ed., *The Inability to Mourn: Principles of Collective Behav-ior* (New York: Grove/Random House, 1975), vii–xiii, here vii–viii.

90 Robert Jay Lifton, *The Nazi Doctors: Medical Killing and the Psychology of Genocide* (New York: Basic, 1986). The correspondence between Lifton

and Mitscherlich is in the Nachlass Alexander Mitscherlich held at the University Library of the Goethe-University of Frankfurt am Main.

91 Christa Rohde-Dachser, *Das Borderline-Syndrom*, 7th, rev. ed. (Bern: Huber, 2004).

92 Christa Rohde-Dachser, *Expedition in den dunklen Kontinent: Weiblichkeit im Diskurs der Psychoanalyse* (Berlin: Springer, 1991).

93 An English-language sampling – the abbreviated translation of one chapter – can be found in Christa Rohde-Dachser, "Explicating the Image of Woman in Psychoanalytic Discourse: Sigmund Freud's Theory of Femininity," in Herta Nagl-Docekal and Cornelia Klinger, eds., *Continental Philosophy in Feminist Perspective: Re-Reading the Canon in German* (University Park: Penn State University Press, 2000), 231–254.

94 Micha Brumlik, "'Der grosse Alexander,'" *Die Zeit* 39 (September 19, 2008), available at: www.zeit.de/2008/39/Mitscherlich-100 (accessed January 24, 2016).

95 Alexander Kluy, "Martin Dehli: Leben als Konflikt," *Cicero* (July 20, 2009), available at: www.cicero.de/salon/martin-dehli-leben-als-konflikt/43869 (accessed January 24, 2016).

5 Exploding Oedipus

1 Gilles Deleuze and Félix Guattari, *Anti-Oedipus: Capitalism and Schizophrenia* (Minneapolis: University of Minnesota Press 1983 [1972]), 43.

2 For example, see André Green, "A quoi ça sert?" *Le Monde*, April 28, 1972: 19; cf. Catherine Backès-Clément, Gilles Deleuze, and Félix Guattari, "Gilles Deleuze and Félix Guattari on *Anti-Oedipus*" [1972], in Gilles Deleuze, *Negotiations, 1972–1990* (New York: Columbia University Press, 1995).

3 Summarily articulated – representing his own view and that of other prominent French analysts – in a paper delivered at the 1981 IPA congress in Helsinki by Serge Lebovici, "The Origins and Development of the Oedipus Complex," *International Journal of Psycho-Analysis* 63 (1982): 201–215, here 202. Additional complaints included Deleuze and Guattari's presumed "denial of the distinction between the sexes and the generations." Lebovici's own investment in Oedipal explanations was made clear in later moments in the paper, including one in which he interpreted a female patient's dream of fellating the analyst ("kissing his sex from which spurted a liquid having the smell of both milk and sperm") as signaling her "desire for mastery … especially as regards her parents' pleasure" and as representing a "transference repetition," with the analyst, of a literal experience of "incestuous intercourse with her mother's second husband, even before the age of puberty" – a transference repetition that Lebovici went on to analyze as having as its objective "the wish to combine both paternal and maternal objects" (202, 205). Whether intentionally or not, Lebovici was exemplifying precisely the kind of psychoanalysis that Deleuze and Guattari had found so inexcusably awful.

4 Terry Eagleton, "Capitalism, Modernism and Postmodernism," *New Left Review* 152 (July–August 1985): 69; and Perry Anderson, *In the Tracks of Historical Materialism* (London: Verso, 1983), 51.

5 Cf. Massimo Perinelli, "Longing, Lust, Violence, Liberation: Discourses on Sexuality on the Radical Left in West Germany, 1969–1972," in Scott Spector, Helmut Puff, and Dagmar Herzog, eds., *After the History of Sexuality: German Genealogies With and Beyond Foucault* (New York: Berghahn, 2012), 248–281; and Philipp Felsch, *Der lange Sommer der Theorie: Geschichte einer Revolte 1960–1990* (Munich: C. H. Beck, 2015).

6 Adam Shatz, "Desire was Everywhere," *London Review of Books* 32 (December 16, 2010): 9–12.

7 A sampling: Sherry Turkle, "Whither Psychoanalysis in Computer Culture?" *Psychoanalytic Psychology* 21 (2004): 16–30; Jerry Aline Flieger, *Is Oedipus Online? Siting Freud after Freud* (Cambridge, MA: MIT Press, 2005); R. Braidotti, *Transpositions: On Nomadic Ethics* (Cambridge, UK: Polity Press, 2005); Margrit Shildrick and Janet Price, "Deleuzian Connections and Queer Corporealities: Shrinking Global Disability," *Rhizomes* 11/12 (Fall 2005/Spring 2006), available at: http://rhizomes.net/issue11/shildrickprice/index.html (last accessed July 29, 2016); Griet Roets and Dan Goodley, "Disability, Citizenship and Uncivilized Society: The smooth and nomadic qualities of self-advocacy," *Disability Studies Quarterly* 28.4 (2008), available at: http://dsq-sds.org/article/view/131/131 (accessed July 29, 2016); Petra Kuppers, "Toward a Rhizomatic Model of Disability: Poetry, Performance, and Touch," *Journal of Literary & Cultural Disability Studies* 3.3 (2009): 221–240; K. Martial Frindéthié, *Francophone African Cinema: History, Culture, Politics and Theory* (London: McFarland, 2009); Stephen Dougherty, "Computing the Unconscious," *Psychoanalytic Quarterly* 79 (January 2010): 171–201; and Stephen Hartman, "Reality 2.0: When Loss Is Lost," *Psychoanalytic Dialogues* 21 (2011): 468–482.

8 For example, Noreen Giffney, "Desiring (with) Bion: An Experience in Reading," *American Journal of Psychoanalysis* 73 (September 2013): 288–304; Barnaby B. Barratt, "A Practitioner's Notes on the Free-Associative Method as Existential Praxis," *International Forum of Psychoanalysis* 23 (2014): 195–208; Suely Rolnik, "Avoiding False Problems: Politics of the Fluid, Hybrid, and Flexible" (2011), available at: www.e-flux.com/journal/avoiding-false-problems-politics-of-the-fluid-hybrid-and-flexible/ (accessed February 4, 2016); Stephen Hartman, "Reality 2.0: When Loss Is Lost"; Fadi Abou-Rihan, *Deleuze and Guattari: A Psychoanalytic Itinerary* (London: Continuum, 2009); Carlo Strenger, "Why Psychoanalysis Must not Discard Science and Human Nature," *Psychoanalytic Dialogues* 23 (2013): 197–210; and Gohar Homayounpour, *Doing Psychoanalysis in Tehran* (Cambridge, MA: MIT Press, 2012), xxii.

9 Some of the most compelling efforts, for instance, apply Deleuze and Guattari to creative pedagogy with cognitively disabled children. Daniela Mercieca and Duncan Mercieca, in writing about "students with profound and multiple learning disabilities as agents in educational contexts," have not only put to fresh use such concepts as "assemblages," "flows," "rhizomes," and "collective utterance," but have also argued, with explicit reference to Deleuze and Guattari, that research can be rethought as a "becoming

through engagement with intensities rather than as interpretation of a pre-existent reality out there." See Daniela Mercieca and Duncan Mercieca, "Opening Research to Intensities: Rethinking Disability Research with Deleuze and Guattari," *Journal of Philosophy of Education* 44 (2010): 79; and Duncan P. Mercieca, *Living Otherwise: Students with Profound and Multiple Learning Disabilities as Agents in Educational Contexts* (Rotterdam: Sense Publishers, 2012).

10 Henning Schmidgen, *Das Unbewusste der Maschinen: Konzeptionen des Psychischen bei Guattari, Deleuze und Lacan* (Munich: Fink, 1997); Michel Feher, "Mai 68 dans la pensée," in Jean-Jacques Becker and Gilles Candar, eds., *Histoire des gauches en France*, vol. II (Paris: La Découverte, 2004), 599–623; Julian Bourg, *From Revolution to Ethics: May 1968 and Contemporary French Thought* (Montreal: McGill-Queen's University Press, 2007); François Dosse, *Gilles Deleuze and Félix Guattari: Intersecting Lives* (New York: Columbia University Press, 2010); and Camille Robcis, *The Law of Kinship: Anthropology, Psychoanalysis, and the Family in France* (Ithaca: Cornell University Press, 2013).

11 It has become standard in the scholarship to explain Guattari's unique contribution in developing the concepts not just of "institutional psychotherapy" but specifically of "institutional psychoanalysis" – as well as coining the term "transversality" to capture the multiplicity of directionality of reciprocal transformation occurring within groups as an alternative to the more limited (and in his view simply inaccurate) concept of transference as an element in cure. Less attention has been paid by scholars to the distinctive position taken by Guattari in the transnational psychiatric reform movements in which he remained involved for decades. Unlike the British R. D. Laing and David Cooper, for instance, Guattari refused the term "anti-psychiatric," continuing to defend the value of (reformed) residential settings and also repudiating publicly the grossly insensitive parent-blaming which recurrently marred the work of Laing and Cooper despite their general self-styling as counterculture gurus. Félix Guattari, "La Borde: A Clinic Unlike Any Other" [1977], in *Chaosophy* (Los Angeles: Semiotext(e), 1995), 197.

12 Peter Osborne, "Guattareuze?" *New Left Review* 69 (May–June 2011): 139–151.

13 Cf. Shatz, "Desire was Everywhere," 9–12; Eugene Wolters, "13 Things You Didn't Know about Deleuze and Guattari – Part II," *Critical Theory* (June 20, 2013), available at: www.critical-theory.com/13-deleuze-guattari-part-ii/ (last accessed July 23, 2015).

14 Slavoj Žižek, *Organs without Bodies: On Deleuze and Consequences* (New York: Routledge, 2004). Also see Osborne, "Guattareuze?"

15 Gary Genosko, ed., *The Guattari Reader* (Oxford, UK: Blackwell, 1996); Charles J. Stivale, "Pragmatic/Machinic: Discussion with Félix Guattari (19 March 1985)," in Charles Joseph Stivale, ed., *The Two-Fold Thought of Deleuze and Guattari: Intersections and Animations* (New York: Guilford, 1998), 191–224; François Dosse, *Gilles Deleuze and Félix Guattari: Intersecting Lives* (New York: Columbia University Press, 2010); and Eric Alliez and Andrew Goffe, eds., *The Guattari Effect* (London: Continuum, 2011).

16 Osborne, "Guattareuze?"

17 See esp. Dosse, *Gilles Deleuze and Félix Guattari: Intersecting Lives*, 7; Félix Guattari, "Everybody Wants to be a Fascist" [1973], *Semiotext(e)* 2.3 (1977): 87–98; Sylvère Lotringer and Félix Guattari, "The New Alliance," *Impulse* 10.2 (Winter 1982): 41–44; Félix Guattari, "The Postmodern Dead End," *Flash Art* 128 (1986): 40–41; Félix Guattari and Suely Rolnik, *Molecular Revolution in Brazil* (Los Angeles: Semiotext(e), 2007 [1986]); Félix Guattari, *Soft Subversions: Texts and Interviews 1977–1985* (Los Angeles: Semiotext(e), 2009); Marie Depussé, "Félix Guattari: de Leros à La Borde. Présentation," in Félix Guattari, ed., *De Leros à La Borde* (Fécamp: Nouvelles Éditions Lignes, 2012), 9–23.

18 The only other scholar to make this argument explicitly – to see *Anti-Oedipus* as "not only a harsh and most insightful critique of the assimilationist vein in psychoanalysis" but also as ushering in "a much needed moment of reflexivity ... where the theory finds itself on the couch it has produced" – is the Canadian psychoanalyst Fadi Abou-Rihan. His focus is, however, different from mine, as his main intent is to read the text of *Anti-Oedipus* as itself as "a practice where the science of the unconscious is made to obey the laws it attributes to its object. The outcome here is nothing short of the 'becoming-unconscious' of psychoanalysis, a becoming that signals... the transformation of its principles and procedures into those of its object." Or, at another point: as a text in which "the style ... is inextricably tied to the theory it advocates .... in other words, the '*Anti-Oedipus*' effect is ... of that moment at which the distinctions between style and content, theory and practice, observer and observed cease to hold." Fadi Abou-Rihan, *Deleuze and Guattari: A Psychoanalytic Itinerary* (London: Continuum, 2009), ix–x, 33.

19 Félix Guattari, "Débat" [1973], in Armando Verdiglione, ed., *Psychanalyse et Politique* (Paris: Éditions du Seuil, 1974), 59; and Guattari, "Everybody Wants to be a Fascist," 95–97.

20 Quoted in Anna Freud, "Report on the Sixteenth International Psycho-Analytical Congress," *Bulletin of the International Psycho-Analytical Association* 30 (1949): 179. Also see Josef Christian Aigner et al., "Zur gegenwärtigen Situation der Psychoanalyse," *Psyche* 68.5 (May 2014): 477–484.

21 On the "apolitical" tendencies in British psychoanalysis – despite "never [having] formed an alliance with capitalist culture as it did in the US," see the curtly scathing retrospective remarks of Robert D. Hinshelwood, "Between the Devil and the Deep Blue Sea: Relations with the Dominant Class," in Psychoanalytisches Seminar Zürich, ed., *Between the Devil and the Deep Blue Sea* (Freiburg: Kore, 1987), 185–186.

22 Félix Guattari, "So What" [1985], in *Soft Subversions*, 69.

23 Félix Guattari, "Reflections on Institutional Psychotherapy for Philosophers" [1966], in Félix Guattari, ed., *Psychoanalysis and Transversality: Texts and Interviews 1955–1971* (South Pasadena: Semiotext(e), 2015), 130.

24 Félix Guattari, "Réflexions pour des philosophes à propos de la psychothérapie institutionelle" [1966], in *Psychanalyse et transversalité: essais d'analyse institutionelle* (Paris: Maspero, 1972), 94; and Guattari and Rolnik, *Molecular Revolution in Brazil*, 58. Cf. Schmidgen, *Das Unbewusste der Maschinen*, 55–70.

25 Cf. Bourg, *From Revolution to Ethics*,160.
26 See Jacques Lacan, *The Seminar of Jacques Lacan: Book 1, Freud's Papers on Technique, 1953-1954* (Cambridge, UK: Cambridge University Press, 1988 [1953-1954]), 31, 73, 79.
27 See Brady Brower, "From Corporate Order to Organic Solidarity: Biology and Social Thought in France," paper delivered at the Institute for Advanced Study, Princeton, January 26, 2015. Perhaps even more importantly, there was clear inspiration coming from the seventeenth and eighteenth centuries. Among the many things Deleuze brought to the table were his critical expertise in Spinoza and Kant. Spinoza's notion of *natura naturans* – the self-causing activity of nature, or "nature naturing" – became as important to both Deleuze and Guattari as did their conviction that desire co-constituted its objects, evident also in their grappling with Kant's idea that desire, "'through its representations,'" can be "'the cause of the reality of the objects of these representations.'" Quoted in Deleuze and Guattari, *Anti-Oedipus*, 25. Also see Benedict de Spinoza, *Ethics*, Part I, Prop. 29 (London: Penguin, 1996 [1677]). While Kant had chosen "superstitious beliefs, hallucinations, and fantasies as illustrations of this definition of desire," and distinguished these from longings which were incapable of producing the objects longed for, Deleuze and Guattari – in this way again borrowing from psychoanalysis – maintained the impossibility of distinguishing between psychic and other reality. Or, as Deleuze and Guattari put it in *Anti-Oedipus*: "There is no such thing as the social production of reality on the one hand, and a desiring-production that is mere fantasy on the other." Deleuze and Guattari, *Anti-Oedipus*, 25, 28.
28 Deleuze and Guattari, *Anti-Oedipus*, 288–289.
29 Gilles Deleuze, "Three Group Problems" [1972], *Semiotext(e)* 2.3 (1977): 100.
30 Deleuze and Guattari, *Anti-Oedipus*, 381, 293.
31 Erich Fromm, "Zum Gefühl der Ohnmacht," *Zeitschrift für Sozialforschung* 6 (1937): 95–119; Ernst Simmel, "Anti-Semitism and Mass Psychopathology," in Ernst Simmel, ed., *Anti-Semitism: A Social Disease* (New York: International Universities Press, 1946), 33–78; Max Horkheimer, "The Lessons of Fascism" [1948], in Hadley Cantril, ed., *Tensions That Cause Wars* (Urbana: University of Illinois Press, 1950), 209–242; Theodor Adorno, "Freudian Theory and the Patterns of Fascist Propaganda" [1951], in Andrew Arato and Eike Gebhardt, eds., *The Essential Frankfurt School Reader* (New York: Continuum, 1982), 118–137.
32 Wilhelm Reich, *The Mass Psychology of Fascism* (New York: Simon & Schuster, 1970 [1933]), 24, 36, 60.
33 Reich, *The Mass Psychology of Fascism*, 19. Cf. Deleuze and Guattari, *Anti-Oedipus*, 29.
34 Quoted in Deleuze and Guattari, *Anti-Oedipus*, 29. Cf. Étienne de La Boétie, *The Politics of Obedience: The Discourse of Voluntary Servitude* (New York: Free Life Editions, 1975 [1576]); Benedict Spinoza, *A Theologico-Political Treatise*, Part I (1981 [1670]), available at: http://oll.libertyfund.org/titles/1710 (last accessed October 6, 2015).
35 Deleuze and Guattari, *Anti-Oedipus*, 29.

36 Reich, *The Mass Psychology of Fascism*, 30–31. Cf. Guattari, "Everybody Wants to be a Fascist," 95.
37 Reich, *The Mass Psychology of Fascism*, 36.
38 Reich, *The Mass Psychology of Fascism*, 40.
39 Thomas Frank, *What's the Matter with Kansas? How Conservatives Won the Heart of America* (New York: Henry Holt, 2004).
40 Frank, *What's the Matter with Kansas?* 26–27, 55.
41 Frank, *What's the Matter with Kansas?* 21.
42 Wilhelm Reich, (1970 [1946]) "Preface to the Third Edition" [1946], in *The Mass Psychology of Fascism*, xiv.
43 Reich, *The Mass Psychology of Fascism*, 101.
44 Félix Guattari, "Vietnam 1967 (extraits)" [1967], in *Psychanalyse et transversalité*, 206–207.
45 Backès-Clément, Deleuze, and Guattari, "Gilles Deleuze and Félix Guattari on *Anti-Oedipus*," 19.
46 Michel-Antoine Burnier, Gilles Deleuze, and Félix Guattari, "Capitalism: A Very Special Delirium" [1973], in Félix Guattari, ed., *Chaosophy: Texts and Interviews 1972–1977* (Los Angeles: Semiotext(e), 2009), 37–38.
47 In the book, Deleuze and Guattari took on Reich's problems with the concept of ideology directly: "Reich is at his profoundest as a thinker when he refuses to accept ignorance or illusion on the part of the masses as an explanation of fascism, and demands an explanation that will take their desires into account, an explanation formulated in terms of desire: no, the masses were not innocent dupes; at a certain point, under a certain set of conditions, they *wanted* fascism, and it is this perversion of the desire of the masses that needs to be accounted for. Yet Reich himself never manages to provide a satisfactory explanation of this phenomenon, because at a certain point he reintroduces precisely the line of argument that he was in the process of demolishing, by creating a distinction between rationality as it is or ought to be in the process of social production, and the irrational element in desire, and by regarding only this latter as a suitable subject for psychoanalytic investigation." Deleuze and Guattari, *Anti-Oedipus*, 29.
48 Deleuze and Guattari, *Anti-Oedipus*, 29, 291, 293, 352–353.
49 Deleuze, "Three Group Problems," 101.
50 Cf. Dagmar Herzog, *Sex after Fascism: Memory and Morality in Twentieth-Century Germany* (Princeton: Princeton University Press, 2005).
51 Guattari, "Everybody Wants to be a Fascist," 94. In general, as Deleuze and Guattari's reappropriations also help us see, it has become all too easy in hindsight to make fun of Reich – and no doubt we are still influenced today both by Freud's repudiation of him during the desperate flight from Nazism (and the perception that Reich's Marxism was too toxic to be associated with) and by the stark naivety of some of the liberationist projects pursued in his name in and around 1968. What is lost from memory in the current smirkily complacent consensus, however, is not only the genuinely innovative insights Reich offered at the time into the sophisticated, and after all stunningly effective, emotional work done by Nazism. Also lost is the fact that quite a few of those insights were subsequently taken up, albeit without giving Reich credit, by the far more consistently celebrated although otherwise mutually opposed figures of

Erich Fromm and Theodor Adorno (with Fromm, in the introduction to *Escape from Freedom* (1941), stealing Reich's questions, and Adorno, in *The Authoritarian Personality* (1950) and thereafter, stealing a number of Reich's answers – and even as Adorno simultaneously, as Reich too had been, remained undecided on whether what was most important about fascist propaganda was its idea-content or its affective appeal). See Adorno, "Freudian Theory and the Patterns of Fascist Propaganda." Meanwhile, Deleuze and Guattari were well aware of Marcuse – and aware also of the accusation that he was too "Rousseauis[t]" in his optimism as well as of his critiques of "culturalists" and neo-Freudians. Deleuze and Guattari, *Anti-Oedipus*, 30, 112, 118, 173, 388fn55. But, although one might argue that Guattari's later 1980s reflections on "Integrated World Capitalism's" insinuation into individuals' psyches bore strong resemblance to some of Marcuse's concerns, in *Anti-Oedipus* Deleuze and Guattari display little interest in his work, finding it less useful than Reich's and still based too much on a presumed contrast between rationality and irrationality.

52 Reich, "Preface to the Third Edition," in *The Mass Psychology of Fascism*, xiv–xvi, xxvi; and Guattari, "Everybody Wants to be a Fascist," 94–97. Cf. Gilles Deleuze and Félix Guattari, *A Thousand Plateaus: Capitalism and Schizophrenia* (Minneapolis: University of Minnesota Press, 1987 [1980]), 214–215.

53 Melanie Klein, "Zur Frühanalyse," *Imago* 9 (1923): 222–259; Melanie Klein, "A Contribution to the Theory of Intellectual Inhibition," *International Journal of Psycho-Analysis* 12 (1931): 206–218; and Melanie Klein, *The Psycho-Analysis of Children* (London: The Hogarth Press, 1932).

54 Cf. Vamik Volkan, "The Intertwining of the Internal and External Wars," Paper presented at Austen Riggs, October 16, 2004, available at: www.vamikvolkan.com/The-Intertwining-of-the-Internal-and-External-Wars.php (accessed July 29, 2016).

55 Cf. Wilfred R. Bion, "Attacks on Linking," *International Journal of Psycho-Analysis* 40 (1959): 308.

56 Deleuze and Guattari, *Anti-Oedipus*, 1.

57 In fact, Deleuze and Guattari thought Klein had stopped short of the most radical possibilities in her own findings: "Melanie Klein was responsible for the marvelous discovery of partial objects, that world of explosions, rotations, vibrations." But it was not enough to shift attention from the Oedipal to the pre-Oedipal – or, as Klein did, to locate the Oedipal much earlier in infant development than her colleagues did – and Deleuze and Guattari suspected that Klein had been all too "eager to avoid any sort of contretemps with the International Psycho-Analytic Association that bears above its door the inscription 'Let no one enter here who does not believe in Oedipus.'" Thus, they lamented, Klein "does not make use of partial objects to shatter the iron collar of Oedipus; on the contrary, she uses them – or makes a pretense of using them – to water Oedipus down, to miniaturize it, to find it everywhere, to extend it to the very earliest years of life." In sum: "If we here choose the example of the analyst least prone to see everything in terms of Oedipus, we do so only in order to demonstrate what a forcing was necessary for her to make Oedipus the sole measure of desiring-production … Say that it's Oedipus, or you'll get a slap in the

face. The psychoanalyst no longer says to the patient: 'Tell me a little bit about your desiring-machines, won't you?' Instead he screams: 'Answer daddy-and-mommy when I speak to you!' Even Melanie Klein." Deleuze and Guattari, *Anti-Oedipus*, 45.

58 Lacan, *The Seminar of Jacques Lacan: Book 1*; cf. Marie-Claude Thomas, "Melanie Klein mit Lacan. Eine Anmerkung," *Lacaniana* (January 17, 2015), available at: http://lacan-entziffern.de/signifikant/marie-claude-thomas-melanie-klein-mit-lacan-eine-anmerkung/ (accessed July 29, 2016).

59 Backès-Clément, Deleuze, and Guattari, "Gilles Deleuze and Félix Guattari on *Anti-Oedipus*," 13; Stivale, "Pragmatic/Machinic: Discussion with Félix Guattari," 203; Levi R. Bryant, "Lacan and Deleuze: A Pet Peeve," *Larval Subjects*, May 22, 2006, https://larvalsubjects.wordpress.com/2006/05/22/lacan-and-deleuze-a-pet-peeve/ (accessed July 29, 2016).

60 Deleuze and Guattari, *Anti-Oedipus*, 51.

61 Jacques Lacan, "The Neurotic's Individual Myth" [1953], *Psychoanalytic Quarterly* 48 (1979): 405–425.

62 Cf. Deleuze and Guattari, *Anti-Oedipus*, 47.

63 Deleuze and Guattari, *Anti-Oedipus*, 96.

64 Félix Guattari, "Nous sommes tous des groupuscules" [1970], *Psychanalyse et transversalité*, 280. Cf. Gilles Deleuze and Michel Foucault, "Les Intellectuels et le pouvoir: entretien Gilles Deleuze et Michel Foucault, du 4 mars 1972," *L'Arc* 49 (1972): 4.

65 Cf. Backès-Clément, Deleuze, and Guattari, "Gilles Deleuze and Félix Guattari on *Anti-Oedipus*," 17. Deleuze and Guattari, *Anti-Oedipus*, 116.

66 Russell Jacoby, *The Repression of Psychoanalysis: Otto Fenichel and the Freudians* (Chicago: University of Chicago Press, 1983).

67 Alexander Mitscherlich, "Psychoanalysis and the Aggression of Large Groups," *International Journal of Psycho-Analysis* 52 (1971): 161–167; Paul Parin, "Der Ausgang des ödipalen Konflikts in drei verschiedenen Kulturen: eine Anwendung der Psychoanalyse als Sozialwissenschaft," *Kursbuch* 29 (1972): 179–201; Reimut Reiche, "Ist der Ödipuskomplex universal?" *Kursbuch* 29 (1972): 159–176; Pier Francesco Galli, ed., *Psicoterapia e scienze umane. Atti dell'VIII Congresso Internazionale di Psicoterapia* (Milan: Feltrinelli, 1973).

68 Cf. Backès-Clément, Deleuze, and Guattari, "Gilles Deleuze and Félix Guattari on *Anti-Oedipus*"; and Georges Veltsos and Félix Guattari, "Félix Guattari à la télé grecque," *ΑΣΥΜΜΕΤΡΙΑ* (1991), available at: https://deterritorium.wordpress.com/2011/09/22/felix-guattari-a-la-tele-grecque-1992/ (accessed July 23, 2015). As Guattari put it in 1991, emphatically, in an interview with Giorgos Veltsos on Greek television, in the midst of a trip to evaluate infamous asylums on the island of Leros and in Athens: "Me, I never ever said that the psychotic or the schizophrenic was a revolutionary hero who would replace the leaders of the working class or the militants in the factory... I never said that .... No, because sometimes they wanted us to say stupid things like that ... To put it simply, what I find is that the relationship with the psychotic, for example in a clinic like the one that I work in at La Borde, raises questions, very insistently, questions that one usually makes an effort not to see; the psychotic puts into question the whole world of dominant significations, the world of social relations, the

world of exchange, the world of affect; he introduces … dimensions that are in rupture with this mediatized world, this world of power that we are in." Guattari, "Félix Guattari à la télé grecque."

69 As Guattari put it in an interview in 1972: "According to traditional psychoanalysis, it's always the same father and always the same mother – always the same triangle. But who can deny that the Oedipal situation differs greatly, depending on whether the father is an Algerian revolutionary or a well-to-do executive? It isn't the same death which awaits your father in an African shanty town as in a German industrial town; it isn't *the same* Oedipus complex or the same homosexuality. It may seem stupid to have to make such obvious statements and yet such swindles must be denounced tirelessly; there is no universal structure of the human mind!" Félix Guattari, "Psycho-Analysis and Schizo-Analysis" [1972], *Semiotext(e)* 2.3 (1977): 82–83.

70 Deleuze and Guattari, *Anti-Oedipus*, 96–97.

71 Guattari, "Vietnam 1967 (extraits)" [1967], 207–209.

72 Deleuze, "Three Group Problems," 100–101.

73 Guattari and Rolnik, *Molecular Revolution in Brazil*, 36.

74 Félix Guattari, "Four Truths for Psychiatry" [1985], in *Soft Subversions: Texts and Interviews 1977–1985*, 202.

75 Guattari and Rolnik, *Molecular Revolution in Brazil*, 58, 35, 44–46, 53, 43.

76 Félix Guattari, "Plan for the Planet" [1979], in *Soft Subversions: Texts and Interviews 1977–1985*, 234; Lotringer and Guattari, "The New Alliance," 44; cf. Félix Guattari, "I am an Idea-Thief" [1980], in *Chaosophy*, 45.

77 Guattari and Rolnik, *Molecular Revolution in Brazil*, 23, 318.

78 Guattari, "So What," 79, 76. Similarly, in 1986 he demanded again: "Is it inevitable then that we remain passive in the face of the rising wave of cruelty and cynicism that is in the process of flooding the planet and that seems determined to last? Guattari, "The Postmodern Dead End," 40.

79 Guattari has been a particular inspiration for politically engaged Latin American analysts. Thus, for instance, the Argentinean analyst Osvaldo Bonano specifically invoked Guattari's ideas about analytic dynamics as he meditated on the transformative processes set in motion by the protests of the "Mothers of the Plaza de Mayo." See Osvaldo Bonano, "Political Repression and Institutional Analysis," in Diana R. Kordon et al., eds., *Psychological Effects of Political Repression* (Buenos Aires: Sudamericana/Planeta, 1988), 129–141. Or, to take another example, as Guattari's close friend and collaborator, the São Paulo-based psychoanalyst (and art critic and curator) Suely Rolnik had put the point in 1986 in the book she created out of his 1982 trip to Brazil – while invoking a comment Deleuze had once made to the effect that both he and Guattari wrote for "unconsciouses that protest": "We all live in an almost constant state of crisis … with the result that no sooner do we succeed in articulating a certain way of living than it becomes obsolete." The trouble was that when "we find ourselves perplexed and disoriented … we tend to adopt merely defensive positions" and "thus we ourselves become the very producers of certain sequences on the assembly line of desire." Yet there was hope, for "sometimes … the unconsciouses 'protest' … they divest from the assembly lines of subjectivity, … creating other worlds inside this world. Whenever this happens,

the principle of the current system, the standardization of desire, suffers a blow. And when it happens (something of the kind was happening then in Brazil) we find an 'ally' in Guattari. Not as a founder or master of a school with which we might align ourselves and thereby find reassurance, but as a certain quality of presence that mobilizes within us the will and courage to express the singularity of our experience, not only in speech but also in action." Guattari and Rolnik, *Molecular Revolution in Brazil*, 15–17. The book became highly influential in Brazil, going through seven Portuguese editions, contributing to the passage of a law for psychiatric reform and shaping alternative psychoanalytic clinical practice as well as university study in psychology (much of this due to Rolnik's own activism). Rolnik is to this day one of the most eloquent exponents of Guattari's vision. In a variety of fora, she notes how the ascent of transnational finance capitalism that coincided with the defeat of the Cold War authoritarian regimes in Latin America as well as in Eastern Europe (and whose irrepressible expansionist aims she surmises may in fact have contributed to the dictatorships' defeat) has also – and for many people disorientingly – insinuated itself in the logic of "flexibility, fluidity, and hybridization" that had once been a hallmark of the countercultural movements of the 1960s and 1970s. What had once been subversive has now been "pimp[ed]" and thus it is "a mistake to take the latter as a value in itself – since it came to constitute the dominant logic of neoliberalism and its society of control." One of Rolnik's greatest concerns is how at the current juncture human beings can maintain, or recover, their capacity to be vulnerable to each other, to de-anaesthetize themselves, to be willing to be fragile, to hold on to desire and to act on it and, in all these ways, to "deconstruct the colonial unconscious" that so stubbornly keeps its hold on human beings also in a postcolonial world. See Rolnik, "Avoiding False Problems"; Suely Rolnik, "The Geopolitics of Pimping" (2006), available at: http://eipcp.net/transversal/1106/rolnik/en (accessed February 4, 2016); and the video of Rolnik's talk at the Guggenheim Museum (2014), available at: www.guggenheim.org/video/suely-rolnik-deconstructs-the-colonial-unconscious (accessed February 5, 2016).

80 Félix Guattari, "New Spaces of Liberty for Minoritarian Desire" [1977], in *Soft Subversions: Texts and Interviews 1977–1985*, 95–98.

81 Deleuze and Guattari, *Anti-Oedipus*, 350–351, 295–296.

82 Summarized and discussed in Guattari and Rolnik, *Molecular Revolution in Brazil*, 101; see also Gilles Deleuze, "Letter to a Harsh Critic," in Deleuze, *Negotiations*, 11.

83 Guattari, "Débat," 57; cf. Deleuze and Guattari, *A Thousand Plateaus*, 156–158.

84 Michel Foucault, "Preface" [1977], in Deleuze and Guattari, *Anti-Oedipus*, xiii–xiv. Aside from the fact that Foucault had picked up on what was actually a recurrent contrapuntal theme in the book, there was also a practical explanation for the drift of his preface. The introduction to the English translation had its origins in a dissertation chapter written by Mark Seem – one of the co-translators of the English version – a doctoral student of Foucault's at SUNY-Buffalo. Mark D. Seem, "The Logic of Power (An Essay on G. Deleuze, M. Foucault and F. Guattari)" (Ph.D. dissertation,

State University of New York at Buffalo, 1976). Seem had been deeply moved by *Anti-Oedipus*, seeing applicability in it to Nixon's America, not just in the "silent majority" of conservatives but in the crisis of the (often only presumptively antiauthoritarian) New Left as well. Seem, who had been involved in support efforts on behalf of those involved in the Attica prison revolt as in other New Left projects (and he would later work among the Black Panthers and Young Lords in alternative drug rehab projects), was repelled by what he saw as the New Left's own share of "fascistic" or authoritarian potential (or what Seem referred to as "the fascisizing elements we all carry deep within us"). Mark D. Seem, "Introduction," in *Anti-Oedipus*, xvi–xvii. It was, in short, Seem's take on *Anti-Oedipus* that Foucault expanded on as he wrote the preface in a New York hotel room with Seem by his side (after insisting by telephone that Viking take Seem's chapter as the book's introduction). Mark Seem, conversation with the author, November 5, 2014, New York City.

85 Janine Chasseguet-Smirgel, *Les Chemins de l'Anti-Œdipe* (Toulouse: Privat, 1974). Cf. Abou-Rihan, *Deleuze and Guattari*.

86 Guattari was a practicing analyst for a dozen years. He continued to see patients in the 1980s, but he no longer called it psychoanalysis. The interview conducted by Michel Butel in 1985 gives good insight into Guattari's views on his own analytic practice: Guattari, "So What," 66–70. Cf. also Félix Guattari, "Institutional Intervention" (1980), in *Soft Subversions: Texts and Interviews 1977–1985*, 37–55, esp. 40; and Dosse, *Gilles Deleuze and Félix Guattari: Intersecting Lives*, 488.

87 Deleuze and Guattari, *Anti-Oedipus*, 55.

88 Ernst Kris, "Danger and Morale," *American Journal of Orthopsychiatry* 14 (1944): 147–155; Ernst Simmel, "Anti-semitism and Mass Psychopathology," in Ernst Simmel, ed., *Anti-Semitism: A Social Disease* (New York: International Universities Press, 1946), 33–78; Donald W. Winnicott, "Berlin Walls," in *Home is Where We Start From* (New York: W. W. Norton, 1969), 221–227; Alexander Mitscherlich and Margarete Mitscherlich, *The Inability to Mourn: Principles of Collective Behaviour* (New York: Grove, 1975); many of Volkan's writings available at: www.vamikvolkan.com/ (accessed January 30, 2016); Martin Bergmann, *Generations of the Holocaust* (New York: Basic Books, 1982); Martin Bergmann, "Psychoanalytical Reflections on September 11, 2001," in Danielle Knafo, ed., *Living with Terror, Working with Trauma: A Clinician's Handbook* (Lanham, MD: Rowman & Littlefield, 2004), 401–413.

89 Sigmund Freud, *Civilization and its Discontents* (London: Penguin, 2002 [1930]).

90 And without question there are grounds for continuing to mock Deleuze and Guattari's certainty in this regard. See especially the hilarious interpretation by Ben Kafka and Jamieson Webster, "No, Oedipus does Not exist," *Cabinet* 42 (Summer 2011): 27–30.

91 Karen Horney, *New Ways in Psychoanalysis* (New York: W. W. Norton, 1939); and Erich Fromm, *Escape from Freedom* (New York: Avon, 1941).

92 Max Horkheimer, "The Lessons of Fascism," in Hadley Cantril, ed., *Tensions That Cause Wars* (Urbana: University of Illinois Press, 1950), 209–242.

93 Alexander Mitscherlich, *Auf dem Weg zur vaterlosen Gesellschaft* (Munich: Piper, 1963).

94 Harry Slochower, "Replacing Oedipus by Cain," *American Imago* 23 (1966): 84–86.

95 Susan Quinn, "Oedipus vs. Narcissus," *New York Times* (June 30, 1981); and Elisabeth Roudinesco, *Why Psychoanalysis?* (New York: Columbia University Press, 2001), 116.

96 For example, see Paul H. Ornstein, "A Discussion of the Paper by Otto F. Kernberg on 'Further Contributions to the Treatment of Narcissistic Personalities,'" *International Journal of Psycho-Analysis* 55 (1974): 241–247; as well as the position statements prepared for the panel on "The Changing Expectations of Patients and Psychoanalysts Today" circulated before the 1975 IPA congress in London in the *IPA President's Newsletter* 7 (1975): 30–36. Archive of the International Psychoanalytical Association, London.

97 Hans W. Loewald, "The Waning of the Oedipus Complex," *Journal of the American Psychoanalytic Association* 27 (1979): 751–775.

98 Richard Gilman, "The FemLib Case against Sigmund Freud," *New York Times Magazine* (January 31, 1971): 10–11, 42, 44, 47.

99 See esp. Erich Fromm, *The Crisis of Psychoanalysis* (New York: Holt, Rinehart, Winston, 1970); Heinz Kohut, "Ist das Studium des menschlichen Innenlebens heute noch relevant?" [1971], in Heinz Kohut, ed., *Die Zukunft der Psychoanalyse* (Frankfurt am Main: Suhrkamp, 1975).

100 Nancy Caro Hollander, *Love in a Time of Hate: Liberation Psychology in Latin America* (New Brunswick: Rutgers University Press, 1997); and Mariano Ben Plotkin, *Freud in the Pampas: The Emergence and Development of a Psychoanalytic Culture in Argentina* (Palo Alto: Stanford University Press, 2002).

6 Ethnopsychoanalysis in the Era of Decolonization

1 Paul Parin, Fritz Morgenthaler, and Goldy Parin-Matthèy, *Die Weissen denken zuviel: psychoanalytische Untersuchungen bei den Dogon in Westafrika* (Hamburg: Europäische Verlagsanstalt, 1993 [orig. 1963]), 45. Translation of the quote provided by Francessa Rich, available at: http://francessarich.blogspot.com/search/label/Paul%20Parin (accessed January 20, 2016).

2 On the contradictory effects – including especially economic – of decolonization on the Dogon, see "Vorwort zur 3. Auflage," in Paul Parin, Fritz Morgenthaler, and Goldy Parin-Matthèy, *Die Weissen denken zuviel*, 12.

3 The first trip to the Sepik in December 1972 to mid-March 1973 – "for 79 days I was … on one of the most amazing journeys one could ever imagine" – is mentioned by Morgenthaler in a letter to Heinz Kohut, April 17, 1973. Personal collection of Thomas Kohut.

4 Paul Parin, Fritz Morgenthaler, and Goldy Parin-Matthèy, *Les Blancs pensent trop: 13 entretiens avec les Dogon* (Paris: Payot, 1966); Paul Parin, Fritz Morgenthaler, and Goldy Parin-Matthèy, *Fürchte deinen Nächsten wie dich selbst: Psychoanalyse und Gesellschaft am Modell der Agni in Westafrika* (Frankfurt: Suhrkamp, 1971); Paul Parin, Fritz Morgenthaler, and Goldy Parin-Matthèy, *Fear thy Neighbor as Thyself: Psychoanalysis and Society among the Anyi of West Africa* (Chicago: University of Chicago Press, 1980).

5 Paul Parin, Fritz Morgenthaler, and Goldy Parin-Matthèy, "Il complesso edipico nei Dogon dell'Africa Occidentale," *Rivista di Psicoanalisi* 9 (1963): 143–150; Fritz Morgenthaler and Paul Parin, "Typical Forms of Transference Among West Africans," *International Journal of Psycho-Analysis* 45 (1964): 446–449; Paul Parin and Fritz Morgenthaler, "Ego and Orality in the Analysis of West Africans," in Werner Muensterberger and Sidney Axelrad, eds., *The Psychoanalytic Study of Society*, vol. III (New York: International Universities Press, 1964), 197–202; Paul Parin and Fritz Morgenthaler, "Ist die Verinnerlichung der Aggression für die soziale Anpassung notwendig?" in Alexander Mitscherlich, ed., *Bis hierher und nicht weiter: Ist die menschliche Aggression unbefriedbar?* (Munich: Piper, 1969), 222–244.

6 Fritz Morgenthaler, Florence Weiss, and Marco Morgenthaler, *Gespräche am sterbenden Fluss: Ethnopsychoanalyse bei den Iatmul in Papua Neuguinea* (Frankfurt: Fischer, 1984); Fritz Morgenthaler, Florence Weiss, and Marco Morgenthaler, *Conversations au bord du fleuve mourant: ethnopsychanalyse chez les Iatmouls de Papouasie-Nouvelle Guinée* (Geneva: Editions Zoé).

7 For example, see Paul Parin, *Der Traum von Ségou: Neue Erzählungen* (Hamburg: Europäische Verlagsanstalt, 2001); Paul Parin, *Die Leidenschaft des Jägers: Erzählungen* (Hamburg: Europäische Verlagsanstalt, 2003).

8 A wonderful early tribute to Morgenthaler is Hans-Jürgen Heinrichs, "Löwengrüße von FM," *Die Zeit*, November 9, 1984, available at: www.zeit.de/1984/46/loewengruesse-von-fm (accessed January 20, 2016). Heinrichs observes that "after the death of Alexander Mitscherlich and Heinz Kohut, with Morgenthaler one of the most significant psychoanalysts of the post-Freudian generation has died." An excellent introduction to the work of Paul Parin can be found in the lecture delivered at the first anniversary of Parin's death by Christian Maier, "Warum Paul Parin am liebsten Hacker geworden wäre," *Ethnopsychoanalyse* (2010), available at: http://web123604.rex15.flatbooster.info/Ethnopsychoanalyse/index.php?page=507299593&f=1&i=1908324131&s=1209623709&ss=507299593 (accessed January 20, 2016).

9 For example, see Peter Winzeler et al., eds., *Das Kreuz mit dem Frieden: 1982 Jahre Christen und Politik* (Berlin: Elefanten, 1982); Pascal Eitler, "Politik und Religion – semantische Grenzen und Grenzverschiebungen in der Bundesrepublik Deutschland 1965–1975," in Ute Frevert and Heinz-Gerhard Haupt, eds., *Neue Politikgeschichte: Perspektiven einer historischen Politikforschung* (Frankfurt am Main: Campus, 2005), 268–303; Dagmar Herzog, "The Death of God in West Germany: Between Secularization,

Postfascism, and the Rise of Liberation Theology," in Michael Geyer and Lucian Hölscher, eds., *Die Gegenwart Gottes in der modernen Gesellschaft: Transzendenz und religiöse Vergemeinschaftung in Deutschland* (Göttingen: Wallstein, 2006), 425–460.

10 See the documentary film *Missions chez Tito – Les missions de la centrale sanitaire suisse en Yougoslavie 1944–48* (2006), directed by Daniel Künzi, with description at: www.artfilm.ch/missions-chez-tito-60-ans-apres-de-daniel-kuenzi-a-la-chaux-de-fonds (accessed January 20, 2016).

11 On Parin's defense of lay analysis and support for Anna Freud on this matter, see letter from Heinz Kohut to George H. Pollock, March 11, 1975, in Heinz Kohut, *The Curve of Life Correspondence of Heinz Kohut, 1923–1981*, vol. 1 (Chicago: University of Chicago Press, 1994), 322. On generational and political splits within the Swiss Psychoanalytic Society that led, in 1977, to the splitting-off from the Society of the Psychoanalytic Seminar Zürich that the trio had originally co-founded in 1958, see Thomas Kurz, "Aufstieg und Abfall des Psychoanalytischen Seminars Zürich von der Schweizerischen Gesellschaft für Psychoanalyse," *Luzifer-Amor* 12 (1993): 7–54. On the links between the Swiss and the Plataforma movement, see Berthold Rothschild, "'Plataforma' in den letzten zwanzig Jahren: Vortrag anlässlich des 20. Jahrestags ihrer Gründung," *Luzifer-Amor* 12 (1993): 55–62. For Morgenthaler's original radical memorandum recommending greater democracy within the Swiss Psychoanalytic Society and suggesting that students take charge of their own training program within the Zurich seminar (a proposal that may have been overwhelming for the trainees), see Fritz Morgenthaler, "Memorandum über Ziel, Sinn und Organisation des Seminars Zürich" (January 1970), available at: www.psychoanalyse-zuerich.ch/uploads/files/Morgenthaler_Memorandum.pdf (accessed January 20, 2016).

12 See the summary blurb for the documentary film about Paul Parin, *Der Rauch der Träume* (2008), directed by Mischka Popp and Thomas Bergmann, available at: http://kw2007.com/supply-GADB240B239 F247448C23EA0B6C63EB53.htm (accessed January 20, 2016).

13 See "Aus welchen Quellen schöpfte Fritz Morgenthaler? Ein Gespräch von Paul Parin, Jan Morgenthaler und Ralf Binswanger am 1.10.2003," *Werkblatt* 53 (2004): 5–21, available in expanded version at: www.werkblatt.at/archiv/53morgenthaler.htm (accessed January 20, 2016); and Paul Parin, "Begrüßung," *Journal für Psychoanalyse* 45/46 (2005): 11–13.

14 Ralf Binswanger, "Eine Mini-Ethnie im Dienst von Psychoanalyse und Sexualforschung: Zum Tod von Paul Parin (1916–2009)," *Zeitschrift für Sexualforschung* 22.3 (2009): 284–290.

15 Parin, Morgenthaler, and Parin-Matthèy, *Die Weissen*, 34. This core contention would be quoted over and over again in the years that followed. For example, see Harry Nutt, "Mein Leben ist eine Nachschrift: Zum Tode von Paul Parin," *Frankfurter Rundschau*, May 27, 2009, available at: www.fr-online.de/kultur/zum-tode-von-paul-parin-mein-leben-ist-eine-nachschrift,1472786,3226154.html (accessed January 20, 2016).

16 Hear the audiofile of lectures Morgenthaler and Parin delivered in Vienna in 1971: "Eine ethnologische Anwendung der Psychoanalyse: Fritz Morgenthaler spricht über 'Afrikaner im psychoanalytischen Prozess,' Paul

Parin zu 'Zwei psychische Folgen des Kulturwandels in Westafrika,'" available at: www.mediathek.at/atom/017828F7-20A-0063A-00000BEC-01772EE2 (accessed January 20, 2016); and see Parin, Morgenthaler, and Parin-Matthèy, "Preface," *Fear Thy Neighbor*, ix: "Very soon we discovered, to our surprise, that it was not at all difficult to motivate our partners to talk with us for an hour each day … The interpretation of resistance to a continuation of the interviews or to an intensification of transference prepared the way for more searching interpretations, which – with the help of additional information provided by our subjects on their memories, dreams, fantasies, and sometimes through their acting out – enabled us to make quite plausible reconstructions of their psychic development and the dynamics of their unconscious."

17 Personal communication, Gunter Schmidt, March 9, 2013.

18 Wilhelm Reich, *Der Einbruch der Sexualmoral: zur Geschichte der sexuellen Ökonomie* (Copenhagen: Verlag für Sexualpolitik, 1935).

19 See the important discussion in Joanne Meyerowitz, "'How Common Culture Shapes the Separate Lives': Sexuality, Race, and Mid-Twentieth-Century Social Constructionist Thought," *Journal of American History* 96.4 (March 2010): 1057–1084.

20 See Maureen Molloy, *On Creating a Usable Culture: Margaret Mead and the Emergence of American Cosmopolitanism* (Honolulu: University of Hawaii Press, 2008), 51. See in this context also the outstanding new study by Peter Mandler, *Return from the Natives: How Margaret Mead Won the Second World War and Lost the Cold War* (New Haven: Yale University Press, 2013).

21 For example, see Géza Róheim, *Psychoanalysis and Anthropology: Culture, Personality and the Unconscious* (New York: International Universities Press, 1950).

22 For example, see the volumes of the journal *Psychoanalysis and the Social Sciences*, published from 1947 to 1962.

23 Some commentators in the era even thought to do so would be impossible. See Parin, Morgenthaler, and Parin-Matthèy, "Vorwort zur 3. Auflage," 24.

24 Marcel Griaule, *Méthode de l'ethnographie* (Paris: Presses Universitaires de France, 1957), 92; cf. James Clifford, *The Predicament of Culture: Twentieth-Century Ethnography, Literature, and Art* (Cambridge: Harvard University Press, 1988), 68.

25 Megan Vaughan, *Curing their Ills: Colonial Power and African Illness* (Stanford: Stanford University Press, 1991); Jock McCulloch, *Colonial Psychiatry and "the African Mind"* (Cambridge, UK: Cambridge University Press, 1995); Richard C. Keller, *Colonial Madness: Psychiatry in French North Africa* (Chicago: University of Chicago Press, 2007); Warwick Anderson, Deborah Jenson, and Richard C. Keller, eds., *Unconscious Dominions: Psychoanalysis, Colonial Trauma, and Global Sovereignties* (Durham: Duke University Press, 2011).

26 Octave Mannoni, *Prospero and Caliban: The Psychology of Colonization* (New York: Praeger, 1964 [French orig. 1950]); Frantz Fanon, *Black Skin, White Masks* (New York: Grove, 1967 [French orig. 1952]); Philip Chassler, "Reading Mannoni's Prospero and Caliban Before Reading Black Skin, White Masks," *Human Architecture: Journal of the Sociology of Self-Knowledge* 5.3 (2007): 71–81; François Vatin, "Dépendance et

émancipation: retour sur Mannoni," *Revue du MAUSS* 2.38 (2011), 131–148. See also Anny Combrichon and Véronique Collomb, *Psychanalyse et décolonisation: Hommage à Octave Mannoni* (Paris: L'Harmattan, 1999).

27 Erik Linstrum, *Ruling Minds: Psychology in the British Empire* (Cambridge, MA: Harvard University Press, 2016).

28 Wulf Sachs, *Black Hamlet* (Baltimore: Johns Hopkins University Press, 1996 [orig. 1937]). The original subtitle was: "The Mind of an African Negro Revealed by Psychoanalysis."

29 Marie-Cécile and Edmond Ortigues, *Œdipe africain* (Paris: Librarie Plon, 1966). The historian Alice Bullard has recently deemed the Ortigues's book "a vital text from the early years of postcolonialism and transcultural psychiatry" and noted that it, too, is deeply concerned with issues of transference across lines of race and culture, as well as (though more problematically) with what its authors presumed as the difficulties of transition from tradition to modernity. Alice Bullard, "L'Oedipe Africain, a retrospective," *Transcultural Psychiatry* 42.2 (June 2005): 171–203.

30 For contrasting analyses, see Saul Dubow, "Wulf Sachs's Black Hamlet: A Case of 'Psychic Vivisection'?"*African Affairs* 92.369 (October 1993): 519–556; and Jonathan Crewe, "*Black Hamlet*: Psychoanalysis on Trial in South Africa," *Poetics Today* 22.2 (2001): 413–433.

31 Ernest Jones, "Mother-Right and the Sexual Ignorance of Savages," *International Journal of Psycho-Analysis* 6 (1925): 109–130.

32 Melford E. Spiro, *Oedipus in the Trobriands* (Chicago: University of Chicago Press, 1983).

33 Karen Horney, *New Ways in Psychoanalysis* (New York: Norton, 1939); Erich Fromm, *Escape from Freedom* (New York: Avon, 1969 [orig. 1941]). See the related criticism of the outdatedness of the Oedipus story in Max Horkheimer, "The Lessons of Fascism," in Hadley Cantril, ed., *Tensions That Cause Wars* (Urbana: University of Illinois Press, 1950), 209–242. Later further skepticism was voiced, despite initial affirmation, by Heinz Kohut, *The Restoration of the Self* (New York: International Universities Press, 1977); and Jay Greenberg and Stephen Mitchell, *Object Relations in Psychoanalytic Theory* (Cambridge, MA: Harvard University Press, 1983).

34 Melanie Klein, *The Psycho-Analysis of Children* (London: The Hogarth Press, 1932).

35 Jacques Lacan, "The Neurotic's Individual Myth" (1953), *Psychoanalytic Quarterly* 48 (1979): 405–425.

36 George Devereux, "Why Oedipus Killed Laius – A Note on the Complementary Oedipus Complex in Greek Drama," *International Journal of Psycho-Analysis* 34 (1953): 132–141.

37 Anne Parsons, "Is the Oedipus Complex Universal?" (1964), reprinted in Robert A. LeVine, ed., *Psychological Anthropology: A Reader on Self in Culture* (Oxford: Wiley-Blackwell, 2010), 131–153. See the contrasting assessments of Parsons by Marvin K. Opler, review of Anne Parsons, *Belief, Magic and Anomie: Essays in Psychosocial Anthropology* (New York: Free Press, 1969), in *American Anthropologist* 72.4 (1970): 865–867; and Winifred Breines, "Alone in the 1950s: Anne Parsons and the Feminine Mystique," *Theory and Society* 15.6 (November 1986): 805–843.

38 Kenneth Lewes, *The Psychoanalytic Theory of Male Homosexuality* (New York: Simon and Schuster, 1988); Kenneth Lewes, "A Special Oedipal Mechanism in the Development of Male Homosexuality," *Psychoanalytic Psychology* 15.3 (1998): 341–359; Scott J. Goldsmith, "Oedipus or Orestes? Aspects of Gender Identity Development in Homosexual Men," *Psychoanalytic Inquiry* 15.1 (1995): 112–124; Scott J. Goldsmith, "Oedipus or Orestes? Homosexual Men, Their Mothers, and Other Women Revisited," *Journal of the American Psychoanalytic Association* 49.4 (December 2001): 1269–1287.

39 Sander L. Gilman, *Freud, Race and Gender* (Princeton: Princeton University Press, 1993); Daniel Boyarin, "Freud's Baby, Fliess's Maybe: Homophobia, Anti-Semitism, and the Invention of Oedipus," *GLQ* 2.1/2 (April 1995): 115–147.

40 For example, see Ayelet Barkai, "Oedipus Has Two Mommies," manuscript in preparation, 2015.

41 Parin, Morgenthaler, and Parin-Matthèy, "Preface," in *Fear Thy Neighbor*, viii.

42 On the ideas of a "clan-conscience" (as opposed to an individual superego or ego-ideal), see Parin, Morgenthaler, and Parin-Matthèy, *Die Weissen*, 491, 583, 607. On the idea of an "oral organization of the group-ego" which is "dependent on reciprocal identifications," see Parin, Morgenthaler, and Parin-Matthèy, "Vorwort zur 3. Ausgabe," 14.

43 Vera Saller, "Die Afrika-Bücher: einst Pioniertaten, heute überholt?" *Journal für Psychoanalyse* 45/46 (2005): 227–241, here 235.

44 Parin, Morgenthaler, and Parin-Matthèy, *Fürchte*, 217–218; Paul Parin, "Der Ausgang des ödipalen Konflikts in drei verschiedenen Kulturen," *Kursbuch* 29 (1972): 191–192.

45 Parin, "Der Ausgang," 196.

46 Parin, Morgenthaler, and Parin-Matthèy, "Vorwort zur 3. Auflage," 18.

47 Parin and Morgenthaler, "Ist die Verinnerlichung."

48 Parin, Morgenthaler, and Parin-Matthèy, "Vorwort zur 3. Auflage," 18. Goldy was an essential part of the trio-team, but published fewer texts in her own voice, for example: "Nicht so wie die Mutter," in Paul Parin and Goldy Parin-Matthèy, eds., *Subjekt im Widerspruch* (Frankfurt am Main: Syndikat, 1986); and "Alt sein," in Karola Brede et al., eds., *Befreiung zum Widerstand: Aufsätze über Feminismus, Psychoanalyse und Politik. Margarete Mitscherlich zum 70. Geburtstag* (Frankfurt am Main: Fischer, 1987). For further insight, see the interviews: with Goldy and Paul, "Gegen den Verfall der Psychoanalyse: Gespräch mit Paul Parin und Goldy Parin-Matthèy," *tell* 15 (August 4, 1983): 9–15; with Goldy by Anke Schulz, Dagmar Scholz, and Sophinette Becker, "Psychoanalyse, Frauenrolle und Weiblichkeit: Ein Gespräch mit Goldy Parin-Matthèy," *links* 12 (June 1980): 19–25; with Goldy by Heinz Hug, "'… ein Guerillakampf mit anderen Mitteln': Interview mit Goldy Parin-Matthèy," *Schwarzer Faden* 27 (January 1988): 60–65; and about Goldy with Ursula Hauser by Marta Vardynets and Mariia Demianchuk, "An Attempt to Capture Goldy Parin-Matthey" (February 24, 2012), available at: http://media.wix.com/ugd/828439_6d43f9a475e16dd89063eecadf0c146c.pdf (accessed July 30, 2016), as well as the memory-piece by Bigna Rambert, "Macht doch net so a Gschiss! Abschied von Goldy Parin-Matthéy," *Werkblatt* 37.2 (1996): 9–11; and the documentary film, *Mit*

Fuchs und Katz auf Reisen: Portrait von Paul Parin und Goldy Parin Matthey (1997), directed by Marianne Pletscher.

49 Parin, Morgenthaler, and Parin-Matthèy, *Die Weissen*, 24. See also the related comments about the difficulties of deciding whether to treat their findings among the Dogon as variations on, or opposites, to European psychic structures (33).

50 Parin, Morgenthaler, and Parin-Matthèy, *Die Weissen*, 31.

51 See George Devereux, *Reality and Dream: Psychotherapy of a Plains Indian* (New York: International Universities Press, 1951); George Devereux, *From Anxiety to Method in the Behavioral Sciences* (New York: Humanities Press, 1967); George Devereux, *Ethnopsychoanalysis: Psychoanalysis and Anthropology as Complementary Frames of Reference* (Berkeley: University of California Press, 1978).

52 Devereux saw himself as a "classical" Freudian and had reservations about the neo-Freudian variant of culture-and-personality theorizing exemplified by someone like Abram Kardiner. In his letters to Parin, Devereux criticized Kardiner directly (for "rejecting the entirety of instinct theory") and listed as the only individuals who truly engaged in "decent ethnopsychiatry (on a psychoanalytic basis)" Parin himself, "your wife, Dr. Morgenthaler, Dr. L. Bryce Boyer (USA), Prof. Dr. Weston La Barre (USA), and a few other people." Even his own analyst, Geza Róheim, although he had worked with native peoples, had been concerned with interpreting their mores and their mythology, but had "written practically nothing about [these peoples'] neuroses and psychoses." In a later letter, Devereux added an appreciation for the work of "[Werner] Muensterberger (for fifteen years a good friend)." Here again Devereux emphasized that "there are at present hardly 10–15 people in total, that one could describe as strict psychoanalytic ethnopsychiatrists." He went on to explain: "La Barre has worked clinically with American Indians; Muensterberger with Chinese; Boyer with Indians ... All three are classical analysts." George Devereux to Paul Parin, April 7, 1967, and George Devereux to Paul Parin, April 14, 1967, both from Studio und Archiv Paul Parin und Goldy Parin-Matthèy at the Sigmund Freud Privatuniversität, Vienna. For more context on Kardiner, see William C. Manson, "Abram Kardiner and the Neo-Freudian Alternative in Culture and Personality," in George W. Stocking, ed., *Malinowski, Rivers, Benedict and Others: Essays on Culture and Personality* (Madison: University of Wisconsin Press, 1986), 72–94. On Muensterberger (analyst to Marlon Brando – when he was in New York – as well as to James Dean, editor of the series *Psychoanalysis and the Social Sciences*, collector of African art, and – not incidentally – after Morgenthaler's death the author of the introduction to the English-language translation of Morgenthaler's *Homosexuality, Heterosexuality, Perversion*), see Lisa Zeitz, *Der Mann mit den Masken: das Jahrhundertleben des Werner Muensterberger* (Munich: Berlin Verlag, 2013).

53 Instead, intriguingly, Parin-Matthèy conducted Rorschach tests (together with translators) with 100 non-French speaking Dogon informants in the village of Sanga and its environs; Parin too sometimes used Rorschachs in the midst of his interactions with informants. The trio saw the Rorschachs as an important supplement to the analyses/conversations, believing they

could function as "X-rays of the soul." The translators relied on by Parin-Matthèy, Barobo from the village of Ogolna and Ombotiembe from Mori, were deliberately chosen because they were "young enough, not to intimidate anyone" (as an elder interpreter-translator might have). "Vorwort zur 3. Auflage," 29, 33–34. Notably, however, already by the time the second edition of *Die Weissen* was published, the extended section on the Rorschach materials had been cut – a clear sign of the greater sensitivity to the complexities of transcultural communications and inegalitarian power relations in colonial-postcolonial contexts that the authors had acquired in subsequent decades.

54 Parin, Morgenthaler, and Parin-Matthèy, "Vorwort zur 3. Auflage," 10.

55 Parin, Morgenthaler, and Parin-Matthèy, *Die Weissen*, 111. In 1960, when the trio first arrived in Sanga, Morgenthaler treated a number of ill individuals and this was a basis for positive feelings toward the newcomers. Parin later also noted that the Dogon hosts felt highly at ease with Morgenthaler, more so than with himself, and that they tried in 1960 to encourage Morgenthaler to remain with them rather than return to Switzerland. Parin, "Vorwort zur 4. Ausgabe," in Parin, Morgenthaler, and Parin-Matthèy, *Die Weissen*, ix–x. But Parin also noted that in 1966, when the three returned to the village of Sanga, they were greeted warmly, as if they had just been there the day before, and "all who had at the time [i.e., in 1960] engaged in 'psychoanalytic' conversations with us, wanted to talk with us again daily, preferably in the same spot and at the same time of day." Parin, Morgenthaler, and Parin-Matthèy, "Vorwort zur 3. Auflage," 10.

56 Parin, Morgenthaler, and Parin-Matthèy, *Die Weissen*, 28.

57 For a recent strong critique of this ethnographic naivety and – in view of the trio's generally politically critical stance surprising but nonetheless revealing – lack of alertness to the colonial and postcolonial power dynamics structuring their encounters with their informants, see the essay by David Becker, "Die Gutmütigkeit des Afrikaners: Überlegungen zur Ethnopsychoanalyse aus postkolonialer Sicht," in Johannes Reichmayr, ed., *Ethnopsychoanalyse Revisited: Gegenübertragung in transkulturellen und postkolonialen Kontexten* (Giessen: Psychosozial-Verlag, 2016), 319–341.

58 Parin, Morgenthaler, and Parin-Matthèy, *Die Weissen*, 25–26.

59 Parin, "Vorwort zur 4. Ausgabe," ix.

60 Parin, Morgenthaler, and Parin-Matthèy, *Die Weissen*, 36.

61 Walter E. van Beek, "Haunting Griaule: Experiences from the Restudy of the Dogon," *History in Africa* 31 (2004): 44.

62 Parin, Morgenthaler, and Parin-Matthèy, "Vorwort zur 3. Ausgabe," 15, 18–19. See also their remarks about "development" often meaning not much more than neocolonial domination and exploitation (18–19).

63 Marcel Griaule, *Conversations with Ogotemmêli: An Introduction to Dogon Religious Ideas* (London: Oxford University Press, 1965). Griaule was praised in *Die Weissen denken zuviel* both for his extensive and impressive ethnographic knowledge and for having prompted the French colonial administration to build dam technology for collecting water; Griaule had lived in Sanga many times (39). For a critical exposé of Griaule's misapprehension of the truth-value of his findings, see Walter E. van Beek et al., "Dogon Restudied: A Field Evaluation of the Work of Marcel Griaule [and

Comments and Replies]," *Current Anthropology* 32.2 (April 1991): 139–167; for a partial defense of Griaule and repositioning of the debates, see Andrew Apter, "Griaule's Legacy: Rethinking 'la parole claire' in Dogon Studies," *Cahiers d'Études africaines* 45 (2005): 95–129.

64 Parin, Morgenthaler, and Parin-Matthèy, *Die Weissen*, 29.

65 With thanks to Nathan Kravis for pointing out this constitutive dilemma.

66 See the criticisms in Ortigues and Ortigues, *Œdipe africain*; and Geneviève Calame-Griaule, review of Parin, Morgenthaler, and Parin-Matthèy, *Les Blancs pensent trop*, *L'Homme* 9.1 (1969): 111–113. Also see the summary in Parin, Morgenthaler, and Parin-Matthèy, "Vorwort zur 3. Ausgabe," 16.

67 Adler, review of Geneviève Calame-Griaule, "Ethnologie et langage," *La Quinzaine littéraire* 9 (July 15, 1966): 23: "Par ailleurs, on nous donne la traduction française d'un livre de psychanalystes suisses dont le titre Les Blancs pensent trop dans sa démagogie n'est certes pas un garant de la valeur des idées que leurs auteurs nous apportent sur la culture du peuple Dogon et sur les problems des individus qui la vivent."

68 Parin, Morgenthaler, and Parin-Matthèy, *Die Weissen*, 45.

69 Parin, Morgenthaler, and Parin-Matthèy, "Vorwort zur 3. Ausgabe," 20, 16.

70 Among other things, there is discussion of interethnic tensions between the Dogon and the (generally poorer, nomadic, animal-herding) Peul peoples who now served as administrators and tax collectors for the new independent state of Mali and hence had changed their relationship to the (agricultural and proudly non-nomadic) Dogon, who still considered themselves of higher status.

71 In addition, clitoridectomy was described as a fact of Dogon life – *the* rite of passage for young girls into adulthood – but, strikingly, and in hindsight certainly peculiarly, at no point did the Parins and Morgenthaler indicate that this phenomenon did any damage to women's sexual interest or to general Dogon exuberance about heterosexual relations. Parin, Morgenthaler, and Parin-Matthèy, *Die Weissen*, 61–63, 85.

72 Parin, Morgenthaler, and Parin-Matthèy, *Die Weissen*, 56–66.

73 On mask dances and mosques, see the discussion of the developments found on the return trip in 1966 in Parin, Morgenthaler, and Parin-Matthèy, "Vorwort zur 3. Ausgabe," 12–13.

74 Parin, Morgenthaler, and Parin-Matthèy, *Die Weissen*, 170, 172, 611.

75 Nutt, "Mein Leben."

76 See Florence Weiss and Milan Stanek, "Aspects of the Naven Ritual: Conversations with an Iatmul woman of Papua New Guinea, *Social Analysis* 50.2 (2006): 45–76; the discussion of the exhibit "Kinder im Augenblick: Florence Weiss – Fotografien vom Sepik," in *Bild-Akademie/Netzwerk Fotografie* (July 26, 2015), available at: http://bild-akademie.de/blog/2015/07/26/kinder-im-augenblick-florence-weiss/ (accessed July 29, 2016); interview with Weiss by Bettina Dyttrich, "Jägerinnen und autonome Kindergruppen," *Die Wochenzeitung*, 51 (December 22, 2005), available at: www.woz.ch/0551/ethnologie/jaegerinnen-und-autonome-kindergruppen (accessed July 29, 2016); Maya Nadig, "Interkulturalität im Prozess – Ethnopsychoanalyse und Feldforschung als methodischer und theoretischer Übergangsraum," in Hildegard Lahme-Gronostaj and Marianne Leuzinger-Bohleber, eds., *Identität und Differenz: zur Psychoanalyse*

des Geschlechterverhältnisses in der Spätmoderne (Opladen: Westdeutscher Verlag, 2000), 87–101; Maya Nadig, "Ein Blick auf die Ethnopsychoanalyse heute," in Emilio Modena, ed., *"Mit den Mitteln der Psychoanalyse …"* (Giessen: Psychosozial, 2000), 427–433; interview with Nadig by Wolfgang Hegener, "'Konstruktionen sind im aktiven Handeln entstanden … ,'" *Forum: Qualitative Social Research* 5.3 (September 2004), available at: www.qualitative-research.net/index.php/fqs/article/viewArticle/557/1207 (accessed July 29, 2016); Mario Erdheim, *Die gesellschaftliche Produktion von Unbewusstheit – Eine Einführung in den ethnopsychoanalytischen Prozess* (Frankfurt am Main: Suhrkamp, 1982); Vincent Crapanzano, *Tuhami, Portrait of a Moroccan* (Chicago: University of Chicago Press, 1980).

77 Parin, "Vorwort zur 4. Ausgabe," vi.
78 Johannes Reichmayr, *Ethnopsychoanalyse: Geschichte, Konzepte, Anwendungen*, 3rd ed. (Giessen: Psychosozial, 2013); Johannes Reichmayr et al., *Psychoanalyse und Ethnologie: biographisches Lexikon der psychoanalytischen Ethnologie, Ethnopsychoanalyse und interkulturellen psychoanalytischen Therapie* (Giessen: Psychosozial, 2003); Fundación Ursula Hauser, available at: www.fundacionursulahauser.org/#!home/mainPage (accessed January 21, 2016).
79 For example, see Sir Aubrey Julian Lewis, "African Minds," *Times Literary Supplement* (January 30, 1964): 77–79.
80 Parin, Morgenthaler, and Parin-Matthèy, "Vorwort zur 3. Ausgabe," 16.
81 Parin, "Der Ausgang"; cf. Markus Brunner et al., "Critical Psychoanalytic Social Psychology in the German Speaking Countries," *Annual Review of Critical Psychology* (2013), available at: www.academia.edu/3701103/_2013_Critical_psychoanalytic_social_psychology_in_the_German_speaking_countries (accessed July 29, 2016).
82 Reimut Reiche, "Ist der Oedipuskomplex universell?" *Kursbuch* 29 (1972): 159–176.
83 Fritz Morgenthaler, "Die Stellung der Perversionen in Metapsychologie und Technik," *Psyche* 28 (1974): 1077–1098, here 1079.
84 Heinz Hartmann, "Problems of Infantile Neurosis: A Discussion (Arden House Symposium)," *Psychoanalytic Study of the Child* 9 (1954): 31–36; Morgenthaler, "Die Stellung," 1079.
85 Phyllis Greenacre, "Further Considerations Regarding Fetishism," *Psychoanalytic Study of the Child* 9 (1955): 187–194.
86 On the opening page of "Further Considerations," Greenacre referred back to an earlier paper of hers from 1953 in which she had talked about how a fetish "so clearly acts as some kind of stabilizer or reinforcement for the genital functioning of the patient"; she also prefigured Morgenthaler's *Plombe* when she wrote about "the nature and timing of the special faults in the body image, which were *patched up* by the use of the fetish in later life" (187, emphasis mine). Morgenthaler said, in the English abstract of his essay that he regarded perversions "chiefly as compensatory acts of the ego. Perverse drive satisfaction is subject to a change of function. It fills – somewhat like a dental filling – a cavity in the regulation of self-esteem acquired in childhood. A defective distinction between self and other results in an unresolvable contradiction of reality and fantasy. The perverse gratification 'solves' this contradiction periodically." But – in

contradistinction to Greenacre – Morgenthaler emphasized that "Not the disappearance of the perversion is the goal of therapy, but the substitution of a narcissistic for a sexualized transference." Or, again in the essay itself, he stressed "that it cannot be the goal of the psychoanalytic treatment to eliminate the perversion. The analysis is no declaration of war against the perversion, but rather a process, that leads to an as thorough as possible comprehension of the *function* that the manifest perverse activity serves within the framework of the interactions of the psychic systems and the self" (1078, emphasis mine). For a positive interpretation of Greenacre as profoundly sensitive to her patients, see Nellie Thompson, "Phyllis Greenacre: Screen Memories and Reconstruction," in Gail S. Reed and Howard B. Levine, eds., *On Freud's "Screen Memories"* (London: Karnac, 2015), 150–171. For a skeptical view, see Rachel Devlin, *Relative Intimacy: Fathers, Adolescent Daughers, and Postwar American Culture* (Chapel Hill: University of North Carolina Press, 2005), 35–38.

87 See Kohut, *The Restoration*, 5, 7, 42–44 (case of "Mr. M"), 79–80 ("Mr. U."), 122, 126 ("Mr. A"), 199–219 ("Mr. X"), 247; and Dagmar Herzog, "Die Politisierung des Narzissmus: Kohut mit und durch Morgenthaler lesen," *Luzifer-Amor* 29.1 (2016), 67–97.

88 Morgenthaler, "Die Stellung," 1083–1087.

89 Morgenthaler, "Die Stellung," 1092. Whether it is possible for an analyst to be a function for a patient rather than an object is an open question. For the best balanced appraisal of Kohut's work, see Lawrence Friedman, "Kohut: A Book Review Essay," *Psychoanalytic Quarterly* 49 (1980): 393–422.

90 For a glimpse of the close and dynamic interconnection and sense of intuitive solidarity between younger politically engaged West Germans around the Mitscherlichs and Fritz Morgenthaler and Paul Parin, see the back-and-forth correspondence already in 1973–1974 between Helmut Dahmer and Fritz Morgenthaler in the the archive of the journal *Psyche: Zeitschrift für Psychoanalyse und ihre Anwendungen*, Frankfurt am Main. Interestingly, it was the acceptance of Morgenthaler's essay on perversions in the summer of 1974 that triggered Dahmer's thought that Morgenthaler might be interested in reviewing for *Psyche* Reimut Reiche and Martin Dannecker's pathbreaking – at once empiricist and analytically informed – book on "the ordinary homosexual," *Der gewöhnliche Homosexuelle: eine soziologische Untersuchung über männliche Homosexuelle in der BRD* (Frankfurt am Main: Fischer, 1974). In other words, the mutual learning and appreciation began already in the first half of the 1970s.

91 Reimut Reiche, "Diskussion über Socarides' Theorie der Homosexualität," *Psyche* 26 (1972): 476–484.

92 Guy Hocquenghem, *Le Désir homosexuel* (Paris: Éditions Universitaires, 1972). Dannecker has been called "Hocquenghem's sternest critic." Judith Still and Michael Worton, *Textuality and Sexuality: Reading Theories and Practices* (Manchester, UK: Manchester University Press, 1993), 57.

93 Martin Dannecker, *Der Homosexuelle und die Homosexualität* (Frankfurt: Syndikat, 1978). Dannecker, on his own recognizance, took the view that "homosexuality is just as little or much a sickness as is heterosexuality," and that indeed "heterosexuality ... too undoubtedly bears unmistakable pathological features in its prevalent cultural form." He was thus appreciative that "in Morgenthaler's work, as generally in the theory of narcissism,

the strict distinction between homosexuals and heterosexuals is dissolved, and attention is focused on structural disturbances that can equally appear on both sides."

94 Letter from Sigusch to Morgenthaler, May 2, 1977. Personal collection of Volkmar Sigusch.

95 Erwin J. Haeberle, review of Volkmar Sigusch, ed., *Therapie sexueller Störungen*, 2nd ed. (1980), *Journal of Sex Research* 18.1 (February 1982): 90–93. Also see the extended discussion in Dagmar Herzog, "'Where They Desire They Cannot Love': Recovering Radical Freudianism in West German Sexology (1960s–80s)," *Psychoanalysis and History* 16.2 (July 2014): 237–261.

96 Sigusch to Morgenthaler, May 2, 1977.

97 Sigusch to Morgenthaler, May 18, 1978. And in a later letter going over little details that needed clarifying, Sigusch said once again: "I must once more emphasize how profoundly, after every new rereading of your essay, I am excited and fascinated. This essay will preoccupy us for a very long time." Sigusch to Morgenthaler, July 3, 1978. Personal collection of Volkmar Sigusch. Meanwhile, another gay rights activist, Manfred Herzer, had complained that Morgenthaler was not radical enough. And Morgenthaler worked on his formulations in order to be responsive to those objections. Manfred Herzer, "Die Psychoanalyse der Schwulen," *Emanzipation* (September–October 1979): 15–18; Manfred Herzer, "Morgenthaler auf dem Weg zur Besserung?" *Emanzipation* (March–April 1980): 17.

98 Fritz Morgenthaler, "Innere und äussere Autonomie," *Neue Zürcher Zeitung* 153 (July 6, 1979): 31–32; Fritz Morgenthaler, "Homosexualität," *Berliner Schwulenzeitung* 22 (June–July 1980): 6–9; Fritz Morgenthaler, "Homosexualität," in Volkmar Sigusch, ed., *Therapie Sexueller Störungen*, 2nd ed. (Stuttgart: Thieme, 1980), 329–367; "Fritz Morgenthaler," available at: http://en.wikipedia.org/wiki/Fritz_Morgenthaler (accessed January 21, 2016); "Fritz Morgenthaler," available at: http://de.wikipedia.org/wiki/Fritz_Morgenthaler (accessed January 21, 2016).

99 Morgenthaler, "Homosexualität," in Sigusch, *Therapie*.

100 Fritz Morgenthaler, "Ein Traumseminar mit Morgenthaler in Italien," in *Psychoanalyse, Traum, Ethnologie: Vermischte Schriften* (Giessen: Psychosozial, 2005), 21–54; Fritz Morgenthaler and Paul Parin, *Der Traum: Fragmente zur Theorie und Technik der Traumdeutung* (Frankfurt am Main: Campus, 1986); Reimut Reiche, "Die Rekonstruktion des Traums im Traumseminar," *Psyche* 66 (2012): 992–1021; Ralf Binswanger, "Dream Diagnostics: Fritz Morgenthaler's Work on Dreams," *Psychoanalytic Quarterly* 85.3 (July 2016): 727–757.

101 Jan Abram, *The Language of Winnicott: A Dictionary of Winnicott's Use of Words* (London: Karnac, 2007).

102 Fritz Morgenthaler, *Technik: zur Dialektik der psychoanalytischen Praxis* (Frankfurt am Main: Syndikat, 1978), 39, 113–114; Ralf Binswanger, "Technik: Zur Dialektik der psychoanalytischen Praxis – Lesehilfe," *Werkblatt* (2004), available at: www.werkblatt.at/morgenthaler/lesehilfe.htm (accessed July 29, 2016).

103 Hans-Juergen Heinrichs, *Fritz Morgenthaler: Psychoanalytiker – Reisender – Maler – Jongleur* (Giessen: Psychosozial, 2005).

104 See also Ulrike Körbitz, "Das Sexuelle und die Technik: Fritz Morgenthaler – Jean Laplanche – Jacques Lacan in ihren Überlegungen zur Steuerung des analytischen Prozesses durch den Analytiker," unpublished manuscript, 2007–2008, available at: www.psychoanalyse-graz.at/upload/fck/Das_Sexuelle_und_die_Technik.pdf (accessed January 21, 2016).

105 The New Left bookstore Land in Sicht in Frankfurt am Main invited Morgenthaler to speak in 1981 – specifically on the topic of homosexuality. Personal communication from Dieter Schiefelbein, July 28, 2013. Hans-Jürgen Heinrichs had facilitated the connection. The psychoanalyst Herbert Gschwind also remembers: "My history with Parin and Morgenthaler starts in Land in Sicht 1981/1982, where I heard Morgenthaler for the first time." Personal communication, August 1, 2014. Paul Parin himself remembered clearly that he had been invited to speak on "Psychoanalysis and Politics" at Land in Sicht already in November 1979 and that Morgenthaler had presented his "new sexual theory" a year later, i.e., 1980 or 1981; as a trio with Parin-Matthèy they had visited Land in Sicht multiple times. See Paul Parin, "Seit 20 Jahren Gast bei 'Land in Sicht': Schöne Literatur und das Wissen, dass Kultur nie unpolitisch sein kann," *Frankfurter Rundschau* (June 30, 1998): 98.

106 Reimut Reiche, personal communication, May 23, 2013.

107 Nutt, "Mein Leben."

108 Parin, "Vorwort zur 4. Ausgabe," iii.

109 Dieter Schiefelbein quoted in Matthias Arning, "Neue Orte der Linken," *Frankfurter Rundschau* (April 30, 2008), available at: www.fr-online.de/zeitgeschichte/spontikultur-neue-orte-der-linken,1477344,2794480.html (accessed July 29, 2016).

110 See Gabriele Goettle, "Paul Parin," in *Experten* (Frankfurt am Main: Eichborn, 2004), 46–47.

111 Helvetas: Schweizer Gesellschaft für Entwicklung und Zusammenarbeit, image available at: http://poster-gallery.com/de/shop/view_product/Meat-Cultura-Zuerich-Die-Weissen-denken-zuviel-806683 (accessed January 22, 2016). In a special issue of Helvetas' journal on "aboriginals" or "natives" (*Ureinwohner*), the quote – ascribed to "a village chief in Mali" – was accompanied by the remark that "aboriginals [or: natives] have much to say to us."

112 Andreas Hilmer, "Begegnungen," *Die Zeit* (June 7, 2007), available at: www.zeit.de/reisen/newsletter/fragebogen_hilmer (accessed January 21, 2016).

113 For example, see Reimut Reiche, "Das Rätsel der Sexualisierung," in Volkmar Sigusch und Ilka Quindeau, eds., *Freud and das Sexuelle* (Frankfurt am Main: Campus, 2005), 135–152; Sonja Düring and Margret Hauch, "Sexualisierung als unerkannte Abwehr: Überflüssige Odysseen," *Deutsches Ärzteblatt* 86 (February 2007): 84.

114 Parin, "Vorwort zur 4. Auflage."

115 See "'Sexualkunde, na, das macht der Kollege,'" *Der Spiegel* 9 (February 27, 1978): 62–76; Gunter Schmidt, "Sexuelle Folklore," *Literatur Konkret* (Autumn 1979): 70–71; Wolf Wagner, *Familienkultur* (Hamburg: Europäische Verlagsanstalt, 2003).

116 Fritz Morgenthaler, *Homosexualität, Heterosexualität, Perversion* (Frankfurt am Main: Qumran, 1984).

117 Paul Parin, "Die Verflüchtigung des Sexuellen," in Parin and Parin-Matthèy, *Subjekt im Widerspruch*, 81–89.

118 Reimut Reiche, "Fritz Morgenthaler," in Volkmar Sigusch, ed., *Personenlexikon der Sexualforschung* (Frankfurt am Main: Campus, 2009), 533–539.

119 Paul Parin, "'The Mark of Oppression': Ethnopsychoanalytische Studie über Juden und Homosexuelle in einer relativ permissiven Kultur," *Psyche* 39 (1985): 193–219; Paul Parin, "Kommentar zu 'Psychoanalyse in Schwulitäten' von der Bundesarbeitsgemeinschaft Schwule im Gesundheitswesen," *Psyche* 39 (1985): 561–564; Parin, "Die Verflüchtigung."

120 Parin, "Die Verflüchtigung." Parin further observed that, although clearly all Western societies had grown far more accepting of sexual diversity, it was nonetheless telling that conservative and reactionary governments always strove to reinstitute moral rules (implicitly recognizing the value of sexual repression for political control).

121 Paul Parin, "Die Beschädigung der Psychoanalyse in der Emigration," *Wiener Tagebuch* 6 (1989): 19–22.

122 For example, see Paul Parin, "Das Ich und die Anpassungsmechanismen," *Psyche* 31 (1977): 481–515; Daniel M. A. Freeman, "Contributions of Crosscultural Studies to Clinical Theory and Practice: The Work of Paul Parin," *Psychoanalytic Study of Society* 14 (1989): 281–299.

123 For example, see many issues of the journal *Transcultural Psychiatry*.

124 Tobie Nathan, "George Devereux and Clinical Ethnopsychiatry," *Ethnopsychiatrie.net*, available at: www.ethnopsychiatrie.net/GDengl.htm (accessed January 21, 2016); Gesine Sturm, Maya Nadig, and Marie Rose Moro, "Current Developments in French Ethnopsychoanalysis," *Transcultural Psychiatry* 48.3 (July 2011): 205–227.

125 Vera Saller, *Wanderung zwischen Ethnologie und Psychoanalyse* (Tübingen: Diskord, 2003); Johannes Reichmayr, "Die Ethnopsychoanalyse in der eigenen Kultur," in *Ethnopsychoanalyse*, 179–253.

126 Organized by Johannes Reichmayr, Michael Reichmayr, Christine Korischek, Liam Zimmermann, and Lisa Ndokwu of the Studio und Archiv Paul Parin und Goldy Parin-Matthèy at the Sigmund Freud Privatuniversität in Vienna. The conference celebrations are supplemented by the publication of the anthology edited by Johannes Reichmayr, *Ethnopsychoanalyse Revisited*.

Afterword

1 Paul Parin, "Die Beschädigung der Psychoanalyse in der angelsächsischen Emigration und ihre Rückkehr nach Europa," *Psyche* 44 (1990): 191–201, here 199. This essay reviewed the history of psychoanalysis since the 1930s, its depoliticization in the diaspora as well as its return to Europe with transformed content, and the paradoxical results. As the abstract observed, in Parin's view, "the history of [psychoanalysis'] achievements

is, at the same time, the history of its deterioration." Among other things, Parin noted: "Quantitatively it was an extraordinary success; qualitatively there was, despite some indisputable advances, a decline, a self-estrangement that has still not to this day been overcome." And: "Psychoanalysis is more vulnerable to social context than many other disciplines. The comparable case is the discipline of historical research, which notoriously gets corrupted and is condemned to wither away under dictatorships of all kinds" (191, 192–193).

2 Charles B. Strozier, *Heinz Kohut: The Making of a Psychoanalyst* (New York: Farrar, Straus and Giroux, 2001), 172–174, 424fn21; Elizabeth Lunbeck, *The Americanization of Narcissism* (Cambridge, MA: Harvard University Press, 2014), 41.

3 For the complexities of the multiple backstories, see: Elisabeth Young-Bruehl, *Anna Freud: A Biography* (New York: Summit Books, 1988); Ernest Wolf interview in Virginia Hunter, ed., *Psychoanalysts Talk* (New York: Guilford Press, 1994); Anna Freud, letter to Heinz Kohut, November 24, 1968, and Heinz Kohut, letters to Anna Freud, December 3, 1968, and January 4, 1969, in Geoffrey Cocks, ed., *The Curve of Life: Correspondence of Heinz Kohut, 1923–1981*, vol. 1 (Chicago: University of Chicago Press, 1994), 218–222; Martin S. Bergmann, "The Dynamics of the History of Psychoanalysis: Anna Freud, Leo Rangell, and André Green," in Gregorio Kohon, ed., *The Dead Mother: The Work of André Green* (London: Routledge, 1999), 193–204; Douglas Kirsner, *Unfree Associations: Inside Psychoanalytic Institutes* (London: Process Press, 2000); Leo Rangell, *My Life in Theory* (New York: Other Press, 2004); Orna Ophir, *The Paradox of Madness in American Psychoanalysis 1960–2000: Liberating Ethos, Praxis under Siege*, Ph.D. thesis, Tel Aviv University, 2008; Leo Rangell, "The IPA Administration from 1969 to 1973: Rome, Vienna, Paris – A Peak and a Turn," in Peter Loewenberg and Nellie L. Thompson, eds., *100 Years of the IPA: The Centenary History of the International Psychoanalytical Association 1910–2010* (London: International Psychoanalytical Association, 2011), 457–467.

4 Rangell, "The IPA Administration," 457–458.

5 Rangell, "The IPA Administration," 459. Rangell requoted his own encomium delivered at Hartmann's memorial service: "In 1939, Sigmund Freud died. That same year, Dr Hartmann published a small monograph, on the ego and its adaptive function, which announced a new phase in the understanding of man and defined the direction of the next three decades … Subsequent history showed that in that year the baton had been passed between the two men" (459).

6 Rangell, "The IPA Administration," 464. See also Rangell, *My Life*; as well as the obituary by Paul Vitello, "Leo Rangell, a Stalwart of Freudian Talk Therapy, Dies at 97," *New York Times*, June 4, 2011, available at: www.nytimes.com/2011/06/05/us/05rangell.html?_r=0 (accessed March 25, 2016).

7 Amazon blurb for Leo Rangell, *The Road to Unity in Psychoanalytic Theory* (New York: Jason Aronson, 2007), available at: www.amazon.com/The-Road-Unity-Psychoanalytic-Theory-ebook/dp/B00D6DUJGI (accessed March 25, 2016).

8 Marco Conci, "Elvio Fachinelli: A Biographical Profile," *Journal of European Psychoanalysis* 3/4 (1996–1997): 157–162, here 160. For samples of Fachinelli's work, see his *Il bambino dalle uova d'oro: brevi scritti con testi di Freud, Reich, Benjamin e Rose Thé* (Milan: Feltrinelli, 1974); Elvio Fachinelli, *La freccia ferma: tre tentativi di annullare il tempo* (Milan: L'Erba voglio, 1979). Fachinelli had been analyzed by Cesare Musatti, one of the most prominent postwar Italian analysts. For an intriguing glimpse of Musatti, see his defense of Freud and of psychoanalysis against the Pavlovian Soviet F. V. Bassin: Cesare L. Musatti, "An Answer to F. V. Bassin's Criticism of Freudianism," *Soviet Review* 1 (1960): 14–26.

9 Bolko is coeditor (with Pier Francesco Galli and Paolo Migone) of the Italian psychoanalytic journal *Psicoterapia e Scienze Umane* (Psychotherapy and Human Sciences) – a venture which, since the 1960s, has brought together Kleinians, Balintians, Sullivanians, Reichians, and Jungians with varieties of more traditional Freudians. See "Presentation of the Journal and History of the Group of *Psicoterapia e Scienze Umane*," available at: www.psicoterapiaescienzeumane.it/presentaz-engl.htm (accessed March 25, 2016). She has written both on technical-clinical issues and on sociopolitical problems such as racism; most recently, she cohosted the visit to Italy of the US borderline specialist Otto Kernberg. See "Otto Kernberg, 'Psicoanalisi e religione: perché Freud aveva torto' (18-3-2015)," available at: www.youtube.com/watch?v=hWGbXu_SGpQ (accessed March 25, 2016). Rothschild – like Bolko an analysand of Parin's – has spent more than forty years as a clinician and well-known public intellectual in Zurich. He was active in the debates surrounding the psychoanalytic work on character disorders of Kohut and Kernberg, authored practical guides for psychiatrists and the general public, and was also – indicatively – editor of an anthology which critically interrogated "the self-mystification of psychoanalysis." For example, see Berthold Rothschild, "Der neue Narzissmus – Theorie oder Ideologie?" in Psychoanalytisches Seminar Zürich, ed., *Die neuen Narzissmustheorien: Zurück ins Paradies?* (Frankfurt am Main: Syndikat,1981): 25–62; and Berthold Rothschild, ed., *Selbstmystifizierung der Psychoanalyse* (Göttingen: Vandenhoeck & Ruprecht, 1996); as well as the interview with Helen Schmid Blumer, "Interview mit dem Psychiater und Psychoanalytiker Berthold Rothschild," *Psychotherapie Forum* 18.1 (March 2010): 32–37; and Dagmar Herzog, "Die Politisierung des Narzissmus: Kohut mit und durch Morgenthaler lesen," *Luzifer-Amor* 29.1 (2016): 67–97.

10 Letter (about Morgenthaler's public statement at the IPA Congress in Paris 1973) from Helmut Dahmer to Fritz Morgenthaler, September 22, 1973, from the the archive of the journal *Psyche: Zeitschrift für Psychoanalyse und ihre Anwendungen*, Frankfurt am Main. For essential primary documents, a list of many of the individuals who have been involved in the Plataforma network, and a brief history of its formation from the perspective of a Mexican analyst, see the website created by Rodolfo Álvarez del Castillo, "Movimiento Plataforma Internacional," available at: http://roalvare.wix.com/plataforma (accessed March 25, 2016).

11 Johannes Cremerius, "Die psychoanalytische Abstinenzregel," *Psyche* 38 (1984): 769–800, here 778, 791. This essay is also outstanding on sexual

and gender dynamics within the history of psychoanalysis. Three further extraordinary essays by Cremerius are: Johannes Cremerius, "'Die Sprache der Zärtlichkeit und der Leidenschaft': Reflexionen zu Sándor Ferenczis Wiesbadener Vortrag von 1932," *Psyche* 37 (1983): 988–1015; Johannes Cremerius, "Der Verzicht der Psychoanalyse auf ihre emanzipatorisch-aufklärerische Aufgabe und die Wiederkehr der Traumatheorie," *Journal des Psychoanalytischen Seminars Zürich* 14 (1986): 39–41; and Johannes Cremerius, "Die Auswirkungen der Verflüchtigung des Sexuellen in der Psychoanalyse auf die Beurteilung von Homosexualität," *Psychoanalyse im Widerspruch* 7 (1992): 7–20. On Cremerius' work in Italy, see Marco Conci, "Gaetano Benedetti, Johannes Cremerius, the Milan ASP, and the future of the IFPS," *International Forum of Psychoanalysis* 23 (2014): 85–95.

12 For a fascinating retrospective critique of Rangell's misunderstanding of the transformations underway in the early 1970s – including an excellent summary of the face-off at the 1975 London IPA between Rangell (in this case supported by Anna Freud), on the one hand, and the French Winnicottian André Green, on the other, a face-off which Rangell and Freud seemed to have won at that moment, but which in hindsight manifestly marked the end of ego psychology and its focus on neuroses, and the rise of varieties of object relations approaches replete with an increasing turn to character disorders and psychoses – see Bergmann, "The Dynamics of the History of Psychoanalysis," 194–199. Among other things, Bergmann here also recounts Rangell's overconfident dismissal of self psychology, object relations, etc.

13 For remarkable reflections on the relations between fantasy and reality in the contexts of threats of nuclear war, the Chernobyl explosion, and HIV/AIDS, see: Hans Becker and Sophinette Becker, "Der Psychoanalytiker im Spannungsfeld zwischen innerer und äusserer Realität," *Psyche* 41 (1987): 289–306; and Sophinette Becker and Ulrich Clement, "HIV-Infektion – psychische Verarbeitung und politische Realität," *Psyche* 43 (1989): 698–709. For the relevance of this problem of fantasy-reality in Argentina, see Diana R. Kordon and Lucila I. Edelman, "Observations on the Psychopathological Effects of Social Silencing Concerning the Existence of Missing People," in Diana R. Kordon et al., eds., *Psychological Effects of Political Repression* (Buenos Aires: Sudamericana/Planeta, 1988): "Thousands of people are kidnapped mainly during the years 1976, 1977 and 1978. Nevertheless, mass media never give information about this. Silence is imposed as an official, repressive rule ... And yet, information circulates underground from mouth to mouth, amongst those one can trust in. 'Fantasy, truth, exaggeration?', ask themselves those who receive the piece of news. Panic is the common denominator ... Terrifying things happen while apparently everything continues just as it has always been." The simultaneous presence and absence of news "triggered psychosis," and "during the days of the 1978 Football World Cup, the maniac atmosphere of triumph rendered dissociation even more drastic" (27–28).

14 Judith S. Kestenberg, "Psychoanalyses of Children of Survivors from the Holocaust: Case Presentations and Assessment," *Journal of the American Psychoanalytic Association* 28 (1980): 775–804; Ilse Grubrich-Simitis, "Extremtraumatisierung als kumulatives Trauma," *Psyche* 33

(1979): 991–1023; Ilse Grubrich-Simitis, "Nachkommen der Holocaust-Generation in der Psychoanalyse," *Psyche* 38 (1984): 1–28; Emily A. Kuriloff, *Contemporary Psychoanalysis and the Legacy of the Third Reich: History, Memory, Tradition* (New York: Routledge, 2014).

15 Sammy Speier, "Der ges(ch)ichtslose Psychoanalytiker – die ges(ch)ichtslose Psychoanalyse," *Psyche* 41 (1987): 481–491, here 485. For other analysts' support of Speier's theory of postwar silence, as well as for the counter-vailing view that in fact the postwar decades were marked by frequently quite overt antisemitism, see the conference discussion summary by K. H. Schäfer and R. Rehberger, "Zur Wiederkehr der verdrängten Identifikation mit dem Nationalsozialismus im psychoanalytischen Prozess," in Helmut Luft and Günter Maass, eds., *Narzissmus und Aggression: Arbeitstagung der Deutschen Psychanalytischen Vereinigung in Wiesbaden vom 21.–24. November 1984* (Hofheim: DPV, 1985).

16 For succinct samplings of some of the terms of dispute, see Freder-ick Crews et al., *The Memory Wars: Freud's Legacy in Dispute* (New York: NYREV, 1995); Todd Dufresne, *Killing Freud: Twentieth Century Culture and the Death of Psychoanalysis* (London: Continuum, 2006); and Dietrich Rueschemeyer et al., "The Freud Question: An Exchange," *New York Review of Books* (December 8, 2011), available at: www.nybooks.com/articles/2011/12/08/freud-question-exchange/ (accessed March 26, 2016).

17 That intellectual history is consequential – that ideas matter – was under-stood full well on the other side of the Iron Curtain. Indeed, Soviet lead-ers were surprisingly preoccupied with psychoanalysis for the duration of the Cold War. Psychiatrists, psychologists, and allied professionals were expected to make public repudiations of Freud and to declare their adher-ence to the (purportedly contradicting) views of the Russian physiologist Ivan Pavlov. Soviet observers of the Western intellectual and popular cul-tural scenes noted the dramatic rise of fascination with Freud in the USA in the postwar era and, rather than shrugging this off as a quirk of the enemy with no relevance for high politics, recurrently pursued the issue, sponsor-ing conferences and fostering research agendas in order to encourage the articulation of countervailing perspectives. Over and over – in a revealing inversion of the situation in the first two decades in the postwar USA, in which most analysts styled themselves in perpetual deference to Freud and in which every little departure from what was understood to be the proper tradition was felt, anxiously, to require special justification and explication and ideally was expressed as honoring some theretofore neglected aspect of Freud rather than representing a divergence – Soviet bloc commenta-tors outdid themselves in enumerating the wrongs that Freud was said to stand for. These included: Freud's basic pessimism – arguably even fatal-ism – about human nature and thus the inherent skepticism about possi-bilities for social change; the overemphasis on libido – but then again the conviction that human beings were also inevitably driven by aggression; the emphasis on the individual as opposed to any collective; the focus on intrapsychic dynamics at the expense of social context; and indeed the very emphasis on the patient's past more than his or her present and future. These messages were, moreover, communicated around the Eastern bloc.

In Czechoslovakia, already in 1948, "psychoanalysis had been forced to go into hiding," and the reconstructed memorial plaque honoring Freud at his birthplace in Příbor – having been removed once before by the Nazis – was removed again by the Communists. In 1950, an "incendiary campaign" against psychoanalysis was launched in Czechoslovakia, with a brochure entitled *Kritické poznámky k psychoanalyse* (Critical Notes on Psychoanalysis) condemning Freudianism – specifically "in light of the teachings of Ivan Pavlov" – as "bourgeois pseudoscience." Later, after a momentary thaw around the uprisings of 1968 (a dozen analysts from Czechoslovakia, along with four from Hungary, had been permitted to attend a meeting of the Central European Psychoanalytical Association in Brunnen, Switzerland, in April of that year, where they met with, among others, Alexander and Margarete Mitscherlich, Goldy and Paul Parin, Fritz Morgenthaler, and Paula Heimann), the period of so-called "normalization" set in and "psychoanalysis went underground for the third time in Czechoslovakia." In Hungary as well, "during the period from 1948 to about 1980, psychoanalysis essentially went underground," and also former Freudians were cooperating "to emphasize Pavlov's significance and to denounce Freud." Meanwhile, at the latest in 1950, in the newly founded German Democratic Republic, tentative postwar efforts to relaunch psychoanalytic institutes or establish research chairs dedicated to analysis were there, too, forced to give way to the "cortico-visceral psychotherapy à la Pavlov." In January 1953, a Pavlov conference was held in Leipzig, attended by 1,800 medical professionals. Unanimously, they accepted two resolutions. One was addressed to the US president Dwight D. Eisenhower asking him for "justice" – i.e., mercy – on behalf of Ethel and Julius Rosenberg (the Rosenbergs would be executed half a year later). The other endorsed the "most important guidelines for the nurture and utilization of Pavlovian achievements in the German Democratic Republic." Back in the Soviet Union, at a 1958 conference on "Problems of Ideological Struggle with Modern Freudism," warnings were sounded that "Freudism" was being used "by bourgeois ideologists to dupe the masses in the interests of imperialism and as an ideological weapon in the fight against Marxism." For details, see Vladimír Borecký, "Psychoanalýza v ilegalitě: Osudy Freudova učení v českých zemích," *Dějiny a současnost* (2006), available at: http://dejinyasoucasnost.cz/archiv/2006/4/psychoanalyza-v-ilegalite/ (accessed March 3, 2016); M. M. Montessori, "32nd Bulletin of the International Psycho-Analytical Association," *Bulletin of the International Psychoanalytical Association* 49 (1968): 748; André Haynal, "On Psychoanalysis in Budapest," in Peter Loewenberg and Nellie L. Thompson, eds., *100 Years of the IPA: The Centenary History of the International Psychoanalytical Association 1910–2010: Evolution and Change* (London: International Psychoanalytical Association, 2011), 103; Ferenc Erös, "Some Social and Political Issues Related to Ferenczi," in Judit Szekacs-Weisz and Tom Keve, eds., *Ferenczi and His World: Rekindling the Spirit of the Budapest School* (London: Karnac, 2012), 50–52; Heike Bernhardt and Regine Lockot, *Mit ohne Freud: zur Geschichte der Psychoanalyse in Ostdeutschland* (Giessen: Psychosozial-Verlag, 2000), 21, 172–174, 183, 194–195; and Martin A. Miller, *Freud and the Bolsheviks: Psychoanalysis in Imperial Russia and the Soviet Union* (New Haven: Yale University Press, 1998), 126. All through, however, and crucially, various aspects of Freud's ideas inadvertently were transmitted in professional literature via the indirect route of explicating their flaws. Moreover, some ideas – for instance, the notion of an unconscious, or the idea that there were such phenomena as neuroses, or the importance of early childhood in emotional development – continued to find partial acceptance from the authorities, as long as they were couched either in self-distancing remarks or presented as independent home-grown discoveries. Especially in the 1960s, as Martin A. Miller reported in his dazzling history *Freud and the Bolsheviks*, "the way to gain access to the censored work of Freud was to become a critic of Freudian theory." Miller's counterintuitive but fascinating core discovery was that the recurrent negative attention accorded to psychoanalysis, as well as the authorities' awareness of the popularity of psychoanalysis particularly in the postwar USA, had, among other things, the unintended effect that Soviet and other Eastern bloc experts had repeated occasion to scrutinize Freud's work so as to be able to dismantle and rebut it more effectively. As Miller observed: "for over thirty years, a far longer period of time than the number of years in which psychoanalytic practice was actually permitted, Soviet politicians and scholars carried on an unrelenting 'ideological struggle' against Freudian ideas and influences. This campaign, in which careers were both made and lost, went on while Soviet psychoanalysis was supposedly extinct." Most pointedly: "No other government in this century devoted as much attention, critical or otherwise, to Freud's ideas as did the Soviet regime" (163).

18 David Becker, *Die Erfindung des Traumas – verflochtene Geschichten* (Freiburg: Freitag, 2006), 226.

19 Medawar quoted in Freeman Dyson, "How to Dispel Your Illusions," *New York Review of Books* (December 22, 2011): 42.

20 Frederick Crews, "Afterword: Confessions of a Freud Basher," in Crews et al., *The Memory Wars*, 298.

21 Steinem quoted in Jerry Adler, "Freud in Our Midst," *Newsweek* (March 26, 2006), available at: www.newsweek.com/freud-our-midst-106495 (accessed March 26, 2016).

22 In a conversation published in 1995, Steinem was quoted as saying: "When I was in my twenties and thirties, therapy was so Freudianized that it never occurred to me that it would be helpful. Sending a woman to a Freudian seemed like sending a Jew to an anti-Semite. Now it's very different. I am so grateful to the women who have fought this battle inside very difficult, biased, professionally rarified organizations." Gloria Steinem and Anna Myers-Parrelli, "Steps Toward Transformation," *Women and Therapy* 17.1–4 (1995), later published in book form as Ellen Cole, Esther D. Rothblum, and Phyllis Chesler, *Feminist Foremothers in Women's Studies, Psychology, and Mental Health* (New York: Routledge), 485.

23 Dinitia Smith, "Freud May Be Dead, But His Critics Still Kick," *New York Times* (December 10, 1995), available at: www.nytimes.com/1995/12/10/weekinreview/idead-trends-freud-may-be-dead-but-his-critics-still-kick.html (accessed March 24, 2016). As Smith put it, "Why is everyone working so hard to crush a movement that may be dying on its own?"

24 Ellen Willis, "Historical Analysis [Review of Eli Zaretsky, *Secrets of the Soul*]," *Dissent* (Winter 2005): 113–116, here 113–114.

25 Kramer quoted in Adler, "Freud in Our Midst."

26 Joan Wallach Scott, *The Fantasy of Feminist History* (Durham: Duke University Press, 2011), 4–5; cf. 150fn10.

27 Heinz Hartmann, "Comments on the Psychoanalytic Theory of the Ego," *Psychoanalytic Study of the Child* 5 (1950): 74–96, here 87.

28 Sigmund Freud, "Instincts and their Vicissitudes," in *The Standard Edition of the Complete Psychological Works of Sigmund Freud*, vol. XIV *(1914–1916): On the History of the Psycho-Analytic Movement, Papers on Metapsychology and Other Works* (1915), 109–140.

29 Strikingly, in the midst of his restatement, in 1970, of this essentially Horneyan thesis, Erich Fromm also floated his view that a major trouble with postwar US psychoanalysis lay in its social and political "conformism" – a position that would be taken up eloquently, and with even more empirical evidence, by the (albeit more Fenichel- and Adorno-influenced and hence more Fromm-ambivalent) historian Russell Jacoby a dozen years later. See Erich Fromm, "The Crisis of Psychoanalysis," in *The Crisis of Psychoanalysis* (New York: Holt, Rinehart and Winston, 1970), 1–29, here 5, 29; Russell Jacoby, *The Repression of Psychoanalysis: Otto Fenichel and the Political Freudians* (New York: Basic Books, 1983).

INDEX

310 / Index

Oraison, Marc, 50
original sin, doctrine of, 40
Ortigues, Edmond, 189, 196
Ortigues, Marie-Cécile, 189, 196, 211
Osborne, Peter, 155
Oury, Jean, 155

Papua New Guinea, 14, 180, 186, 198, 201–3
Parin, Paul, 7, 14, 179–87, 190–8, 208, 210–11, 214, 216–17, 282, 287, 294, 299
Parin-Matthèy, Goldy, 179–86, 191–8, 208, 214, 216, 286–7, 299
Paris, 177, 213, 214, 281
Paris, Bernard J., 53
Parsons, Anne, 190–1, 199
Pavlov, Ivan, 296, 298
Person, Ethel Spector, 82
Plack, Arno, 134
Plataforma, 7, 184, 222, 296
Plé, Albert, 50
Plotkin, Mariano Ben, 10
Pope Pius XII, 50–2, 54
postcolonial theory, 116, 155, 279
post-traumatic stress disorder, 13, 89–94, 110–14, 117–18, 120–2
projective identification, 142, 146, 165
Prozac, 218
psychiatric reform, 156, 272, 279
psychiatry, 12, 22, 33, 37, 41–2, 44–7, 54, 72–4, 76, 81, 91, 107,109, 205, 211, 217–18
Psychoanalytic Seminar Zurich, 184

queer theory, 10, 155, 173, 174, 191

Radó, Sándor, 63
Rangell, Leo, 35, 212–14, 215, 297
Rank, Otto, 61
Rapaport, David, 35
Rascovsky, Arnaldo, 4, 222
Reagan, Ronald, 146, 210, 215
Reich, Wilhelm, 3, 14, 27, 29, 133, 138, 153, 156, 160–2, 178, 186, 216, 275, 296
Reiche, Reimut, 199
Reichmayr, Johannes, 198
relational psychoanalysis, 53, 83, 84,

85, 182
religion, 10, 21–2, 34, 36, 37–52, 57–8, 197–8
Rickman, John, 182
Rieff, Philip, 11
Riesman, David, 149
Robcis, Camille, 10
Rohde-Dachser, Christa, 149
Róheim, Géza, 188, 193, 287
Rolnik, Suely, 278
Rome, 5–7, 52, 178, 212–14, 221, 295
Rose, Jacqueline, 146
Rosenberg, Ethel, 299
Rosenberg, Julius, 299
Rosenfeld, Herbert, 141, 145, 149, 216
Rothschild, Berthold, 214, 296

Sachs, Wulf, 189
Said, Edward, 116, 121
Saller, Vera, 191
Schäffer, Fritz, 95–6
schizoanalysis, 168, 277
Scott, Joan Wallach, 219
secondary gain, 92, 101, 102
Seem, Mark, 279
Segal, Hanna, 141, 144, 146, 149
self psychology, 74, 177–8, 193, 203, 210, 212, 219, 297
Selg, Herbert, 137
sexology, 15, 55–6, 59, 79, 204, 208
sexual revolution, 1, 14, 16, 36, 56, 67, 70, 73–4, 76, 134, 156, 162, 172, 186, 209
sexuality, history of, 15, 21, 23–4, 29–30, 35, 55, 209
sexuality, theories of, 15–16, 33, 40, 41–2, 44–5, 47–9, 51–3, 57, 79–80, 126–7, 138–9, 200, 204, 208–10, 219–20
Shapira, Michal, 10
Shatan, Chaim, 112
Sheen, Fulton J., 39–40, 42–3, 45–9, 53–4
Sherfey, Mary Jane, 69, 76
Sigmund Freud Archives, 8, 13, 44, 107, 218
Sigmund-Freud-Institut, 128, 130, 145, 150
Sigusch, Volkmar, 204–5
Silverberg, William V., 33
Simmel, Ernst, 176

P 17 - aff m ps1
Paul Parsin
Cordi Parin - matthey
Fritz Morgenthaller

Anti Oedipus - Gilles Deleuze & Felix Guattari